D0786665

WITHDRAWN
UTSA LIBRARIES

Eastern European
National Minorities, 1919-1980

Eastern European National Minorities 1919-1980

A Handbook

By

Stephan M. Horak

and

Richard Blanke

David Crowe

Kenneth C. Farmer

Stephen Fischer-Galati

Peter John Georgeoff

Toussaint Hočevar

Josef Kalvoda

Martin L. Kovacs

Theodor Veiter

1985

LIBRARIES UNLIMITED, INC.

Littleton, Colorado

Copyright © 1985 Stephan M. Horak
All Rights Reserved
Printed in the United States of America

No part of this publication may be reproduced, stored in a retrieval
system, or transmitted, in any form or by any means, electronic,
mechanical, photocopying, recording, or otherwise, without the
prior written permission of the publisher.

LIBRARIES UNLIMITED, INC.
P.O. Box 263
Littleton, Colorado 80160-0263

Library of Congress Cataloging in Publication Data

Horak, Stephan M., 1920-
    Eastern European national minorities, 1919-1980.

    Includes index.
    1. Minorities--Europe, Eastern--Bibliography.
2. Europe, Eastern--History--Bibliography.
I. Blanke, Richard.   II. Title.
Z2483.H53   1985   [DJK26]   016.3058'00947   84-25004
ISBN 0-87287-416-8

Libraries Unlimited books are bound with Type II nonwoven material that
meets and exceeds National Association of State Textbook Administrators'
Type II nonwoven material specifications Class A through E.

LIBRARY
The University of Texas
At San Antonio

This work was developed under a contract with the U.S. Department of Education. However, the content does not necessarily reflect the position or policy of that department, and no official endorsement of these materials should be inferred.

Table of Contents

Introduction

The problem of national or ethnic minorities became and has remained inseparable from the spread of national consciousness in the early nineteenth century, which soon translated into the political concept of nationalism aimed at the creation of nation-states. Although nationalism spread to all continents, eastern Europe became the classic historical example of its force and implication. The complexity of the issue grew as national minorities became "subject nationalities." This division of ruling nationality and subjugated ethnic minorities led to a multiplicity of issues, conflicts, and problems. In short, these problems became a historic force dangerous to overlook or underestimate as an element of cause and effect.

Realizing the importance of the national minorities in eastern Europe and the absence of scholarly tools necessary for an in-depth study of and understanding of the problem, a group of experts was assembled for the production of a one-volume handbook comprised of basic information to serve as a guide to the pertinent international literature on the subject. While being aware of the difficulty of covering the vast material within one volume and providing a complete bibliography, the decision was made to introduce the student and researcher to the better-known international sources, monographs, and periodical literature. Additionally, the *Handbook* reveals the substance, extent, and importance of the issues related to national minorities as they emerged after World War I and assesses the developments up through 1980. The bibliography, international in scope, should make the *Handbook* useful not only in the English-speaking world but in other countries as well.

The contributors made an extra effort to include material for all the minorities populating the respective countries. However, the number and quality of entries vary, depending on the number of works that have been printed and their availability. For this reason an unevenness remains as a witness to existing gaps, a problem to be considered by experts in future research and publications.

The *Handbook*'s organization and scheme are patterned on my *Guide to the Study of the Soviet Nationalities: Non-Russian Peoples of the USSR* (1982), which, in fact, pointed to the need for the *Handbook*. Thus, this volume can be seen as a logical extension of the *Guide*, since several east European national minorities after World War II were incorporated into the Soviet Union, and in some instances still reside on both sides of the present Soviet frontiers.

As to the technical organization of the *Handbook*, the following should be observed:

1) A general chapter brings the national minorities issue into the focus and context of east European history and the present situation. This chapter is followed by a list of works discussing various aspects of eastern Europe as introductory literature and then by works on national minorities in general.

2) Chapters on individual countries discuss the treatment of the national minorities, statistical data, and political, social, economic, and educational aspects and changes that have occurred during the three periods: the interwar period, World War II, and post-World War II up to 1980. Each essay is followed by an annotated, selected international bibliography of titles representing different views and interpretations.

3) Entries under the respective national minorities are arranged in alphabetical order. However, when the number of entries surpassed 30, a subdivision by subject headings seemed appropriate, offering the user a more direct access to the material. A complete description of the work cited is accompanied by an annotation informing the user of the work's special features, value, and point of view. Most of the titles in non-Western languages have been translated into English to facilitate wider use.

The inclusion of Austria and Italy, with their small ethnic groups of Slovenes and Croats, extends the *Handbook*'s coverage to countries which otherwise are not geographically considered a part of eastern Europe. Likewise, Theodor Veiter's contribution on "Nationality Research Centers in Eastern European Countries" provides information not always available, increasing the *Handbook*'s value as a guide to further study.

The magnitude of the problem with which this volume concerns itself has been very recently acknowledged by the British author Raymond Pearson in his study *National Minorities in Eastern Europe 1848-1945* (London: Macmillan Press, 1983), offering a general overview of national minorities in eastern Europe with the background development since 1848. Pearson's volume, together with titles included in the general chapter of the present work, provides additional material for experts and as well as general readers.

In my capacity as contributor, organizer, and editor of the project, I would like to express my thanks to all the contributors for their part of the project and for their collegial collaboration during all stages of the work for the last eighteen months. While the *Handbook* is the product of a team of scholars, I personally am obliged to Professor Joseph Rothschild from

Columbia University for his advice in the preparation of my contribution, and to Professor Donald F. Tingley from Eastern Illinois University for his generous assistance in the execution of my editorial responsibility. A generous grant from the U.S. Department of Education in support of the project made it easier for contributors to complete their assignments. Certainly my wife, Marie Louise, after many years of loyal collaboration and support, deserves my gratitude not only for the preparation of the final draft but also for her involvement in the work from the beginning.

Stephan M. Horak

1 ————————————— Eastern European National Minorities, 1919-1980

Stephan M. Horak

HISTORICAL SUMMARY

Demographic Problems and Changes

Political, linguistic, religious, and cultural as well as socioeconomic implications pertaining to and emerging from the presence of national minorities (ethnic groups not belonging to a dominant nationality in a nation) are better understood through statistics. Without statistical data, issues discussed remain vague and arbitrary in perception. Hence, any compilation of arguments aimed at the fortification of conclusions or solutions necessitates a knowledge of the number of peoples in question. Specifically, any judgment concerning the borders of a given state, especially in the east European area in an age of nationalism and national consciousness, can best be addressed with the use of proper statistical information. Popular opinions and false data will not survive the test of time and do not serve any purpose, as the history of post-World War I eastern Europe shows.

Contrary to the popular conception, the end of World War I, the collapse of the Russian and German empires, and the disintegration of the Habsburg empire were not followed by the emergence of national states. Poland, Czechoslovakia, and Yugoslavia cannot be considered to have true national states. Likewise, the states in existence prior to the war, such as Romania and

Bulgaria, contained a significant number of minorities. Hungary and Albania came closest to the concept of national states, with less than 8% of "foreign" elements.

The following tables, covering both periods, illustrate the problem of national minorities. They are based on Paul S. Shoup's data in *The East European and Soviet Data Handbook*.[1]

Albania

	1945	%	1955	%
Total population	1,122,044	100.00	1,391,499	100.00
Albanians	1,075,467	95.82	1,349,051	97.00
Others	46,577	4.18	42,448	3.00

Czechoslovakia

	1930	%	1970	%
Total population	14,729,536	100.00	14,361,557	100.00
Czechs & Slovaks	9,756,604	66.20	13,538,102	94.32
Others	4,972,932	33.80	823,455	5.68

(1930 census within prewar boundaries; 1970 census within the postwar boundaries)

Bulgaria

	1934	%	1965	%
Total population	6,077,939	100.00	8,227,866	100.00
Bulgarians	5,274,854	86.80	7,231,243	87.90
Others	803,085	13.20	996,623	12.10

Hungary

	1930	%	1970	%
Total population	8,685,109	100.00	10,322,099	100.00
Hungarians	8,000,335	92.10	10,166,237	98.50
Others	684,774	7.90	155,862	1.50

(Nationality determined by language)

Poland

	1931	%	1975	%
Total population	31,985,779	100.00	33,846,000	100.00
Poles	21,993,444	68.90	33,142,000	97.90
Others	9,992,335	31.10	704,000	2.10

(1931 census by native tongue; 1975 census only by estimation. Since the census of 1931 was based on native tongue, its results do not reflect correct numbers when religious and ethnic affiliation are used in determining nationality. By these latter identities, the number of Poles would be approximately 19,430,000 (61%) and all non-Poles 12,486,000 (39%). See Stephan M. Horak, *Poland and Her National Minorities, 1919-1939* [New York: Vantage Press, 1961], pp. 80-100.)

Romania

	1930	%	1977	%
Total population	18,057,028	100.00	21,559,416	100.00
Romanians	12,981,324	71.90	19,001,721	88.10
Others	5,075,704	18.10	2,557,695	11.90

(1930 census within the prewar boundaries; preliminary results only of 1977 census)

Yugoslavia

	1931	%	1971	%
Total population	13,934,038	100.00	20,522,972	100.00
Serbs, Croats, Slovenes, Macedonians, Montenegrins, Muslims	11,866,233	85.16	17,781,619	87.00
Others	2,067,805	14.84	2,741,353	13.00

By dividing the total population of these seven east European countries for the interwar and post-World War II periods into two groups — state nationalities and national minorities — the following picture emerges:

	Interwar Period		Post-World War II Period	
	1930s	%	1970s	%
Total population	94,521,473	100.00	110,231,409	100.00
State nationalities	70,948,261	75.00	102,209,973	92.80
National minorities	23,643,212	25.00	8,021,436	7.20

This cumulative table, together with the data on individual countries cited above, illustrates several crucial changes which took place in eastern Europe. Apart from political and socioeconomic upheavals resulting from World War II and its aftermath, perhaps the most lasting impact upon the region was the demographic simplification in several countries. This is especially true when considering that the problem of minorities of the interwar period was the most troublesome and unresolveable issue affecting the internal as well as external affairs of several states.

The decline of the number of peoples identifiable as national minorities reduced the level of dissatisfaction and potential conflicts. The number of people in that category of the interwar period has declinded significantly — from 23.6 million to only 8 million (7.2%) — and does not currently pose a serious political problem. Moreover, after 1945 all seven countries emerged almost as national states, with the percentage of minorities ranging from 1.5% (Hungary) to 13% in Yugoslavia, which had always been a multinational state.

The largest shift in the demographic composition took place in post-World War II Poland and Czechoslovakia, countries which had experienced the greatest ethnic problems during the interwar period. This shift was the result of the war, the defeat of Nazi Germany, subsequent territorial changes, and the forceful resettlement of some 10 million Germans. Extermination of the Jews was the second largest cause affecting Poland, Hungary, and Romania.

On the other hand, the only large current national minority living outside its mother country is the Hungarians in Romania (1,706,874) and in Czechoslovakia (572,569). Numbering over 3,800,000 in the 1930s, the large Jewish population of eastern Europe was reduced to only 72,600 by the 1970s as a result of Nazi extermination and the emigration after 1945. The Jews who remained were no longer set apart from the rest of society as they had been before the war, but in most cases integrated themselves into the native population and institutions. The disappearance of the Jews, together with the removal of the Germans from almost all countries except Romania (358,732) in 1977), emerges as the most characteristic change on the demographic map of eastern Europe. Additionally, over 5 million Ukrainians and 2 million

Belorussians, formerly Polish citizens, together with their ethnic territories, were incorporated into the Ukrainian SSR and Belorussian SSR, respectively.

Political Implications and Problems
of the Interwar Period and World War II

The year 1919 did not precipitate nationalism; nationalism antedated it and had existed for decades. This date is selected for practical purposes as a point from which nationalism emerged in a new and active role, marking the opening of the interwar era. Several important events took place that year which affected the fate and future of all the peoples of east and southeast Europe. It was the year of the Versailles peace treaty with Germany and the Treaty of St. Germain-en-Laye with Austria of September 10, by which the independent republic of Austria recognized the independence of Czechoslovakia, Poland, Yugoslavia, and Hungary—states which had come into existence toward the end of 1918. These two settlements, together with the Trianon Treaty of 1920 with Hungary, redrew completely the political map of east and southeast Europe and finalized the victories of nationalism by accepting the principle of national self-determination in drawing up new frontiers and resolving international disputes.

Despite the noble intentions regarding the rights of peoples to self-government, in practice, justice was not always carried out. The right to self-determination of many ethnic groups in that geographical area was violated on numerous occasions. Several reasons can be cited for the uneven application of this principle. World War I and the local wars and skirmishes which followed left in their wakes both victorious and defeated nations. The latter, of course, were denied equal treatment, as was the case with the Germans, Hungarians, Ukrainians, Belorussians, Macedonians, and the Albanians of the Kosovo province. Another contributing factor was the uneven development of national consciousness among the peoples of eastern Europe. Like any other trend, world view, system, or ideology, nationalism is characterized by varying degrees of development. Its intensity and degree of penetration among the masses, as well as the commitment by the elite, differed widely from one geographical location to another, making one nation stronger than the other and placing some people in a more favorable position than others. For example, the Poles found themselves in a better position than the Belorussians or the Ukrainians. The Czechs' fortune and position greatly outweighed those of the Sudeten Germans and the Slovaks. The Romanians quickly took advantage of their position opposite the Hungarians. The Serbs considered themselves superior to the Croats and the Slovenes; hence, they seized the role of the dominant nationality in Yugoslavia.

Apart from real or perceived causes dividing the peoples into state-nationalities and ethnic minorities, the post-World War I settlement left in its wake the most serious problem—23.6 million out of 94.5 million people remained as subject nationalities. Two out of every seven east central Europeans were forced to live in a country not of their choice and were deprived of national freedom and full citizenship. In fact, only 70.9 million people could claim status of state-nation for themselves.

In countries where the minorities numbered above 30%, the celebrated victories were premature. Multinational states such as Poland and Czechoslovakia found themselves having to deal simultaneously with two enemies — social or economic internal difficulties and hostile neighbors. The animosities created by the local wars and conflicts and unstable conditions encouraged foreign intervention. To wit — the Polish-Ukrainian war of 1918-1919 for the possession of Eastern Galicia (West Ukraine); the Polish-Soviet Russian war of 1919-1920, which led to the partition of Belorussian and Ukrainian territories under the terms of the Treaty of Riga of March 18, 1921; the Polish-Czechoslovak conflict over the Teschen area in January 1919; the Polish-Lithuanian feud of 1922 precipitated by Poland's incorporation of Vilna (Wilno); Czechoslovakia's disregard for the principle of self-determination in regards to Sudeten Germans; the Hungarian-Czechoslovak short war of March 1918 over an area in South Slovakia with a population of some 700,000 Magyars, occupied previously by the Czech army; the Romanian invasion of Hungary and the occupation of Transylvania in November 1918, and the invasion of Hungary in April 1919 to forestall reconquest of that province; the imposition on Hungary of the Treaty of Trianon's harsh terms leading to losses of territory and population to Czechoslovakia, Romania, and Yugoslavia (as a result Hungary was willing to join any alliance aimed at the nullification of the Trianon terms); Yugoslavia's dispute with Italy in February 1919 regarding Fiume and the territory on the Dalmatian coast; the Treaty of Neuilly of November 27, 1919, which, among other restrictions, deprived Bulgaria of a seaboard on the Aegean Sea and gave some border areas to Yugoslavia. Refugees from previously Bulgarian-held parts of Thrace and Macedonia organized the Internal Macedonian Revolutionary Organization (IMRO), whose activities in the years to come created a state of chronic tension between Bulgaria and her neighbors. As a result of these activities, Greece invaded Bulgaria in October 1922. And, finally, in January 1918, Bessarabia was invaded by, and later incorporated into, Romania; and in a separate peace treaty of the same year, Romania was given the province of Bukovina.

This long list of short wars and lasting conflicts occurring immediately after World War I created three distinct complications: 1) directly or indirectly, all countries involved had to deal with the issues of national minorities, mainly the ethno-territorial group; 2) almost all resurfaced on the agenda of history and contributed enormously to new decisions, conflicts, wars, and settlements less than two decades later; 3) all found themselves pulled into World War II, after which most of them underwent basic political, social, and economic changes as well as territorial and demographic changes, becoming predominantly, except for Yugoslavia, almost homogeneous states.

In regards to the ethnic problem of interwar eastern Europe and its implications, Professor Joseph Rothschild correctly observed that

> all in all, the rather complicated structure of the ethnic minority question both reflected the attempted but fragile interwar European power-balance and, due to the ensuing political tensions, also helped to overturn it.[2]

It is unfortunate that the countries of eastern Europe were either unable or unwilling to comprehend the poignancy of the issue and to resolve it in a spirit of compromise and partnership. This is not to suggest that all ills and wounds were instantly curable and that an ideal magic formula could have been applied. Nevertheless, much of the ensuing hostility, bloodshed, hatred, and readiness to ally with either Nazi Germany or the Communist Soviet Union would not have emerged at all, or would have been kept to a minimum, if internal peace and justice had been promoted. Rothschild portrays a dismal picture of prevailing social and economic conditions in eastern Europe which hampered attempts to defuse nationalistic animosity through economic improvement.[3] Overpopulation in some areas, the absence of industrial progress, low agricultural productivity, and high illiteracy, together with the impact of the worldwide depression, could hardly provide a favorable climate for reconciliation. Yet the failure of most of the regimes in power to explore means other than the use of power and terror stands out as the most obvious deterrent to improved relations. Having divided the population into first-, second-, and third-class citizens, mainly on account of their ethnic origin, the governments of Poland, Romania, Yugoslavia, and, to a lesser degree, Czechoslovakia, invited the consequences they were neither ready nor able to handle when their policies began to crumble.

Ukrainian, Slovak, Croat, and Hungarian irredenta were conceived not in Berlin or Moscow, but in Warsaw, Bucharest, Prague, and Belgrade. Berlin jumped on the wagon when it was already rolling; therefore, rewriting the history on this aspect serves no useful purpose.

Admittedly, the constitutions of all the respective countries provided, in various degrees, for the equality of all citizens, and some states, like Poland and Czechoslovakia, were obliged to sign agreements explicitly protecting the rights of their national minorities. The Polish parliament (Sejm) approved, on September 29, 1922, a provincial autonomy for the voivodships of Lwow, Stanislawow, and Tarnopol (West Ukrainian territory), although it was never implemented. Also, Article 7 of the Riga Peace Treaty required both parties to guarantee the rights of national minorities.

Article 12 of the Covenant of League of Nations entitled this body to assume the role of guarantor of the rights of national minorities. The following international instruments also stipulated that the national minorities be protected by the League of Nations:

"Minorities" treaties signed at Paris during the peace conference

1) Treaty between the Principal Allied and Associated Powers and Poland, signed at Versailles on June 28, 1919.

2) Treaty between the Principal Allied and Associated Powers and the kingdom of the Serbs, Croats, and Slovenes, signed at St. Germain on September 10, 1919.

3) Treaty between the Principal Allied and Associated Powers and Czechoslovakia, signed at St. Germain on September 10, 1919.

4) Treaty between the Principal Allied and Associated Powers and Romania, signed at Paris on December 9, 1919.

5) Treaty between the Principal Allied and Associated Powers and Greece, signed at Sèvres on August 10, 1920.

Special chapters inserted in the general treaties of peace
1) Treaty of peace with Austria, signed at St. Germain-en-Laye on September 10, 1919 (Part III, Section V, Articles 62 to 69).
2) Treaty of peace with Bulgaria, signed at Neuilly-sur-Seine on November 27, 1919 (Part III, Section IV, Articles 49 to 57).
3) Treaty of peace with Hungary, signed at Trianon on June 4, 1920 (Part III, Section VI, Articles 54 to 60).
4) Treaty of peace with Turkey, signed at Lausanne on July 24, 1923 (Part I, Section III, Articles 37 to 45).

Special chapters inserted in other treaties
1) German-Polish convention on Upper Silesia, dated May 15, 1922 (Part III).
2) Convention concerning the Memel Territory, dated May 8, 1924 (Article 11, and Articles 26 and 27 of the statute annexed to the convention).

Declarations made before the Council of the League of Nations
1) Declaration by Albania, dated October 2, 1921.
2) Declaration by Estonia, dated September 17, 1923.
3) Declaration by Finland (with respect to the Aaland Islands), dated June 27, 1921.
4) Declaration by Latvia, dated July 7, 1923.
5) Declaration by Lithuania, dated May 12, 1922.

During the years 1920-1931, nineteen nationalities from thirteen countries submitted 525 petitions to the League of Nations citing violations of their rights. Of these petitions, 155 accused Poland of violations. From October 1931 on, some two hundred charges were filed against Poland concerning atrocities committed during the pacification of the Ukrainians. During the years 1920-1930, 63 petitions were submitted against Romania, 60 against Czechoslovakia, and 53 against Yugoslavia.[4]

In 1934, hoping to bring an end to the flow of petitions, Poland refused to cooperate with the League of Nations and to recognize its obligations as outlined in the minority treaty of 1919. This resulted in a weakened Polish position on the international scene and did nothing to stem the growing internal difficulties. In searching for a way out of this predicament, Warsaw turned to an intensive polonization program. The results were predictable—increased violence, creation of two concentration camps, mass arrests, and a subsequent increase in terroristic activities by the Organization of Ukrainian Nationalists (OUN). The policy of "an eye for an eye" continued into the last days of the existence of interwar Poland.

A similar situation existed in Czechoslovakia between the Czechs, the Germans, and the Slovaks, and in Yugoslavia between the Serbs and the Croats. Conflicting national aspirations had not withered away. On the contrary, polonization was moving stubbornly toward confrontation and explosion. World War II merely helped speed it up and increased its intensity.

Eastern Europe's desire for a departure from the status quo coincided in the late 1930s with similar aims in Nazi Germany and Communist Soviet Russia. Moreover, Germany and Soviet Russia shared an interest in the belt separating them, a fact which forced them in the initial stages to coordinate their actions. The prevailing conditions in Europe, and particularly in some east European countries, provided them with issues, such as national self-determination, territorial claims, and oppressed minorities, which would easily be exploited.

In 1938, under the pretext of justifiable causes, east Europe entered the most brutal period of its history, lasting until 1945 and beyond. The process began in Austria, whose annexation to the Reich was approved by 99.75% of the voting population in an Austrian plebiscite on April 10, 1938. Despite the presence of German troops and selective terror, this action was considered an exercise in self-determination, a privilege denied them by the Western democracies in 1919 when the Austrian constituent assembly had voted Austria an integral part of Germany. By and large, the Western democracies remained silent, being aware of their own inconsistency in handling the problem of self-determination. Although at the time it appeared that justice had been served, the Austrians' self-determination would soon be obscured by the totalitarianism of the Nazi state.

The fate of the Sudetenland and Czechoslovakia was inescapable, especially after the peaceful solution of the Austrian problem. After all, it was argued, over 3 million German people living in a compact area for centuries were entitled to self-determination just as the Czechs, the French, and others were. Neville Chamberlain, Edward Daladier, Benito Mussolini, and Adolf Hitler found themselves in agreement on that issue on September 29, 1938 at the conference in Munich. The warm welcome the British and French statesmen received upon their return from Munich was for "saving the peace," as well as a testimony to popular acknowledgment of previous wrongdoing. A chain reaction followed. Now Prague, humiliated and weakened by the loss of the Sudetenland, had to grant full autonomy to Slovakia on October 4, and to Carpatho-Ruthenia (Ukraine) on October 8, 1938. Indeed, both acts were long overdue, having been promised in the Pittsburgh Pact of May 30 and in the Philadelphia Understanding of October 26, 1918, respectively.

At this point, Czechoslovakia's issues had been resolved in the spirit of a just implementation of the principle of self-determination. The basic democratic framework of the republic remained intact and had even been improved through the elimination of the remnants of national discrimination. Neighbors to the north and south believed the time was right to submit their territorial claims as well.

On September 29, Poland, with the largest percentage of the national minorities and the worst record in the treatment of them, submitted a virtual ultimatum to Prague claiming the Teschen region, to which the Czech government yielded. Hitler was pleased to have a new partner in his *Neuordnung* of Europe. Poland's reward for this precariously fragile partnership was an area of 400 square miles and some 240,000 inhabitants, with less than 100,000 Poles.

The other territorial demand came from Hungary, a request for the southern region of Slovakia where 700,000 Magyars lived. On November 2, the German-Italian Commission gave Hungary a broad strip of southern

Slovakia and Ruthenia, an area of 5,000 square miles with a population of 1,000,000. Warsaw, in the past eager to establish a common frontier with Hungary, welcomed the decision, but she had to wait until March 1939 to see it enacted. Budapest celebrated the partial recovery of Hungary's pre-1918 territory while rapidly falling into Hitler's web.

The remainder of the country, now renamed Czecho-Slovakia, whetted the appetites of Hitler and his new partner, Hungary. The epilogue to Munich began in Prague when the government deposed Msgr. Josef Tiso, the premier of Slovakia, accusing him of separatist intent. Tiso appealed for Hitler's intervention, which was duly forthcoming. President Hacha was summoned to Berlin, and in a dramatic confrontation accepted protectorate status for Bohemia and Moravia, which were promptly occupied by German troops. Slovakia, now under German protection, proclaimed her independence on March 14, 1939. Germany's involvement and its most benevolent support of Slovak national aspirations should, however, neither minimize nor condemn the act of March 14, for the majority of Slovaks did not regret the collapse of the republic and welcomed their national independence. The mood of the people began to undergo changes only in 1944, but never to the point of relinquishing national aspirations.

The fate of Carpatho-Ruthenia, which proclaimed its independence as Carpatho-Ukraine on March 15, 1939, was tragically different. On the next day, with Hitler's permission and Poland's political support, Hungarian troops invaded this tiny republic of 400,000 people. Stalin acquiesced because of his fear of resurgent sentiment for Ukrainian national statehood so dangerously close to Soviet Ukraine. The paramilitary units of the "Carpathian Sich" fiercely resisted the invaders. Within this sequence of events, Ukrainians were the first to forcibly resist Hitler's *Neuordnung*, but Hitler's decision not to tolerate Ukrainian national self-determination had the support not only of Budapest but also of Warsaw and Moscow.

Both Hitler and Stalin were eager to exploit national issues, adroitly using them for their own designs and thereby adding a new dimension to their strategies. Although the dismantlement of Czechoslovakia, except for resistance in Carpatho-Ukraine, had been accomplished peacefully, supporting in some quarters the belief in Hitler's innocence, the events of the coming months and years convinced skeptics and the naive alike of the real nature of Nazism. The realization of its naked brutality began to spread over Europe from Berlin and Moscow. As Karl Jasper points out, totalitarian ideologies, while in power, necessitate the administration of "terror as such."

The Hitler-Stalin Pact of August 23, 1939 not only unchained the Second World War but also initiated a new re-mapping of eastern Europe accommodating Hitler's *Lebensraum* and the Soviet Union's territorial expansion program, followed by Sovietization of the incorporated areas. The slightest hopes for improvement of the fate of national minorities became an illusion. The destruction of Poland and subsequent partition of her territory amounted to a total disregard of the national self-determination of the Poles and Poland's minorities. The incorporation of the Polish ethnic territories, Upper Silesia, the Poznan province, and eastern Pomerania, into the German Reich and the forceful resettlement of the Poles into the General Gouvernement were acts of conquest and violence. These historically Polish lands had experienced German colonization from the time of Poland's first partition in 1772, yet had preserved their ethnic Polish character into the twentieth century. The number of Germans in these territories in 1931 amounted to 630,000, i.e., 10% of the total population. The irony of history has this same pattern of conquest and depopulation applied against the defeated Nazi Germany in 1944-1945, with the expulsion of the German population from east of the Oder-Neisse rivers.

Germany's partner, the Soviet Union, while sharing the spoils, excused the occupation of the eastern part of Poland, with a population of 13,199,000, as an act of "liberation of the Belorussian and Ukrainian brethren from the Polish yoke." But the Belorussian and Ukrainian inhabitants had not been consulted about their coming "liberation," were not told about the Hitler-Stalin Pact, and no delegations begging for "liberation" reached Moscow before the Red Army crossed the borders. There were no welcome banners, as was the case in 1941 when the German troops were greeted in towns and villages. Meetings, propaganda, elections, and "unification" followed the *fait accompli*, while all procedural details of "liberation" were formally worked out in Moscow. The old yoke was replaced with the burdens of Soviet citizenship and deplorable life under the totalitarian regime. National self-determination, never mentioned in the official propaganda, was substituted by slogans of the "unification" with the quasi republics of the BSSR and Ukrainian SSR. Ukrainian nationalism was proclaimed the "enemy of the people," and the Russians introduced themselves as "big brothers." The "reunification" of Ukraine with the USSR in 1922, and then West Ukraine and North Bukovina with the Ukrainian SSR in 1939/1940, was one of the most costly unifications in history in terms of human lives. Conservative estimates for the period 1922-1955 run between 10 and 12 million Ukrainians who were executed, starved to death during the 1932-1933 Stalin-instigated famine, or perished in Siberian concentration camps. Belorussian losses for the same period are estimated as between 3 and 4 million people.

The fate and treatment of the peoples under Nazi and Soviet occupation during the Second World War are discussed in separate chapters, and a selected list of the literature on this subject is appended. The striking similarities of methods used by the Nazi and Soviet powers to achieve their aims are well known. The differences as to detail as well as documentary sources available result from the fact that the defeat of Nazi Germany made original documents available to the victors and researchers, whereas in the case of the Soviet Union much of the source material remains out of reach, and only limited data, some archival pieces and eyewitness accounts, offer fragmentary insight into Soviet policy and action.

The fact remains undisputed, however, that the Hitler-Stalin partnership resulted in tragic consequences for the whole of eastern Europe. Poland's disappearance from the political map was only the beginning of the new rearrangement, followed by the incorporation of the Baltic states, northern Bukovina, and Bessarabia into the Soviet Union. With Hitler's support and the Western powers' indifference, and under the threat of force, Stalin proceeded with the destruction of Estonia, Latvia, and Lithuania on September 29, 1939, first with the establishment of Soviet naval and military bases and then complete integration into the Soviet Union on June 15-16, 1940.

The liquidation of the Baltic states resulted from several motives: it extended Soviet borders, thus providing increased security; it restored Imperial

Russia's frontiers, referred to in Soviet historiography as an act of "reunification"; and it complied with the Marxist vision of world socialism. Ironically, the latter motive evolved not from the "proletarian revolution," but from the Nazi-Soviet collaboration.

A different outcome of the Hitler-Stalin Pact affecting territorial change and a national minority involved Romania. The two northern territories, Bukovina and Bessarabia, formerly belonging to Austria-Hungary and Russia, respectively, came under the Soviet "sphere of influence." Bukovina, an Austrian province from 1774 until 1918, with a mixed population of 800,000 by 1910, comprised 305,000 Ukrainians living mainly in the northern part, and 268,100 Romanians in the southern area. By 1930, the number of Ukrainians increased to 582,115, living predominantly in Bukovina and in lesser numbers in neighboring Bessarabia. Unlike Bessarabia, Bukovina had never been a part of the tsarist empire, and only the large Ukrainian population could serve as a convenient argument for Stalin's decision to demand it from Romania for the sake of "liberation and unification" in an ultimatum of June 27, 1940. Bessarabia, with a population of 2,452,000 (1939), mainly Romanian-speaking (65%), was part of the historical principality of Moldavia. Since the province had been acquired by Russia in 1812, Moscow was offered another opportunity to insist on a historical claim.

A partial dismantling of Great Romania began on August 30, 1940 under pressure from Berlin and Rome (Vienna Arbitrage). Bucharest agreed to yield to Hungary an area of 16,646 square miles (two-thirds of the Transylvania province) with a mixed Hungarian-Romanian-German population of 2,392,600. According to the 1930 census, the area contained 1,555,000 Magyars and some 700,000 Germans. On September 8, a further territorial cession of some 3,000 square miles (southern Dobrudja) was demanded by and yielded to Bulgaria (the Treaty of Craiova). All in all, during 1940, Romania lost 40,000 square miles of her territory and 4 million people, of which 40% were native Romanians. Admittedly, Romania once again became a nation-state; however, a large number of Romanians concomitantly were made national minorities, at least until 1944/1945.

A still different course of fragmentation, rearrangement, and territorial and demographic change took place in Yugoslavia. On April 6, 1941, German troops invaded Yugoslavia, and eleven days later the Yugoslav government capitulated. The collapse of interwar Yugoslavia provided an opportunity for a very different settlement by the parties involved, thereby satisfying the territorial claims of Hungary, Italy, and Bulgaria, and creating an "Independent Croat State," with the remaining, mainly Serbian territory falling under German military administration. The political rearrangement remedied little. Internal civil war involving the Chetniks, the Partisans, and the Ustashe on the one hand, and emerging partisan warfare against the German occupation on the other, contributed to internal disintegration, mass resettlements, and huge losses of human lives.

Hitler's *Neuordnung* implemented in Yugoslavia only in the case of the Croats resembled the application of national self-determination. Northern Slovenia, occupied by Germany, was incorporated into the Reich's frontiers, and the southern part, with Lubliana, in addition to half of the coastal area of Croatia, was annexed by Italy. Hungary reacquired the northern part of her former province Voivodina, comprising the whole of Batchka. Bulgaria was allowed to administer Macedonia, which she claimed from the pre-World War I era, and incorporated small areas along the Bulgarian-Yugoslav frontiers. Albania, under Italian protection and occupation, was rewarded with the Kosovo province, populated by some 750,000 Albanians. Montenegro remained occupied by Italy. As mentioned before, Serbia, in addition to the Banat, was under German military authority up until the time the Axis powers were defeated.

Prior to the Nazi-Soviet war, the territorial changes made in eastern Europe reflected Hitler's program for the destruction of the settlements made by the Versailles peace treaty and its extensions — St. Germain, Trianon, and Neuilly. Among the losers were Poland, Czechoslovakia, Romania, and Yugoslavia, and among the winners were those former losers which had revisionistic expectations — Germany, Hungary, and Bulgaria. When considering the principles of national rights, self-determination, and national freedom in general, it might be concluded that the unsatisfactory situation only worsened as it was changed. Increasingly, oppression could not be accepted as a permanent and satisfactory solution by those longing for an improvement in the fate of national minorities. Germany invaded the Soviet Union on June 22, 1941, embarking on a two-front war, while conditions in that part of Europe stayed basically the same. Eastern Galicia was incorporated into the remnants of the former Poland, now named General Gouvernement, and Bukovina and Bessarabia were returned to Romania, which was generously compensated by Hitler with a large piece of territory from Ukraine, Transnistria, together with the seaport Odessa.

Restoration of the territorial *status quo ante* in eastern Europe became a possibility in 1944, when the German army retreated from the eastern front. However, what a few years earlier would have been considered inconceivable became reality — the Soviet army, having reconquered Soviet territory during the summer of 1944, reached the Romanian border, and on August 24 the Romanian government surrendered, offering the Soviet troops free access to Hungary and the Balkan Peninsula. By the end of 1944, the whole of eastern Europe was free of German occupation, but was now overrun by the Soviet army and faced with new political decisions.

Post-World War II Period

The post-World War II period witnessed several basic political, social, economic, and demographic changes of historical significance. The reduced presence of Jews in all of eastern Europe reflects the most obvious demographic change. The forceful expulsion of Germans (Volksdeutsche) from Poland, Czechoslovakia (sanctioned by the Potsdam Conference of August 2, 1945), and Hungary, resulting in a decline of their number to 500,000 at the most, represents another basic change in the ethnic composition after 1945. As a consequence of these two singular events, two former multi-national states, Poland and Czechoslovakia, emerged as nation-states, especially after the Soviet reannexation of Western Belorussia, Western Ukraine, and Carpatho-Ukraine from Czechoslovakia on June 29, 1945. By 1970, some voluntary resettlements reduced the numbers of Hungarians in Czechoslovakia to 572,569, a decline of 9% from 1930.

As a result of these developments, the proportion of national minorities in eastern Europe was reduced to 7.2% from the 27.7% of the interwar period. The Yugoslavian and Bulgarian situations remained almost unchanged, due to the restoration of their respective borders in 1939, with the exception of the territory around the city of Trieste, as provided by the agreement of 1954.

The elimination of the German element from eastern Europe was not limited to the demographic aspect. The restoration of Poland within her historical frontiers of the Piast dynasty (10th-14th centuries) along the Oder-Neisse rivers moved the boundaries of eastern Europe some 70 miles westward, nullifying the centuries-long German drive to the east. Instead of becoming an area for German colonization, eastern Europe pushed its German minorities back into the remnants of the Third Reich, the Federal Republic of Germany and the German Democratic Republic. It should be noted that the ouster of the Germans was aided by their mass flight to escape the approaching Soviet army and the liquidation of some 2 million who perished in reprisal for all atrocities and persecutions by the Nazis during wartime. In fact, Nazi Germany's brutality and disregard of basic national and human rights made the expulsion of Germans seem morally and legally justifiable. Berlin's refusal to compromise, to take advantage of the rejection of the Soviet regime by the Balts, Belorussians, Ukrainians, and many others, and her lack of awareness of the limits of Germany's potential and power contributed to the exclusion of Germany as an ally in that part of Europe for decades to come.

The forceful Sovietization of eastern European states did nothing to improve conditions. Moscow's policies were equally oppressive, and the deeply rooted national consciousness and economic hardships continued. The problem of national minorities remained in several countries, despite Marxist claims of having resolved national issues and conflicts of the past.

With the signing of the peace treaties on February 10, 1947 in Paris with Hungary, Bulgaria, and Romania, the question of the borders, and thereby of the ethnic minorities, was determined once again. Accordingly, Hungary now officially recognized the loss of the territories annexed in 1939 and 1941, including Transylvania and the southern region of Slovakia. Hungary once again was made into a nation-state, with 98.5% of the population being Magyars. As far as the problem of Hungarian minorities in Romania and Czechoslovakia is concerned, the difference lies in the fact that interwar Hungary could speak and complain on behalf of its countrymen, whereas the present regime pretends the problem does not exist, and only recently has the issue been raised in Budapest. When and how the old Hungarian revisionism can resurface depends on external developments rather than Budapest's ability and planning.

Bulgaria retained southern Dobrudja but lost all the Yugoslav and Greek territories that had been annexed and occupied during the war. By 1965, Bulgaria's national minorities accounted for 12% of her total population (8,277,866), the largest percentage of which were Muslims.

Romania was compensated for her loss of northern Bukovina and Bessarabia (Moldavian SSR) with the return of Transylvania and, apart from the large Hungarian and German minorities (1,706,876 and 358,732 as of 1977), comprised 88.1% ethnic Romanians. With the recent rise of nationalism, Bucharest is returning to the policy of Romanization, especially of

Transylvania, a province in dispute for centuries, and only a restrained mention of Bessarabia by semiofficial quarters has been detected publicly.

Poland, despite her geographical dislocation, emerged after World War II as one of the most homogeneous societies, not only ethnically but religiously, which contributed enormously to the revival of Polish historical nationalism, especially of its anti-Russian characteristic. The minor remnants of non-Poles (2.1%), comprising an estimated 350,000 Ukrainians, 200,000 Belorussians, and 400,000 others, do not pose any particular problem, especially after the forceful resettlement of Ukrainian Lemkos into the northern and western voivodships. The outburst of anti-Semitism in the 1950s forced the remnants of the Jews to emigrate, and their number at the present can be estimated at some 20,000.

Czechoslovakia, left with only one larger ethnic group, the Magyars (579,617) as of 1980), found herself in a more favorable position than before 1938. However, strife between Czechs and Slovaks, even under different political conditions, bears watching. It is important to observe that Czechs and Slovaks living outside of Czechoslovakia maintain their separateness at all levels, including political, cultural, social, and scholarly.

By creating a federation of six republics—Serbia, Slovenia, Croatia, Bosnia-Hercegovina, Montenegro, and Macedonia—independent socialist Yugoslavia endeavored to resolve national conflicts by implementing the principle of self-determination. Only the Albanians, among the larger ethnic groups (1,309,523), were denied the right to set up their own "people's republic," and they continue to challenge the system in the form of strikes, riots, and general disobedience. Apart from this, Yugoslavia's national minorities (those not identified with one of the republics), the Hungarians, Ruthenians-Ukrainians, Italians, and others, enjoy a greater degree of national, religious, and cultural freedom than the ethnic minorities in any other east European state.

Although the old Serb-Croat animosity has diminished, it remains potentially explosive. The massacre of the Croatian Ustashe at the end of the war by Tito's partisans, an act of retaliation against Ustashe wartime massacres of non-Croatians, exacerbated simmering rivalry. The hostility was intensified further by economic strife and administrative posturing, as in the case in Croatia in the early 1970s. Similar to the Czech-Slovak situation, the Serbs, Croats, and Slovenes do not fraternize outside of Yugoslavia, preferring to group themselves in their own organizations. The animosity often translates into acts of violence and even assassinations, as has frequently been the case in West Germany. Such a protracted state of unrelenting mutual suspicion might easily be transplanted into Yugoslavia once again whenever the power of the Communist system either weakens or disintegrates to the point of chaos. For these and other reasons, including the possibility of external interference, the results of the Yugoslav federative socialist experiment remain unpredictable at best.

In summarizing the impact of World War II on population changes, it should be noted that the size of the modern-day mass movement in eastern Europe can be compared only with the mass migration of the fifth and sixth centuries, which resulted in significant changes in Europe's demographic structure. By using Joseph B. Schechtman's findings[5] and updating them for the 1945-1946 period, we can estimate that the number of peoples affected by all forms of transfer, evacuation, expulsion, and voluntary and involuntary resettlements totals 14 million. This number does not even include the approximately 9 million Jews and others who were physically liquidated by either Nazi Germany or Soviet Russia, which would raise the total to 23 million people. Based on this figure, four out of ten persons of the pre-World War II population of all eastern European countries were either removed from their native places and regions or perished altogether in less than a decade. A further footnote to the above figures is that approximately 1 million east European political refugees fled to the West to escape the advancing Soviet armed forces, and perhaps as many were deported to Siberia, mainly from West Ukraine, West Belorussia, Poland, Romania, and Hungary. Hence, the number of 23 million, as asserted here, should easily stand up to any critical challenge.

Concluding Observations

The importance of the national minorities in eastern Europe in all three periods—interwar, World War II, and since 1945—has been discussed at some length. While the degree varies from one country and one period to another, the national minorities problem warrants an extensive study within the context of modern history, since it applies to many other parts of the world.

It is possible to speak of two different phases pertaining to the eastern European ethnic minorities problem, and the question of differences in both periods must be answered on several levels. While in the interwar period the issue of nationalities involved not only the desire for self-determination but also the demand for significant territorial changes within the existing states, the post-World War II situation virtually eliminated the necessity for major territorial adjustments. Compared to the Albanians in Yugoslavia and the Hungarians in Romania and Czechoslovakia, the ethnic problems in other countries are of lesser importance. For instance, the small territorial pockets of Belorussians in Poland, Ukrainians in Poland, Romania, and Czechoslovakia, Slovenes in Austria and Italy, and Turks in Bulgaria do not contain the potential for eruption or challenge to the respective states. In those cases, the regional problem has been defused and replaced with concerns for cultural development, human rights, survival of educational institutions, and preservation of the language. These concerns are equally present in any west European country comprising ethnic elements. The difference remains in the absence of political freedom in all east European states.

Denationalization, widely practiced in eastern Europe in the past, survives into the present. All regimes, including the USSR, officially profess to Marxist internationalism, insisting on having resolved national issues and removed nationalistic conflicts by abolishing all forms of former political, national, and economic discrimination.

> In fact, theory and practice have diverged in a number of cases and where in a communist country the population suffered totalitarian rule, the weight of this bore especially heavily on the minority which found itself under a double pressure. With the growth of the national element in the policies ... in the late 1950s and early 1960s, the pressure on the minorities tended to increase.[6]

This pressure leads to denationalization of ethnic groups that are attempting to escape the additional hardships caused by their origin. While motives differ, the results remain the same—an increase of the dominant nationality and a decline of the ethnic minority. This was especially true in Poland and Romania throughout the interwar and postwar periods. More recently, the process of deliberate denationalization was initiated in Yugoslavia, as the results of the 1981 census indicate. For the first time since 1945, the number of various non-Serbian nationalities began to decline at the expense of publicly encouraged "Yugoslavism," the Yugoslav equivalent of Moscow's program of Sovietization, which was to result in a monolithic society. Since the number of Yugoslavs increased from 273,077 in 1971 to 1,150,000 in 1981, a corresponding decline of almost all non-Serbian nationalities, including Croats (by 98,647) and even Ruthenian-Ukrainians (by 2,483), cannot be explained as the result of mixed marriages only.

The results of the 1981 census have been officially commended as a "victory over nationalism," thereby implying that socialism and the process of Yugoslavization are compatible and that society as a whole is progressing. It is uncertain whether this trend will continue in the future, for in the censuses of 1953, 1961, and 1971, the number of "Yugoslavs" vacillated—998,698 in 1953, and only 263,077 in 1971. Obviously, the return to a traditional national identity can repeat itself again under different conditions, a possibility not only in the case of Yugoslavia, but equally so in the rest of eastern Europe. The Soviet Union is no exception, as recent events indicate. To many non-Russians, the Soviet Union remains the notorious "prison of nations."

Neither nationalism nor ethnic awareness has been obliterated in eastern Europe, despite the 35-year-long experiment in socialism which has denied nationalistic values, identities, and appeals. The present situation is not unlike the interwar period, with its discrimination, restrictions, and lack of basic human and national freedom. This fact stands in stark contrast to the pronouncement of the Universal Declaration of Human Rights adopted and proclaimed by the General Assembly of the United Nations on December 10, 1948. Its Article 15 assures that "everyone has the right to a nationality," and Article 2 states that "everyone is entitled to all the rights and freedoms set forth in this Declaration, without distinction of any kind, such as race, color, sex, language, religion, political or other opinion, national or social origin, property or other status." For many peoples of eastern Europe, there has been no evidence to suggest that these rights exist.

The history of eastern Europe since 1919 clearly demonstrates that minorities are most often oppressed by equally oppressed majorities. Perhaps the recent events in Poland serve to keep alive a flicker of hope for a better future for both minorities and majorities.

Notes

[1]Paul S. Shoup, *The East European and Soviet Data Handbook: Political, Social, and Developmental Indicators, 1945-1975* (New York: Columbia University Press, 1981), p. 482. Especially Section C: "National and Religious Affiliation," pp. 133-68.

[2]Joseph Rothschild, *East Central Europe between Two World Wars* (Seattle: University of Washington Press, 1974), p. 14.

[3]Ibid., pp. 14-25. On the economic and social relationships of ethnic groups in eastern Europe, see also Julius Rezler, "Economic and Social Differentiation and Ethnicity," in *Ethnic Diversity and Conflict in Eastern Europe*, ed. Peter F. Sugar (Santa Barbara, CA: ABC-Clio Press, 1980), pp. 279-345.

[4]For additional details see Herbert Truhart, *Völkerbund und Minderheiten* (Vienna, 1931).

[5]Joseph B. Schechtman, *European Population Transfers, 1939-1945* (New York: Oxford University Press, 1946), Appendix 1.

[6]George Schöpflin, "National Minorities in Eastern Europe," in *The Soviet Union and Eastern Europe: A Handbook*, ed. George Schöpflin (New York: Praeger, 1970), p. 12.

BIBLIOGRAPHY

The study of eastern European national minorities, like other specific areas or topics, requires a step-by-step approach in order to be properly comprehended within the broader context of history. The Western world, and in particular the English-speaking countries, has accumulated sufficient published and other available material to provide a basic as well as an advanced level of background information. A list of annotated titles that provide background information on eastern Europe is offered here, followed by a list of titles related to eastern European national minorities in general. The user will find material on individual countries in the respective chapters of this work, in addition to the individual essays on the various ethnic minorities.

For a general history of eastern Europe, the following books are recommended:

Oskar Halecki, *Borderlands of Western Civilization: A History of East Central Europe* (New York: Ronald Press, 1952).

Francis Dvornik, *The Slavs: Their Early History and Civilization* (Boston: American Academy of Arts and Sciences, 1956); and *The Slavs in European History and Civilization* (New Brunswick, NJ: Rutgers University Press, 1962).

W. H. McNeill, *Europe's Steppe Frontier, 1500-1800* (Chicago: University of Chicago Press, 1964).

Leften S. Stavrianos, *The Balkans since 1453* (New York: Rhinehart, 1958).

Robert Lee Wolff, *The Balkans in Our Time* (Cambridge, MA: Harvard University Press, 1956).

Charles and Barbara Jelavich, eds., *The Balkans in Transition: Essays on the Development of Balkan Life and Politics since the Eighteenth Century* (Berkeley: University of California Press, 1963).

Hans Kohn, *Pan-Slavism: Its History and Ideology*, 2nd rev. ed. (New York: Vintage Books, 1960).

Hugh and Christopher Seton-Watson, *The Making of a New Europe: R. W. Seton-Watson and the Last Years of Austria-Hungary* (Seattle: University of Washington Press, 1981).

General Reference Works

1. **The American Bibliography of Slavic and East European Studies** (1957-). Published by Indiana University in Slavic and East European Series (1957-1966); since 1967 under the sponsorship of The American Association for the Advancement of Slavic Studies, Columbus, OH; since 1975 prepared at the Library of Congress for the American Association for the Advancement of Slavic Studies.

This bibliography seeks to present on an annual basis as complete a record as possible of North American publications in Slavic and east European studies. It includes works, primarily in English but also in other languages, which are of research or information value and were published in North America or, if published elsewhere, were written, edited, or compiled by North Americans. The average number of entries per issue is 5,000. An author index and a bibliographical index are provided. This is a basic tool for anyone involved in east European studies, as it also lists articles on east European national minorities in all states.

2. **Bibliographie d'etudes Balkaniques, 1966- .** Sofia: Academie Bulgare des sciences, Institut d'etudes Balkaniques. Centre international de recherches scientifiques et de documentation, 1968- .

This bibliography offers the most comprehensive listing of material published on the Balkan countries, including monographs and articles. Material on the national minorities is listed under various subject headings, making location difficult.

3. Birkos, Alexander S., and Tambs, Lewis A. **Academic Writer's Guide to Periodicals, II.** East European and Slavic Studies. Kent, OH: Kent State University Press, 1973. 572p.

The guide is meant to cover periodicals and monographic series in the social sciences and humanities. Volume 2 deals with east European and Slavic studies (comprising the Balkans, the Baltic area, and eastern Europe—Czechoslovakia, Hungary and Poland, and the Soviet Union). The typical journal entry includes the complete title of the periodical, the name of the editor, the editorial address, the subject areas of interest (both chronologically and geographically), and the editorial policies (style, preferred length, remuneration, and so on). Four types of indexing (general unrestricted, chronological, geographical, and topical) facilitate the location of information.

4. Birkos, Alexander S., and Tambs, Lewis A., eds. **East European and Soviet Economic Affairs: A Bibliography (1965-1973).** Littleton, CO: Libraries Unlimited, 1975. 170p.

A collection of English-language books and articles dealing with the economic affairs of eastern Europe and the USSR. The compilers present a broad, comprehensive bibliography of material available in most medium-sized and large libraries. The entries (1,168 in all) are arranged geographically and subdivided by subjects. A list of publishing outlets for scholarly papers and author, title, publisher, and periodical indexes are appended.

5. Blejwas, Stanislaus, comp. and ed. **East Central European Studies: A Handbook for Graduate Studies (A Preliminary Edition).** Columbus, OH: American Association for the Advancement of Slavic Studies, 1973. 301p.

The handbook provides a list of major libraries, archives, and institutions in the United States and abroad. Of particular interest is the inclusion of Jewish and Ukrainian studies.

6. Budurowycz, Bohdan. **Slavic and East European Resources in Canadian Academic and Research Libraries.** Research Collections in Canadian Libraries, vol. 4. Ottawa: National Library of Canada, 1976. xvi, 595p., paper.

Intended as a guide to Slavic and east European resources in Canadian libraries for scholars, students, and librarians, the book's primary purpose is to report on the extent of existing research collections and to draw recommendations for a well-planned and coordinated national collection policy. The survey gives a detailed descriptive analysis of resources in each of the 50 academic and 17 specialized libraries in 10 Canadian provinces. It analyzes the holdings for all the disciplines in the humanities and social sciences in all languages dealing with the USSR and all east European countries. This is a valuable reference guide, as special attention is paid to collections on east European national minorities.

7. Hnik, Thomas, ed. **European Bibliography of Soviet, East European and Slavonic Studies.** Vol. I (1975), vol. II (1976). Birmingham: University of Birmingham, 1977-1979. Vol. III (1977). Paris: Éditions de L'école des Hautes Études en Sciences Sociales, Institut d'Études Slaves, 1981.

This new bibliography was born from the merger of two older ones, "Travaux et publications parus en francais en ... sur la Russie et l'URSS," which appeared as a section in the *Cahiers du monde russe et soviétique*, and *Soviet, East European and Slavonic Studies in Britain*, and it promises to be a worthy counterpart to the *American Bibliography of Slavic and East European Studies*. The bibliography covers French, British, and German publications on the Communist countries of eastern Europe. Each volume contains either scattered entries on national minorities in all east European countries or entries grouped in special chapters on national minorities.

8. Horak, Stephan M., comp. **Russia, the USSR, and Eastern Europe: A Bibliographic Guide to English Language Publications, 1964-1974.** Littleton, CO: Libraries Unlimited, 1978. 488p.

_____. **Russia, the USSR, and Eastern Europe: A Bibliographic Guide to English Language Publications, 1975-1980.** Littleton, CO: Libraries Unlimited, 1982. 279p.

Both volumes offer extensive listings of works on eastern European countries, in addition to titles covering, to various degrees, the issue of minorities in all respective countries. A unique feature of this bibliography is that most annotations accompanying the bibliographic citations are excerpted from professionals journals, over half from *Slavic Review*. The bibliography is substantially complete through 1980. Author, title, and subject index.

9. Horecky, Paul L., ed. **East Central Europe: A Guide to Basic Publications.** Chicago and London: University of Chicago Press, 1976. 956p. (3,380 entries).

Chapter 5, "The Nationality Question," by Francis S. Wagner, lists 24 entries. There is no special listing under individual countries. Chapter 6 on Jews lists one title, and part 6 includes 12 entries for Sorbians (Lusatians) and Polabians. About 60 specialists contributed entries in European languages.

10. Horecky, Paul L., ed. **Southeastern Europe: A Guide to Basic Publications.** Chicago: University of Chicago Press, 1970. 755p.

This volume covers Albania, Bulgaria, Greece, Rumania, and Yugoslavia. More than 50 experts submitted sections containing about 3,000 entries. A considerable number of the contributors are natives of the regions about which they write.

11. Horecky, Paul L., chief ed. **East Central and Southern Europe: A Handbook of Library and Archival Resources in North America.** Santa Barbara, CA: ABC-Clio Press, [1976]. xi, 467p.

Holdings of some 40 research libraries, archives, and special institutions on Albania, Bulgaria, Czechoslovakia, East Germany, Greece, Hungary, Poland, Romania, and Yugoslavia are here recorded and evaluated with only sporadic references and indications of collections on national minorities of the respective countries.

12.   Horna, Dagmar, ed. **Current Research on Central and Eastern Europe.** New York: Mid-European Studies Center, Free European Committee, 1956. 251p.

The book lists 1,214 works in English arranged by standard subjects. A limited number of books on national minorities is included in such headings as History, Politics and Government, Population, and Religion. A "Roster of Authors" includes the profession, position, and address of each of the authors whose works are listed.

13.   Lewanski, Richard C., comp. **Eastern Europe and Russia/Soviet Union: A Handbook of West European Archival and Library Resources.** Ridgewood, NJ: K. G. Saur, 1980. xv, 317p.

The guide covers the resources in 22 west European countries and concludes with a subject index. Under the name of each country, institutions are listed by geographical area (cities), with accurate addresses and the names of institutional heads, librarians, and archivists. This is followed by a brief description of the collection, photocopying and telex facilities, information services, and business hours.

14.   Meyer, Klaus, comp. **Bibliographie der Arbeiten zur osteuropäischen Geschichte aus den deutschsprachigen Fachzeitschriften 1858-1964.** Bibliographische Mitteilungen des Osteuropa-Instituts an der Freien Universität Berlin, vol. IX. Berlin: Otto Harrassowitz, 1966. 314p.

This selective bibliography attempts to make available the contents of German-language periodicals for the past century in the field of east European history. It uses a chronological subject arrangement of more than 4,000 articles from 55 periodicals and yearbooks.

15.   Meyer, Klaus, comp. **Bibliographie zur osteuropäischen Geschichte: Verzeichnis der zwischen 1939 and 1964 veröffentlichten Literatur in west-europäischen Sprachen zur osteuropäischen Geschichte bis 1945.** Bibliographische Mitteilungen des Osteuropa-Instituts an der Freien Universität Berlin, vol. X. Berlin: In Kommission by otto Harrassowitz, Wiesbaden, 1972. 649p.

The bibliography lists 12,152 entries on Russian/Soviet and Polish history. The section on Poland includes special chapters on Poland's national minorities, Jews, Germans, and others (entries 10529-10615), and the chapter on "Poland in the Second World War" lists entries on Jews (12033-12071).

16.   Schöpflin, George, ed. **The Soviet Union and Eastern Europe: A Handbook.** New York: Praeger, 1970. 614p.

A team of contributors examine the political and economic systems of the eastern European countries, the structure of their societies, and historical background essential to an accurate understanding of the Soviet Union and eastern Europe. Basic country-by-country information is provided on the governments, economies, communications, and the social structure of the Communist-ruled states. The rest of the book is devoted to an analysis of politics, military and strategic affairs, planning and economic policy, trade, social affairs, education, law, religion, and culture.

17. Shoup, Paul S. **The East European and Soviet Data Handbook: Political, Social, and Developmental Indicators, 1945-1975.** New York: Columbia University Press; Stanford, CA: Hoover Institution Press, 1981. 482p.

Section C, National and Religious Affiliation (pp. 113-66), provides data on nationalities for all the east European countries for the interwar and post-World War II periods. Nationality is determined by ethnic affiliation, not by native tongue. The data is reliable and in most cases based on official censuses in both periods.

18. Späth, Manfred, comp. **Bibliography of Articles on East-European and Russian History: Selected from English-Language Periodicals 1850-1938.** Edited by Werner Philipp. Bibliographische Mitteilungen des Osteuropa-Instituts an der Freien Universität Berlin. Wiesbaden: Otto Harrassowitz, 1981. 98p.

The articles selected are limited to those that deal with the tsarist Russian territory and the states within these boundaries founded after World War I. The chapter on Poland lists articles on Ukrainian and German national minorities (pp. 81-83).

19. Teich, Gerhard. **Topographie der Osteuropa-, Südosteuropa- und DDR-Sammlungen.** Zentralbibliothek der Wirtschaftswissenschaften in der Bundesrepublik Deutschland. München and New York: Verlag Dokumentation, 1978. 388p.

This useful guide to the West German learned institutions and libraries gives detailed descriptions of 210 collections affiliated with universities, institutes, and societies, and private holdings. In each instance are given the name and address of the institution, the person in charge, the area of specialization, the size of the collection (books and periodicals), special features indicating area or nationality and even information on lending and use of the library. The holdings on national minorities are in each case described in detail. The work is an indispensable companion to the specialist working in German libraries and archives.

20. Walker, Gregory, ed. **Resources for Soviet, East European and Slavonic Studies in British Libraries.** Birmingham: University of Birmingham Centre for Russian and East European Studies, 1981. 240p.

The guide's aim is to record library collections in the United Kingdom likely to be of use for advanced study or research, and to describe their contents in sufficient detail for the enquirer to make an informed choice among the resources available. Included are over 140 libraries' holdings relating to the USSR, Poland, Czechoslovakia, GDR, Hungary, Yugoslavia, Romania, Bulgaria, and Albania. As regards subject coverage, the intention has been to include collections in all areas of the humanities and social sciences. Though no special listing of collections on national minorities is offered, the guide's importance lies with its description of characteristics and size of holdings and addresses and names of librarians to contact.

General Publications

21. Jásci, Oscar. **The Dissolution of the Habsburg Monarchy.** 4th ed. Chicago: University of Chicago Press, 1966. 482p.

Jásci maintains that the main factor responsible for the destruction of the Habsburg monarchy was the problem of nationality and that its dissolution was hastened, but not caused, by World War I. The book discusses and analyzes each nationality in terms of national aspiration, development, and participation in the empire's disintegration. Numerous statistical tables provide additional insight, and a comprehensive bibliography enhances the work's value. Highly recommended for historical background information on the events that led to the dissolution of the second largest multinational empire.

22.   Kann, Robert A. **The Habsburg Empire: A Study in Integration and Disintegration.** New York: Praeger, 1957. 227p.

_____. **The Multinational Empire: Nationalism and National Reform in the Habsburg Monarchy, 1848-1918.** 2 vols. New York: Octagon Books, 1964. Maps.

Both volumes review some basic problems and concepts, among them nationalism and its setting and the process of integration and disintegration between 1867 and 1918.

23.   Klein, George, and Reban, Milan J., eds. **The Politics of Ethnicity in Eastern Europe.** East European Monographs, no. 93, and ASN Series in Issue Studies (USSR and East Europe), no. 2. Boulder, CO: East European Monographs, 1981. 279p.

From among 10 chapters comprising this informative study, the following contributions deal exclusively with the national minorities in eastern Europe: John Georgeoff, "Ethnic Minorities in the People's Republic of Bulgaria"; Zeline Amen Wand, "Minority Politics in the German Democratic Republic"; Ivan Volgyes, "Legitimacy and Modernization: Nationality and Nationalism in Hungary and Transylvania"; Milan J. Reban, "Czechoslovakia: The New Federation"; and George and Patricia V. Klein, "Nationalism vs. Ideology: The Pivot of Yugoslav Politics."

24.   Macartney, Carlile A. **National States and National Minorities.** London: Oxford University Press, 1934. 570p.

The book provides an extensive and objective survey of the national minorities issue in Europe, with the emphasis on the eastern European states. An especially valuable part of the study is the statistical data for all countries for the 1920s.

25.   Mellor, Roy E. H. **Eastern Europe: A Geography of the Comecon Countries.** New York: Columbia University Press, 1975. 358p.

This systematic survey of the human geography of the socialist countries of eastern Europe links together the historical and contemporary scenes, and illuminates the complexity of these countries and their interrelationships. Particular attention is given to the political-geographical evolution of the map of eastern Europe and to population, ethnography, and transport. Of special interest and value to students of national minorities is the chapter on population, with its tables and maps indicating numbers of national minorities in all countries before and after World War II. Background information is also provided. This work presents knowledgeable and objective treatment of the subject as well as reliable data and maps.

26.   Rothschild, Joseph. **East Central Europe between the Two World Wars.** A History of East Central Europe, vol. IX. Seattle: University of Washington Press, 1974. 420p.

The book is part handbook and part political history of all countries between the Baltic Sea and Greece, with only a brief discussion of the Baltic states. Problems and issues of national minorities are sufficiently illuminated and supported by statistical data. Their impact upon political, social, and economic aspects of the respective countries is discussed in detail. Numerous tables supplement the material, and the work can well be used in courses on national minorities as an introduction and background for the interwar period.

27. Seton-Watson, Hugh. **The East European Revolution.** New York: Praeger, 1951. 435p.
This classic work provides a basic survey of the social structure, politics, history, and economics of eastern Europe, as well as an analysis of the development that led to the Sovietization of the satellite countries. The author is well aware of the ethnic factors that shaped and contributed to the internal as well as external problems with which all east European states were confronted. Sufficient background knowledge is provided to help the reader better understand the complexities of the situation, especially since World War II.

28. Seton-Watson, Hugh. **Eastern Europe between the Wars, 1918-1941.** Cambridge: Cambridge University Press, 1945. 3rd ed. Hamden, CT: Shoe String Press, 1963. 442p.
In a general and rather critical survey of the interwar history of all east European states, the author points out how the newly acquired provinces, such as Croatia and Transylvania and especially Bessarabia, were neglected or misgoverned after the First World War, so that they proved weak spots when the unity of the new states came to be tested. Seton-Watson wrote this book before eastern Europe fell under Soviet domination.

29. Sugar, Peter F. **Ethnic Diversity and Conflict in Eastern Europe.** Santa Barbara, CA: ABC-Clio Press, 1980. 553p.
The volume comprises papers presented at the Conference of the Joint Committee on Eastern Europe of the American Council of Learned Societies in 1976 in Seattle, Washington. The conference recognized that ethnicity has been a factor in determining the developments in eastern Europe from the middle of the eighteenth century until the present and that there is a need for a more general understanding of its impact. The discussion is limited to four key topics: 1) language as the basis for ethnic identity; 2) the influence of state policy on ethnic persistence and nationality formation; 3) economic and class differentiation and ethnicity; 4) religion and ethnicity. Ten essays elaborate on various aspects of the four main topics, although they do not deal specifically with the issues of the national minorities of eastern Europe during the interwar and postwar periods. On the whole, the essays are informative, well balanced, and objective in treating issues of conflicting interests. Of special value are the bibliographical contributions to each chapter.

30. Sugar, Peter F., and Lederer, Ivo J., eds. **Nationalism in Eastern Europe.** Publications on Russia and Eastern Europe, no. 1. Far Eastern and Russian Institute. Seattle: University of Washington Press, 1969. 465p.
Concentrating on the history of nationalism in the nineteenth and twentieth centuries, this volume contains separate chapters on each of the east European countries, with the emphasis on the state-nationalities. Almost all essays, in various degrees of impartiality, discuss the interplay and relationship between the "master nationality" and the ethnic minorities populating these countries. The main value of the book within the context of the study of east European national minorities lies in the exposition of the attitudes of the state nationalities towards the "subject nationalities."

National Minorities — Rights and Protection

31. Azcárate y Flórez, Pablo de. **League of Nations and National Minorities: An Experiment.** Carnegie Endowment for International Peace. Division of International Law. Studies in the Administration of International Law and Organization, no. 5. Washington: Carnegie Endowment for International Peace, 1945. 216p.

The former director of the Minorities Questions Section of the League of Nations discusses the situation of national minorities in Europe with emphasis on central and eastern Europe, the rights and duties of minorities, and the actions of the League of Nations in the interest of minorities. An appendix contains the official "Report of Work of the League of Nations in Relation to Protection of Minorities." A name and subject index is appended. See also: Viefhaus, Erwin. *Die Minderheitenfrage und die Entstehung der Minderheitenschutzverträge auf der Pariser Friedenskonferenz 1919: Eine Studie zur Geschichte des Nationalitätenproblems im 19. und 20. Jahrhundert.* Marburger Ostforschungen, Bd. 11. Würzburg: Holzner, 1960. 244p.; Buza, László. *A kisebbségek jogi helyzete a békeszerződések és más nemzetközi egyezmények értelmében* (Legal Position of Minorities in the Light of Peace Treaties and Other International Agreements). Budapest: Magyar Tudományos Akadémia, 1930. 432p. This volume deals with international agreements concluded between governments of east central Europe to protect minorities.

32. Feinberg, Nathan. **La question des minorités á la conférence de la paix, 1919-1920 et l'action juive en faveur de la internationale des minorités.** Paris: Rousseau & Cie., 1929. 167p.

This book discusses the problem of the national minorities at the Paris Peace Conference. It also includes the complete text of the minorities treaty with Poland of June 28, 1919 (pp. 141-47), the Memorandum of the Committee of the Jewish Delegation to the Paris Peace Conference of May 1919 (pp. 148-52), and several other documents pertaining to Jewish and other national minorities questions. The footnotes provide a basic bibliography unavailable elsewhere.

33. Flachbarth, Ernst. **System des internationalen Minderheitenrechtes: Geschichte des internationalen Minderheitenschutzes. Positives materielles Minderheitenrecht.** Introduction by Graf Stephan Bethlen. Budapest: R. Gergely Verlag, 1937. 475p.

A global treatment concentrating on east central Europe, the book includes interstate agreements on protection of minorities and reviews the role of the League of Nations. It contains relevant documents in their original languages. See also: Erler, Georg H. J. *Das Recht der nationalen Minderheiten.* Deutschtum und Ausland. Studien zur Auslandkultur, Heft 37/39. Münster in Westfalen: Aschendorffsche Verlagsbuchhandlung, 1931, 1931. 530p. This title contains an extensive review of nationality statistics, historical background, education, protection of minorities, politics, etc., in Czechoslovakia, Hungary, and Poland.

34. Mair, Lucy Philip. **The Protection of Minorities: The Working and Scope of the Minorities Treaties under the League of Nations.** London: Christophers, 1928. 244p.

The author reviews the treaties and actions on behalf of the national minorities placed under the protection of the League of Nations.

35. Stone, Julius. **International Guarantees of Minority Rights: Procedures of the League of Nations in Theory and Practice.** London: Oxford University Press, 1932. 297p.

The book offers an account of the role of the Council of the League of Nations as protector of minorities and of its successes and failures since 1919. Four valuable appendixes enhance the usefulness of the book to the casual student. Excellent treatment of a complicated subject.

36. Stone, Julius. **Regional Guarantees of Minority Rights: A Study of Minorities Procedure in Upper Silesia.** Cambridge, MA: Bureau of International Research, Harvard University, 1933. 313p.

A companion volume to the author's *International Guarantees of Minority Rights*, this study deals with the procedure in force that protects minority rights in Upper Silesia. The appendixes include the text of the German-Polish Convention of May 15, 1922, and the rules of procedure of the mixed Commission for Upper Silesia. The book remains the standard work on the Geneva Convention of 1922.

37. Veiter, Theodor, ed. **System eines internationalen Volksgruppenrechts.** 1. Teil: *Grundlagen und Begriffe.* Völkerrechtliche Abhandlungen. Band 3/1. Vienna, 1970.

European experts describe the juridical relationship between the law of ethnic groups on one side and international law and human rights on the other as it exists in authoritarian states and in democracies. The practice in east European countries before and after World War II is frequently referred to and used for clarification of the problem.

National Minorities — Publications

38. Batowski, Henryk, ed. **Irredenta niemiecka w Europie środkowej i południowo-wschodniej przed II wojną światową** (German Irredenta in Central and South-Eastern Europe before World War II). Cracow: Państwowe Wydawn. Naukowe, Oddz. w Krakowie, 1971. 281p.

The purpose of this work is to show what part the German minorities living in east Europe played during the interwar period, specifically in Czechoslovakia, Poland, Hungary, Romania, and Yugoslavia. A team of authors discuss in brief outline the position and activities of those Germans who maintained particularly close links with the Reich and the Nazi party organization. Included are maps, a name index, a geographical index, and a list of German organizations. Each chapter provides an updated bibliography in German and other languages.

39. Brunner, Georg, and Meissner, Boris, eds. **Nationalitäten-Probleme in der Sowjetunion und Osteuropa.** Köln: Markus Verlag, 1982. 221p.

This is the first German publication dealing with the non-Russian nationalities of the USSR and national minorities of the east European states. Each chapter offers a general introduction, a short historical background, statistical data, the legal and political treatment of the minorities, and an updated selected bibliography. Appendixes provide statistical data based on official censuses for the nationalities of the post-World War II period in each country. Pertinent and well-condensed information introduces the reader to a complex and less known area of Soviet and east European studies.

40. Chaszar, Edward. "The Problem of National Minorities before and after the Paris Peace Treaties of 1947." *Nationalities Papers* 9:2 (Fall 1981): 195-206.

The League of Nations had minority petitions presented in its council, yet the League lacked sanctions and had to rely on internal (national) constitutions. The U.N. has not followed suit. The Paris Peace Treaties after World War II favored forcible transfer of minority populations. Thus, minority rights remained unprotected, although they were included in the human rights provisions of the charter.

41. Chmelař, Josef. **Evropské menšiny ve svých organisacích** European Minorities in Their Organizations). Národnostní otázky (Nationalities Questions), vol. 2. Prague: Čs. společnost pro studium menšinových otázek, Orbis, 1933. 57p.

The subject of this booklet is the organizations of national minorities in Europe after World War I and their cooperation, with emphasis on central east Europe. A bibliography is included.

42. Chmelař, Joseph. **National Minorities in Central Europe.** Prague: Orbis, 1937. 105p. Map.

Following the country-by-country approach, the author discusses national minorities in Czechoslovakia, Poland, Romania, Yugoslavia, Hungary, Austria, Italy, Germany, and the Baltic states during the post-World War I period. This is a very useful, though brief, survey of the area of intermingled nationalities. A map of central Europe's nationalities mosaic is attached.

43. **Congress of European Nationalities. Sitzungsbericht des Kongresses der organisierten nationalen Gruppen in den Staaten Europas.** 13 vols. Wien and Leipzig: In Kommission bei Wilhelm Braumüller Universitäts-Verlagsbuch-handlung, 1626-1938.

Thirteen congresses were held annually between 1925 and 1937, usually in Geneva. Representatives of the ethnic minorities—chiefly from Poland, Czechoslovakia, Hungary, and Romania—made situation reports reflecting the problems of nationalities in those states as well as the degree of implementation of minority rights and the possibilities for peaceful solutions. Included are addresses, statistical materials, reports on group and individual cases, and resolutions presented to the congresses.

44. Dami, Aldo. **Les nouveaux martyrs; destin des minorités.** Paris: Fernand Sorlot, [1936]. xvii, 277p. Tables.

An extensive discussion of the fate of the Ruthenians (Ukrainians) in Czechoslovakia and of Hungarians in Czechoslovakia, Romania, and Yugoslavia. In each case, historical background is provided together with statistical data. Appendixes include texts of treaties and agreements concerning the rights of the national minorities in Czechoslovakia, Romania, and Yugoslavia.

45. Dawidowicz, Lucy S., ed. **The Golden Tradition: Jewish Life and Thought in Eastern Europe.** New York: Holt, Rinehart & Winston, 1967. 502p. Maps.

This is an anthology of memoirs and biographical sketches of Jewish writers, politicians, revolutionaries, and scholars from eastern Europe. Taken all together, the effect is a picture of the spiritual atmosphere and crosscurrents of east European Jewry from the beginning of the eighteenth century up to the Second World War. A scholarly introduction traces the history of spiritual and political movements of the period.

46.   Dawidowicz, Lucy S. **The War against the Jews, 1933-1945.** New York: Holt, Rinehart & Winston, 1975. xviii, 460p.

In addition to discussing Nazi extermination of Jews, the author analyzes the prevailing forms of anti-Semitism in east European countries.

47.   **Deutsche Ostsiedlung in Mittelalter und Neuzeit.** Studien zum Deutschtum im Osten, Heft 8. Köln: Böhlau Verlag, 1971. 240p.

In 1970/1971, the University of Bonn arranged a series of lectures devoted to the topic of the German settlement in the east during the Middle Ages and modern times. These 12 lectures are included in this collection, which is a splendid introduction to this topic although it closes with the year 1914. It appears from these studies that the "German" settlement in the east could be regarded in a broader sense as a west European settlement.

48.   Gäll, Ernö. **Nemzetiséq, erkölcs, értelmiséq** (Nationality, Morals, Intelligentsia). Budapest: Szépirodalmi Publishers, 1978. 472p.

While the author analyzes the meanings and implications of "nation" and "nationality," the problems connected with literature on nationality are at the center of his interest. In fact, he draws out examples from studies or other literary products to illustrate points encountered during the scrutiny of histories of ideas, including the ones underlying programs and claims of nationalities. A favorite study of Gäll's is the history of ideas in Transylvania.

49.   Grulich, Rudolf, and Pulte, Peter. **Nationale Minderheiten in Europa: Eine Darstellung der Problematik mit Dokumenten und Materialen zu den europäischen Volksgruppen und Sprachminderheiten.** Foreword by Prof. Dr. Johannes Hampel. Opladen: Heggen Verlag, 1975. 215p. Map. Statistical tables.

The volume comprises six sections. The 63-page introduction provides the most essential data about the most important countries in Europe that contain national minorities. The data include the numbers and percentages of national minorities, as well as terse information about the positions, cultural, educational, and the like, of the larger minorities within the various countries. Other sections deal with international and supranational documents and documents and material records of individual European states. A short list covers the addresses of research and interest organizations (not separated nationally) and of nationality-group organizations tabulated according to individual countries.

50.   Janowsky, Oscar I. **Nationalities and National Minorities: With Special Reference to East-Central Europe.** New York: Macmillan, 1945. 232p.

This general account of the interwar development in Europe and in eastern Europe in particular concludes with the author's proposed solution, the creation of a large federation of nations of east central Europe.

51.   Junghann, Otto. **National Minorities in Europe.** New York: Covici-Friede Publishers, 1932. 121p.

One of the ideals for which the First World War was fought was the right of peoples to self-determination. In addition, internationally guaranteed treaties were enacted for the protection of minorities. yet the newly enlarged states could not resist temptations either to take advantage of possibilities under the protection of the victors or to avenge injustices. Consequently, radical hostility was expressed towards minorities and national tolerance was often fully disregarded.

52. King, Robert R. **Minorities under Communism: Nationalities as a Source of Tension among Balkan Communist States.** Cambridge, MA: Harvard University Press, 1973. 326p.

The subtitle of this book is more descriptive of the contents than is the main title. King is less interested in the political, cultural, and socioeconomic conditions per se of the ethnic minorities in the several Balkan Communist states (including Czechoslovakia and Hungary) than he is in ascertaining how the relations between a *Staatsvolk* and the ethnic minorities in any particular Communist state become a source of international tension between several Communist states. King's thesis is that communism has not solved the nationality problem in eastern Europe. Cases of Communist interstate tension that are studied in this book in order to illustrate and confirm its main thesis are the Czechoslovak-Hungarian conflict, the Romanian-Hungarian controversy, and the Yugoslav-Albanian disagreement.

53. Komjathy, Anthony, and Stockwell, Rebecca. **German Minorities and the Third Reich.** New York: Holmes & Meier Publishers, 1980. xii, 217p.

The central aim of this study is to describe the relationship between German ethnic minorities in Czechoslovakia, Hungary, Poland, Romania, and Yugoslavia and the Third Reich in the period between World War I and the end of World War II. After World War II, about five and a half million folk Germans were expelled from east central European countries. They were accused of supporting Nazi Germany, promoting Nazism, serving the Reich's imperialism, and providing a fifth column for the German army. Stereotyping German ethnic minorities as a fifth column or as a blind instrument of the Third Reich's imperialism was found to be grossly misleading. German minorities belonged to diverse political groups, Marxist, conservative, liberal, and Nazi, although most of them had one common characteristic, the desire to preserve their cultural identity, their Germanness. Strong efforts of some governments to assimilate them only strengthened their resistance to acculturation.

54. Lendvai, Paul. **Anti-Semitism without Jews: Communist Eastern Europe.** Garden City, NY: Doubleday, 1971. 393p.

This study examines the present conditions and status of Jews in Poland, Czechoslovakia, Hungary, and Romania. Despite the enormous numerical decrease of Jews since World War II (to about 0.2% of the total population), many of the problems remained, including anti-Semitism in various forms. In addition to a large number of appended documents, the author offers his own analysis, which is not entirely supportable by history. Nevertheless, the book provides a wealth of information for future historians.

55. Meyer, Peter, et al. **The Jews in the Soviet Satellites.** Syracuse, NY: Syracuse University Press, 1953. 637p.

This is a collection of surveys on the situation of the Jews in five Soviet bloc countries up to spring 1953. Each survey begins with a review of the situation before the Second World War and during the Nazi occupation, but deals mainly with the Communist attitude toward Jewish problems and the effect of the Soviet system on Jewish life. The work is based on Communist-sponsored Jewish publications, official documents, and Jewish press from the West. There is an excellent, extensive bibliography under the headings "Czechoslovakia," by Peter Meyer; "Hungary," by Eugene Duchinsky; and "Poland" and "Polish Jews under Soviet Rule," by Bernard Weinryb.

56. Niederhauser, Emil. **A Nemzeti mégujalási mozgalmak kelet-európában** (National Renewal Movements in Eastern Europe). Budapest: Akademia Publishers, 1977. 385p.

A novel approach is used here for the analysis of movements of national renewal. Instead of dealing with them one by one, the author provides comparisons on various levels of such related topics as the emergence of cultural institutions, national language, education, literature, theatre, music, fine arts, history and historical consciousness, and so on. Also, social programs and activities (uprisings and revolutions) are discussed. The comparisons of the various national movements help in identifying their principal patterns. Additional aspects examined and compared include history writing and historical consciousness as well as the ballot and the constitution.

57. Rhode, Gotthold. **Nationalitätenproblem in Ost- und Südosteuropa.** Darmstadt: Wissenschaftliche Buchgesellschaft, 1973. 110p.

The various nationalities of east Europe are extensively reviewed from historical and political perspectives. The author's scholarship and objectivity are well demonstrated.

58. Schechtman, Joseph B. **European Population Transfers, 1939-1945.** Studies of the Institute of World Affairs. New York: Oxford University Press, 1946. xi, 532p. Illus. Maps. Bibliography.

This study mirrors a phase of the profound social transformation in central and southeastern Europe and its implications for the years to come. Its immediate concern is the decisions of the Potsdam Declaration of 1945, which envisaged population transfer as instrumental to the final peace settlement. In addition to the resettlement of Germans from east European countries, the transfer of non-German minorities is discussed. Appendixes provide statistical tabulations for all transferred or resettled nationalities during the years 1939-1945.

59. Schmelz, Uziel O., comp. **Jewish Demography and Statistics: Bibliography for 1920-1960 + Addenda.** 2 vols. Jerusalem: Hebrew University, Institute for Contemporary Jewry, 1961.

Approximately 5,000 items relating to Jewish communities throughout the world are listed in this very useful, extensive bibliography. It includes books and articles in many languages, adding English translations of titles in lesser-known languages. Demography is used here in a wide sense to include health, economy, education, social matters, and community organization. A third volume with new material up to 1966 and an addendum for 1920-1960 was published in 1968. Another bibliography, narrower in scope, is *Jews in the Communist World: A Bibliography, 1945-1962* (New York: pro Arte, 1963. 125p.), by Randolph L. Braham and Mordecai M. Hauer. This selected bibliography of books and articles lists 845 entries. Part A lists references to non-English literature, with titles in lesser-known languages translated into English. Part B supplements an earlier compilation by Braham entitled *Jews in the Communist World: A Bibliography, 1945-1960* (New York: Twayne Publishers, 1961, 64p.), which listed materials in English only.

60. Schulz, Eberhard G., ed. **Leistung und Schicksal: Abhandlungen und Berichte über die Deutschen im Osten.** Köln: Böhlau Verlag, 1967. 414p.

The book is divided into five parts: history of settlement and languages, climate and economic history, cultural history, political history, and postwar developments. It deals with the contribution of the Germans to the development of east central Europe, and in particular their previous settlement areas within the German borders of 1937, in Poland and in Czechoslovakia. The fate of Germans in the Soviet Union from 1917 to 1965 is discussed briefly. The contributions give a good picture of the political, economic, and cultural achievements of the Germans, which for political reasons are today either minimized or misinterpreted.

61. Seraphim, Peter H. **Das Judentum im osteuropäischen Raum.** Essen: Essener Verlagsanstalt, 1938. 736p. Illus. Maps. Ports.

This is a history of the Jews in eastern Europe from their first settlement there until the Second World War. Prepared in cooperation with the Institut für osteuropäische Wirtschaft of Königsberg University, the study presents more details on the economic aspect of Jewish life and the participation of Jews in the economy of the various countries than on the cultural and religious life of the Jews. A special chapter is devoted to demography and statistics. Although it is anti-Semitic, this is the only general history of east European Jewry in a Western language.

62. Stillschweig, Kurt. **Die Juden Osteuropas in den Minderheitenverträgen.** Berlin: J. Jastrow, 1936. 207p.

The minority treaties between the Allied Powers of the First World War and new states, and the provisions in peace treaties with defeated nations, guaranteed the religious, linguistic, and educational rights of Jews in eastern Europe. This book discusses these rights and the factors involved in their adoption. For information on the struggle for Jewish autonomy and minority rights in Europe and the United States, see also Janowsky, Oscar I., *The Jews and Minority Rights (1898-1919).* New York: Columbia University Press, 1933. 419p.

63. Straka, Manfred, ed. **Handbuch der europäischen Volksgruppen.** Ethnos, vol. 8. Published on behalf of the Föderalistische Union Europäischer Volksgruppen, Povl Skadegard, Secretary General. Vienna: Wilhelm Braumüller Universitäts-Verlagsbuchhandlung, 1970. 658p.

This book deals with all European ethnic groups, but two-thirds of it is devoted to eastern and southeastern Europe. Essays discuss individual ethnic groups within particular states and are generally divided up as follows: history, statistics, legal position, political representation, religious and church life, language, schools, mass-media, and the position in the state.

64. Trunk, Isaiah. **Judenrat: The Jewish Councils in Eastern Europe under Nazi Occupation.** Introduction by Jacob Robinson. New York: Macmillan, 1972. 664p.

The study centers on the questions: Why and how did the councils (Judenrat) work and was Jewish-Nazi cooperation decisive in the destruction of European Jewry? To arrive at an answer to these questions, the author spent five years of study and research in various Jewish archives in the United States, Israel, and Germany, in addition to compiling a personal collection of notes and summaries of documents in Poland during the years 1946-1950. The notes cover 62 pages. In addition, Trunk utilized 927 questionnaires that were filled out by survivors. The author set for himself the task of writing an objective history of the councils; his intention was not to pronounce judgment on those institutions but rather to probe deeply into the entire complex topic.

65.   Vago, Bela. **The Shadow of the Swastika: The Rise of Fascism and Anti-Semitism in the Danube Basin, 1936-1939.** Published for the Institute of Jewish Affairs. London, Westmead, Hants, England: Saxon House, D.C. Health, 1975. 431p.

Vago has used British Foreign Office material relevant to the precarious position of Jews in Romania, Czechoslovakia, and Hungary within the general framework of domestic developments from 1936 until August 1939. Of the documents included, 164 are printed in part or in full.

66.   Veiter, Theodor, ed. **Volkstum zwischen Moldau, Etsch und Donau. Festschrift für Franz Hieronymus Riedl.** Ethnos, vol. 10. Publication series of the Research Group for Questions of Nationality and Language. Marburg/Lahn. Vienna: Wilhelm Braumüller Universitäts-Verlagsbuchhandlung, 1971. 416p.

The 32 essays deal with the area between Silesia, Transylvania, and Trent. Arranged by subject, they are concerned with ethnopolitical and nationality questions. This is an impressive volume, although, as is the nature of such commemorative publications, the essays are of varying quality. Some articles stand out above the others, such as Ermacora's contribution on the "Plebiscite (1920 in Carinthia) as a model for the application of the right to self-determination in the community of nations," and the contributions by Burmeister and Meusburger on the Italian minority in Vorarlberg, 1870-1918, and on the transfer of those willing from South Tyrol to Vorarlberg and their integration.

67.   de Zayas, Alfred M. **Nemesis at Potsdam: The Anglo-Americans and the Expulsion of the Germans. Background, Execution, Consequences.** 2nd rev. ed. Boston: Routledge and Kegan Paul, 1979. 268p. Illus.

This is a new edition of a book that describes the expulsion of 15 million Germans 2 million of whom did not survive, from most parts of eastern Europe, a process which has received scant attention by Western scholars. It is astonishing that 34 years later, so little is known in the English-speaking world about this tragic event. The author attempts to remedy this situation by discussing the flight preceding the expulsion and the actual transfer and its consequences against the historical precedents and principles of population transfers. He pays special attention to the role and attitudes of the Western Allies.

Periodical Literature

68.   **Danubian Review.** A review devoted to research into problems of the Danubian Basin. 1934-1943. Budapest: Hungarian Frontier Readjustment League. Monthly.

69.   **Europa Ethnica (Nation und Staat).** No. 1 (Sept. 1927)- . Monthly, 1927-1944; Quarterly 1961- . Publication suspended, October 1944-1957. Title varies: 1927-August/September 1944, *Nation und Staat.* Wien: W. Braumüller, 1927- . Since 1957 issued by the Federal Union of European Nationalities. Text in English, German, or French.

70. **Kisebbségi Körlevél** (Minority Circular). 1937-1944. Pécs. Bimonthly.

Issued by the Research Institute of Minorities at the University of Pécs, the journal is devoted to the problems of national minorities in the Danubian Basin, with emphasis on east central Europe. It includes book reviews, maps, statistics, surveys, laws, decrees, statutory provisions, and published texts. The following periodicals also contain much material relative to the whole area: *Magyar Kisebbség; nemzetpolitikai szemle* (Magyar Minorities; A Nationality Review). vols. 1-17; 1922-1938. Lugos: Husvéth és Hoffer Könyvnyomdája. Semimonthly. *Láthatár* (Horizon). 1933- . Budapest. Biweekly.

71. **Kulturwehr; Zeitschrift für Volkstumsfragen.** vols. 1-14, no. 4; 1925-1938. Berlin: Verband der nationalen Minderheiten im Deutschen Reich. Monthly.

72. **Minorité; informations concernant les minorités et l'évolution du droit minoritaire.** January 1934- . Geneva. Monthly.

73. **Prosveshchenie natsional'nostei: obshchestvenno-politicheskii i nauchno-pedagogicheskii zhurnal** (Education of the Nationalities; A Socio-Political and Scholarly-Pedagogical Journal). 1929-1935, no. 4. Moscow. Monthly.

74. **Voix des peuples; revue de politique international.** vols. 1-12; 1934-1945. Geneva: Bureau Central des Minorités. Ten times yearly.

2 ⸻ National Minorities in Poland, 1919-1980

Kenneth C. Farmer,
with the assistance of David Crowe (Jews)
and Richard Blanke (Germans)

HISTORICAL SUMMARY

Poland in the twentieth century has had a troubled history of minority nationality relations, all of it complex and much of it violent. Part of the problem throughout history has been the difficulty of defining the location of the Polish state; as in much of eastern Europe, there are no unambiguous geographical frontiers, and the villages and settlements have been mixed, so that there have been no distinct ethnic boundaries either. Included with Polish territory, therefore, have been Ukrainians, Belorussians, Lithuanians, Czechs, Germans, and Russians, in addition to Poles and Jews—to mention only the major ones. There have also been numerous numerically smaller ethnographic groups such as Gypsies, Kashubs, Karaims, and *Goralen* (a small but fiercely independent Carpathian mountain people). In addition, Poles have lived in all the neighboring east and central European countries, including the Russian empire and the present-day Soviet Union.

As a result of her unfortunate location between Germany and the Russian empire, Poland has in the modern age been successively partitioned between these two competing and expanding powers, disappearing from the map entirely as a political entity in 1795. In 1807, with Napoleon's help, a Duchy of

Warsaw was created, followed in 1815 by so-called "Congress Poland." By 1830, however, even the pretense that Congress Poland was other than a suzerainty of the tsar had been dropped.

Minorities in Interwar Poland, 1919-1939

The avowed intent of the Allied powers at the close of World War I was to create an independent Polish state on the ethnographic principle, comprised of unquestionably Polish territories and having free access to the sea.[1] This was the thirteenth of President Woodrow Wilson's famous Fourteen Points, which became the nominal guidelines for the territorial settlements in postwar Europe. The underlying principle of the Fourteen Points was that of "national self-determination," the radical, indeed for its time revolutionary, idea that national self-identity should be the basis for the formation of an independent state. While it was given much lip service, the principle was not really applied at the peace conference because it was essentially unworkable: its rigorous application would have led to the creation of dozens of small states, unviable economically, geopolitically, and militarily.

In fact, the creation of an independent Polish state reflected less the principle of national self-determination than the desire of the Allies to isolate Germany and Bolshevik Russia with a *cordon sanitaire*. Polish spokesmen (unlike the Germans and Soviets admitted to the peace conference) were even less concerned with national self-determination except insofar as it applied to Poles. Roman Dmowski's memorandum to the Commission on Polish Problems of the Supreme Council of the Paris Peace Conference, for example, made the following territorial demands for Poland: in the west, Upper Silesia and part of Breslau province, Western Prussia, the southern half of Eastern Prussia, and most of Pomerania. In the east, the Poles demanded Lithuania, two-thirds of Belorussia, and virtually all of Western Ukraine including Galicia.[2] The Poles claimed for Poland any territory that contained Polish inhabitants; fully half the population of the proposed Polish state would have been non-Polish.

German protests against a draft treaty based on these demands were vocal, leading to a series of plebiscites on the status of Upper Silesia and East Prussia, the results of which favored German administration of these territories. Meanwhile, Polish rebels were staging uprisings in Upper Silesia. Eventually, the differences over Upper Silesia were reconciled, as were differences over East Prussia and West Prussia, although Polish gains in these territories were smaller than in Upper Silesia. All told, the German empire lost to Poland a total of 3,947,537 people, including about 1,670,000 *Volksdeutsche*.

In the east, lukewarm Allied interest in the non-Russian peoples of the Russian empire, the withdrawal of German forces, and Bolshevik preoccupation with the civil war in Russia all permitted the Poles to gain significant territory, essentially by conquest. The Riga Treaty of March 18, 1921 resulted in the incorporation of Vilna province in Lithuania into Poland. The same treaty recognized the partition of Belorussian and Ukrainian territories between Poland and Soviet Russia. These annexations were accomplished primarily as a result of military activities, but in the end the Polish-Soviet frontier was recognized by the Western powers.[3]

Bitter confrontations between Poles and Ukrainians also marked the creation of the eastern frontiers. Ukraine, as well as Poland, had aspirations for independent statehood following the collapse of the Russian and Austrian empires. The conflict centered around Western Ukrainian territories to which Poland made a "historic claim": Eastern Galicia, Khomshchyna, and Volhynia. A Ukrainian national republic had been established on January 22, 1918 in Kiev, and its western borders had been recognized in the Treaty of Brest-Litovsk of February 9, 1918. Following the collapse of the Habsburg monarchy, Ukrainians proclaimed an independent Ukrainian Western Republic, soon to be attacked by the Poles. The Ukrainians, in conflict also with the Bolsheviks, were unable to sustain a two-front struggle for independence. Prolonged clashes for the possession of Ukraine were concluded by the Riga Treaty, and Western Ukraine fell to Polish rule (the voivodships of Wolyń, Lwów, Stanislawów, and Tarnopol). In March 1923, the Council of Ambassadors vested complete sovereign power over Western Ukraine in Poland.

Thus, the newly independent Polish Republic, created nominally on the basis of the principle of national self-determination, came into existence as a multinational state in which, at best, only about two-thirds of the population was Polish.[4] The 1921 census (the figures of which are disputed by non-Polish historians) give the following breakdown of the population: Poles, 69.2%; Ukrainians, 15.2%; Jews, 8.0%; Belorussians, 4.0%; and Germans, 3.0%. The remaining 0.6% was comprised of Lithuanians, Russians, Czechs, Tatars, and Karaites.[5]

In spite of the federalist orientations of leaders like Jozef Pilsudski and the efforts of sympathetic Poles such as Leon Wasilewski, interwar Poland was not a multinational federation of nationalities living together on the basis of equality; rather, a nation-state mentality dominated the thinking of the Poles, and Poland was a *Polish* republic with a large number of minorities. This attitude fostered constant hostility and strife between Poles and non-Poles. The efforts of the Polish state were oriented not toward accommodation, but toward pacifying and Polonizing its dissatisfied minorities, particularly its large Ukrainian, Belorussian, and German nationalities.

German mistrust of Polish nationality policies in large part brought this problem to international attention. The dissatisfaction of Germany with the Versailles settlement, along with the efforts of Jewish organizations in Britain, France, and the United States, was the major stimulus for the minorities treaty of June 28, 1919. The east Slavic nationalities and the Lithuanians had less influence on the treaty because the eastern borders had not as yet been settled.

The treaty significantly limited Polish sovereignty, insofar as its provisions were stated to be fundamental principles of the state, and were in fact to be guaranteed by the League of Nations.[6] Protection of national minorities became a precondition for recognition of Poland and for its admission to the League of Nations. The treaty, consisting of twelve articles, guaranteed equality to non-Polish citizens in political, cultural, economic, and religious life.[7] The Polish government, lukewarm about the treaty at best, regarded it as a gesture of appeasement to Germany, voicing the fear that it would handicap Poland in international affairs, since any member state of the League of Nations could formally charge Poland with infractions of the treaty.[8] Until Hitler's accession to power in 1933, Germany rarely missed an opportunity to embarrass Poland through charges in the League of Nations of minority abuses.[9] This German harassment was no doubt meant as much to discredit Polish ability to rule and to foster irredentism in Poland as it was a genuine protest against real abuses. Germany was not the only state to charge Poland with abuses. During 1920-1931, there were 247 petitions: the Germans filed 104; Ukrainians, 85; Jews, 33; Lithuanians, 19; and Belorussians, 6.[10]

The Polish government signed other international conventions pledging to safeguard the rights of all its minorities. Article VII of the Treaty of Riga with the USSR bound both countries to respect minority rights. An international convention on the status of Upper Silesia, signed with Germany in May 1922, contained similar provisions. Further guarantees of minority rights, based on the provisions of the minorities treaty, were incorporated directly into the first constitution of the Polish state.[11] Finally, a series of laws, the so-called "Lex Grabski," was passed in July 1924 in response to Ukrainian, Belorussian, and Lithuanian complaints about educational, linguistic, and political discrimination.[12]

The period 1919-1926 saw worsening relations between the state and the minority nationalities, due to the chauvinism of central and local officials, and continuing opposition among some minorities to their inclusion within Polish borders. Some abatement of the hostility occurred after the *coup d'etat* of Jozef Pilsudski in May 1926, as the *Sanacja* government sought to deal with the grievances of the minorities.[13] Most of the minority nationalities cooperated with the Pilsudski government by throwing their electoral support behind its legislative coalition, the Bloc of Non-Partisan Cooperation with the Government (BBWR). The honeymoon period was shortlived, however, and relations between the minorities and the Pilsudski government deteriorated. By the 1928 general election, the minorities opted out of the BBWR and ran their own candidate lists. A year later, all the Christian minorities boycotted the official celebrations of the tenth anniversary of Polish independence, evoking harsh retaliatory measures from the regime, particularly against the east Slavs. To ensure a substantial BBWR victory in 1930, after dissolving the rebellious parliament, the regime employed obstruction and terror against the opposition among the minorities.[14]

Except for a momentary respite following Pilsudski's death in May 1935, the decade of the 1930s witnessed progressive deterioration of state/minority relations. In 1934, Poland unilaterally abrogated the minorities treaty, further exacerbating the mistrust. The post-Pilsudski regime proved even more chauvinistic than its predecessors, and, on the eve of World War II, Poland found itself virtually without support among its non-Polish citizens.

Jews

The status of Jews in the new Polish state that emerged at the end of the war was, on paper, secure in view of the minorities treaty and the guarantees of the 1921 constitution.[15] Unfortunately, their real status frequently contrasted with these guarantees. Problems between Poles and Jews were based on centuries-old anti-Semitism, though immediate difficulties can be seen during the period of German-Austrian occupation of Poland, when new Polish-Jewish conflicts emerged in the midst of a Jewish economic decline that continued until the outbreak of World War II.[16]

The outset of Polish independence and its accompanying bloody pogroms between 1918 and 1920 dashed Jewish hopes that conditions would be better under Polish rule, and caused one Jewish newspaper to comment, "Poland has been reborn with bloodstains on her forehead."[17] Furthermore, these fears were exacerbated by the failure of the Polish government to enforce treaty and constitutional guarantees of Polish rights, and its refusal to grant promised adequate financial support to the independent Jewish school programs. The government also tried to restrict the activities of Poland's 599 *Kehiloth*, or communities for religious affairs, which hurt the efforts of Poland's Jewish community to develop a strong national identity.[18]

The government hoped to force the assimilation of the Jewish population into Polish society. It combined restrictive community and educational policies against the Jews, with economic programs in the urban areas that favored Poles over others.[19] Most of Poland's Jews — 2,853,318, making up 10.5% of the population in 1921 — lived in urban areas; 81% in central Poland and 61.5% in eastern Poland lived in cities. Consequently, they were disproportionately an important factor in Poland's predominantly rural society.[20] To counter this, the Polish government adopted policies throughout the interwar period to reduce Jewish and other non-Polish urban strength, which in turn affected the economic and social status of the urban Jewish population. As a result, although the Jewish population continued to grow in the cities during the interbellum period, its percentage in urban areas in relation to non-Jews dropped.[21]

Essentially, the policies of the various Polish governments after World War I created an economic and social structure that favored the ethnic Polish population and weakened the economic and social strength of its non-Polish elements.[22] Wide-scale dismissals of Jewish civil servants took place soon after Polish independence, and this trend spilled over into other areas where Polish public funding was involved. As a consequence of these policies, Jews increasingly were barred from a number of professional fields and stood out only in the areas of medicine and law; 56% of the country's physicians were Jews, as were 35.5% of the lawyers. The former, however, were usually not allowed to work in state hospitals, and the latter were excluded from holding court positions.[23] In education, similar restrictions limited Jewish teachers and professors to 5.7% of the total, and only 3.1% in the universities.[24] Restrictions were also placed on Jewish university students in the interwar period, and their proportion of total higher education enrollment dropped from 24.6% in 1921-1922 to 8.2% in 1938-1939.[25]

Jewish community and cultural life suffered similar restrictions, although it continued to provide Poland's Jews with important outlets for ethnic expression. Jewish communal life in Poland functioned around the *Kehilah*, which oversaw Jewish religious, educational, and social welfare matters. Unfortunately, Polish officials tried to restrict the *Kehiloth* to a religious role, but by 1928 they had given the country's 599 *Kehiloth* jurisdiction over Jewish schools and social welfare institutions.[26]

The Jewish educational system, the cornerstone for the maintenance of ethnic identity, suffered—particularly in the 1930s—from lack of governmental financial support, though in some regions, such as Vilna, Bialystok, and others, local government support in the 1920s had been strong.[27] With the rapid decline of government support for Jewish schools and the economic deterioration of the Jewish population the following decade, the number of Jewish schools continued to decrease steadily.[28]

A number of Jewish organizations sponsored schools for Jewish children. Agudath Israel had Horeb and Beth Yakov schools, while the Zionist Mizrachi organization maintained Yabneh schools. Another Zionist school system was the Tarbuth schools. Those who sought a Yiddish education could attend the Jewish Bund's Central Yiddish School Organization (CYSZO) schools. Others included the Yeshivoth and Poale Zion's Shukult schools. Each of these systems reflected the religious or political tincture of its sponsoring organization.[29] There was also the Institute of Judaism in the Polish capital for training rabbis, as well as the Yiddish Scientific Institute (YIVO) in Vilna, with its emphasis on Yiddish higher education and research, and the Orthodox Yeshiva Chachmey Lublin. Although it is difficult to verify the accuracy of figures, in 1936 there were 468,309 Jewish children enrolled in Jewish and non-Jewish schools in Poland, with 180,181 students attending 1,465 Jewish institutions. With the addition of students in the numerous *heder* and *Kehilah* schools, there were 232,428 students in 3,045 schools.[30]

The Jewish community was equally active in social welfare. The Society for the Protection of Jewish Public health (TOZ) oversaw many of these efforts, while other groups, such as Bikur Holim, Tomche Aniyim, and Hachnassath Kalah, provided relief in many of Poland's urban areas. These organizations maintained hospitals, clinics, and other facilities to aid the sick and needy, sometimes with local governmental support.[31]

To exploit their numerical strength for political gain, Jewish leaders created political organizations to represent the Jewish population in the new Sejm. Unfortunately, the traditional factionalism among Poland's Jews hurt these efforts, and Jews as a political bloc were ineffective in halting the economic and social decay that affected the Jewish community. In the first Sejm of 1919, the Zionist and Mizrachi (religious Zionist)-led Temporary Jewish national Council had six of eleven Jewish delegates in the legislature, led by Yitshak Grunbaum. Poale Zion, a Marxist group with Zionist leanings, had one delegate, while the Folkspartey—a conservative Yiddish, anti-Zionist faction—and the Orthodox League each had two.[32] These internal divisions hurt Jewish political efforts and strained their ability to work with the Sejm's National Minorities Bloc to resolve mutual hostilities between Poland's government and its ethnic groups.[33] Jewish political leaders remained determined and at the initiative of the government sought ways in the mid-1920s to resolve the oppressive economic situation of the Polish Jews. The government, however, failed to propose or support any proposals that would have brought significant economic relief to the Jewish community.[34] With the onset of the depression and the emergence of a more virulent strain of anti-Semitism, Jewish politics became more radicalized, and the General Zionists lost their dominant political position, to be replaced by the Bund, the Jewish Social Party, which had long represented the Jewish working class.[35] On the eve of the Nazi occupation and the Holocaust, Poland's doomed Jewish community was still working within the Polish political system to preserve its identity and its rights.

Ukrainians

The Ukrainians were the largest, and perhaps the most troublesome, minority in interwar Poland. Stephan Horak estimates the Ukrainian population in 1931 at approximately 5,660,000, concentrated heavily in southeastern Poland,[36] in the provinces of Lwów, Lublin, Polesie, Wolyń, Stanislawów, and Tarnopol. The Ukrainians were predominantly rural (as were the Belorussians), and, indeed, agrarian reform was one of the major areas of contention with the government. The Ukrainian peasantry was more mobilized and better organized politically than were their Polish neighbors. The well-developed Ukrainian cooperatives in Poland were viewed with suspicion by the Polish peasants and were harassed by federal and local government officials. The Ukrainian press also thrived in Poland, as did the network of Ukrainian-language schools; these latter, while continuing to help maintain Ukrainian identity, were also a target of government repression.

The Ukrainian community, less cohesive politically than socially or religiously, was united on the ultimate goal of independence from Poland. At the center of the political spectrum was the Ukrainian National Democratic Union (UNDO). Working for an independent, democratic Ukraine, it was closely associated with the Uniate Church and was strongest in East Galicia and Volhynia. Because it was moderate in its techniques and relatively so in its program, it was with this party that the Polish government usually preferred to deal.

There were four major parties on the Left. Two with non-Marxist socialist programs—the Ukrainian Socialist Radical party and the Ukrainian Social Democratic party—were influential. The Marxist parties—the Communist party of Western Ukraine (KPZU) and its offshoot, the Sel-Rob—were active but less influential. On the Right was the Organization of Ukrainian Nationalists (OUN) and the Ukrainian Military Organization—illegal, underground organizations devoted to Ukrainian independence, espousing an increasingly integral nationalist ideology influenced by Fascist movements to the west and sometimes employing political terror. All of these parties and organizations entered into political, educational, and religious activities, sometimes violent, aimed at preserving the Ukrainian way of life against discrimination and Polonization. The government responded alternately with oppression and accommodation.

During the period of parliamentary supremacy, which lasted until Pilsudski's *coup d'etat* in May 1926, the Ukrainians of Eastern Galicia had, as a result of their boycott of the elections of 1922, no representatives in the Polish Sejm, with the exception of five deputies elected by the Ukrainian Agricultural party, which collaborated with the Polish government. However, twenty Ukrainian deputies and six senators, elected from Volhynia, Polissia, and the province of Lublin, stated their demand for national territorial autonomy within the Polish state, though their experience with the successive coalition governments ruling Poland during this period proved to be bitterly disappointing.

Perhaps the greatest single reverse they suffered was the passing of the school law of July 31, 1924, which ultimately dealt a devastating blow at Ukrainian public schools in Eastern Galicia and Volhynia, transforming most of them into either bilingual or outright Polish institutions. According to the last Austrian school survey, there were 2,496 public elementary schools in Eastern Galicia with Ukrainian as the language of instruction. By 1938, only 452 of them had survived and the number of schools with Polish as the language of instruction had increased from 1,590 to 2,100. Bilingual schools, which began to operate only in 1924, increased to 2,485 by 1938; only the Ukrainian language and religion were taught in Ukrainian. The number of Ukrainian high schools (gymnasia) declined from twenty in 1929 to only five by 1934. By 1934, Ukrainians were left with only one teachers college. The virtual nonexistence of Ukrainian vocational schools affected the rural areas the most, since the majority of the rural population could not speak Polish. The question of existence of these schools was a social-economic problem for the Ukrainians. For Poland, this seemed to be chiefly a political matter. One of the most bitter controversies between the Ukrainians and the Poles concerned the establishment of a Ukrainian university in Lwów. Poland agreed to create a university under the autonomy law of September 26, 1922. However, the promised university was not established until 1939.

It was after Pilsudski's coup, in March 1928, that the Ukrainian deputies and senators from Galicia, representing two major political parties—the Ukrainian National Democratic Union (UNDO) and the Ukrainian Socialist Radical party—as well as some splinter groups, entered for the first time the Polish parliament. While pledging support for the idea of Ukrainian statehood, they were, at the same time, prepared to seek a dialogue with the Polish government on the basis of existing political realities, with a view toward reaching some kind of settlement on at least the most pressing issues. Their influence was being constantly eroded, however, by the nationalist underground, which rejected any accommodation with Warsaw and vowed to continue by all means at its disposal a revolutionary struggle against what it considered to be an illegal Polish occupation of Western Ukraine. Obviously, they could not ignore the fact that the policy of the newly created Organization of Ukrainian Nationalists (which in 1929 replaced the UVO) of actively and openly seeking a confrontation with the Polish regime was rapidly winning the allegiance of the younger generation, while the political platforms of the legal parties were becoming largely irrelevant. Therefore, it is perhaps not surprising that the leaders of these parties maintained regular contacts and in some instances even tried to coordinate their activities with the command of the nationalist underground.

Strife between the Ukrainians and the Polish government continued throughout the 1920s until at the end of the decade the OUN (under the military and ideological leadership, respectively, of Evgeni Konovalets and Dmytro Dontsov) launched a campaign of sabotage and political terror against the regime. The Pilsudski government responded forcefully with arrests, deportations, and military occupation of Ukrainian communities. This period of virtual civil war in eastern Poland, euphemistically termed "pacification" (June through November 1930), resulted in widespread property destruction, severely tarnished Poland's image abroad, and poisoned relations between Ukrainians and Poles for the remainder of the decade.

   In the second round of Polish-Ukrainian discussions started in the spring of 1935, an attempt was made to reconcile Poland's security concerns with the legitimate aspirations of the Ukrainian minority. As a result of these negotiations, a gentlemen's agreement, generally known as the "normalization," was concluded by the representatives of the UNDO and the Polish government, leading to the election of fourteen Ukrainian deputies and five senators to the Warsaw parliament; in addition, five deputies and one senator from Volhynia were elected on the government list. The leader of the UNDO, Vasyl Mudryi, became Deputy Speaker of the Sejm, an amnesty for political prisoners was approved, and certain credits were extended to Ukrainian economic institutions. In return, the Ukrainian deputies voted for the budget and either ceased or mitigated their criticism of the government's policies. At the same time, however, the hopes of the Ukrainians for bilingualism and a greater participation in local administration, as well as for some meaningful concession in the field of education, remained unfulfilled. As time went on, the chances for a lasting normalization of Polish-Ukrainian relations began to decrease, for the Polish government never regarded the agreement of 1935 as part of a broader political settlement but rather viewed it as a purely tactical move, limited in its scope and significance. In addition, forces decidedly opposed to any concessions in favor of the national minorities were beginning to gain ascendance in the ruling camp after the death of Marshal Pilsudski.[37]

   The policy of antagonizing Ukrainian peasants had been initiated in July 1919, when the Sejm passed two agrarian reform laws following occupation of the West Ukrainian territory by the Polish army. These laws ignored the fact that villages in Galicia were already overpopulated, and the land estates, owned mainly by the Polish nobility, became the focal point of conflict involving socioeconomic and national-political dimensions. The land obtained for parceling was distributed primarily among Poles, with the following priority: 1) invalids of the Polish army, 2) farm hands formerly employed by land estates, and 3) other rural workers and small farmers. As a result of this policy, the Polish government succeeded in parceling out 800,000 *ha.* of land within the Ukrainian territories. During eighteen years of Polish rule, 300,000 Poles were resettled in rural Ukrainian areas, and about 100,000 in towns.[38]

   Pacification, coupled with the unfair policy of land distribution, intensified three types of retaliation: the strengthening of nationalistic sentiments among Ukrainian peasants; passive resistance and consumer boycott of products under state monopoly, such as liquor and tobacco; and renewed interest in, and extension of, economic organizations such as cooperatives and agricultural banks, and fierce determination to keep the land in Ukrainian hands at any price. A similarly effective measure resulted from application of the policy of boycotting non-Ukrainian businesses, enterprises, and stores. The Polish-Ukrainian confrontation soon reached a level of all-pervasive hostility, punctuated frequently by acts of violence on both sides. Warsaw's decision to treat the whole agrarian issue as a political one and to see in the Ukrainian peasants not a social class but a different non-Polish nationality, reverberated and contributed significantly to the rising anti-Polish sentiments among the Ukrainian masses, who otherwise might have been molded into loyal citizens.

   This exacerbation of Polish-Ukrainian relations enabled the OUN to win once more the support of the masses of the Ukrainian population in Eastern

Galicia for its policy of confrontation with Poland. The southeastern provinces of Poland were becoming a battleground of two nationalities, with both communities living their separate lives, alien if not outright hostile toward each other, with even social contacts between the members of the two opposing groups frowned upon, with nationalist fighting squads on both sides setting the tone, and with Ukrainian and Polish political parties making only a lukewarm attempt to defuse the situation. The Polish government reacted to these developments by taking a series of repressive measures, which had a certain similarity, both as far as their extent and the methods used were concerned, to the "pacification" of 1930.

It was at this inauspicious moment, on December 9, 1938, that the Ukrainian deputies in the Sejm presented to the Speaker a bill providing for the establishment of an autonomous "Galician-Volhynian Land," enjoying full rights of self-government except in foreign policy and in military and financial matters. The bill was roughly modelled after the home-rule law granted by the prague Parliament to Slovakia and Subcarpathian Rus', but it also evoked unhappy memories of similar demands put forward by the Sudeten German party, which later escalated and eventually led to the dismemberment of Czechoslovakia. While proposals for a territorial autonomy for Eastern Galicia and Volhynia had been voiced in the Polish Sejm as early as 1922, the attempt to revive the issue at a time when Poland's international situation was becoming increasingly insecure produced deep-seated resentment and indignation in the Polish press and among Polish politicians, including even those groups which usually showed a sympathetic attitude toward the Ukrainian minority and its legitimate aspirations.

Hitler's territorial demands to Poland and the threat of war hanging over the country persuaded the Ukrainian politicians to keep a generally low profile in order not to antagonize the Poles during their hour of trial. It was hoped that, by doing so, the Ukrainian minority would not be regarded as a "fifth column" within the Polish state and treated accordingly. The Nazis were, of course, quite anxious to exploit the Ukrainian underground in Poland, but these hopes did not materialize, with the exception of a few isolated incidents. The OUN leadership refused to initiate any large-scale anti-Polish action. In fact, the apprehensions that the dubious allegiance of the Ukrainians to Poland might provoke a mass anti-Ukrainian action on the part of the Polish population, if not the Polish authorities, led to the declaration of loyalty to the Polish Republic; this declaration was made by the head of the Ukrainian Parliamentary Representation and Deputy Speaker of the Sejm, Vasyl Mudryi, during the extraordinary session of that body on September 2, 1939. By then, of course, it was much too late to expect any meaningful reconciliation, as both the Poles and the Ukrainians were rapidly drawn into the Second World War as victims of both aggressors — Nazi Germany and Soviet Russia.

Belorussians

The Belorussians, concentrated primarily in northeastern Poland, comprised a sizeable minority in Wilno and Bialystok provinces, and a majority in Polesie and Nowogrodek. Stephan Horak, utilizing a variety of sources, has estimated the number of Belorussians in Poland in 1931 at 2,150,000, and nearly 3,000,000 by 1939.[39]

Like the Ukrainians, the Belorussians in Poland were overwhelmingly rural. They were of a lower socioeconomic and cultural level, however, and lacked the political maturity and institutions of self-help created by the Ukrainians and the Germans. Nonetheless. several parties competed for Belorussian support. These included the moderate Belorussian Social Democratic party; the Communist Belorussian Independent Socialist party and Belorussian Social Revolutionary party; the Belorussian Christian Democratic Union at the Far Right; and the terrorist Belorussian Revolutionary Organization, which sought the unification of the Polish Belorussian territory with the Belorussian Soviet Socialist Republic.

Having initially gained the support of the Belorussians early in the Polish-Soviet war through generous promises of autonomy, the Polish government began showing its chauvinism by late 1919. The campaign of Polonization among the Belorussians evoked from them an outbreak of anti-Polish violence. While the repression was brief, it strengthened sentiment among Belorussians for union with Soviet Belorussia. This pattern continued; Polish efforts at accommodation only gave wider latitude to Belorussian autonomist, secessionist, or terrorist groups. These activities evoked a harsh Polish reaction, which only intensified the Belorussians' sense of national unity and determination to resist. During the N.E.P., the Polish Belorussians compared their unfavorable situation with that of their Soviet compatriots across the border, which probably accounted for the appeal that communism found among the Belorussians. The leftist Belorussian groups had coalesced by 1925 into a Belorussian Peasant-Worker Association, called the Hramada, dedicated to uncompromising confrontation with the Polish state.

As the Polish government failed in its initial efforts to create and foster pro-Polish groups among the Belorussians, it turned to oppression. The years 1924 and 1925 saw "pacification" in the form of martial law, arrests, and property destruction, followed by an intensive campaign to eradicate Belorussian national consciousness. The Belorussian leaders of the Hramada, the deputies to the Sejm, and the senators did not escape the tortures of the Polish police; because of their protests, they were accused of disloyalty in 1928. By order of the Polish government, the Hramada was declared dissolved, that is, illegal. Fifty-six leaders of the Hramada were taken to the courts and tried behind closed doors, although the press made no mention of these trials. "Deputy Tarashkevich had been brought into the courtroom in shackles, the Deputies Dvarchanin and Hauryliuk were beaten to death, and others were treated in a like manner."[40] Those who survived the beatings were sent to jail. The local Belorussian leaders who were accused of un-Polish activities were sent to a concentration camp at Bereza Kartuska. "Pacification" was renewed with vigor in 1930, escalating to full-fledged civil war in some regions. The net effect of this was dramatically to increase Communist strength among the Belorussians in the 1930s.

Anti-Polish sentiment continued to grow in all sectors of the Belorussian community. Following Pilsudski's death in 1935, even the Belorussian Roman Catholic clergy—whom the Poles had counted upon as a Polonizing force—were demanding cultural autonomy. The Polish government accordingly moved against the clergy, outlawing the Belorussian Christian Democratic Movement in 1936; it also stepped up its repression of the Orthodox Church. Between 1935 and 1939, the state intensified its cultural battle against the

Belorussians to the point where schools were closed, community organizations and societies were dissolved, and Belorussian candidates were excluded from elections. The final result was that, as Nicholas P. Vakar observed, "World War II found Western Belorussian loyalties divided between communism and nationalism — but with none whatsoever for Poland."[41]

Germans

One of the reasons that made the case of the German minority in Poland so sensitive was that there was a sharp reversal of previous roles: the new Polish state found itself in charge of a significant minority of Germans after more than a century of it being a German state with a Polish minority to deal with. To a large extent, the Poles simply applied to their German minority the same policies which the Germans had previously applied to them with, it is generally agreed,[42] very unimpressive results. The Poles were determined to make Poland a homogeneous state in the shortest time possible.

The study of the German minority in interwar Poland is complicated by the fact that the numbers involved, indeed, the very definition of a "German," differ considerably from one source to another. Official Polish government figures sought consciously to understate the number of non-Poles, while the figures offered by the minorities themselves doubtless inflated their own numbers. It does seem clear, however, that Poland had a lot more to show for her efforts to reduce the number of Germans than did Imperial Germany in its effort to reduce the number of Poles before 1918. According to the prewar census figures from the three partitioning powers, approximately 2.2 million Germans inhabited territories which became part of Poland by 1923, including 1.4 million living in areas acquired from the German empire.[43] By 1927, following a major exodus, especially from these formerly German regions (Poznania, Pomerania [West Prussia], and Polish Upper Silesia), there remained an estimated 1.1 million Germans in Poland, comprising 3.7% of the total population of the state. They were scattered fairly widely around the country: some 370,000 lived in Poznania and Pomerania, and another 300,000 in Polish Upper Silesia (more on the "Germans" of Upper Silesia below); but another 320,000 Germans lived in the former Congress Kingdom, especially in the Lódz industrial region; 95,000 more lived in formerly Austrian Galicia; and even in the eastern provinces, especially Volhynia, there was a German population of more than 50,000 living in mostly German-majority villages.[44]

By 1939, these latter figures had changed only slightly; there remained more than one million Germans in Poland (321,000 in Poznania and Pomerania, 180,000 in Polish Upper Silesia, 364,000 in central Poland, 99,000 in Galicia, and 67,000 in the eastern provinces).[45] They were about 70% Protestant, 30% Catholic, much like the Germans of the Reich; in Upper Silesia and the Lódz industrial region, they were mostly engaged in industrial/commercial activities as workers and entrepreneurs, whereas in the other regions the German population consisted mainly of farmers with medium-sized holdings (this was true of 70% of those in Poznania, Pomerania, and Galicia and of almost 100% of those in Volhynia).[46] It may also be noted that by this time a majority of the Germans in Poland lived in areas that had not been part of Bismarck's German empire. In other words, political control was not as decisive for the development of a German presence in Poland as is often suggested, especially in Polish accounts.

The most striking development in the German population of Poland was the drastic decline of the German population of Poznania and Pomerania in the first half-dozen years of Polish rule: from about 1.1 million persons at war's end to the 370,000 cited above. The reason that most Germans in this area were farmers is that it was more difficult for farmers to simply pick up and leave, but the once-substantial German urban population of Poznania and Pomerania declined by some 85% during this short period.[47] These figures are no longer controversial, but the cause of the exodus receives widely differing interpretations even today: Polish accounts generally argue that it was mostly voluntary, consisting of Germans who did not want to be citizens of Poland, serve in the Polish army, accept the lower standard of living offered by Poland, or who had never really been at home in the area in the first place; German accounts generally argue that the exodus was the result of much chicanery and coercion. Only about 20% of these Germans originally opted to retain their German citizenship, many to avoid being conscripted to fight in the Polish-Russian war in 1920-1921, discovering only later that this was grounds for their expulsion; only about 15% had been civilian or military state employees and thus presumably without real roots in these provinces.[48] Most who traced their presence in the area back for decades or even centuries were willing to accept Polish citizenship (whatever their opinion of the Versailles treaty), but simply found it impossible to stay. Recent accounts, even from Poland, concede that it was National Democratic policy "to forcibly reduce the number of Germans in Poland,"[49] and at least part of this sizeable population movement must be seen as a consequence of conscious Polish government action.

The objective of reducing the number of Germans in Poland was pursued by economic as well as political means. "Poland's practice," writes one recent author otherwise sympathetic to Poland, "was one of dispossessing the German minority."[50] Germans lost about 500,000 *ha.* of land, mostly as the result of various state measures, in the early years of Polish rule. And this was before the onset of the Polish "land reform" program, which turned out to bear some similarity to the Prussian Settlement Law of 1886 (which had led to the state's purchase of Polish land for German settlement): 68% of the land held by German estate-owners in Poznania and Pomerania was "reformed" between the wars, but only 11% of the land held by the Polish.[51]

The rights of the Germans and other minorities of Poland to the use of their language and schools (rights which Prussian Poles did not enjoy before 1918) were supposedly guaranteed by both the Polish Constitution and special minority protection treaties. These treaties provided a basis for bringing complaints even before the League of nations, and no group took advantage of this opportunity as often as the Germans of Poland: 155 of the 525 grievances formally taken up by the League between 1921 and 1933 came from this minority.[52] But these efforts provided little real redress in the last analysis: the number of German public schools in Poland dropped by two-thirds between 1924 and 1933, by which time at least half the German children in Poland were compelled to attend Polish schools.[53] Soon after Poland signed the non-aggression pact with Hitler's Germany in 1934, she also unilaterally renounced her adherence to the minority protection treaties.[54]

The problem of the German minority in Poland came to a sudden end in 1939 in a way that is familiar to all. Nazi Germany increased its pressure on Poland, and Poland simultaneously increased its pressure on its German population. Many Germans there had been attracted to Nazi ideology (proportionately more so than in Germany itself), and this served as justification for still harsher measures by Polish authorities and people. Germans were forced from their places of work by Polish fellow workers and from universities by Polish fellow students; their businesses were widely boycotted and the people themselves victims of occasional pogroms. By the summer of 1939, some 70,000 German exiles from Poland were housed in refugee camps across the frontier.[55] When Hitler declared war on Poland in September 1939, the strained situation inside that country erupted in a so-called "bloodbath," certainly exaggerated by Nazi propaganda[56] and exploited for the Nazis' purposes (thus frequently discounted altogether in the West). But something like a pogrom did occur: four to five thousand German civilians were killed inside Poland during the first weeks of the war, and, of the several thousand *Volksdeutsche* who died or turned up missing as members of the Polish army, most were victims of their Polish comrades rather than the Wehrmacht.[57] The virtually unanimous point of view in Polish accounts even today is that these Germans functioned as a "fifth column" steered from Berlin, and thus presumably deserved their fate,[58] but this assertion does not seem to have a very firm factual foundation and is rejected by the most recent study of the problem.[59]

Lithuanians

The Lithuanians in Poland occupied the western section of Wilno province and the northern part of Nowogrodek. Although Vilna is historically considered Lithuanian, the city has been a source of conflict among Poland, Lithuania, and Belorussia. The city was surrounded in the pre-1945 period with Belorussians, complicating ethnographic claims as well as census figures. The 1921 census showed 72,000 Lithuanians in Poland; the 1931 census showed 83,000. other sources offer figures as high as 300,000.[60] There is little evidence by which to dispute these figures, although the census estimates seem low. Stephan Horak suggests, based on statistical statements of 1861-1910, that over the previous two centuries many Lithuanian families in these territories had become Polonized, and hence indicated the Polish language as native in census surveys that employed native tongue as the criterion of nationality.[61]

Relations between Poland and Lithuania were hostile, due in no small measure to unremitting conflict over the city of Vilna. This interstate hostility affected the situation of the Lithuanians in Poland as well, as the Polish government subjected them to a policy of rapid assimilation. Schools were closed (although the Lithuanians maintained a fairly viable private school system), and the Lithuanian press was muzzled. Lithuanian capacity to resist politically was limited insofar as they had no representatives in the Sejm.

Other Nationalities

In addition to the five nationalities discussed, there were about a quarter of a million other non-Poles in interwar Poland: Russians, Czechs, Slovaks, Karaites Armenians, Bulgarians, Tartars, Gypsies, and others. These groups had arrived in Poland at different times and under varying circumstances, including military campaigns, escape from religious persecution, and the search for economic advantages.

The largest of these groups was the Russians, their number estimated at 139,000 in 1931. The 1931 census also listed 38,000 Czechs in Poland. The other nationalities were not separately enumerated, being classified in the census as "others" or as so-called "locals" (*tutejsi*). Because of their small size, these groups did not present a serious political challenge to the Polish government. Actions against the largest of these numerically unimportant minorities, the Russians, were limited to expropriation of the property of large landowners and repression of the Russian Orthodox Church.

World War II and
the Nazi Occupation, 1939-1945

The outbreak of World War II marked the end of the Polish state; once again, her territory was divided between the two voracious powers to east and west. Under the terms of the Nazi-Soviet Non-Aggression Pact of August 1939, the eastern third of the country was assigned to the Soviet Union, under whose control it remained until the Nazi invasion of June 1941. The population under Soviet control included, in addition to Poles, some Jews, a few Germans, and nearly all of Poland's Ukrainians and Belorussians. Most of the Poles, Jews, and ethnic Germans fell under German control.

The Germans divided their territory into two separate administrative districts. Northern and western Poland (surrounding Gdansk, Poznan, and Upper Silesia) were incorporated into the Reich. The remainder (including Warsaw, Lublin, and Cracow) became the *Generalgouvernement Polen*, or general government, administered separately by a "governor general" who reported directly to Hitler.[62] The General Gouvernement was envisioned as a dumping ground for Poles and Jews who were to be deported from the incorporated regions; the latter would then provide a home for ethnic German "repatriates" from other areas of Europe.[63]

The *Volksdeutsche*—Polish Germans—did not fare as well as might be expected under this policy. The Nazi government preferred officials imported from Germany proper, the Reichsdeutsche, for leadership positions. Waves of ethnic Germans pouring into the Reich from the General Gouvernement and other parts of Europe also came into conflict with the local Germans.

In the east, nearly all the Belorussians and most of the Ukrainians came under Soviet control. Belorussians in German Poland were allowed to move to the Soviet zone, in exchange for the resettlement of Germans from the Soviet zone in the Reich. In the first weeks of their occupation, Soviet authorities conscientiously avoided policies that would antagonize Belorussian national pride. Thus, the Belorussians euphorically voted for incorporation into the BSSR, believing that the dream of a united, sovereign, and democratic Belorussian nation was being realized. Stalinization was not long in coming, and soon all areas of the lives of the disillusioned Belorussians were methodically and forcibly Sovietized and Russified.

There was some disagreement in the Nazi hierarchy over how to handle the half a million Ukrainians who remained under German control. Himmler and the police establishment argued obsessively that all non-Germans to the east be treated brutally as *Untermenschen*. A more moderate position was reflected in the views of Hitler's early deputy, Alfred Rosenberg, who saw the non-Russian subjects of the USSR as natural allies in the struggle against the hated Bolsheviks and that in return they should be promised autonomy in Hitler's new territorial reorganization of Europe. Himmler's racist views were ultimately to prevail, but in the first years of the war German policy favored the Ukrainians, especially in contrast to the brutal policy toward the Poles. Ukrainian cultural, political, and educational institutions were supported and even upgraded. In contrast to the Belorussians, large numbers of Ukrainians poured into the General Gouvernement and later into the Reich from the Soviet zone. Early in 1940, Governor General Frank warned his subordinates that the Ukrainians should be considered subjects of the Reich, not as the representatives of any future independent Ukraine; tolerance of their cultural and social autonomy was to be contingent upon their loyalty to Hitler.[64] In spite of Berlin's worries that Ukrainian nationalism might complicate German-Soviet relations, special detachments of Ukrainian combat troops trained for use against the Soviet Union were formed in 1940 and transferred to the General Gouvernement in early 1941.[45]

Germans

With the end of the Polish state in 1939, the concept of a German minority in Poland, strictly speaking, also comes to an end; it is almost impossible to trace this population group through the war period, with its radically changed boundaries and infusion of new settlers from German settlements farther east. Wherever they lived, in reclaimed western Poland or in the General Gouvernement, Germans were again part of the dominant political group. The Poles were again on the receiving end of hostile nationality policies, except that these new policies were quite without precedent in recent European history and harsh even by the standards prevailing elsewhere in Hitler's Europe. Among other things, more than 1 million Poles were expelled from western provinces to make room for German newcomers from further east; 1.5 million Poles were sent to do forced labor in Germany; and an effort was made to liquidate the entire Polish intelligentsia.[66] On the list of the victims of Nazism, Poles ranked third in absolute numbers, behind Jews and Soviet POWs. But in 1944-1945, as in 1918, the victimizer/victim relationship was again reversed: the final chapter in the story of the Germans in Poland was written when Russia and her temporary allies in the West agreed to shift Poland westward to the Oder and Neisse rivers and "transfer" westward any Germans living east of that line.

Jews

Although estimates vary, there were approximately 3,300,000 Jews in Poland in the fall of 1939. They made up about 10% of the Polish population, while their heavy concentration in Poland's cities made them easy prey for the brutal actions committed by German *Einsatzgruppen* and other forces when they entered Poland on September 1, 1939. Fortunately, with the Soviet occupation of eastern Poland under the terms of the Nazi-Soviet Pact, 1,200,000 to 1,250,000 Jews came under Soviet jurisdiction, while another 200,000 to 300,000 fled into the area from German Poland.[67]

After the initial wave of destructive violence against Jews and their property, synagogues, and businesses in the early stages of World War II, the 1,550,000 to 1,600,000 Jews under German occupation were subjected to a series of German actions that isolated them from the rest of Polish society. Many were forced into labor camps, paving the way for later policies designed to exterminate them completely.[68]

Essentially, the Nazi scheme for ridding its region in Poland, and later Europe, of Jews was to ship them to ghettos in the General Gouvernement's four major cities—Warsaw, Lublin, Radom, and Cracow. The ghettoization process began in Poland in early 1940, and the Warsaw ghetto, with its 400,000 inhabitants, was set up on November 15, 1940; 150,000 to 200,000 Jews were later transferred to Warsaw, though its population remained relatively stable because of the high death rate from disease and malnutrition.[69]

German authorities administered life in the ghettos through the *Judenräte*, or Jewish Councils, established in 1939 to oversee and maintain Jewish life in these enclaves. At first, they appeared to be a German attempt to continue the Jewish tradition of ethnic autonomy, though in time they came to be seen as a Nazi tool for acquiring forced labor and victims for the death camps.[70] The next phase of the Holocaust came with the German invasion of the Soviet Union on June 22, 1941. Nazi officials, using the cover of war to mask the wide-scale massacre of Russian and other Jews living in the western USSR, established a number of death camps. The first deaths by gassing took place at Auschwitz in the fall of 1941, and formal death camps were established at Chelma, Belzec, Sobibor, Majdanek, and Treblinka by 1942.[71] Over the next three years, the majority of Poland's Jews who survived the ghettos, as well as Jews from other parts of Europe, died in these camps. Although estimates vary, at least 90% of Poland's prewar Jewish population died during the Holocaust.[72]

Ukrainians, Belorussians, and Lithuanians

The Ukrainian population in eastern Poland initially welcomed the Nazi invasion as "liberation" from Polish and Soviet oppression. During the first two years of the war, Nazi policy was indeed more favorable to the Ukrainians than it had been to the Poles. The Uniate Church was granted autonomy, and the Ukrainians were encouraged to develop self-help organizations and were appointed to leading roles in civilian government, although under close German supervision.

The initial reaction of the Belorussians was likewise favorable, although, as in all cases, the honeymoon was short-lived. The Belorussians had not figured nearly so prominently in German strategy as had the Ukrainians, and before long a brutal reign of terror was instituted in the Belorussian territories. The average Belorussian found himself caught between the repression of the Nazis and the retaliatory responses of the Belorussian partisans.[73]

The politically more advanced Ukrainians attempted to take advantage of the occupation. Organization of Ukrainian Nationalists (OUN) leader Stepan Bandera organized in Cracow a Ukrainian National Committee, and on June 30, 1941, in Lviv, the committee declared Ukraine a sovereign state. This was predicated on the belief that the Nazis would permit an independent Ukraine in Hitler's new territorial reorganization of Europe, a hope for which there was little basis. Bandera and his associates were arrested and placed in concentration camps, Ukrainian civil leaders were replaced by German military personnel, and Galicia was incorporated into the General Gouvernement; the brutal Erich Koch was appointed *Reichskommissar* for the remaining Ukrainian territory. The Gestapo then instituted a reign of terror against the local inhabitants. The German effort to recruit Ukrainians to fight alongside German troops, which had gotten off to a good start in 1941, was impeded by these policies and was a failure before war's end. In March 1945, Hitler personally ordered the disarming of the Ukrainian division "Halychyna."

Hitler and Himmler's views, not those of a few Nazis who favored cooperation with the non-Russian peoples, prevailed in the occupation; this meant that the Ukrainians, Belorussians, and Lithuanians were treated like the other *Untermenschen*. Their hopes for national freedom from Poland and Russia were cruelly and bloodily disappointed from 1941 to 1945.

National Minorities in the
Polish People's Republic, 1945-1980

Through a process of infiltration, subversion, terror, purges, and sham elections, Communist regimes were established in all the east European countries that were liberated and occupied by the Red Army, with the sole exception of Austria. This included Poland, which, with its intense nationalism, democratic aspirations, and attachment to the Roman Catholic religion, might have been—had the Poles had any freedom of choice—among the least likely countries to fall under an atheist, totalitarian regime subservient to Moscow.[74]

Postwar territorial and population shifts dramatically changed the ethnic makeup of Poland. In the words of one noted historian:

> In addition to the movement of some 3 million Poles from the eastern marshes to the newly acquired western lands, between 1946 and 1949 about 2.5 million Germans, Ukrainians, Russians and Byelorussians left Poland. The total population of Poland fell from 34,849,000 in 1939 to 25,505,000 in 1951, while the ethnic composition by the latter date was more than 98% Polish and 94% Catholic. As a result of the wartime as well as postwar changes, Poland became ethnically and religiously homogeneous as never before in its history.[75]

Essentially, Poland's boundaries after the war were moved to the west, at the expense of Germany and to the benefit of the Soviet Union. The USSR retained those territories it had annexed as a result of the 1939 Nazi-Soviet Pact. The Oder-Neisse River line, suggested as early as 1918 by Roman Dmowski as a Polish frontier, became the western boundary. This boundary, as well as procedures for removing German citizens from these areas, was provisionally accepted by all parties at the Potsdam Conference in August 1945.[76] The Soviet Union recognized and guaranteed the new boundaries immediately, and this was reaffirmed in 1965. East Germany recognized the new border in 1950, and West Germany in 1970. International acceptance of the Polish borders was finalized in the Helsinki Agreements of Security and Cooperation in Europe in 1975.

Postwar changes in the makeup of the population resulted from four factors: 1) deaths during the war; 2) the retention by the USSR of the eastern territories inhabited by Ukrainians, Belorussians, and Lithuanians; 3) the repatriation of Poles from the eastern territories, the USSR, and other countries; and 4) the evacuation from Poland of many of the remaining non-Poles. Most of the latter were Germans. Nearly 6 million Germans emigrated or were evicted in 1944-1945. During 1946-1949, an additional 3 million people of various nationalities left Poland as a result of the Potsdam Treaty. In 1957-1958, there was a new wave of emigration of indeterminate size, arranged by the West German and Polish Red Cross to reunite families. Finally, by 1958, 500,000 Ukrainians, Belorussians, and Lithuanians had moved to the USSR, and 200,000 Jews had emigrated to Israel.[77]

There is no question that the population transfers after World War II reduced the non-Polish population of Poland dramatically. By Polish assertion, only about 450,000 people, or 1.5% of the population, were non-Polish in 1950. A later report by a Polish sociologist placed the number in 1965-1966 at 440,000, according to estimates of administrative authorities and minority organizations, broken down as follows:

Ukrainians	approximately	180,000
Belorussians		160,000
Jews		25,000
Slovaks		20,000
Czechs		2,000
Russians		10,000
Lithuanians		10,000
Germans		4,000
Gypsies		18,000
Greeks and Macedonians		10,000
Miscellaneous		1,000
Total		440,000[78]

These estimates are conservative, and Western estimates are invariable higher. West German sources, for example, placed the non-Polish population of Poland in 1963 at 2.5 million, or 8% of the population.[79] (Western estimates are further discussed below under individual countries.) Much of the difficulty lies in the fact that, while the government at least nominally respects nationality rights, it does not officially recognize nationality as a demographic category: all citizens of the Polish People's Republic are officially regarded as Poles, and this pertains especially to census data.

Most of the national minorities in present-day Poland inhabit the border provinces; the central provinces are more homogeneously Polish. The Western Territories contain about 50% of the minorities, and these are mostly Germans. Three nationalities — Belorussians, Slovaks, and Lithuanians — are clustered, compact, and located in the east. More dispersed are the Ukrainians, Jews, Russians, Germans, Gypsies, Greeks, and Macedonians.

In spite of Poland's self-definition as a national state, and despite the pretense that Polish state citizenship obliterates nationality, the party and government began in the 1950s to pay attention in a haphazard way to the needs and problems of national communities. After 1950, school systems for minorities were established and Jewish emigration to Israel was liberalized, but serious attention to the German problem had to wait until 1957. Article 69 of the 1952 constitution bestowed equal rights on national minorities:

1. The citizens of the People's Republic of Poland possess, independently of nationality, race or religion, equal rights in all spheres of governmental, political, economic, social and cultural life. The violation of these principles through direct or indirect expansion or restriction of the law with regard to nationality, race or religion is punishable.

2. The dissemination of hatred or indifference, the instigation of discord, or the humiliation of any person of different nationality, race or religion is forbidden.[80]

There have been some noteworthy governmental initiatives on behalf of national minorities: a 1952 Politburo resolution on education in the Ukrainian language; a 1955 letter of the PUWP Central Committee Secretariat on Ukrainian problems; a 1957 Secretariat resolution encouraging aid for Germans and Ukrainians, German emigration, and the return of some Ukrainians from the Western Territories to take over unoccupied farms in the southeast; a 1952 government resolution on aid for Gypsies and Gypsy settlement; and a 1957 Central Committee letter on anti-Semitism.

These efforts at accommodation in the 1950s followed several years of hostile relations between the government and the minorities. Not counting the long (and ongoing) campaign for first the expulsion, then the assimilation of Germans, the high point of this hostility was the "pacification" of Ukrainians in the Lemko region in 1947.

The problems of Germans and Jews in contemporary Poland have received considerable international attention. In part, this has been because of their numbers; more importantly, it is the result of vocal concern on the part of intensely interested homelands. The Ukrainians, always a cohesive and vocal minority wherever they have settled, have received somewhat less, but some, attention. The remainder have received almost none. In perspective, national minorities in today's Poland are small and unconnected islands in a large ethnic Polish sea, and in a political system which discourages any form of pluralism. While they enjoy limited cultural autonomy, grudgingly granted by the regime as a measure to pacify them and buy their support, they enjoy little communal political power and are subject to assimilationist pressure.

Germans

In an exchange that was only superficially symmetrical, Poland received lands inhabited before the war by about 9.5 million Germans in return for eastern provinces which she had conquered in 1920-1921 and which contained only a few million ethnic Poles. Virtually the entire population of Germany east of the Oder-Neisse line, as well as those Germans who had lived in interwar Poland, was expelled as part of the removal of some 15 million Germans from throughout eastern Europe, the largest such expulsion in the history of Western civilization.[81] It remains unclear how many of these Germans fled before the arrival of the Red Army and how many waited around for the formal expulsion notices that followed within a short time of that arrival, but the distinction is not a very important one in any case. Certainly they did not remain in the newly established Polish state long enough to be the object of a new period of Polish nationality policy or to function for any time as an organized national minority (which does not rule out the existence of numerous Germans living in today's Poland strictly as individuals). The only remnant of this problem that survived after 1945 was the case of the "Polish-speaking Germans"; in Upper Silesia and Masuria, for example, many persons of subjectively German orientation were able to avoid expulsion due to their objectively Polish nationality. This phenomenon reemerged, however, in the wake of the West German-Polish Warsaw Treaty of November 1970. Among other things, this treaty allowed for the repatriation of Germans living in Poland, but it did not define what a "German" was, with the result that many more people than anticipated applied to emigrate, including a large contingent from Upper Silesia that showed up in West Germany unable to speak any German.[82]

Jews

In the interwar years, Jews, 10% of the population of Poland, constituted about 25% of the Polish Communist party. Even after Stalin had liquidated the party's leadership in 1938, Jews continued to be disproportionately represented in the Communist elite in exile—the "muscovite" Communists who followed the Red Army back into eastern Europe, and especially into Poland. The reason for this was that the Polish Jews, living under regimes that were anti-Semitic as well as authoritarian, were attracted to socialism's internationalist promise and believed that the victory of socialism over capitalism would surely herald the end of ethnic discrimination. In fact, the Jewish Communist leaders became the victims of anti-Semitic campaigns and purges. The imposition of Stalinism engendered resentment among Polish Communists and non-Communists alike, and this became joined to a latent but powerful popular anti-Semitism. In Poland in 1956, and again in 1967-1968, anti-Semitism became an open political issue and was cynically manipulated as a weapon in factional struggles at the top.[83]

Anti-Semitism, anti-communism, and anti-Sovietism were prominent among the forces at work in the complex factional struggles of 1956. Although Jews had been prominent in the Pulawy group, the Politburo nomination of Roman Zambrowski – a member of this group – was vetoed by Khrushchev because Zambrowski was Jewish. The opposing Natolin faction openly employed demagogic anti-Semitic rhetoric during and after the October crisis. The following years under Gomulka saw the ascendancy of both former Natolinites and "Partisans" (former Polish resistance fighters) at the expense of moderates, repentant Stalinists, and reformist intellectuals – a very large percentage of whom happened to be Jewish.

In the aftermath of the Arab-Israeli war of 1967, official anti-Semitism came to the fore again in the form of anti-Zionism. Gomulka was alarmed at Polish popular support for Israel, although this was probably prompted more by Polish delight at a Russian setback than by sudden widespread love for the Jews. Such open anti-Sovietism, extending even to the Polish officer corps, could have had repercussions that would have sorely complicated Gomulka's standing with the USSR. Perhaps inspired by his "Partisan" secret police chief, Mieczyslaw Moczar, Gomulka launched an anti-Zionist campaign, clearly hoping to use latent Polish anti-Semitism to counteract popular sympathy for Israel. General Moczar and his allies manipulated the anti-Zionist campaign into a full-scale purge of Jewish officials at all levels of party and government, as well as the scientific and educational establishment. Moczar's manipulation was also behind three days of student riots beginning March 8, 1968 at Warsaw University and extending into the provinces. By May, the purge had claimed at least eighty government officials and hundreds of other Jewish victims in the sciences, the arts, economics, and finance. The attacks centered mainly on those sectors of the polity which had resisted control by the "Partisan" faction of Moczar and Ryzard Strzelecki.[84] The anti-Zionist campaign pervaded the mass media, was marked by vicious slander, and, before ebbing in early summer, sank even to the level of defaming the memory of the Polish Jewish victims of the Holocaust.

Eight to nine thousand Jews left Poland in 1967-1968; between 10,000 and 15,000 remain.[85] An estimated 70,000 to 80,000 Jews living in Poland survived the Holocaust, and in 1946 another 150,000 returned from the USSR. Initially, the survivors tried to revive their community life in league with the Polish Committee of National Liberation in Lublin, which created a Central Committee of the Jews of Poland in 1944 to oversee cultural reconstruction.[86] Another organization, the Union of Religious Communities, oversaw religious questions. The committee, which had representatives from Poland's most important political parties, dealt first with aid to Holocaust victims and then worked to create a stable Jewish communal life. Jewish cooperatives, farms, professional societies, and newspapers formed the cornerstone of this movement.[87]

Unfortunately, many of these efforts were undermined by a latent anti-Semitism that erupted in violence in Klementow, Czestochowa, Lublin, Kielce, and other cities, resulting in hundreds of deaths.[88] Despite efforts by government and Jewish leaders to reassure the Jewish community that the excesses would cease, these events triggered a mass migration of Jews that would empty Poland of the bulk of its Jewish population over the next decade.[89] By early 1948, 150,000 had left.[90]

Emigration and the Stalinization of Poland after 1947 seriously hampered the rebuilding of the Jewish community. Aided in part by Jewish Communists, most independent Jewish communal institutions were either abolished or communized between 1947 and 1950.[91] These policies fostered further emigration, and about 30,000 Jews left in 1949-1950.[92] Ten years later, a new wave of emigration left only about 30,000 Jews in the country. With the final wave of exodus during 1967-1969, Poland's Jewish community—once a rich and thriving subculture—virtually disappeared.[93]

Today, the remnant of Polish Jewry inhabits urban areas, with the greatest concentration in Warsaw, Lódz, Szczecin, and such towns in Lower Silesia as Wroclaw, Lenica, Walbrzych, and Klodzko. About half of all Polish Jews live in the Oder-Neisse region; another one-third live in Lower Silesia.

About 3,000 Polish Jews are organized in eighteen religious organizations; until 1981, they had no rabbi. The largest cultural organization is the Jewish Social and Cultural Society, active since 1945. The Yiddish Buch publishing house issues fewer than ten titles per year. A Yiddish newspaper, *Folks Shtyme*, and a literary monthly, *Yiddishe Schriften*, exist with miniscule circulation.

Ukrainians

At present, Ukrainians are the largest minority in Poland; according to the Polish count, there are between 180,000 and 200,000. Some 30,000 to 35,000 of these are Lemkos (originally from the Beskidy Mountains), and an indeterminate number are Hutsuls, a Carpathian mountain people.

Ironically, most of the Ukrainians in Poland live in territories far from their place of origin. About two-thirds of the Ukrainians live in the Oder-Neisse region; most of these were forcibly resettled there in the 1947 "pacification" of the Lemkos. Only a small fraction of Poland's Ukrainians remain in their native southeastern regions adjoining Soviet Ukraine.

The Ukrainians in Poland are mainly rural—90-95% live in villages. There are apparently no *gromada* (the smallest territorial administrative unit) inhabited exclusively by Ukrainians, and only in rare instances are villages inhabited exclusively or nearly so by Ukrainians. In a few localities, Ukrainians are the majority, with most of them located in northern and western Poland.[94] The usual pattern is that Ukrainians occupy 5 to 15% of a village; there are thousands of villages with only a few Ukrainian families.

The largest cultural association is the government-sponsored Ukrainian Social and Cultural Society, founded in 1956, with its governing board in Warsaw. It has five provincial branches in Olsztyn, Gdansk, Koszalin, Szczecin, and Wroclaw; there are thirty county branches and approximately 200 "circles." The society, with a membership of about 5,000, publishes a weekly Ukrainian-language newspaper, *Nashe slovo* (with a supplement for Lemkos), and a literary monthly, *Nasha kultura*.

Ukrainians have had the legal right to education in the Ukrainian language since 1956. There are three Ukrainian elementary schools with over 200 pupils each, two high schools with over 300 students, and some 100 "centers" for part-time instruction in the language, at which about 2,000 people study. In addition, there are departments of Ukrainian philology at Warsaw University and the teacher's colleges in Olsztyn and Szczecin.[95] Some teachers are trained in Kiev. Minority languages will be taught in Polish schools, upon petition, with a specified minimum number of interested students; for Ukrainians, the state-set minimum is seven pupils.[96]

The Special Case of the Lemkos

The Lemkos (Lemky) are a culturally and linguistically cohesive group that had inhabited the Beskidy (Bieszczady) Mountains in southeastern Poland for centuries. Their language is closely related to Ukrainian. In spite of the marked ethnic and cultural differences between the Lemkos and their Polish neighbors, there were not the daily antagonisms with the Poles that characterized other parts of the borderlands.

After the 1944 repatriation agreement between Poland and the Ukrainian SSR, it was frequently the Lemkos who were forcibly sent to the USSR, even though the agreement had called for the voluntary exchange of Polish and Ukrainian populations. The Lemkos also bore the brunt of the 1947 anti-Ukrainian pogrom, euphemistically called "Operation Freedom" (or "Operation Vistula," Akcja "Wisla," or simply Akcja "W"). In response to the death on, March 28, 1947, of the popular Polish general Karol Swierczewski in a UPA ambush, the operation was authorized by a decree of the Presidium of the Council of Ministers dated April 17, 1947.[97] The purpose of the operation was to deprive the underground UPA of its support in the Carpathians by forcibly resettling the Ukrainians in northern and western Poland. A total of 17,350 soldiers were sent into the region to liquidate no more than 1500 UPA members, and the campaign was carried out with extraordinary brutality. It encompassed areas that had had no contact with the UPA, and at times the mere presence of a Ukrainian newspaper in a home was sufficient evidence to brand the inhabitants as UPA "bandits." Conditions in the new settlement areas were poor: 70% of the buildings allotted to the Ukrainian refugees were in ruins. The authorities ruled that no more than 10% of the population of any given village could be Ukrainian, in order to prevent the concentration of Ukrainians into compact communities.[98] The Ukrainians were ill-treated by Polish settlers from the eastern territories and by the security forces, both of whom regarded anyone speaking Ukrainian as a UPA terrorist.[99] The Lemkos have, in 1968 and in 1971, appealed to congresses of the PUWP for rehabilitation and restitution of their rights, but without success.[100]

Belorussians

Polish estimates place the Belorussian population of Poland at between 165,000 and 200,000. Unlike the Ukrainians, the Belorussians have remained in their traditional territories; the majority of them live in Bialystok province, in the southern and eastern counties near Soviet Belorussia. For the most part, they are a rural, peasant, farming population, although a small portion of them are engaged in trades or crafts in small towns.

Since 1956, there has been an officially sponsored Belorussian Social and Cultural Society, with a governing board in Bialystok, which claims 5,500 members and publishes a Belorussian-language weekly (*Niva*) with a circulation of 7,000. The Belorussians have the largest number of native-language schools (thirty-four, with 2,400 students), and there is a chair of Belorussian philology at Warsaw University. Many of the teachers are trained in Minsk.[101] In spite of these advances, there is a high degree of Polonization of Belorussians in Bialystok province.

Lithuanians

The Lithuanians are concentrated in an enclave of about 10,000 people on the border of Poland and Soviet Lithuania, in the northern part of Bialystok province; most of these are to be found in Sejny county, which is 40% Lithuanian. Small colonies of Lithuanian settlers also live in the Western Territories, in Gorzow, Wroclaw, and Slupsk. There is a Lithuanian Social and Cultural Society with 1,300 members, which irregularly publishes a Lithuanian-language newspaper *Ausra*.

Other Nationalities

The approximately 19,000 Russians living in Poland are widely dispersed, although most live in towns such as Lódz, Olsztyn, Gdansk, and Szczecin. There is a substantial Russian settlement in the rural area on the border of Olsztyn and Bialystok provinces, comprised mainly of the descendants of Old Believers who fled religious persecution in Russia in the eighteenth century.

The 17,000 or 18,000 Gypsies in Poland are divided into four tribal groups: Polish Highland Gypsies, Polish Lowland Gypsies, Kelderasze, and Lovari. The latter two groups, mainly from Russia, Hungary, Romania, and Germany, and numbering about 7,000, persist in a nomadic way of life despite official settlement policies. The Polish Gypsies live a settled existence (in Nowa Huta, Szczecin, Warsaw, Lublin, Lódz, and other centers), and are employed in farming, factories, roadbuilding, metalworking, and cottage industries.[102]

Slovaks, numbering about 20,000, are concentrated in Spisz and Orawa, in Cracow province. Between 2,000 and 5,000 Czechs live in Lower Silesia near the Polish-Czech border. There are about 5,000 Greeks and a similar number of Macedonians — still retaining Greek citizenship — who left Greece after World War II, most of whom live in the Western Territories.

The Kashubs (Kaszuby), an ethnographic group numbering perhaps 200,000, live in the Polish Corridor and in eastern Pomerania. Even in the 1919-1939 period, the Kashubs preferred not to be considered Polish. Although their language is related to Polish, it is strongly influenced by German and by the language of Lithuanian tribes that occupied eastern Prussia prior to the settlement of that region by the *Ritterorden* in the mid-thirteenth century. The Kashubs have a cultural society and publish a Kashubian-language newspaper, *Kaszebe*.

There are a small number of Slovenes to be found in western Pomerania and Stolp. Finally, there are about 1,200 Moslem Tartars, concentrated near Landsberg/Warthe, and a smaller number of Karaims, a Tatar people of Jewish faith, who live in small communities in central Poland, Silesia, and Pomerania.

Notes

[1]Stephan Horak, *Poland and Her National Minorities, 1919-1939* (New York: Vantage Press, 1961), pp. 28-29.

[2]See the text of the memorandum in Paul Roth, *Die Entstehung des polnischen staates* (Berlin, 1926), pp. 133ff.

[3]For an account, see Nicholas P. Vakar, *Belorussia: The Making of a Nation: A Case Study* (Cambridge: Harvard University Press, 1956), pp. 112-16.

[4]Polish census figures of the 1920s and 1930s were notoriously unreliable, and estimates of the non-Polish population of interwar Poland vary. The census of 1921 reported 69.2% of the population as Polish (by self-definition). That of 1931 (which employed linguistic criteria) reported 68.9%. See *Rocznik Statystyki Rzeczypospolitej Polskiej*, vol. IV (Warsaw, 1926), and *Mały Rocznik Statystyczny 1939* (Warsaw, 1939). Using ethnoreligious criteria, Edward Wynot arrives at the lower figure of 55% of the population as Polish on the eve of World War II; Edward D. Wynot, Jr., "Poland's Christian Minorities, 1918-1945: From Disappointment to Separation," National Convention of American Association for the Advancement of Slavic Studies, October 14-16, 1982, Washington, DC, p. 8.

[5]*Mały Rocznik Statystyczny* (Warsaw, 1926).

[6]Siegfried E. Heit, "National Minorities and Their Effect on Polish Foreign Relations," *Nationalities Papers* VIII:1 (Spring 1980): 10.

[7]Excerpts of the most important parts of the minorities treaty are reprinted in Horak, pp. 188-91.

[8]Tadeusz Komarnicki, *The Rebirth of the Polish Republic* (London, 1957), p. 296.

[9]Heit, "National Minorities," p. 13.

[10]Herbert Truhart, *Völkerbund und Minderheitenpetitionen* (Vienna, 1931). Cited by heit, p. 13.

[11]Articles 95, 96, 104, 105, and 109-112. Excerpts are reprinted in Horak, *Poland and Her National Minorities*, pp. 195-96.

[12]*Dziennik Ustaw Rzeczypospolitej Polskiej* (Warsaw, 1924), no. 73, item 724; no. 78, item 757; and no. 79, item 766.

[13]See, for example, the views of Leon Wasilewski, head of the Pilsudski cabinet's "Committee of Experts on the Eastern Provinces and the National Minorities," in *Sprawy narodowościowe w teorii i w życiu* (Warsaw, 1929).

[14]Wynot, "Polands Christian Minorities," p. 10.

[15]Ezra Mendelsohn, *Zionism in Poland: The Formative Years, 1915-1926* (New Haven: Yale University Press, 1981), p. 14; Oscar Janowsky, *The Jews and Minority Rights (1898-1919)* (New York: Columbia University Press, 1933), pp. 360-69. Janowsky provides an excellent analysis of the minorities treaty.

[16]Mendelsohn, *Zionism in Poland*, p. 43; Pawel Korzec, "Antisemitism in Poland as an Intellectual, Social and Political Movement," in *Studies on Polish Jewry, 1919-1939*, ed. Joshua Fishman (New York: YIVO Institute for Jewish Research, 1974), pp. 18-29. This extensive article (pp. 12-104) traces the history of Polish anti-Semitism throughout the interwar period.

[17]*The Jews in Poland: Official Reports of the American and British Investigating Missions* (Chicago: The National Polish Committee of America, 1920), pp. 4-61 passim. This is a collection of official U.S. government reports on pogroms in Poland. Arthur L. Goodhart, *Poland and the Minority Races* (London: George Allen & Unwin, 1920), pp. 42-69 passim; Mendelsohn, *Zionism in Poland*, p. 90.

[18]*The Jews in Poland*, pp. 14-15; Jacob Lestchinsky, "Economic Aspects of Jewish Community Organization in Independent Poland," *Jewish Social Studies* IX:4 (October 1947): 319-21.

[19]Mendelsohn, *Zionism in Poland*, p. 14.

[20]Ibid., p. 5; Jacob Lestchinsky, "The Jews in the Cities of the Republic of Poland," in *YIVO Annual of Jewish Social Science*, I (New York: Yiddish Scientific Institute—YIVO, 1946), p. 159. Lestchinsky states that 2,380,075 of Poland's 3,113,933 Jews lived in cities, while only 22% of Poland's non-Jewish population lived in urban areas. See Georges Castellan, "Remarks on the Social Structure of the Jewish Community in Poland between the Two World Wars," in *Jews and Non-Jews in Eastern Europe, 1918-1945*, eds. Bela Vago and George L. Mosse (New York: John Wiley and Sons, 1974), pp. 187-201, for an excellent demographic survey of Poland's urban and rural Jewish population.

[21]Lestchinsky, "Jews in the Cities," pp. 164-69; Mendelsohn, *Zionism in Poland*, pp. 6, 9.

[22]Mendelsohn, *Zionism in Poland*, p. 8; Raphael Mahler, "Jews in Public Service and the Liberal Professions in Poland, 1918-1939," *Jewish Social Studies* VI:4 (October 1944): 301.

[23]Mahler, "Jews in Public Service," pp. 298, 303, 308-9.

[24]Ibid., pp. 335, 337.

[25]Ibid., p. 341.

[26]Lestchinsky, "Economic Aspects," pp. 320-21; Bernard D. Weinryb, "Poland," in *The Jews in the Soviet Sattelites*, ed. Peter Meyer, et al. (Syracuse: Syracuse University Press, 1953), p. 215.

[27]Lestchinsky, "Economic Aspects," pp. 335-36.

[28]Mahler, "Jews in Public Service," p. 338.

[29]Weinryb, "Poland," pp. 221-22.

[30]Ibid., p. 223.

[31]Ibid.; Lestchinsky, "Economic Aspects," pp. 336-37.

[32]Mendelsohn, *Zionism in Poland*, pp. 108-9.

[33]Ibid., pp. 213-22 passim.

[34]Ibid., pp. 301-8.

[35]Weinryb, "Poland," pp. 218-20. Emanuel Melzer argues that as a result of the Polish-German Non-Aggression Pact of September 1, 1934, Foreign Minister Joseph Beck "in essence rescinded Poland's obligations deriving from the 1919 Treaty for the Protection of national Minorities," and that this marked the beginning of a new level of anti-Semitic policies in Poland. Emanuel Melzer, " Relations between Poland and Germany and Their Impact on the Jewish Problem in Poland (1935-1938)," *Yad Vashem Studies* XII, ed. Livia Rothkirchen (January 1977): 193; Korzec, "Antisemitism in Poland," pp. 74-84.

[36]Horak, *Poland and Her National Minorities*, p. 100.

[37]For a detailed discussion of the activities of the Ukrainian political parties during the period 1937-1939, see Edward D. Wynot, Jr., "The Ukrainians and the Polish Regime, 1937-1939," *Ukrains'kyi istoryk* VII:4 (1980): 44-60.

[38]Stephan M. Horak, "Belorussian and Ukrainian Peasants in Poland, 1919-1939," Ivan Volgyes, ed., *The Peasantry of Eastern Europe*, Vol. I: *Roots of Rural Transformation* (New York: Pergamon Press, 1979), pp. 139-44.

[39]Horak, *Poland and Her National Minorities*, p. 90.

[40]Ivan S. Lubachko, *Belorussia under Soviet Rule, 1917-1957* (Lexington: University of Kentucky Press, 1972), p. 137.

[41]Vakar, *Belorussia*, p. 136.

[42]See, for example, William Hagen, *Germans, Poles, and Jews: The National Conflict in the Prussian East, 1772-1914* (Chicago: University of Chicago Press, 1980); and Richard Blanke, *Prussian Poland in the German Empire, 1871-1900* (Boulder, CO: East European Quarterly, 1981).

[43]Stanislaus Mornik (Erich Jaensch), *Polens Kampf gegen seine nichtpolnischen Volksgruppen* (Berlin, 1931), p. 12.

[44]Ibid., p. 25.

[45]Theodor Bierschenk, *Die deutsche Volksgruppe in Polen, 1934-9* (Würzburg, 1954), p. 10.

[46]Ibid., p. 11f.

[47]Hermann Rauschning, *Die Entdeutschung Westpreussens und Posens* (Berlin, 1930), p. 15; Mornik, *Polens Kampf*, p. 84; Andrzej Chojnowski, *Koncepcje polityki narodowościowej rządów polskich w latach 1921-39* (Wroclaw, 1979), p. 13.

[48]Harald von Riekhoff, *German-Polish Relations, 1918-1933* (Baltimore: Johns Hopkins University Press, 1971), p. 57f; Rauschning, *Die Entdeutschung*, p. 10.

[49]Chojnowski, *Koncepcje polityki*, p. 21.

[50]Riekhoff, *German-Polish Relations*, p. 195.

[51]Rauschning, *Die Entdeutschung*, p. 9; Bierschenk, *Die deutsche Volksgruppe*, pp. 110, 125; Richard Breyer, *Das Deutsche Reich und Polen, 1932-7* (Würzburg, 1955), p. 52.

[52]B. Schmitt, ed., *Poland* (Berkeley and Los Angeles: University of California Press, 1945), p. 154.

[53]Bierschenk, *Die deutsche Volksgruppe*, p. 53; Breyer, *Das Deutsche Reich*, p. 166.

[54]Pawel Korzec, "Polen und der Minderheitenschutzvertrag (1919-34)," *Jahrbücher für Geschichte Osteuropas* 22 (1974): 515-55.

[55]Bierschenk, *Die deutsche Volksgruppe*, pp. 332, 340, 351.

[56]*Polish Acts of Atrocity against the German Minority in Poland.* (Berlin: German Foreign Office, 1940), p. 5.

[57]Hans Roos, *A History of Modern Poland* (New York: Knopf, 1966), p. 167.

[58]Marian Dziewanowski, *Poland in the 20th Century* (New York: Columbia University Press, 1977), p. 107.

[59]Anthony Komjathy and Rebecca Stockwell, *German Minorities and the Third Reich* (New York and London: Holmes and Meier, 1980), p. 191.

[60]Joseph Chmelar, *National Minorities in Central Europe* (Prague, 1937), p. 27.

[61]Horak, *Poland and Her National Minorities*, pp. 91-94.

[62]The first and only governor general was Hans Frank. His own writings are a key to Nazi guidelines in administering the territory; see S. Piotrowski, ed., *Hans Franks Diary* (Warsaw, 1961).

[63]Edward D. Wynot, "Word of Delusions and Illusions: The National Minorities of Poland during World War II," *Nationalities Papers* VII:2 (Fall 1979): 177-78.

[64]*Hans Franks Diary*, pp. 134-35.

[65]Wynot, "World of Delusions and Illusions ...," p. 184.

[66]See Martin Broszat, *Nationalsozialistische Polenpolitik, 1939-45* (Frankfurt, 1965); Jan Gross, *Polish Society under German Occupation* (Princeton, NJ: Princeton University press, 1979).

[67]Raul Hilberg, *The Destruction of the European Jews* (New York: Franklin Watts, 1973), p. 126; Yeshuda Bauer, *A History of the Holocaust* (New York: Franklin Watts, 1982), p. 142; Weinryb, "Poland," p. 226; Ben-Cion Pinchuk, "Jewish Refugees in Soviet Poland, 1939-1941," *Jewish Social Studies* XL:2 (Spring 1978): 142, 145-46.

[68]Weinryb, "Poland," p. 227. Weinryb states that by the eve of the German invasion of the USSR, there were 85 labor camps for Jews in the General Gouvernement, with 80,000 internees.

[69]Jacob Apenszlak, et al., eds., *The Black Book of Polish Jewry* (New York: American Federation for Polish Jews, 1943), pp. 43-49; Mary Pokrovshy, "Ghettos in Nazi Poland," *Background: The Key to Current Events* 5 (1942): 1-15 passim.

[70]Isaiah Trunk, *Judenrat* (New York: Stein and Day, 1977), pp. 570-75; Nora Levin, *The Holocaust: The Destruction of European Jewry 1933-1945* (New York: Schocken Books, 1973), pp. 172-73; Aharon Weiss, "Jewish Leadership in Occupied Poland — Postures and Attitudes," in *Yad Vashem Studies*, XII, ed. Livia Rothkirchen (Jerusalem: Yad Vashem, 1977), pp. 361-65.

[71]Lucy Dawidowicz, *The War against the Jews, 1933-1945* (New York: Bantam Books, 1976), p. 181.

[72]Weinryb, "Poland," p. 229; Hilberg, *Destruction of the European Jews*, p. 670; Levin, *The Holocaust*, pp. 715-18. The latter includes a valuable statistical summary of demographic figures from major studies on the Holocaust.

[73]Wynot, "World of Delusions and Illusions ...," p. 182.

[74]Richard F. Staar, *Communist Regimes in Eastern Europe*, 3rd ed. (Stanford, CA: Hoover Institution Press, 1977), pp. 126-27.

[75]Dziewanowski, *Poland in the 20th Century*, p. 147.

[76]U.S. Senate, Committee on Foreign Relations, "The Berlin (Potsdam) Conference, July 17-August 2, 1945," in *A Decade of American Foreign Policy: Basic Documents, 1941-1949* (Washington, DC: U.S. Government Printing Office, 1950), pp. 43-44.

[77]Andrzey Kwilecki, "National Minorities in Poland," *Polish Round Table* (Warsaw), Yearbook 1968, p. 145.

[78]Ibid., p. 146.

[79]Horst Glassl, "Die nationalen Minderheiten in Polen" (Unpublished manuscript), p. 1.

[80]Kwilecki, *Polish Round Table*, pp. 35-36.

[81]See Alfred de Zayas, *Nemesis at Potsdam* (London: Routledge and Kegan Paul, 1977).

[82]W. W. Kulski, *Germany and Poland: From War to Peaceful Relations* (Syracuse, NY: Syracuse University Press, 1976), pp. 247ff.

[83]Paul Lendvai, "The Party and the Jews," *Commentary* (September 1968): 57.

[84]Ibid., p. 63.; on the March events, see Stanislaw Staron, "Political Developments in Poland: The Party Reacts to Challenge," *Orbis* (Winter 1970); A. Ross Johnson, "Poland: End of an Era?" *Problems of Communism* (January-February 1970).

[85]Radio Free Europe, *News from Poland* (May 16, 1973).

[86]Weinryb, "Poland," pp. 229, 240-41.

[87]Ibid., pp. 279-89.

[88]Ibid., pp. 247-53.

[89]Ibid., pp. 253, 261-63.

[90]Ibid., pp. 254-57.

[91]Ibid., pp. 299-307.

[92]Ibid., p. 313; Emil Lengyel, "The Polish Jew Today," *The Chicago Jewish Quarterly* 16:3 (Spring 1958): 143-47.

[93]*Encyclopedia Judaica*, vol. 13 (New York: The Macmillan Company, 1971), pp. 784-85; "The Jewish Community in Poland," *A.J.A. Quarterly* 18:3 (December 1969): 13-15, 24; "Poland: Whither Polish Jewry?" *Jews in Eastern Europe* III:5 (October 1966): 59-60; Pawns in a Power Struggle," *Jews in Eastern Europe* III:9 (May 1968): 7-20.

[94]Kwilecki, *Polish Round Table*, p. 146.

[95]Radio Free Europe, *Polish Situation Report* (May 3, 1979): 6.

[96]Roman Solchanyk, "Aktywizacja mniejszości ukraińskiej w Polse," *Kultura* (Paris) 7-8 (1981): 125-30.

[97]See Genowefa Lukasziewicz, "Wokól genezy i przebiegu Akcji 'Wisla' 1947 rok," *Dzieje Najnowsze* 6:4 (1974): 35-50.

[98]Ibid.

[99]Maciej Kozlowski, "Lemkowie," *Solidarność* (August 14, 1981): 11; see a discussion of this article in *Radio Liberty Research* 358/81 (September 10, 1981).

[100]"Stanovyshche ukrains'koi menshosty v Pol'shchi," *Suchasnist'* 12:10 (October 1972): 88-102; and "Stanovyshche ukrains'koi menshost v Pol'schi," *Suchasnist'* 13:3 (March 1973): 108-15.

[101]Kwilecky, *Polish Round Table*, p. 151.

[102]J. Ficowski, *Cyganie na polskich drogach* (Warsaw, 1964), passim.

BIBLIOGRAPHY

General Reference Works

75.   Grzegorczyk, Piotr. **Bibliografja mniejszości narodowych w Polsce** (Bibliography on the National Minorities in Poland). Warsaw: Instytut Badań Spraw Narodowościowych, 1932-38.

This is a useful bibliography of works published annually in Poland on national minorities in Poland, published from 1931 through 1937. Available in the New York Public Library, it contains an extensive listing of books and articles in Polish and other languages.

76.   **Mały Rocznik statystyczny** (Short Statistical Yearbook). Warsaw: Główny Urząd Statystyczny Rzecz. Polskiej, 1930-1939.

Rocznik statystyki Rzeczypospolitej Polskiej (Statistical Yearbook of the Polish Republic). Warsaw: Główny Urząd Statystyczny Rzeczypospolitej, 1920-1938.

Skorowidz mniejszosci Rzeczypospolitej Polskiej (Index of Minorities of the Polish Republic). Warsaw: Główny Urząd Statystyczny, 1924-1926.

77.   Markert, Werner, ed. **Polen. Osteuropa-Handbuch.** Köln-Graz: Böhlau Verlag, 1959. 829p. Maps. Tables. Bibliography.

This compendium of information on Poland, updated up to the 1950s, was compiled by a team of German scholars. In addition to chapters on political, social, educational, religious, economic, and demographic aspects of the country, it includes chapters on the Ukrainian Uniate Church, the Orthodox Church, the Evangelical (German) Church, Jews, and Germans. Each chapter provides statistical data, a brief historical survey, and pertinent literature. This work remains a standard reference source for the study of Poland.

78.   **Sprawy Narodowościowe** (Journal dedicated to the research of the nationalities problem). Warsaw: Instytut badań spraw narodowościowych, 1927-1939.

The journal published a great number of articles on Poland's national minorities, mainly by Polish experts such as A. Krysiński, S. Gorzuchowski, L. Wasilewski, and B. Zaborski.

79.   Zaleski, Wladyslaw J. **Międzynarodowa ochrona mniejszości** (International Protection of the Minorities). Warsaw: Instytut Badań Spraw Narodowościowych, 1932. 191p.

This book offers text and comments on all international documents pertaining to the legal protection of the national minorities in Poland. It is a defense of Poland's nationalities policy.

General Works

80.   Alius. **Die Curzon-Linie: Das Grenzproblem Sowjetunion-Polen.** Zürich: Europa Verlag, 1945. 99p. Translation from the French original edition, *La Ligue Curzon* (1945).

A short yet satisfactory presentation of Poland's eastern provinces populated by Belorussians and Ukrainians. The problem is presented against the demographic structure of the territory and the political border issue beginning with the so-called Curzon Line solution and up to the events of 1944, which determined the final Soviet-Polish border.

81. Barnett, Clifford R. **Poland: Its People, Its Society, Its Culture.** New Haven, CT: Yale University Press, 1958. 471p.

The picture starts with a thumbnail sketch of Polish culture and society and proceeds to the presentation of the historical setting, geography and population, ethnic groups and languages, religions, dynamics of political behavior, the legal and theoretical base of government, structure of the government, and foreign policy. Four lasting popular Polish political attitudes are stressed: nationalism, Roman Catholicism, and the general anti-Russian and anti-German attitudes of the people. This is a very useful general overview.

82. Chojnowski, Andrzej. **Koncepcje polityki narodowościowej rządów polskich w latach 1921-1939** (Conception of the Nationalities Policy of the Polish Governments during the years 1921-1939). Seria: Polska myśl polityczna XIX i XX wieku, vol. 3. Wroclaw: Ossolineum, 1979. 242p. (Summaries in Russian, English, and German.)

The author reviews the nationalities policies of all Polish governments of interwar Poland. He is very critical of the policies of Pilsudski and his successors, which aimed at assimilation of the non-Poles and pursued efforts to colonize Ukrainian territories with Poles. The chapters on education and economy are based on statistical data.

83. Goodhart, Arthur Lehmann. **Poland and the Minority Races.** London: George Allen & Unwin, 1920. 194p.

This is a memoir account by the legal counsel to the American Morgenthau mission to investigate the pogroms in Poland in 1918-1919. The work touches on Poland's relations with its Belorussian, Lithuanian, and Ukrainian minorities, and ends with a brief history of Polish Jewry.

84. Hołówko, Tadeusz. **Kwestia narodowa w Polsce** (The Nationality Question in Poland). Warsaw: Ksiegarnia Robotnicza, 1922.

This book expresses the views of a close supporter of Jozef Pilsudski, expounding the "federalist" solution of the national minorities problem.

85. Horak, Stephan. **Poland and Her National Minorities, 1919-1939.** New York: Vantage Press, 1961. 259p. Tables. Maps.

This volume, the definitive work on the subject in English, features a good source base (given limited access to Polish archives) and substantial use of statistics. The author examines major issues in general terms, then focuses on each separate minority. Strongest on the eastern Slavs.

86. Kierski, Kazimierz. **Ochrona praw mniejszości w Polsce** (Protection of the Minorities in Poland). Poznan: Nakl. Związki Obrony Kresów Zachodnich, 1933. 103p.

The author endeavors to prove that the national minorities in Poland enjoyed freedom and equality as formulated by international agreements and guarantees.

87. Mauersberg, Stanislaw. **Szkolnictwo powszechne dla mniejszości narodowych w Polsce w latach 1919-1939** (Elementary Public Schooling for the National Minorities in Poland, 1919-1939). Wroclaw: Ossolineum, 1968. 230p. Tables. Stats. Maps.

The thorough, indepth examination of this topic is based on extensive primary archival sources. It offers an even treatment of each group, with solid analysis and a good bibliography.

88. Mornik, Stanislaus. **Polens Kampf gegen seine nichtpolnischen Volksgruppen**. Berlin and Leipzig: Walter de Gruyter, 1931. 154p. Maps. Tables.

This critical yet objective study concentrates on Poland's ethnographic and sociological structures of its national minorities and on religious and economic aspects, followed by a discussion of Poland's measures aimed at the destruction of minority organizations, culture, languages, and churches. Of special benefit are the numerous statistical tables comprising demographic, educational, religious, and economic data on national minorities. This is one of the most informative studies on the subject.

89. Paprocki, Stanislaw. **Polen und das Minderheitenproblem: Informationen in Umrissen**. Warsaw: Institut zur Erforschung der Minderheitsfragen, 1935. 173p. Also published in English, *Minority Affairs and Poland* (Warsaw, 1935) and French, *La Pologne et le problème des minorités* (Warsaw, 1935).

The author presents the official Polish view on the minorities, supported by statistical data on various cultural, religious, social, educational, and economic aspects of the minorities.

90. Sworakowski, Witold S. **Międzynarodowe zobowiązania mniejszościowe Polski: Komentarz do art. 12-go Malego Traktatu Wersalskiego; z przedmową Juliana Makowskiego** International Obligations Concerning Poland's Minorities: Commentary to the Art. 12 of the Little Versailles Treaty). Warsaw: Instytut Badań Spraw Narodowościowych, 1935. 232p.

91. Urbański, Zygmunt. **Mniejszości narodowe w Polsce** (National Minorities in Poland). Warsaw: Wydawnictwo "Mniejszości Narodowe," 1932. 375p.

This balanced account of the national minorities problem features historical background on each group, along with excerpts from key statutes concerning minority affairs.

92. Wasilewski, Leon. **Sprawy narodowościowe w teorii i w życiu** (Nationality Affairs in Theory and in Practice). Warsaw: J. Mortkowicz, 1929. 232p. Stats.

Presented here are the views of one of Jozef Pilsudski's most eminent experts on minority problems, along with his recommendations for improving ethno-religious relations. Considered a "liberal" on the minorities question, the author focuses on the eastern Slavs.

93. Wynot, Edward D., Jr. "World of Delusions and Illusions: The National Minorities of Poland during World War II," *Nationalities Papers* 7:2 (1979): 177-96.

This is a concise summary of the actions and fates of the Polish Jews, Ukrainians, Belorussians, and Germans during the war that compares and contrasts each case while describing it.

94. Wytwycky, Bohdan. **The Other Holocaust: Many Circles of Hell.** Washington, DC: Novak Report Publishers, 1980. 96p.

This compact book is a first attempt at a comprehensive account of the fate of 9 to 10 million east European Gentiles who died with the 6 million Jews under the Nazi terror in World War II. In descending numbers, the victims were Ukrainians, Poles, Belorussians, and Gypsies. Their horrible deaths cast a shadow over eastern Europe that has never been penetrated by Western scholarship. The book gathers facts and figures, and sketches out the possible avenues of research into the subject.

Ukrainians

General Reference Works

95. Korduba, Myron. **La litterature historique sovietique-ukrainienne.** Harvard Series in Ukrainian Studies, 10. Munich: Wilhelm Fink Verlag, 1972. 365p.

This is a reprint of the 1938 Warsaw edition, edited by Omeljan Pritsak, of Korduba's outstanding bibliography and survey of Ukraine, beginning with 1800. It includes over 55,000 works, as well as a survey of works on Galicia, 1921-1926, by Ivan Krypiakevych.

96. Magocsi, Paul Robert. **Galicia: A Historical Survey and Bibliographic Guide.** Toronto: University of Toronto Press, in association with the Canadian Institute of Ukrainian Studies, 1982. 300p.

The history of Ukrainian Galicia is surveyed from earliest times to the present, and the bibliography covers the extensive literature about Galicia's archeological, political, social, economic, literary, ethnographic, linguistic, and artistic developments. A separate chapter is devoted to Galicia's minorities—Poles, Jews, Germans, and Armenians. The volume includes over 1,000 notes and 3,000 references, six maps tracing historic development in Galicia, and a detailed name and subject index.

97. Pelenskyj, Eugene J. **Ucrainica. Selected Bibliography on Ukraine in Western-European Languages.** Memoirs of the Scientific Ševčenko Society, vol. 158. Munich: Bystrycia, 1948. 111p.

This compact publication contains 2,600 entries on subjects pertaining to Ukrainian studies. The entries on Ukrainians in Poland are arranged by general subjects.

98. **Ukraine: A Concise Encyclopedia.** Edited by Volodymyr Kubijovyč. Prepared by the Shevchenko Scientific Society. 2 vols. Toronto: University of Toronto Press for the Ukrainian National Association, 1963, 1971. Vol. 1, 1185p. Vol. 2, 1394p.

The encyclopedia provides numerous concise entries on various periods and all aspects of the Ukrainian national minority in Poland before 1939 and after 1945. Each entry includes a selected bibliography, basic statistical data, and maps.

99. Weres, Roman, comp. **Ukraine: Selected References in the English Language.** 2nd ed. Chicago: Ukrainian Research and Information Institute, 1974. 312p.

This comprehensive annotated bibliography of books and articles comprises 1,958 entries, many relating to Ukrainians in interwar and postwar Poland.

History and General Studies

100.   Andrusiak, Nicholas. "The Ukrainian Movement in Galicja," *Slavonic Review* 14 (1936): 163-75; 372-79.
A contemporary description and analysis of the internal political divisions within the Ukrainian community under Polish rule in the 1930s.

101.   Feliński, M. **Ukraińcy w Polsce odrodzonej** (Ukrainians in Reborn Poland). Warsaw, 1931. 170p. Translated and published by the author in English under the title *The Ukrainians in Poland* (London, 1931. 173p.).
Available in the Cleveland Public Library, this book contains useful information on the civil rights, political life, economic conditions, and cultural and social organizations of Ukrainians in post-World War I Poland.

102.   Hunczak, Taras, ed. **A History of Pidhaitsi and Its Region.** New York, Paris, Sydney, Toronto: Shevchenko Scientific Society, 1980. 774p.

   Papiz, Wasyl, ed. **Travelog of Pidhaitsi Region.** New York, Paris, Sydney, Toronto: Shevchenko Scientific Society, 1980. 170p.
The American Shevchenko Scientific Society has published a number of regional studies on various West Ukrainian areas. This history and accompanying photo album covers Pidhaitsi, one of the most active and nationally conscious counties. It contains personal memoirs of close to four score authors with an intimate knowledge of the region and historical documents dating back to Austrian rule (1795-1918). Especially well covered are the last decade of Polish rule (1929-1939) and the Soviet and Nazi occupation during World War II.

103.   Karpatiuk, Zenon. "Ukrainians in Present-Day Poland." *Ukrainian Quarterly* 23:4 (Winter 1977): 348-65.
This is a very informative account of the fate of Ukrainians in Poland relating to all aspects of their existence, including their forced resettlement after 1945 from their native lands into newly gained northern and western provinces. Information on the cultural, economic, educational, and political activities of some 250,000 Ukrainians living in Poland is also provided.

104.   Lozyns'kyi, Mykhailo. **Halychyna v rr. 1918-1920** (Galicia in 1918-1920). New York: Vyd. "Chervona Kalyna," 1970. 228p. (Reprint of 1922 edition).
This is a political history of East Galicia during the existence of the Western Ukrainian Republic, of which Lozyns'kyi was one of the leading personalities. The work provides background developments beginning with World War I and includes a number of original documents on the activities of the Ukrainian government.

105.   **Na vichnu han'bu Polshchi, tverdyni varvarstva v Evropi** (For Poland's Everlasting Shame, the Fortress of Barbarism in Europe. 2nd ed. Series: Materiialy i dokumenty, no. 2. New York: "Howerla," 1956. 150p. Photos.
This is a collection of reports and eyewitness accounts about Polish "pacification" of Ukrainian villages and towns in Galicia in 1930. Included are personal reports of foreign journalists, foreign newspaper accounts, and reports of official visitors to the scenes of destruction. Pacification was carried out by units of the Polish army, who were assisted by the police. As a result of this action, several hundred buildings were destroyed and thousands of Ukrainian men and women were brutally beaten.

106. Pankivs'kyi, Kost'. **Roky nimets'koi okupatsii** (The Years of German Occupation). New York and Toronto: "Kliuchi," 1965. 479p.

The former chairman of the Ukrainian Regional Committee in Lviv during the German occupation in 1941-1944 recalls his activities and those of the Ukrainians under the Nazi occupation. His memoirs are objective and reveal many previously unknown details. The historian will appreciate this publication as an important contribution to the literature on this subject.

————. **Vid derzhavy do komitetu** (From Statehood to Committee). New York and Toronto: "Kliuchi," 1957. 160p.

In this study, Pankivs'kyi discusses Ukrainian political aspirations, expectations, and disappointments under the German occupation of Galicia, including the OUN attempt to proclaim an independent Ukraine in Lviv on June 30, 1941 and its suppression.

————. **Vid komitetu do derzhavnoho tsentru** (From Committee to State Organization). New York and Toronto: "Kliuchi," 1968. 284p.

This is the third volume of Pankivs'kyi's memoirs, covering the years 1944-1948.

107. Potichnyj, Peter J., ed. **Poland and Ukraine: Past and Present.** Edmonton and Toronto: The Canadian Institute of Ukrainian Studies, 1980. 364p. Distributed by the University of Toronto Press.

This volume of the Proceedings of the Eleventh Annual McMaster Conference offers the views of Ukrainian and Polish scholars on one of the most sensitive issues of east European history. The eighteen essays are grouped into five sections: Historical Legacy, Cultural Relations, Economic Ties and Communications, World War II and After, and Political Problems. An introductory essay offers a framework for all other contributions; all are balanced, impartial, and marked by good will.

108. Revyuk, Emil, comp. **Polish Atrocities in Ukraine.** New York: United Ukrainian Organizations of the United States, 1932. 512p. Illus.

Presented here are eyewitness accounts of the so-called pacification of the Ukrainians in Eastern Galicia that was carried out by units of the Polish armed forces and the police in the summer of 1930. The physical punishment of hundreds of Ukrainians and the destruction of Ukrainian cultural facilities and cooperative economic installations are illustrated by numerous original photographs.

109. Rudnyts'ka, Milena. **Zakhidnia Ukraina pid bolshevykamy, 1939-1941: Zbirnyk** (Western Ukraine under the Bolsheviks, 1939-1941: A Collection of Essays). New York: Shevchenko Scientific Society, 1958. 494p.

This is a study of the occupation of Western Ukraine by the Red Army in the beginnings of World War II. The author, a one-time member of the Polish Sejm, has succeeded in presenting a study which explains and analyzes all methods applied by communism in occupied foreign territories.

110. Rudnytsky, Ivan L. "The Role of the Ukraine in Modern History." *Slavic Review* 2:2 (1963): 199-216.

A controversial but important article in which the author discusses the role of historical factors in shaping Ukrainian political attitudes and affirms that differences between Russian and Ukrainian thought are historically conditioned. The principal historical factor is Ukraine's association with the West, particularly Poland.

111.   Stachiw, Matthew, and Sztendera, Jaroslaw. **Western Ukraine at the Turning Point of Europe's History, 1918-1923.** Edited by Joan L. Stachiw. 2 vols. Shevchenko Scientific Society Ukrainian Studies, English Section, vol. 5. Scranton, PA: Ukrainian Scientific-Historical Library, 1969.

This is the only study in English which uses original sources to show the conflicting interests in Western Ukraine, namely among the Poles, Russians, Austrians, Jews, and Ukrainians during the last crucial years of World War I and at the Paris Peace Conference. This book is based on M. Stakhiv's six-volume study, *Zakhidnia Ukraina.*

112.   Stakhiv, Matvii. **Zakhidnia Ukraina: narys istorii derzhavnoho budivnytstva ta zbroinoi i dyplomatychnoi oborony v 1918-1923** (Western Ukraine: An Outline of the History of State Making and of the Military and Diplomatic Defense during 1918-1923). 6 vols. in 7. Scranton, PA: Ukrainian Workingmen's Association, 1960-1961.

This is the most comprehensive history of the Western Ukrainian Republic; it includes the period of independence, 1918-1919, the Polish-Ukrainian war of 1919, the international activities of the republic, and the political activities of the government in exile until 1923. Volumes 1 and 2 deal with the period from 1772 to 1914 as an introduction to the subsequent volumes. All volumes contain numerous original documents and pictures of Ukrainian political and military leaders.

113.   Vytvytsky, Stephen, and Baran, Stephen. "West Ukraine under Poland." In **Ukraine: A Concise Encyclopedia**, edited by Volodymyr Kubijovyc. Toronto: Shevchenko Scientific Society, 1963. Vol. I., pp. 838-50.

The best concise presentation of Ukrainian life in interwar Poland, with focus on political and social aspects.

114.   Wynot, Edward D., Jr. "The Ukrainians and the Polish Regime, 1937-1939." *The Ukrainian Historian* 7:4 (1970): 44-60.

Based on hitherto unavailable Polish archival sources, the essay documents the growing hostility leading to the final break between the Polish government and its Ukrainian minority.

115.   Yaremko, Michael. **Galicia-Halychyna (A Part of Ukraine): From Separation to Unity.** With an introduction by Clarence A. Manning. Shevchenko Scientific Society, Ukrainian Studies, vol. 18. English Section, vol. 3. Toronto, New York, Paris: Shevchenko Scientific Society, 1967. 292p.

The author offers information about Galicia and its religious, political, and economic conditions in the past and present, solidly based on historical literature. His intention was to present the material in a popular and narrative style.

116.   Zhyla, Volodymyr, comp. **Zbarazhchyna: Zbirnyk statei, materiialiv i spomyniv** (Zbarazh County: Collection of Essays, Materials, and Memoirs). New York and Toronto: Shevchenko Scientific Society, 1980. 740p. Map.

The volume comprises contributions on history, geography, religion, language and literature, education, and culture, and biographies of leading personalities. Much of the material relates to the period under Polish rule, 1919-1939.

Politics and Political Parties

117. Armstrong, John A. **Ukrainian Nationalism.** 2nd ed. Littleton, CO: Ukrainian Academic Press, 1980. Originally published 1955, 1963 by Columbia University Press under the title *Ukrainian Nationalism, 1939-1945.* xvi, 361p.

This is a dramatic account of the origins of the UPA (Ukrainian Insurgent Army) in Poland and its efforts to establish Ukrainian independence during World War II. A major scholarly work, it is based on numerous personal interviews, extensive files of contemporary newspapers, and countless unpublished documents.

118. Deruga, Aleksy. **Polityka Wschodnia Polski wobec Ziem Litwy, Bialorusi i Ukrainy (1918-1919)** (Poland's Eastern Policy toward the Lands of Lithuania, Belorussia, and Ukraine). Warsaw: Polska Akademia Nauk, 1969. 330p.

Built on impressive archival sources as well as a rich collection of monographs and periodical literature, the study focuses on the Polish-Ukrainian conflict. The author argues that the Polish attack on Western Ukraine in 1919 was a war of conquest against the Ukrainian nation. The study abstains from propaganda and treats non-Poles without discrimination.

119. Knysh, Zenoviy, ed. **Nepohasnyi ohon viry** (Unextinguishable Fire of the Faith). A Collection in Honor of Col. Andriy Melnyk, Head of the Supreme Council (*Provid*) of Ukrainian Nationalists. Paris: Imprimerie P.I.U.F., 1974. 763p.

This volume contains three parts. The first is comprised of 44 articles and memoirs by various authors who collaborated with Col. Melnyk during 1917-1920 and during his subsequent career as leader of the OUN and UPA. The second part contains Melnyk's "Appeals and Speeches" on the problems of Ukrainian liberation. The third contains various statements and resolutions of the Supreme Council of Ukrainian Nationalists on events in postwar Ukraine.

120. Lewandowski, Krzysztof. **Sprawa ukraińska w polityce zagranicznej Czechoslowacji w latach 1918-1932** (The Ukrainian problem in the Foreign Policy of Czechoslovakia in 1918-1932). Wroclaw, Warsaw, Cracow, Gdansk: Polish Academy of Science, 1974. 336p.

A great deal of useful information is provided on Ukrainian-Czech, Ukrainian-Polish, and Ukrainian-Russian relations during the interwar period. The author is swayed, of course, by the Communist viewpoint, but the work is still impressive due to its extensive use of sources.

121. Makar, Volodymyr. **Bereza Kartuz'ka: Spomyny v 1934-35rr.** Bereza Kartuzka: Memoirs, 1934-35). Toronto: Liga vyzvolennia Ukrainy, 1956. 204p. Illus.

This is the author's personal story about his experiences in the Polish concentration camp Bereza Kartuzka, where several thousand Ukrainians were held, without judicial verdicts, on the order of the Polish administrative and police authorities.

122. Motyl, Alexander J. "The Rural Origins of the Communist and Nationalist Movements in Wolyn *Województwo,* 1921-1939." *Slavic Review* 37:3 (1978): 412-20.

This is a quantitative study of peasant support for the OUN and the KPZU (Communist Party of Western Ukraine) in the eastern Polish *województwo* of Wolyń in the 1930s. The author finds that the Ukrainian Communists were strongest in areas with the largest numbers of landless peasants and that the Nationalists did best where poor peasants were most numerous. He attempts to explain this in terms of land ownership.

123.   Motyl, Alexander J. **The Turn to the Right: The Ideological Origins and Development of Ukrainian Nationalism, 1919-1929**. East European Monographs, no. 65. Boulder, CO: East European Quarterly, 1980. 215p. Distributed by Columbia University Press.

Motyl examines the changes in Ukrainian political thought after World War I and analyzes the shift to the Right, which in his opinion was caused by the war. Exhibiting painstaking objectivity, he tries to come to terms with the ideology of the OUN and searches for the beginnings of the ideology of Ukrainian idealism. This is a valuable study for anyone interested in the subject matter.

124.   Paneyko, B. "Galicia and the Polish-Ukrainian Problem." *Slavonic Review* 9 (1930/31): 567-87.

This is a contemporary account of the violent and occasionally murderous confrontations between Poles and Ukrainians known euphemistically as the "pacification" (June-October 1930).

125.   Papierzynska-Turek, Miroslawa. **Sprawa ukraińska w Drugiej Rzeczypospolitej, 1922-1926** (The Ukrainian Problem in the Second Polish Republic, 1922-1926). Krakow: Wydawnictwo Literackie, 1979. 390p.

With particular focus on the activities of the Sejm, this is a thorough study of the interwar Polish government's policies toward national minorities before 1926. It provides a good discussion of Polish and Ukrainian political parties, Ukrainian community organizations, and the electoral, agricultural, and educational policies of the government. The discussion of the problem of the Orthodox Church in Poland, with the complicating factor of the conservative Russian population, is especially welcome.

126.   Piotrkiewicz, Teofil. **Kwestia ukraińska w Polsce w koncepjach pilsudczyzny, 1926-1930** (The Ukrainian Problem in Poland in Pilsudski's Concept, 1926-1930). Warsaw: Instytut historji, Warsaw University, 1981. 165p.

Published under the aegis of the Institute of History at Warsaw University, this study is an inquiry into the views of Pilsudski's followers concerning the Ukrainians. The study ends in 1930, the year of the mass pogrom of Ukrainians known as "pacification." It is thoroughly documented, resting heavily on primary sources, including government documents not available to previous researchers. The book presents separate discussions of the views of the so-called Ukrainophile Poles—Leon Wasilewski, Tadeusz Holowko, and Piotr Dunin-Borkowski.

127.   Radziejowski, Janusz. **Komunistyczna Partia Zachodniej Ukrainy 1919-1929: Węzlowe problemy ideologiczne** (The Communist Party of Western Ukraine, 1919-1929: Crucial Ideological Problems). Cracow: Wydawnictwo Literackie, 1976. 267p.

This is the first book-length study of the Communist party of Western Ukraine published outside the Soviet Union; it is also the first serious and objective treatment of an important but heretofore neglected aspect of the Communist movement in interwar Poland. The author focuses his attention on those thorny ideological issues which presented such problems for the Comintern leadership: the organizational relationships between the Communist party of Western Ukraine, the Communist party of Poland, and the Communist party (Bolsheviks) of Ukraine, and the Ukrainian question in Poland and the USSR.

128. Skrzypek, Stanislaw. **The Problem of Eastern Galicia**. London: Polish Association for the South-Eastern Provinces, 1948. 94p. Maps. Tables.

The author presents the Polish view on the fate of the Ukrainians in Galicia, claiming that many of their accomplishments were the result of Poland's generous policy. Included are documents favoring and supporting the Polish claim to Eastern Galicia.

129. Srokowski, S. "The Ukrainian Problem in Poland: A Polish View." *Slavonic Review* 9 (1931/32): 588-97.

A pro-Polish government account of the "pacification" of Ukrainians in Galicia during the summer and fall of 1930.

130. Torzecki, Ryszard. **Kwestia ukraińska w polityce III Rzeszy 1933-1945** (The Ukrainian Question in the Policy of the Third Reich, 1933-1945). Warsaw: Ksiaźka i Wiedza, 1972. 375p.

This study contains much material on German assistance to Ukrainian nationalist groups within Poland in their activities against the Polish state.

131. **Ukraińskie i ruskie ugrupowania polityczne w Polsce w dniu I kwietnia 1927 roku** (Ukrainian and Ruthenian Political Groups in Poland as of April 1, 1927). Warsaw, 1927. 170p.

This is the published version of a government study that offers a quantitative profile and then analyzes the strengths and weaknesses of each party.

Social and Economic Conditions

132. Horak, Stephan M. "Belorussian and Ukrainian Peasants in Poland, 1919-1939: A Case Study in Peasantry under Foreign Rule." In **The Peasantry of Eastern Europe**, edited by Ivan Volgyes. Vol. I: **Roots of Rural Transformation**. New York: Pergamon Press, 1979, pp. 133-56.

The essay elaborates on the agrarian question, the cooperative movement, Polish sanctions, and the political consequences of Poland's refusal to accommodate the Ukrainian and Belorussian peasantry.

133. Kwilecki, Andrzej. **Lemkowie: zagadnienie migracji i asymilacji** (The Lemkos: Problems of Migration and Assimilation). Warsaw: Państwowe Wydawnictwo Naukowe, 1974. 322p.

The subject of this study is the fate of the Lemkos before and after the population transfers of 1947 ("Operation Vistula"). Kwilecki writes about the deportation, the reception of the migrants by the local population and authorities, their economic conditions and legal status, and their eventual "stabilization" after 1956. The author has attempted to discover the current ethnic identification of the Lemkos, especially their degree of assimilation to the Polish nationality; as he admits, his sources do not suffice for generalization on the topic.

134. Senkiw, Ivan. **Die Hirtenkultur der Huzulen: Eine volkskundliche Studie.** Marburg/Lahn: J. G. Herder Institut, 1981. 186p. 64 illus. Map. Table.

Based on the author's pre-World War II field studies, this book describes the remnants of the shepherd culture of the Carpathian Mountains, which, affected by the economic development of the late nineteenth century, fell victim to the political developments after 1945. Senkiw concerns himself primarily with the ethnographic origin of the Hutsul people and attempts to draw parallels between the shepherds of the Carpathian Mountains and those of the Balkan countries.

135. Vytanovych, Illia. **Istoriia ukrains'koho kooperatyvnoho rukhu** (History of the Ukrainian Cooperative Movement). New York: T-vo Ukr. Koop., 1964. 624p.

This is the first synthetical work about the development of the Ukrainian cooperatives. It is rich in documentary material and includes personal reflections of the author, who was the organizer and leader of the movement in interwar Poland. Within a short period of time, the Ukrainians succeeded in building one of the most successful cooperative systems in Europe. Of special value are statistical data unavailable elsewhere.

Geography and Population

136. Kubijovyč, Volodymyr. **Ethnic Groups of the Southwestern Ukraine (Halyčyna-Galicia) on the 1st January 1939. Vol. I: Ethnographic Map of Southwestern Ukraine.** 89p. London: Memoirs of the Scientific Shevchenko Society, 1953.

This important pamphlet presents detailed information on the ethnic groups of Galicia on the eve of World War II. Available at the Library of Congress.

137. Kubiiovych, Wolodymyr, ed. **Naukovyi zbirnyk geografichnoi sektsii pry Ukrains'kii Hromadi v Krakovi** (Scientific Collection of the Geographical Section of the Ukrainian Students Society in Cracow). Krakow, 1930. 115p. (With summaries in German and French.)

This is a collection of anthropo-geographical studies of the villages of East Carpathia. The Ukrainian authors, former students at Jagellonian University, present useful statistical breakdowns of the population according to ethnicity (Jews, Ukrainians, Poles, Armenians, Hutsuls, etc.) and social class in the 1920s. Available at the Library of Congress.

Education and Cultural Affairs

138. Mudryi, Vasyl. **Ukrains'kyi universytet u Lvovi, 1921-1925** (Ukrainian University in Lviv, 1921-1925). Nürnberg: "Chas," 1948. 59p.

Mudryi presents a documentary story of the struggle for the organization of the Ukrainian university in Lviv, first under Austro-Hungary rule and after 1921 under Polish administration. Until 1925, there existed a private, clandestine university, which was subsequently transferred to Vienna, Prague, and, after 1945, Munich under the name Ukrainian Free University.

Religion

139.   Prokoptschuk, Gregor. **Der Metropolit: Leben und Wirken des grossen Förderers der Kirchenunion, Graf Andreas Scheptytzkyj.** München: Verlag Ukraine, 1955. 299p. Illus.

An authoritative biography of the metropolitan Andreas Sheptytsky, head of the Ukrainian Catholic (Uniate) Church in Poland. Sheptytsky, a spiritual as well as secular leader of Ukrainians, was instrumental in the Ukrainians' struggle for independence.

Militarism and World War II

140.   **Evhen Konovalets ta ioho doba** (Eugene Konovalets and His Epoch). Munich: E. Konovalets Foundation, 1974. 1019p.

This is a rich collection of articles, letters, and essays by some 35 authors who knew the intrepid Col. Eugene Konovalets, commander of the *Sich* Riflemen during 1917-1920 and organizer of the Ukrainian Military organization (UVO). Konovalets was assassinated in Rotterdam by a Comintern agent in May 1938. This book will be of great interest to scholars, Ukrainian and non-Ukrainian alike, in that it describes Konovalets' activities during two crucial decades.

141.   Heike, Wolf-Dietrich. **Sie wollten die Freiheit: Geschichte der ukrainischen Division, 1943-1945.** Dorheim/H.: Podzun Verlag, [1974]. 252p.

These are the memoirs of Major W. -D. Heike, Chief of Staff of the Ukrainian Division. He has written an objective and factual history of the Ukrainian military unit known as "Division Halychyna" from its formation to the end of the war, including its deployment at the eastern front near Brody in 1944.

142.   Horak, Stephan M.; Armstrong, John A.; Dytryshyn, Basil; Farmer, Kenneth C.; Kulchycky, George; Reshetar, John S.; and Subtelny, Orest. "Symposium. Ukrainians in World War II: Views and Points." *Nationalities Papers* X:1 (1982): 1-39.

These are papers from a symposium at the fourteenth AAASS Conference at Asilomar, California (September 1981), organized around the thorny question of Ukrainian "collaboration" with Nazi occupying forces in Poland and Soviet Ukraine during World War II. Among the issues addressed by the participants are whether the Ukrainians were bound to loyalty to Poland or the USSR, the significance of the Lviv Act of Independence of June 20, 1941, and the activities of the Ukrainian Insurgent Army (UPA).

143.   Kutschabsky, W. **Die Westukraine im Kampfe mit Polen und dem Bolschewismus in den Jahren 1918-1923.** Berlin: Junker und Dünnhaupt Verlag, 1934. 439p. Maps.

This is one of the best presentations of the history of the Western Ukrainian Republic, her diplomatic activities, the Polish-Ukrainian war, the occupation of Eastern Galicia by the Polish army, and the incorporation into the Polish Republic. Included are a useful bibliography and military maps of the various stages of the Ukrainian-Polish war. The book remains the standard work on this subject.

144. **Litopys Ukrains'koi Povstans'koi Armii** (Chronicle of the Ukrainian Insurgent Army). Vols. I, II. **Volyn i Polissia: Nimets'ka okupatsiia** (Volyn and Polissia: The German Occupation); vols. III, IV. **Chornyi Lis, 1947-1950** (Black Forest, 1947-1950); vol. V. **Volyn i Polissia**; vols. VI-VII. **Upa v svitli nimets'kykh dokumentiv, 1942-1945** (UPA in the Light of German Documents, 1942-1945); vols. VIII-IX.

Ukrains'ka Holovna Vyzvolna Rada: Dokumenty, ofitsiini publikatsii, materiialy, 1944-1945 (The Ukrainian Supreme Liberation Council: Documents, Official Publications, Papers, 1944-1945). Toronto: Litopys UPA, 1972-1982. 1980. 319p. Vol. IX, 1982. 535p. Edited by E. Shtendera and P. Potichnyi. (Summaries in English).

Contained in these volumes are historical documents and relevant materials pertaining to the history of the Ukrainian Insurgent Army, which operated mainly in Western Ukraine (Galicia and Volyn). Each volume or sequence of volumes is planned to cover a specific theme. Thus far, no Soviet documents concerning the UPA have appeared in print. Even in Poland, the full edition of the captured UPA documents has yet to appear in print.

145. Mirchuk, Petro. **Ukrains'ka Povstans'ka Armiia, 1942-1952** (The Ukrainian Insurgent Army, 1942-1952). Munich: "Cicero," 1953. 319p.

The book contains the story of the formation and warfare of the Ukrainian Insurgent Army (UPA) against Nazi Germany, Soviet Russia, and, after 1945, the Polish army in the eastern territories of Poland. Included are documents, military reports about UPA actions, and photographs.

146. Shandruk, Pavlo. **Arms of Valor.** Translated by Roman Olesnicki. Introduction by Roman Smal-Stocki. New York: Robert Speller and Sons, 1959. 320p.

These are the memoirs of Pavlo Shandruk, lieutenant-general of the general staff, Ukrainian National Army. They cover three important periods of his life: the era of Ukrainian independence after World War I; his experience under the Polish occupation; and his experiences during World War II.

147. Szcześniak, Antoni B., and Szota, Wiesław Z. **Droga do nikąd: Działalność Organizacji Ukraińskich Nacjonalistów i jej likwidacja w Polsce** (The Road to Nowhere: Activity of the Organization of Ukrainian Nationalists and Their Liquidation in Poland). Warsaw: Wojskowy Instytut Historyczny. Wyd. Ministerstwa Obrony Narodowej, 1973. 588p.

Based on a large body of documents on Ukrainian-Polish relations, the study emphasizes the period 1920-1948, when the activities of the Ukrainian Insurgent Army came to an end in eastern Poland. It also provides information on the Ukrainian political parties and their activities during the Nazi occupation. Basically, the authors take an anti-Ukrainian stance, underscoring the attitude of the current Communist regime in Poland. Nonetheless, the book provides a mass of information unavailable elsewhere.

148. Tys-Krokhmaliuk, Yuriy. **UPA Warfare in Ukraine: Strategical, Technical and Organizational Problems of Ukrainian Resistance in World War II.** Translated from Ukrainian by Walter Dushnyck. New York: Society of Veterans of the Ukrainian Insurgent Army of the U.S. and Canada, 1972. 448p.

This publication offers a wealth of information, documents, and statistical data, as well as the memoirs of the surviving members who reside in the West. Organized in the Western Ukraine in 1943, the UPA fought against Nazi occupation and later against the Soviet army until 1957.

149. **Ukrains'ka Halyts'ka Armiia: Materialy do istorii** (The Ukrainian Galician Army: Sources to History). 4 vols. Winnipeg: Dmytro Mykytiuk, 1958-1968. Photos. Maps.

The Ukrainian Galician Army (UHA) was organized during the short existence of the West Ukrainian Republic (1918-1919) and was first engaged in a war against Polish aggression and subsequently against Soviet Russia. This multivolume work contains documents pertaining to its existence and memoirs of its officers and soldiers. It is a useful collection of sources for the historian of Polish-Ukrainian relations and Ukrainians under Polish rule.

150. Veryha, Vasyl. **Dorohamy Druhoi svitovoi viiny: Legendy pro uchast ukraintsiv u varshavs'komy povstani 1944 r. ta pro ukrains'ku diviziiu "Halychyna"** (The Roads of the Second World War: Legends on the Participation of Ukrainians in the Warsaw Uprising of 1944 and on the Ukrainian Division "Galicia"). Toronto: Navyi Shliakh, 1980. 259p.

The purpose of this volume is to examine (and refute) the allegation that units of the Ukrainian division "Galicia" participated in putting down the 1944 uprising in Warsaw, and to analyze the motives behind the organization of the division and its subsequent military performance. While the intent is commendable, the author has overemphasized marginal or peripheral issues and fails to analyze the basic problem sufficiently.

151. Veryha, Vasyl. "The 'Galicia' Ukrainian Division in Polish and Soviet Literature." *The Ukrainian Quarterly* XXXVI:3 (1980): 253-70.

This article is a valuable review of the treatment of the division SS-"Galicia" by Soviet and Polish historians. The Polish historians are found to be more accurate and objective. Veryha goes to particular lengths to refute the allegation that units of the division "Galicia" participated in combatting the Warsaw uprising.

Jews

General Reference Works

152. Balaban, Majer. **Bibliografia historii Żydów w Polsce i w krajach ościennych w latach 1900-1930** (A Bibliography of the History of the Jews in Poland and in Neighboring Countries in the Years 1900-1930). Warsaw: Nakl. Tow. Szerzenia Wiedzy Judaistycznej w Polsce, 1939. Vol. 1.

Balaban's extensive bibliography deals with Jewish community life, culture, religion, and the economic status of Jews in Poland and other east European countries between 1900 and 1930. Only one volume was published in this series.

153. Bronsztein, Szyja. **Ludność żydowska w Polsce w okresie międzywojennym: studium statystyczne** (The Jewish Population in Poland in the Interwar Period: A Statistical Study). Wroclaw: Zaklad Narodowy im. Ossolinskich, 1963. 295p.

This is an extremely valuable study of various aspects of Jewish life in Poland from 1914 to 1939. Based upon demographic and other statistics, it provides an in-depth look at the impact of Poland's Jewish communtiy on Polish society, with a summary in English.

154.   Hoskins, Janina, comp. **Polish Books in English, 1945-1971**. Washington, DC: Library of Congress, 1974. 161p.

Prepared by the Reference Department of the Slavic and East European Division of the Library of Congress, the bibliography has a number of important entries on the history of Jews in Poland, particularly for the modern period.

155.   Mark, Bernard. **Męczeństwo i walka Żydow w latach okupacji: poradnik bibliograficzny** (The Martyrdom and Struggle of the Jews during the Years of Occupation: A Bibliographic Guide). Warsaw, 1963. 44p.

This short, fully annotated bibliography, drawn primarily from Polish sources, deals with Polish Jewry during World War II. It lists 114 entries.

156.   Trunk, I.I.S. **Poland**. (in Hebrew). 3 vols. New York: Farlag Unser Tsait, 1944-1946.

This exhaustive bibliography deals with the lives of Poland's best Yiddish writers and provides an excellent overview of Polish Jewish life over the past century.

157.   Wasiutynski, Bohdan. **Ludność żydowska w Polsce w wiekach XIX i XX: studium statystyczne** (The Jewish Population in Poland in the Nineteenth and Twentieth Centuries: A Statistical Study). Warsaw: Kasyin, Mianowskiego, 1930. 224p.

The author provides an excellent history of the Jewish communities in Poland for the nineteenth century and first third of the twentieth century, with individual chapters on Congress Poland, Galicia, and other regions. An excellent selection of statistical data and charts is broken down on a city-to-city basis.

History and General Studies

158.   Aisene, Benjamin. **Les Juifs polonais: 1918-1944: Ou, les morts accusent**. Paris: Pensee universelle, 1980. 185p.

This is a rather shallow overview of Jewish life in Poland between 1918 and 1944. Its statistical information can be found elsewhere.

159.   Biderman, Israel M. **Mayer Balaban: Historian of Polish Jewry. His Influence on the Younger Generation of Jewish Historians**. New York: Dr. I. M. Biderman Book Committee, 1976. 334p.

Biderman's study serves a twofold purpose: it is a history of Polish-Jewish historiography over the past century, and a history of the life and works of one of Poland's premier historical scholars, Mayer Balaban. It also discusses the major conclusions drawn from Balaban's research and his impact on other Jewish historians such as Ignacy Schipper.

160.   Cohen, Israel. **Vilna**. Philadelphia, PA: The Jewish Publication Society of America, 1943. 527p.

This is a history of the Polish-Lithuanian Jewish community in Vilna (Lithuanian, Vilnius) from 1350 through the early stages of World War II. It provides excellent insight into the rich historical and cultural heritage of this Jewish "Jerusalem of the North." Approximately the last third of the book deals with Vilna's Jewish community in the twentieth century. It has a section of supplementary notes and a bibliography.

161.   Czerniakow, Adam. **The Warsaw Diary of Adam Czerniakow: Prelude to Doom**. Edited by Raul Hilberg, Stanislaw Staron, and Josef Kermisz. Translated by Stanislaw Staron and the staff of Yad Vashem. New York: Stein and Day, 1979. 420p.

A translation of *Dziennik getta warszawskiego*, these are the memoirs of the Warsaw ghetto's controversial *Judenrat* leader from early September 1939 through July 1942. There are two lengthy historical introductions by the editors, as well as a documentary appendix and a select bibliography.

162.   Dubnow, Simon M. **History of the Jews in Russia and Poland from the Earliest Times until the Present Day**. Translated from the Russian by I. Friedlaender; with a bibliographical essay, *New Introduction and Outline of the History of Russian and Soviet Jewry, 1912-1974*, by Leon Shapiro. 2 vols. New York: KTAV Publishing House, 1975.

This is a new edition of the classic study of Polish Jewry. The latter part of the second volume contains an extensive section on the history of Poland's Jewish community since 1912.

163.   Echt, Samuel. **Die Geschichte der Juden in Danzig**. Leer, Ostfriesland: Rantenberg, 1972. 282p.

A rather detailed history of Danzig's Jewish population, with most of the work devoted to the twentieth century through 1945. Included are detailed statistical information on the Free City's Jewish community and its victimization under the Nazis and an excellent section of notes.

164.   Eizenbach, Artur. **Dokumenty i materialy do dziejów okupacji niemieckiej w Polsce**. Tom III: **Getto Lódzkie Częśc I** (Documents and Materials to the History of the German Occupation in Poland. Vol. III: Ghetto in Lódz, Part I). Lódz: Centralnej Żydowskiej Komisji Historycznej w polsce, 1946. 300p.

This Polish documentary collection deals with the history of the Lódz ghetto from the fall of 1939 through 1944. Most of the material, drawn from official Polish and German sources, documents the slow disintegration of the Lódz ghetto's 233,000 Jews during the Holocaust. The Lódz ghetto survived longer than Europe's other ghettos because of its value to the German war economy. However, after its elimination in 1944, its remaining Jews were shipped to Auschwitz.

165.   Fishman, Joshua A., ed. **Studies on Polish Jewry, 1919-1939: The Interplay of Social, Economic, and Political Factors of a Minority for Its Existence**. New York: YIVO Institute for Jewish Research, 1974. 851p.

The history of Poland's Jewish community during the interwar years is the subject of this selection of articles in English and Yiddish. Many of the entries emphasize the problems the Jews encountered because of anti-Semitic attitudes and their efforts to deal with this phenomenon. Each section includes bibliographical articles and a collection of documents on Polish Jewish history during this period.

166. Golczewski, Frank. **Polnisch-jüdische Beziehungen 1881-1922**. Quellen und Studien zur Geschichte des östlichen Europa, Bd. 14. Wiesbaden: Franz Steiner Verlag, 1981. 391p.

With an emphasis on the period after the outbreak of World War I, this recent study deals with the history of Polish-Jewish relations since 1881. It is particularly valuable for the period immediately after the end of World War I, when Poland's Jews were subjected to a severe wave of anti-Semitic violence. There is a rather detailed bibliography at the end of the book.

167. Heller, Celia S. **On the Edge of Destruction: Jews of Poland between the World Wars**. New York: Schocken Books, 1980. 369p.

This is a detailed account of the history of Poland's Jewish community during the interwar period. It deals with the Jewish religious, community, and political organizations and their relationship to the Polish state and discusses anti-Semitism in Poland during this period and its relationship to the degenerative status of Jews in interbellum Poland. An excellent section of bibliographical notes is appended.

168. Jewish Labour Confederation. **The Pogroms in Poland and Lithuania**. Special no., vol. I, no. 9. London: Jewish Socialist Labour Confederation Poale-Zion, 1919. 46p.

This pamphlet contains the result of an official Jewish investigation of pogroms that took place in Poland, Galicia, and Vilna in November and December 1918. It provides extensive details on the number of Jews injured and killed and discusses the Jewish response to these tragedies.

169. Lestschinsky, Jacob. **On the Eve of Destruction: About Jewish Life in Poland, 1935-1937** (in Hebrew). Buenos Aires: Tsentral Farband Poilishe Yidn in Argentine, 1951. 255p.

The author's second volume on Jewish life in Poland uses a series of vignettes to give the reader a more life-like view of conditions in Poland for Jews several years before the outbreak of World War II. As in his first study, for the period 1927-1933, Lestschinsky depicts a grim picture of growing anti-Semitism. He does point out, however, that there were some Poles who protested these anti-Semitic feelings.

170. Lichtenstein, Erwin. **Die Juden der Freien Stadt Danzig unter der Herrschaft des Nationalsozialismus**. Tübingen: Mohr, 1973. 242p.

Sponsored by the Leo Baeck Institute, this work deals with the history and status of Danzig's Jewish population between 1933 and 1939.

171. Mahler, Raphael. **The Jews of Poland between the Two World Wars: A Socio-economic History on a Statistical Basis** (in Hebrew). Tel-Aviv: Dvir, 1968. 195p.

The study provides a balanced overview of Jewish life in Poland between 1918 and 1939. The author uses a large body of statistical information to discuss the economic degeneration of Polish Jews during this period as well as the decline of their social and professional status.

172. Mendelsohn, Ezra. **Zionism in Poland: The Formative Years, 1915-1926**. New Haven, CT: Yale University Press, 1981. 373p.

A superb study of Polish Zionism from the early days of World War I through 1926. The author begins with an overview of the history of the Polish Jewish community and then traces the history of Polish Zionism through 1926. He pays particular attention to the relationships and conflicts of the various Zionist factions with one another and with other Jewish political and religious factions. The book contains several appendixes and a good bibliography.

173. **Mission of the United States to Poland**. Washington, DC: Government Printing Office, 1920. n.p.

This is a report by President Wilson to Congress on the Morgenthau investigation of the pogroms in Poland in 1918-1919.

174. National Polish Committee of America. **The Jews in Poland: Official Reports of the American and British Investigating Missions**. Chicago: National Polish Committee of America, 1920. 64p.

The pamphlet presents the reports of the American Morgenthau investigation as well as various British investigatory teams on the pogroms in Poland in 1918-1919.

175. Rabinowicz, Harry M. **The Legacy of Polish Jewry: A History of Polish Jews in the Inter-war Years, 1919-1939**. New York: T. Yoseloff, 1965. 256p.

A good study of the Jewish community of Poland between the two world wars, with a valuable bibliography at the end.

176. Segal, Simon. **The New Poland and the Jews**. New York: L. Furman, 1938. 223p.

This scholarly work deals with Polish anti-Semitism during the interwar period from the perspective of its impact on the Jewish community and Poland as a whole. Segal integrates his study with an investigation of the political environment in Poland, particularly after 1926, and its relationship to this phenomenon. He also discusses the economic situation in Poland *vis-à-vis* the Jews and Poland and looks at the status of other minority groups in Poland during this period.

177. Tenenbaum, Joseph. **In Search of a Lost People: The Old and New Poland**. With Sheila Tenenbaum. New York: Brechhurst Press, 1948. 312p.

In this blended memoir/history of the past thousand years of Polish Jewry, the author deals first with the Warsaw ghetto, the Jewish uprising there and its aftermath, and then follows with accounts of events in other major ghettos in Poland. In the next major section of his work, he discusses post-Nazi Poland and then goes into detail on the German use of Poland as its major execution center in eastern Europe. A brief bibliography, with some materials in Polish, is appended.

178. Żydowski Instytut Historyczny. *Biuletyn*, no. 1. Warsaw, 1951- .

This very important Polish Jewish historical journal is the principal scholarly organ of the Jewish Historical Institute of Poland. Published in Polish with English summaries, its articles cover all aspects and periods of Jewish culture and history, particularly the interwar period and the Holocaust.

Politics and Political Parties

179. Johnpoll, Bernard K. **The Politics of Futility: The General Jewish Workers Bund of Poland, 1917-1943**. Ithaca, NY: Cornell University Press, 1967. xix, 298p.

This valuable study deals with the history of the Polish Jewish Bund from its inception through the Holocaust. It provides a rare glimpse of Jewish domestic politics in Poland during this period, particularly the impact of Jewish religious and cultural differences on political issues. There is a substantial bibliography at the end of the volume.

180. Korzec, Pawel. "General Sikorski und seine Exilregierung zur Judenfrage in Polen im Lichte von Dokumenten des Jahres 1940." *Zeitschrift für Ostforschung: Länder und Völker im östlichen Mitteleuropa.* 30. Jhrg. 2 (1981): 229-61. (12 appendixes included).

Korzec deals with the contact between Jewish organizations and Polish government agencies in exile from October 1939 to the end of April 1940, a little-known but important episode in Polish-Jewish relations. The Jewish organizations expected that a friendly attitude of the Polish government-in-exile towards the Jewish question would improve the Polish-Jewish relations in occupied Poland. In spite of an uncommon convergence of bilateral interests, the talks did not bring any concrete results, as demonstrated by the documents included in the annex.

Social and Economic Conditions

181. Bornstein, I. **Rzemioslo żydowskie w Polsce** (Jewish Handicrafts in Poland). Warsaw: Nakl. Inst. Badań Spraw Narodowściowych, 1936. 189p.

This study deals with Jewish craftsmen in Poland and their impact on the Polish economy.

182. Gliksman, Georges. **L'aspect economique de la question juive en Pologne**. Paris, 1929. 196p.

Based upon an excellent body of statistical information, this is a good study of the economic status of Jews in Poland in the decade after World War I.

183. Schiper, Ignacy. **Dzieje handlu żydowskiego na ziemiach polskich** (A History of Jewish Commerce in the Polish Lands). Warsaw: Nakl. Centrali Związku Kupców, 1937. 791p.

This extensive study deals with the effect Poland's Jewish community had on that nation's economy.

Holocaust and Anti-Semitism

184. Aubac, Stephane. **Les dessous d'une campagne: la question juive en Pologne et les opinions socialistes sur les "pogroms."** Paris: Picart, 1919. 94p.

The Jewish pogroms in Poland at the end of World War I are the subject of this brief study.

185. Banas, Josef. **The Scapegoats: The Exodus of the Remnants of Polish Jewry**. Edited by Lionel Krchan. Translated by Tadeusz Szafar. London: Weidenfeld and Nicolson, 1979. 221p.

This is the history of official Polish anti-Semitism since 1948 and its impact on the exodus of Poland's remaining Jewish population over the next 20 years.

186. Bartoszewski, Wladyslaw. **The Blood Shed Unites Us: Pages from the History of Help to the Jews in Occupied Poland**. Warsaw: Interpress, 1970. 243p.

This is an official Polish study about Polish help offered to Jewish Holocaust victims by a member of the illegal Council for the Aid to Jews ("Zegota"), who also was associate head of the Jewish section of the Delegate's Office of the Polish Government-in-Exile in London. A valuable bibliography is appended.

187. Bartoszewski, Wladyslaw. **Righteous among Nations: How Poles Helped the Jews, 1939-1945.** Edited by Wladyslaw Bartoszewski and Zojia Lewin. London: Earlscourts Pubs., 1969. 834p.

First published in Polish as *Ten jest z ojczyzny* (He Is My Fellow Countryman), this volume is an effort to underline the positive role played by some Poles to save Jews from death during the Holocaust. it is a collection of personal accounts, historical pieces, and documents. An American edition was published as *The Samaritans: Heroes of the Holocaust* (1970).

188. Berenstein, Tatiana, and Rutkowski, Adam. **Assistance to the Jews in Poland, 1939-1945.** Translated by Edward Rothert. Warsaw: Polonia Pub. House, 1963. 82p.

This official Polish account of Polish-Jewish relations during World War II emphasizes various forms of Polish help extended to Jews during this period. It covers the early stages of the German occupation and then the efforts of the Polish resistance after 1941 to save Jews from extermination. Also appeared in German and Polish editions.

189. **Biuletyn Głównej Komisji Badania Zbrodni Niemieckich w Polsce.** Warsaw: Wydawnictwo Prawnicze, 1946-1976.

The official bulletin of the Polish High Commission for the Investigation of German Crimes in Poland contains articles in its individual editions on crimes against Poland's Jewish population. The High Commission has also published a number of other works on issues that relate to the Holocaust.

190. **The Black Book of Polish Jewry: An Account of the Martyrdom of Polish Jewry under the Nazi Occupation.** Edited by Jacob Apenszlak, et al. New York: The American Federation for Polish Jews in Cooperation with the Association of Jewish Refugees and Immigrants from Poland, 1943. 343p.

Beginning with the conquest of Poland in September 1943, this unique, classic study details the development of the full Nazi program for the destruction of Poland's large Jewish community. It discusses the Nazi "blitzpogroms" against Jews in various Polish communities and details the creation and administration of the Warsaw ghetto. Following are studies of Nazi policies in Lódz, Krakow, Lublin, Lwów, Eastern Galicia, Wilno, and eastern Poland, the evolution of Nazi extermination policies against Jews in individual communities, the creation of concentration camps at Neblinka, the Warsaw ghetto, and the development of Jewish resistance movements. The final section of the book is a lengthy history of the Jews in Poland and their contributions to Polish society and culture. A new edition appeared in 1982, entitled *The Black Book: The Nazi Crime against the Jewish People.*

191. Central Commission for Investigation of German Crimes in Poland. **German Crimes in Poland.** 2 vols. Warsaw: n.p., 1946, 1947.

These volumes contain a collection of articles on various concentration camps in Poland, and German policies towards prisoners in these camps. Volume I contains a chapter on the execution of Polish Jews, and most other chapters also touch on the Jewish question.

192.   Checinski, Michael. **Poland, Communism, Nationalism, Anti-Semitism.** Translated in part by Tadeusz Szafar. New York: Karz-Cohl Publishing, 1982. viii, 289p.

The argument of this study is that anti-Semitism in its present form in Poland, like the current Polish government, is an import from the Soviet Union. The study collates much material on a frequently misunderstood subject.

193.   Delbo, Charlotte. **None of Us Will Return**. Translated by John Githens. Boston: Beacon Press, 1968. 127p.

Charlotte Delbo, a member of the French Resistance, was captured and sent to a number of concentration camps. This small autobiography is an extremely poignant account of her experiences at Auschwitz.

194.   **Dokumenty i materialy z czasów okupacji niemieckiej w Polsce. I: Obozy** (Documents and Materials from the Time of German Occupation in Poland. I: Camps). Edited by N. Blumenthal. Lódz: Wydawnictwo Centralnej Żydowskiej Komisji Historycznej, 1946. 335p.

This collection of 129 documents deals with German occupation policies, the establishment of various ghettos and concentration camps, and Poland's Jews during the Holocaust.

195.   **From the History of KI-Auschwitz**. Translated from the Polish by Krystyna Michalik. Fertig, 1982. 225p. Originally published by Państwowe Muzeum w Oświecimiu, 1967.

This is a recent Polish history of the concentration camp in Poland. It provides extensive details on life in the camp and its administration, though it tends to deemphasize the fact that the camp existed primarily to execute Jews.

196.   Hammer, Richard (pseud.). **Bürger zweiter Klasse: Antisemitismus in der Volksrepublik Polen und der UdSSR**. Hamburg: Hoffmann und Campe, 1974. 278p.

A valuable inside account of the resurgence of thinly veiled anti-Semitism in postwar Poland. The Jews who remained in Poland were anti-Zionist and considered themselves full-fledged Poles. Initially welcomed by the regime, they later became pawns in the factional infighting among the leadership of the party.

197.   International Auschwitz Committee. **Auschwitz: Inhuman Medicine, Anthology**. Vol. 1, parts 1 and 2. Warsaw: International Auschwitz Committee, 1971.

The volume contains a collection of articles on Nazi medical experiments at Auschwitz. Many, of course, deal with experiments on Jewish victims.

198.   Klonichi-Klonymus, Arie (Klonitski, Aryeh). **The Diary of Adam's Father** (in Hebrew). Edited by Meir Hovav. Translated by Avner Tomaschoff. Kibbutz Lohamei Ha'getaot: Ghetto Fighters' House, [1969]. 87p. Illus. Maps. Portraits.

A translated Hebrew account of the final period of destruction of the Jews of Galicia, written in the summer of 1943.

199.   **Kronika getta Lódzkiego**. Edited by Danuta Dabrowska and Lucjan Dobroszychi. 2 vols. Lódz: Wydawń, 1965.

This is a two-volume history of the Lódz ghetto drawn principally from German documents, many of which are translated into Polish.

200.   **The Martyrdom of Jewish Physicians in Poland.** New York: Medical Alliance Association of Jewish Physicians from Poland, Exposition Press, 1963. 500p.
This is essentially a memorial volume to the 1500 Jewish doctors who died in the Holocaust. Its numerous biographies paint a vivid picture of life in Poland's ghettos during the Holocaust, particularly for the physician, who was faced with immense medical problems.

201.   Nyiszli, Miklos. **Auschwitz: A Doctor's Eyewitness Account.** Greenwich, CT: Fawcett Publishers, 1960. 160p.
This is a memoir account of a Hungarian Jew who was shipped to Auschwitz after the German occupation of Hungary in 1944. As a doctor, he was able to observe German experiments on Jewish prisoners during his incarceration.

202.   **Okupacija i medycyna; wybór artykulów z "Przegladu lekarskiego-Oświecim" z lat 1961-1970** (Occupation and Medicine: A Selection of Articles of "Auschwitz Medical Review," 1969-1970). Warsaw: Książka i wiedza, 1971. 425p.
A study of medical and sanitary conditions in Nazi concentration camps in Poland, particularly Auschwitz. The book also discusses Nazi atrocities, primarily against Jews.

203.   Pietrzykowski, Jan. **Hitlerowcy w Czestochowie w latach 1939-1945** (Hitlerites in Czestochowa, 1939-1945). Poznań: Instytut Zachodni, 1959. 262p.
This is another official study of the Holocaust in Poland. It discusses initial anti-Semitic acts during the early German occupation of Poland and the gradual development of Nazi policies that transformed Poland into Europe's principal extermination center.

204.   Pisar, Samuel. **Of Blood and Hope.** Boston: Little, Brown and Company, 1979. 311p.
A memoir account of the author's full life, describing a childhood in Soviet- and German-occupied Poland and subsequently his incarceration in the Auschwitz concentration camp.

205.   Poliakov, Leon, ed. **Auschwitz.** Paris: Julliard, 1964. 222p.
This is a collection of articles, memoirs, and eyewitness accounts of Jewish inmates at the Auschwitz concentration camp.

206.   Polska, Ministerstwo Obrony Narodowej. **Męczeństwo, walka, zaglada żydów w Polsce, 1939-1945** (Suffering, Struggle, Extermination of Jews in Poland, 1939-1945). Warsaw: Wydawnictwo Ministerstwa Obrony Narodowej, 1960. 541p.
This is a valuable pictographic account of the events of the Holocaust in Poland during World War II. Polish text.

207.   **Przegląd Lekarski** (Medical Review). Warsaw, 1961-1967.
From 1961 through 1967, this journal devoted a series of articles to medical problems during the Nazi occupation in Poland. Many have subsequently been published in *Auschwitz: Inhuman Medicine.*

208.   Rubinowicz, Dawid. **Pamiętnik Dawida Rubinowicza** (Diary of David Rubinowicz).

The diary was written by a young Jewish teenager from the village of Kranjo. It covers the period from the spring of 1940 through June 1, 1942, when he and his family were sent to Treblinka, where they died several months later.

209. Sierakowiak, Dawid. **Dziennik Dawida Sierakowiaka** (The Diary of David Sierakowiak). Edited by Leon Dobroszycki. Warsaw: State Publishing House Iskry, 1960. 226p.

These are the memoirs of a Holocaust victim from the Lódz ghetto, considered in some cases to be worse than the Warsaw ghetto. This account was serialized in the *Biuletyń Żydowskiego Instytuty Historycznego* before it was released in book form.

210. Telen, Christian. **La Purge: chasse an Juif en Pologne populaire**. Paris: Fayard, 1972. 222p.

Examining anti-Semitism in Poland after World War II, this study covers the Stalinist period until 1953, the thaw after Stalin's death, Gomulka's rise to power, and the use of anti-Semitism in 1968 in response to growing difficulties in Poland.

211. Tushnet, Leonard. **The Pavement of Hell**. New York: St. Martin's Press, 1972. 210p.

This is a study of three Judenrat leaders and their policies during the Holocaust — Adam Czerniakow of Warsaw; Mordecai Rumkowski of Lódz; and Jacob Gens of Wilno. Although the author tries to be sympathetic to their decisions because of their peculiar positions *vis-à-vis* German officials, their positions on a number of issues are what brought them their greatest condemnation.

212. Wildecki, H. **Niebezpieczeństwo żydowskie** (Jewish Danger). Poznań: Nakladern autora, 1934. 95p.

The author traces the history of anti-Semitism in Poland and its impact on the contemporary status of Poland's Jewish community. It has no bibliography.

213. Żydowski Instytut Historyczny. Warsaw. **Eksterminaeja Żydow na ziemiach polskich w okresie hitlerowskiej okupacji: Zbiór dokumentów** (Extermination of Jews in Polish Lands during the Hitler Occupation: A Collection of Documents). Edited by T. Berenstein, A. Eisenbach, and A. Rutkowski. Warsaw, 1957. 378p.

This collection of documents deals with Nazi extermination policies against Poland's Jews between 1939 and 1945. The 187 documents, drawn from German and Polish, describe the slow evolution of Hitler's program to make Poland and Europe "*judenfrei*." This publication also appeared in German as *Faschismus-Getto-Massenmord*.

Militarism, World War II, and the Warsaw Ghetto Uprising

214. Ainsztein, Reuben. **The Warsaw Ghetto Revolt**. New York: Holocaust Library, 1979. 238p. Distributed by Schocken Books.

A detailed history of the background, evolution, and outbreak of the Jewish rebellion in the Warsaw ghetto in the spring of 1943. The author also goes into some detail on the impact of the uprising on Poland's remaining Jewish population. Included are a valuable section of notes and a bibliography.

215.   Blumental, Nachman, and Kermish, Joseph, eds. **Ha-Meri veha-mered be-geto Varsha** (Resistance and Revolt in the Warsaw Ghetto). Jerusalem: Yad Vashem, 1965. 495p. Map.

A documentary history of the events that led to the Warsaw ghetto revolt of 1943 and its aftermath. The Hebrew text is followed by a summary in English.

216.   Borzykowski, Tuwie (Tuvia). **Between Tumbling Walls**. Translated from the Yiddish by mendel Kohansky. Lohame Ha-Getaot, Israel: Ghetto Fighters' House, 1972. 229p.

These memoirs of a member of the Jewish Fighting Force in the Warsaw ghetto deal with the uprising in January 1943, April-May 1943, and Jewish involvement in the Polish uprising of August 1944.

217.   Gray Martin. **For Those I Loved**. Translated by Anthony White. Boston: Little, Brown and Company, 1971. 351p.

Memoirs of a young Jew who lived in the Warsaw ghetto, survived, and was actively involved in smuggling food into the ghetto for his family and orphaned Jewish children. He also survived Treblinka and later became a member of the Resistance at Zablow, then an officer in the Red Army.

218.   Grossman, Mendel. **With a Camera in the Ghetto** (in Hebrew). Edited by Zvi Shner and Alexander Seved. Kibbutz Lohamei Ha'getaot: Ghetto Fighters' House, 1970. 96p. Illus.

This is a photographic account of the Polish city of Lódz under German occupation. It includes an essay about the photographer, Mendel Grossman, by Arieh Ben-Menahem.

219.   Gutman, Israel. **The Jews of Warsaw, 1939-1943: Ghetto, Underground, Revolt**. Translated from Hebrew by Ina Friedman. Bloomington: Indiana University Press, 1982. 487p.

A translation of *Yehude Varshah, 1939-1943*, this excellent monograph details the history of the Warsaw ghetto from its inception in 1940 through the bloody Jewish Warsaw rebellion in 1943. The study includes a detailed bibliography.

220.   Iranek-Osmecki, Kazimierz. **He Who Saves One Life**. New York: Crown Publishers, 1971. 336p.

This is a history of Polish-Jewish relations during World War II, with an emphasis on the role played by a minority of Poles to save Jews from the Holocaust. Overall, it merely adds to the debate over the role played by the Polish nation *vis-à-vis* its Jewish population during this period. The book is a translation of *Kto ratuje jedno życie*.

221.   Kaplan, Chaim Aron. **Scroll of Agony: The Warsaw Diary of Chaim A. Kaplan**. Translated and edited by Abraham I. Katsh. New York: Macmillan, 1965. 350p.

Originally written in Hebrew, an established writer, this diary details the experiences of a Polish Jew, who was confined to the Warsaw ghetto. It is a lucid account of Jewish life in Warsaw during the Holocaust.

222.   Katz, Alfred. **Poland's Ghettos at War**. New York: Twayne Publishers, 1970. 175p.

This is a scholarly account of Jewish politics in Poland before and during the Holocaust and its relationship to the organization of Jewish life in the ghettos during this latter period. It also discusses the development of Jewish underground movements in each of Poland's major Jewish ghettos and looks at the impact of these events on Polish-Jewish ties. Several documentary appendixes, notes, and a bibliography are included at the end.

223.   Korczak, Janusz (Goldszmit, Nenryk). **The Ghetto Years** (in Hebrew). Edited by Riva Keinow. Translated from Polish by Jerzy Bachrach and Barbara Krzywicka. Kibbutz Lohamei Ha'getaot, Israel: Ghetto Fighters' House, 1980. 264p.

The translated diary of the great Polish-Jewish writer and educator, Janusz Korczak, includes a selection of his letters, some of his manifestoes issued during World War II, and his autobiography. It also has an essay, "Final Chapter — Korczak in the Warsaw Ghetto," by Yitzhak Perlis.

224.   Lubetkin, Zivia. **In the Days of Destruction and Revolt**. Translated from the Hebrew by Ishai Tubbin. Kibbutz Lohamei Ha'getaot, Israel: Ghetto Fighters' House, 1981. 338p.

This is an autobiographical account of a female Jewish freedom fighter active first in the Soviet zone, occupied Poland (acquired in the secret Soviet-German treaties of 1939), and then, in early 1940, in German-occupied Poland. She became active in the Jewish Fighting Organization (JFO), its command structure, the Jewish National Committee, and the Jewish Coordination Committee, was actively involved in the Warsaw uprisings of January and April 1943, and barely escaped the ghetto the following month. She resurfaced as a JFO combatant in the August 1944 Polish uprising. The book has a very valuable biographical section on important Jewish figures who were involved in these activities.

225.   Mark, Ber., ed. **Documents and Materials about the Revolt in the Warsaw Ghetto** (in Hebrew). Warsaw: Yiddish Buch, 1953. 405p.

This collection was meant to be used with the author's history of the Warsaw ghetto insurrection of 1943. He uses a variety of sources in this volume, including files from the Ringelblum Archives, court records, memoirs, diaries, personal statements, and other material to document the entire background and history of the Jewish Warsaw uprising. As in his history of the rebellion, Mark tries to use his document to upgrade the role of Jewish Polish Communists in these important events.

226.   Mark, Bernard. **Powstanie w getcie warszawskim** (Warsaw Ghetto Insurrection). Warsaw: Żydowski Instytut Historyczny, 1953. 343p.

Published in conjunction with the author's companion volume of documents on the tenth anniversary of the Warsaw ghetto uprising, this volume presents a detailed account of the evolution of events that led to the rebellion, the rebellion itself, and its aftermath. The author, head of the Jewish Historical Institute, uses a wealth of material recently discovered in his study, though there is a tendency to try to paint a greater role of Jewish Polish Communists in these important events.

227.   Meed, Vladka. **On Both Sides of the Wall: Memoirs from the Warsaw Ghetto**. New York: Holocaust Library, 1979. 276p.

Spanning the period from July 22, 1942 until early 1945, this memoir details the German deportations of Jews to death camps from the Warsaw ghetto and efforts of the Jewish Coordinating Committee to help Jews who were hidden in Poland outside of the ghetto. Particular emphasis was placed on helping Jewish children and seeking the aid of Catholic religious orders willing to hide Jewish children during World War II. The Coordinating Committee also tried to aid Jewish workers in German work camps and to locate Jewish partisans in Poland, and contact was established with the Polish underground.

228. Moczarski, Kazimierz. **Conversations with an Executioner**. Edited by Mariana Fitzpatrick. Englewood Cliffs, NJ: Prentice-Hall, 1981. 282p.

Moczarski recalls his prison conversations over a 255-day period, beginning on March 1949, with Jürgen Stroop, the SS general responsible for the destruction of the Warsaw ghetto. He provides an autobiographical study of Stroop's career, particularly his anti-Semitic liquidation career in the SS in Czechoslovakia, Russia, and Greece. Included are a valuable section of notes and an index. Stroop was hanged for his crimes in Poland on March 6, 1952.

229. Poteranski, Waclaw. **The Warsaw Ghetto: On the 25th Anniversary of the Armed Uprising in 1943**. Warsaw: Interpress Publishers, 1968. 75p.

This is an official Polish history of the Jewish uprising in the Warsaw ghetto in 1943. It provides some background into the history of Germany's deadly policies towards the Jews and the creation of Poland's ghetto system and describes Jewish life in the Warsaw ghetto and Warsaw's role as a transfer point to Poland's various concentration camps. The final portion of the book details the planning and implementation of the Jewish Warsaw ghetto uprising in 1943 and its aftermath. This study appeared initially in Polish as *Warszawskie getto*.

230. Ringelblum, Emanuel. **Notes from the Warsaw Ghetto: The Journal of Emanuel Ringelblum**. Edited and translated by Jacob Sloan. New York: McGraw-Hill Book Company, 1958. 369p.

These are the memoirs of Emanuel Ringelblum, a Polish-Jewish teacher, historian, political activist, and archivist, who recorded his experiences in the Warsaw ghetto from January 1940 through the end of 1942. This edition is more complete than the one published in Poland by the Jewish Historical Commission in Warsaw.

231. Ringelblum, Emanuel. **Polish-Jewish Relations during the Second World War**. Edited by Joseph Kermish and Shmuel Krakowski. Translated (from Polish) by Dafna Aloon, Danuta Dabrowska, and Dana Keren. New York: Howard Fertig, 1976. 230p.

The archivist for the Warsaw ghetto's archives (*Oneg Shabbat*) and author of *Notes from the Warsaw Ghetto* presents a history of ties between Poles and Jews from 1939 to 1945. To a great extent, it is based upon Ringelblum's secret archives collected during the Holocaust, and his view is basically unsympathetic towards Polish claims of aid to Jewish Holocaust victims. The author was tortured and executed for his activities in the spring of 1944.

232. Seifert, Hermann Erich. **Der Jude an der Ostgrenze**. Mit einer Landkarte und 8 Abbildungen. Berlin: I. Eher Nachfolger, 1941. 87p.

The first of two books by this Nazi writer on the status of Jews in eastern Europe during World War II, this volume discusses German efforts to revive a traditional

Jewish lifestyle in its ghettos, and then looks at Jewish conditions in Russia, Poland, and in the General Gouvernement. Seifert's second volume appeared in 1942.

233. Wronski, Stanislaw. **Polacy-Żydzi, 1939-1945** (Poles-Jews, 1939-1945). Prepared by Stanislaw Wronski and Maria Zwolakowa. Warsaw: Ksia˙zka i Wiedza, 1971. 426p.

An official Polish study on Poland's Jewish population during World War II, with an emphasis on Polish-Jewish relations. An adequate bibliography is included.

234. Zuckerman, Isaac, ed. **The Fighting Ghettos**. Translated and edited by Meyer Barkai. Philadelphia, PA: Lippincott, 1962. 407p.

Published originally in Hebrew as *Sefer mihamot ha-geta'ot*, this account discusses Jewish rebellions in Poland during the Holocaust. It emphasizes outbursts in Warsaw, Bialystok, Grodno, and in several concentration camps, and deals with Jewish participation in the Partisan movement. A lengthy biographical section and maps of the major ghettos conclude the volume.

Education and Cultural Affairs

235. Eisenstein, Miriam. **Jewish Schools in Poland, 1919-39**. New York: King's Crown Press, 1950. 112p.

This is a brief study of the complexity of school systems for Polish Jews during the interwar period. For the most part, Jewish secular and religious education often followed the religious and political divisions of the Polish Jewish community as a whole. Therefore, the author centers the discussion around the educational thrust of two of the Jewish community's major organizations, the Bund and the Zionists.

236. Herzog, marvin I. **The Yiddish Language in Northern Poland: Its Geography and History**. Bloomington: Indiana University Press, 1965. xxix, 323p.

The historical, linguistic, and cultural impact of the Yiddish language on northern Polish Jewry is examined in this excellent study.

237. Schiper, Ignacy, ed. **Żydzi w Polsce odrodzonej; dzialalność spoleczna, oświatowa i kulturalna** (The Jews in the Reborn Poland: Social, Educational, and Cultural Activity). 2 vols. Warsaw: Nakl. Wydawn. "Żydzi w Polse odrodzonej," 1932-1933.

This is an excellent history of Polish Jewry. The second volume deals with the twentieth century, through the 1930s, and with encyclopedic coverage details, with charts, pictures, paintings, etc., all aspects of Jewish social, economic, religious, political, and cultural life. It has excellent bibliographic information at the end of each chapter.

Belorussians

238. **Bialoruskie ugrupowanie polityczne w Polsce w dniu 1 kwietnia 1927 roku** (Belorussian Political Groups in Poland as of April 1, 1927). Warsaw, 1927. 15p.

This is the published version of a government study that offers a quantitative profile and then analyzes the strengths and weaknesses of each party.

239. Engelhardt, Eugen von. **Weissruthenien, Volk und Land**. Berlin: Volk und Reich Verlag, 1943. 358p. Illus. Maps.

The book provides basic information about Belorussia: its history, economy, education, and social conditions. This is the only German work ever published on Belorussia. Its objective presentation is of special merit.

240. Guthier, Steven L. "The Belorussians: National Identification and Assimilation, 1897-1970." *Soviet Studies* 29:1 (1977): 37-61; 29:2 (1977): 270-83.

This is an account of the development of Belorussian national consciousness from the late nineteenth century to the present. The struggle for the national rebirth of the Belorussian nation is studied against assimilationist pressures imposed on them by both Poles and Russians.

241. Juzwenko, Adolf. **Polska a "Biala" Rosja (od listopada 1918 to kwietnia 1920 r)** Poland and "White" Russia [from November 1918 to April 1920]). Wroclaw, 1973. 296p.

Juzwenko discusses, in a very objective manner, the political relations between Poland and "White" Russia during the years 1918-1920. He points out that Poland could see no political gain if either Kolchak or Denikin came to power; if an independent Poland were created, the Whites would demand that it include no part of Lithuania or Belorussia, nor Chelm or Eastern Galicia. This book is an important contribution to the literature on the history of Polish-Russian relations.

242. Korus-Kabacinska, Janina. "Położenie ludności bialoruskiej w Rzeczypospolitej Polsce w latach, 1924-1926" (The Position of the Belorussian Population in the Polish Republic, 1924-1926). *Zeszyty Historyczne Uniwersytetu Warszawskiego* 2 (1961): 161-221. Tables.

This is an account of the "pacification" campaign of the Polish government to counter nationalism and Communist influence among the Belorussians in Volyn, Polissia, and Wilno provinces during 1924-1926.

243. Krysinski, A. "Liczba i rozmieszczenie Bialorusinow w Polsce" (The Number and the Settlements of Belorussians in Poland). *Sprawy Narodowościowe* 3-4 (1928): 351-79.

244. Laniewski, Stanislaw [Pseud. Stanislaw Elski]. **Die weissruthenische Frage: Historisch-politischer Abriss**. Translated from Polish. Berlin, 1942. 54p.

This pamphlet gives excellent insight into the fear and hatred that Poles felt towards the Belorussians during a tense period in their relationship.

245. Lubachko, Ivan S. **Belorussia under Soviet Rule, 1917-1957**. Lexington: University of Kentucky Press, 1972. 219p.

Of particular value in this scholarly, historical study of Belorussia in the twentieth century are chapter 9 on "West Belorussia under Poland," and chapters 10 and 11 on the Nazi occupation. The book is noteworthy for its use of census data and extensive discussion of the education system.

246. Matsko, A., and Tsamutin, B., eds. **Revoliutsonnii put' kompartii Zapadnoi Bielarusii, 1921-1939 gg.** (The Revolutionary Path of the Communist Party of West Belorussia, 1921-1939). Minsk, 1966. 204p.

Reflecting the Soviet point of view, these articles by Soviet Belorussian authors discuss the impact that the activities of the Communist party of Western Belorussia (KPZB) had on events in interwar Poland.

247. Poluian, Vladimir A., and Poluian, I. V. **Revoliutsonnoe i natsionalno-osvoboditelnoe dvizhenie v Zapadnoi Bielarusii, 1920-1939 gg.** (The Revolutionary and National-Liberation Movement of West Belorussia, 1920-1939). Minsk: Gosizdat BSSR, 1962. 220p.

This Marxist interpretation of the Belorussian nationalist movement focuses on class conflict and "social-economic radicalism" as its main driving forces.

248. Vakar, Nicholas P. **Belorussia: The Making of a Nation: A Case Study**. Cambridge, MA: Harvard University Press, 1956. 296p.

The first major history of the Belorussian people in English, this book emphasizes the modern period and the struggle for the rebirth of Belorussian national consciousness against the assimilationist pressures of their Polish and Russian rulers. Chapter 9, "West Belorussia," pp. 119-36, focuses on the Polish part of Belorussia during the interwar period.

249. Wasilewski, Leon. **Litwa i Białoruś: zarys historyczno-polityczny stosunków narodowościowych** (Lithuania and Belorussia: A Historical-Political Outline of Nationality Relations). Warsaw: J. Mortkowicz, 1925. 251p.

This study offers a good socioeconomic and political profile of the Belorussians by a sympathetic Pole, considered a "liberal" on the minorities question and a leading advisor to Jozef Pilsudski.

250. Wyslouch, S. **Rola komunistycznej partii Zachodniej Bialorusi w ruchu narodowym Bialorusinów w Polsce** (The Role of the Communist Party of West Belorussia in the Belorussian National Movement in Poland). Wilno, 1933. 207p.

This is a contemporary discussion of the activities of the Communist party of Western Belorussia in Poland and the bases of its appeal to the Belorussian minority in Poland.

Germans

General Reference Works

251. Czech, Joseph. **Die Bevölkerung Polens: Zahl und völkische Zusammensetzung**. Veröffentlichungen der schlesischen Gesellschaft für Erdkunde #16. Breslau: M. and H. Marcus, 1932. 232p. Maps. Tables.

More than half of this handbook (pp. 92-191) deals with the German minority in Poland, applying a so-called "anthropo-geographical" methodology while surveying that group's historical development, its numerical decline after 1919, its current distribution in interwar Poland, and the chief characteristics of German communities in the different regions of the state.

252. **Die Nationalitäten in den Staaten Europas: Sammlung von Lageberichten**. Edited by E. Ammende and the "Europäisches Nationalitäten-Kongress." Vienna: Wilhelm Braumüller, 1931. 568p.

A handbook, similar to Urbanski, Czech, etc., surveying (on pp. 75-121) the political, economic, legal, and educational situation of the Germans in interwar Poland. Though focusing on Poznania, Pomerania, and eastern Upper Silesia, objects of German irredentism, and critical of Polish government policy, it contains much useful statistical information.

253.   Swart, Friedrich, and Breyer, Richard. "Die deutsche Volksgruppe im polnischen Staat." In **Das östliche Deutschland: Ein Handbuch**, edited by Göttinger Arbeitskreis. Würzburg: Holzner Verlag, 1955. pp. 477-526.

This is a concise survey of the German minority in interwar Poland, its population distribution, social and econimic characteristics, religious life, legal position, etc. It also summarizes Polish nationality policies and the impact of German-Polish international relations on the Germans of Poland.

History

254.   Bahr, Richard. **Volk jenseits der Grenzen: Geschichte und Problematik der deutschen Minderheiten**. Hamburg: Hanseatische Verlagsanstalt, 1933. 476p.

Pages 125-205 of this survey of German minorities in Europe, especially those created in 1919, deal with the Germans in interwar Poland. The focus is on the problems and political challenges presented by their new situation and their continuing inability to form a united front to deal with it, which Bahr attributes to the considerable variety of German communities and living conditions in Poland.

255.   Bierschenk, Theodor. **Die deutsche Volksgruppe in Polen, 1934-1939.** Beihefte zum Jahrbuch der Albertus-Universität Königsberg, X. Würzburg: Holzner Verlag, 1954. 405p.

The most complete account of the German minority in Poland, including the entire range of its political, cultural, economic, educational, and other organizations and activities, as well as its numerous conflicts with Polish government policies. Written by a former activist in that minority, the work is quite critical of Polish policies but not excessively polemical. The author makes the point that most Polish Germans, despite their poor treatment, were loyal citizens of Poland until 1939.

256.   Enders, Jacob. **Die deutschen Siedlungen in Galizien.** Eckarschriften no. 75. Wien: Verlag Österreichische Landsmannschaft, 1980. 80p. Map.

The author describes the 150-year fate of the Germans in Galicia. The kingdom of Galicia came under Habsburg domination in the Polish partitions of 1772. More than 100,000 Germans, most of whom were farmers and tradesmen, were widely dispersed among some 3.5 million Poles and Ukrainians and over one million Jews. Always economically and ethnically oppressed, the Germans faced further difficulties after 1918, and Nazi politics during 1939-1945 brought on their end.

257.   Heike, Otto. **Das Deutschtum in Polen, 1918-1939.** Bonn: Selbstverlag des Verfassers, 1955. 296p. Map. Bibliography.

The leading expert on the subject offers a balanced account of the Germans in interwar Poland. Of special importance are the detailed statistics and discussions regarding the German political parties and organizations, participation in elections, the activities of the German representatives in the legislative bodies, the economic structure, education, and cultural activities. Included are the texts of ten documents pertaining to the German legal and political status in Poland and a comprehensive bibliography of German publications. The number of Germans in Poland for 1938 is estimated at 1,030,000.

258. Heike, Otto. **150 Jahre Schwabensiedlungen in Polen 1795-1945**. Leverkusen: published by the author, 1979. 364p.

The German migration to Poland is analyzed, using the example of agricultural settlements. Based on rich sources, the book describes in great detail the origins, development, and fate of many Swabian settlements, including ethnologically interesting pictures of daily life and customs. A large volume of information has been compiled and presented in an orderly fashion. An appendix, illustrations, and charts contribute to this exceptionally valuable collection of materials, which includes elements of process analysis.

259. Komjathy, Anthony, and Stockwell, Rebecca. **German Minorities and the Third Reich**. New York: Holmes & Meier Publishers, 1980. 217p.

This work includes a chapter on the Germans of Poland as part of an examination of how Germans throughout eastern Europe behaved toward their countries of residence in the face of the rise of Nazism in Germany and the emergence of Hitler's ambitions in eastern Europe. The authors contend that the Germans of Poland were as loyal as could reasonably be expected and do not deserve the "fifth-column" label commonly applied by Polish historians.

260. Kramer, Julius, Mohr, Rudolf, and Hobler, Ernst. **Aufbruch und Neubeginn: Heimatbuch der Galiziendeutschen**. Stuttgart-Bad Cannstatt: Relief Committee of Galician Germans, 1977. 672p.

Over 60 writers contributed to this sequel to the first volume published by the same group of exiled Germans of Galicia. The well-edited book offers many photographs, illustrations, and statistical data, and includes a history of the German Evangelical Church and the German Mennonites in Galicia. This is a valuable contribution to the literature on the history of Ukrainian-Polish and Ukrainian-German relations.

261. Lesniewski, Andrzej, ed. **Irredentism and Provocation: A Contribution to the History of the German Minority in Poland**. Poznan: Wydawn. Zachodnie, 1960. 72p.

This is a translation of a Polish collection on the subversive activities of Germans in Poland during 1939-1945 which, while somewhat polemical, is valuable for some of its historical perspectives and its bibliographical references.

262. Potocki, Stanislaw. **Położenie mniejszości niemieckiej w Polsce 1918-1938** (The Position of the German Minority in Poland 1918-1938). Wydawnictwa Instytuty Baltyckiego w Gdansku, 4. Gdansk: Wydawn. Morskie, 1969. 502p.

Based largely on primary sources, this is the most extensive treatment of this subject from the Polish perspective. The author stresses the voluntary nature of the post-1919 exodus and the "privileged" economic position and elaborate, officially tolerated organizational network of those Germans who remained in Poland. While not denying that Polish policy toward the Germans had some repressive aspects, Potocki justifies it nonetheless with reference to their willingness to serve as instruments of hostile Third Reich policies.

263. Rhode, Gotthold. "Das Deutschtum in Posen und Pommerellen in der Zeit der Weimarer Republik." In **Die deutschen Ostgebiete zur Zeit der Weimarer Republik.** Studien zum Deutschtum im Osten, Heft 3. Cologne: Böhlau Verlag, 1966. pp. 88-132.

This recent assessment by a leading scholar-spokesman for German refugees from interwar Poland stresses the sense of "renewal" and the trend toward self-sufficiency among the Germans in Poland once the shock of 1919 wore off. The author is mildly critical of Polish policies, but not self-righteous, e.g., he concedes that Polish treatment of Germans was not comparable to the Germans' treatment of the Poles during World War II or what happened to eastern Germans during 1945-1947.

264. Riekhoff, Harald von. **German-Polish Relations, 1918-1933.** Baltimore: Johns Hopkins University Press, 1971. 421p.

Riekhoff focuses on intergovernmental relations, but devotes considerable attention to the role of the German minority in Poland as a complicating factor in these relations. He takes a factual, objective approach, simultaneously criticizing the revanchism of even democratic Germany and its reluctance to accept the new Polish state as well as Polish chauvinism and the often unnecessarily repressive treatment of the German minority.

265. Staniewicz, Restytut. **Mniejszość niemiecka w województwie śląskim w latach 1922-1933** (The German Minority in the Silesian Province, 1922-1933). Biuletyn no. 26. Katowice: Śląski Instytut Naukowy, 1965. 111p. (Summaries in Russian and English).

A slim but comprehensive examination of the German minority in Polish Upper Silesia prior to the Nazi era. Fairly balanced and based on sound archival research.

Politics and Political Parties

266. Breyer, Richard. **Das Deutsche Reich und Polen, 1932-1937: Aussenpolitik und Volksgruppenrecht.** Marburger Ostforschungen, Band 3. Würzburg: Holzner Verlag, 1955. 372p.

Breyer presents a thorough analysis of German-Polish relations during the era of preventive-war crises and the 1934 non-aggression pact. Focus is on relations between the two governments, but considerable attention is paid to the role of the German minority in Poland in these relations. The author denies that harsh Polish nationality policies were notably relaxed by the 1934 rapprochement on the government level.

267. Dworecki, Zbigniew. **Problem niemiecki w świadomości narodowo-politycznej społeczeństwa polskiego województw zachodnich Rzeczypospolitej, 1922-1939** (The German Problem in the National-Political Consciousness of Polish Society in the Western Regions of the Republic, 1922-1939). Seria Historia, 92. Poznan: uniw. Mickiewicza, 1981. 250p. (Summary in German).

This survey focuses on the response of the majority Polish population of western Poland to the German minority. It analyzes class and other traditional factors which went into the formation of Polish stereotypes of the Germans, and while critical of ultranationalist Poles, e.g., in the "Westbund," the author concludes that Polish attitudes were generally an understandable reaction to provocative German attitudes and policies.

268. Golczewski, Frank. **Das Deutschlandbild der Polen 1918-1939: Eine Unter-suchung der Historiographie und der Publizistik.** Geschichtliche Studien zur Politik und Gesellschaft, vol. 7. Düsseldorf: Droste Verlag, 1974. 316p.

The first part of this monumental study analyzes the Polish image of the Germans, as Prussians, West and South Germans, and Austrians, during the interwar period; then it anlyzes the typical German characteristics as seen by the Poles. The seond part is a survey of Polish historiography on German history and in particular the history of Polish-German relations. The book is based on an impressive bibliography, and will be a most valuable source for scholars interested in Polish views on Germany during the period 1918-1939.

269. Grünberg, Karol. **Niemcy i ich organizacje polityczne w Polsce międzywojennej** (The Germans and Their Political Organizations in Interwar Poland). Warsaw: Wiedza Powszechna, 1970. 157p.

Based on secondary sources, this summary is of the standard Polish position, which as remained fairly consistent through the interwar and postwar political changes—most Germans who left Poland after 1919 were bourgeois or bureaucrats who did so voluntarily; those who remained were treated fairly, indeed too generously, given their lack of loyalty and easy manipulation by the Reich in the 1930s.

270. Heiss, F., ed. **Deutschland und der Korridor.** Berlin: Volk und Reich, 1939. 311p. Illus. Maps.

This work is aimed at a general audience and is tendentious and without a scholarly apparatus; but it contains articles by leading German authorities of the period and is useful as a compendium of the official German position during the 1930s. Focus is on opposition to the "corridor" for geopolitical rather than ethnic reasons, but consideration is also given to the German minority in western Poland.

271. Kellermann, Volkmar. **Schwarzer Adler, Weisser Adler: Die Polenpolitik der Weimarer Republik.** Cologne: Markus Verlag, 1970. 196p.

This work represents the equivalent of the Riekhoff book (see entry 264), but it was written by a nonprofessional historian, using secondary sources, who aims to influence contemporary policy toward Poland. Still, it is a clear, objective, and comprehensive survey which contrasts with most other German accounts by virtue of its recognition of the manipulation and subsidization of the German minority situation in Poland by official Germany because of its value to revanchist foreign-policy aims.

272. Kulski, W. W. **Germany and Poland: From War to Peaceful Relations.** Syracuse, NY: Syracuse University Press, 1976. xxii, 336p.

This is the first in-depth analysis in English to fully present the Polish and German points of view regarding their mutual relations, the breakdown of which in 1939 led to the Second World War. It traces the stages of German and Polish relations, affected not only by wartime and postwar events but also by a thousand years of mutual history. The author, a former member of the Polish diplomatic corps between 1928 and 1945, delineates the history of the Oder-Neisse boundary from its diplomatic origins up through Willy Brandt's *Ostpolitik* and the Warsaw Treaty of 1972.

273. Meissner, Lucjan. **Niemieckie organizacje antyfaszystowskie w Polsce, 1933-39** (German Anti-Fascist Organizations in Pland, 1933-39). Warsaw: Książka i Wiedza, 1973. 301p.

Meissner analyzes those factions within the German minority which resisted Nazi ideology and control in the 1930s, e.g., the German Socialist Workers party centered in Lódz (DSAP) and the Christian Peoples party (CVP) in Upper Silesia. He criticizes the Polish government for its failure to support more effectively these loyal factions against pro-Nazi, irredentist elements within the German minority, which were heavily supported by the German government.

274. Mroczko, Marian. **Związek Obrony Kresów Zachodnich, 1921-1934: Powstanie i działalność** The Association for the Defense of the Western Districts, 1921-1934: Growth and Activity). Gdansk: Wydawn. Morskie, 1977. 258p.

This is a thorough analysis of the significant anti-German pressure group in interwar Poland, and its leading figures and activities. From its emergence in the Upper Silesian plebiscite campaign, it functioned as an unofficial organization but with general Polish government encouragement. Mroczko approves of its "patriotism" but is critical of its largely National-Democratic, "bourgeois" ideology.

275. Ratyńska, Barbara. **Stosunki polsko-niemieckie w okresie wojny gospodarczej, 1919-30** (German-Polish Relations during the Era of Economic Warfare, 1919-30). Warsaw: Książka i Wiedza, 1968. 358p.

In the context of a general treatment of German-Polish relations after 1919, this monograph focuses on German government efforts to achieve political goals, for example, a more favorable situation for Germans in Poland, by means of economic pressure at a time of Polish vulnerability, especially during the immediate post-Locarno era (1925-1927).

276. Rauschning, Hermann. **Die Entdeutschung Westpreussens und Posens: Zehn Jahre Polnischer Politik.** Berlin: Reimar Hobbing, 1930. 405p.

This is a comprehensive account of the rapid decline of the German population of Poznania and Pomerania, 1919-1926, and the factors behind this development. Rauschning argues that most of the exodus was not voluntary but due to Polish pressures, which are treated here in great variety and detail, affecting mainly long-established residents—mostly urban—rather than recent arrivals, colonists, or civil servants.

277. Rosenthal, Harry Kenneth. **German and Pole: National Conflict and Modern Myth.** Gainesville: University of Florida Press, 1976. x, 175p.

This is a well-documented account of the opinions Germans have held of the Poles throughout history, and especially since the end of the eighteenth century. The author finds the Germans in the west indifferent to Poles, those in the east contemptuous and fearful. Since World War II, these negative attitudes in West Germany have been replaced by a new indifference.

278. Wapiński, Roman. "Endecja wobec problemów polskich ziem Zachodnich w latach 1919-39" (National Democracy and the Problems of the Western Polish Lands in the Years 1919-39). *Zapiski Historyczne* 31:4 (1966): 61-81.

The article analyzes National Democratic policy toward the western regions of Poland, where Germans constituted the chief national minority problem. Wapinski suggests that this party's traditionally hard line regarding national minorities was an integral part of its struggle for dominance in national politics but that this, together with its alleged ideological sympathies with Nazism in the 1930s, led to such inconsistencies as the annexation of the Olsa district in 1938.

279. Wynot, Edward D., Jr. "The Polish Germans, 1919-1939: National Minority in a Multinational State." *Polish Review* 17:1 (1972): 23-64.

The author is quite critical of the leading spokesmen for the German minority in Poland, who are characterized as revanchists and fifth-columnists, but some distinction was made between them and the mass of Germans in Poland. Wynot shares the view of official Polish historiography and defends the correctness of Polish government policies toward the German minority, except perhaps when these were allegedly modified in the wake of the 1934 Non-Aggression Pact.

Economy and Social Conditions

280. Heike, Otto. **Aufbau und Entwicklung der Lodzer Textilindustrie: Eine Arbeit deutscher Einwanderer in Polen für Europa.** Mönchen-Gladbach: Verlag Heinrich Lapp, 1971. 326p.

The author began preliminary work on this book in Lódz forty years ago. It describes the development of the Lódz textile industry region, placing particular emphasis on the importance of the Germans in creating and expanding the most important center of the Polish textile and light industry. Although the account makes one guess that the author is a self-taught historian, it succeeds in carrying out its aim. The work is particularly valuable as a source of material for future works.

281. Heike, Otto. **Die deutsche Arbeiterbewegung in Polen, 1835-1945.** Ostdeutsche Forschungsstelle im Lande Nordrhein-Westfalen, 1969. 195p. Appendix.

This is a history of the German Socialist Workers party (DSAP) in Poland, including auxiliary, youth, cultural, and press aspects. The focus is on Lódz, the movement's headquarters, and Polish Upper Silesia. The author stresses the willingness of these Germans to support Poland and their difficulties in resisting pressure from Polish chauvinists and pro-Nazi Germans.

282. Jeżowa, Kazimiera. **Die Bevölkerung- und Wirtschaftsverhältnisse im westlichen Polen.** Danzig: Towarzystwo Przyjaciól Nauk i Sztuki, 1933. 191p.

This is a frankly polemical response to Rauschning's *Die Entdeutschung Westpreussens und Posens* (entry 276), denying that Germans were present in western Poland in significant numbers before 1772, that Prussian rule was of any benefit to Poles, that most Germans living there in 1919 could exist without state support, etc. It is designed to make the sharp decline of the German population of western Poland appear as a natural economic—rather than coerced political—process.

283. Karzel, Karl. **Die deutsche Landwirtschaft in Posen in der Zeit zwischen den beiden Weltkriegen.** Wissenschaftliche Beiträge zur Geschichte und Landeskunde Ostmitteleuropas, 51. Marburg: Herder Institute, 1961. 205p.

An agronomist from Poznania recounts the travails and achievements of German agriculture in interwar Poland. Despite government chicanery and land "reform," Karzel claims that the Germans of Poland managed to maintain a leading role in that state in the application of new techniques (e.g., the introduction of hybrids and new animal breeds) and that they generally stayed abreast of production levels in Germany itself.

284. Kowalak, Tadeusz. **Spóldzielczość niemiecka na Pomorzu, 1920-1938** (The German Cooperative Movement in Pomerania, 1920-1938). Warsaw: Książka i Wiedza, 1965. 389p. (Summary in English).

Despite the decline of the German population of this region from 42% to 10% between 1918 and 1922, the remaining German minority retained a disaproportionate economic position, aided by an extensive network of cooperatives. The author stresses the role of these co-ops in distributing Reich subsidies and otherwise facilitating the organization of the German minority for anti-Polish political purposes.

285. Kucner, Alfred. "Mniejszość niemiecka w Polsce i dążenie rządu niemiekiego do utrzymania jej stanu posiadnia w b. zaborze pruskim" (The German Minority in Poland and the Efforts of the German Government to Preserve Its Status in the Former Prussian Partition). *Przegląd Zachodni* 14 (1958): 272-305.

Focusing on the first several years of Polish rule, the article recounts the efforts of Germans in Poland, supported by the German government, to maintain their socioeconomic position in the face of changed political conditions. Based mostly on secondary sources, it is without a clear thesis, although the presentation is reasonably objective and factual.

286. **1979 Zeitweiser der Galiziendeutschen.** 20. Jahrgang. Stuttgart, 1978. 143p.

This is a collection of articles written by former Galician Germans who are now living in West Germany. Much attention is given to the 160-year-old settlement of Germans in Galicia and their relationship with other ethnic minorities. Of particular interest are four major articles dealing with Ukrainians.

287. Swart, Friedrich. **Diesseits und Jenseits der Grenze: Das deutsche Genossenschaftswesen im Posener Land und das deutsch-polnische Verhältnis bis zum Ende des 2. Weltkrieges.** Leer: Rautenberg & Möchel, 1954. 231p. Documents.

This is an account of the German cooperative movement in Poznania by someone long active in that movement. It treats nineteenth-century origins but focuses on the interwar years, when German co-ops in Poland were targets of government chicanery and polonization efforts. The author denies that these organizations were primarily political or actively irredentist.

Education and Cultural Affairs

288. Iwanicki, Mieczyslaw. **Polityka oświatowa w szkolnictwie niemieckim w Polsce w latach 1918-1939** (Educational Policy in German Schools in Poland in the Years 1918-1939). Warsaw: Państwowe Wydawn. Naukowe, 1978. 435p. Appendixes.

Iwanicki provides a detailed analysis of German minority schools in interwar Poland, their curricula, prevalent pedagogical theories, teacher-recruitment practices, and ideological coloration. This subject is dealt with in the general context of Polish minority policies. The author concludes that the Polish government sought only to keep the number of German schools at a "sensible" level and prevent subversive teaching but did not try to suppress them altogether.

289. Kowalak, Tadeusz. **Prasa niemiecka w Polsce, 1918-39** (The German Press in Poland, 1918-39). Warsaw: Książka i Wiedza, 1971. 416p.

In this detailed examination of the German press in Poland, the focus is on its predominant anti-Polish attitudes and control by Reich agencies, although the great number and variety of viewpoints are illustrated, including various anti-Nazi voices in the 1930s which the Polish government failed adequately to encourage and support.

290. Nasarski, Peter. **Deutsche Jugendbewegung und Jugendarbeit in Polen, 1919-1939**. Ostdeutsche Beiträge aus dem Göttinger Arbeitskreis, Band VI. Würzburg: Holzner Verlag, 1957. 134p. Appendix.

Written by a former activist in the German youth movement in interwar Poland, this account has more the character of a wistful memoir than a scholarly analysis but is nonetheless useful as a first-hand report on its subject. The movement described here was not monolithic; it contained a large variety of organizations (Wandervögel, scouts, religious, young-socialist, etc.), all subject to Polish official interference but also, the author concedes, to the attraction and eventual control of Nazi Germany.

291. Reiter, Norbert. **Die polnisch-deutschen Sprachbeziehungen in Oberschlesien**. Slawistische Veröffentlichungen der Freien Universität Berlin, 23. Wiesbaden: Harrassowitz, 1960. 102p. "Lexikon."

This volume contains a linguistic analysis of the languages spoken in Upper Silesia (German, Polish, and the local dialect), with implicit rather than explicit historical-political meaning. It demonstrates that both major languages as spoken locally borrowed heavily from the other and that the Upper Silesian form of Polish was to some extent a conglomerate language situated between them.

292. Wynot, Edward D., Jr. "The Case of German Schools in Polish Upper Silesia, 1922-1939." *The Polish Review* 19:2 (1974): 47-69.

The article points out that Poles and Germans alike saw the schools of Polish Upper Silesia as instruments of their respective national-political aspirations, to which pedagogical considerations often took a back seat. Polish authorities were compelled to resist German intransigence and were naturally resentful of German "abuse" of the international supervision of school arrangements provided by the 1922 Geneva Convention. Based on Polish archival sources.

Law and Legal Protection

293. Kierski, Kazimierz. **Prawa mniejszości niemiekiej w Polsce** (Rights of the German Minority in Poland). Poznan: Związek Obrony Kresów Zachodnich, 1923. 96p.

This is an elaborated view on the legal and political rights of the German minority in Poland. Texts and excerpts from various documents are provided.

294. Ragorowicz, Ludwik. **Wykonanie polsko-niemieckiej górnośląskiej konwencji, Zawartej w Genewie 15 maja 1922 r. w zakresie szkilnictwa** (The Implementation of the Polish-German Convention on Upper Silesia, Concluded at Geneva May 15, 1922, in the School Sphere). Katowice: Slask, 1961. 146p. (Summaries in Russian, German, and English).

This work focuses on Polish minority school policy in Polish Upper Silesia during the time that the region was subject to the Geneva Convention (1922-1937). While the German population allegedly plotted the region's return to Germany, Polish authorities planned its ultimate integration into the rest of Poland by such measures as preventing Polish-speaking children from attending German schools and firing teachers associated with German-nationalist organizations.

295. Rose, William. **The Drama of Upper Silesia: A Regional Study**. Brattleboro, VT: Stephen Day, 1935. 349p.

The second half of this work is concerned with the interwar period, focusing on the 1921 plebiscite campaign, the 1922 partition agreement, and the decade that followed. This first-hand, essentially journalistic account, clearly sympathetic to the Polish point of view, provides much useful information not available elsewhere in English.

296. Rukser, Ulbricht. **Die Rechtsstellung der Deutschen in Polen**. Berlin: Walter de Gruyter, 1921. 256p.

The author concentrates mainly on the German legal position in such areas as legal protection, education, commerce and trade, agrarian reform, and the judicial system. Abuses and discrimination against the German minority are documented.

297. Stone, Julius. **Regional Guarantees of Minority Rights: A Study of Minorities Procedure in Upper Silesia**. New York: Macmillan, 1933. 313p. Appendixes.

This study in international law closely examines the functioning of the 1922 Geneva Convention of Upper Silesia and the associated League of Nations guarantees of minority rights, such as the varieties of recourse available and the legal machinery to implement them. The author takes a generally positive attitude toward the whole enterprise and concludes that, given the level of national feeling in this case, there was really no alternative.

Church and Religious Affairs

298. Kneifel, Eduard. **Die Evangelisch-Augsburgischen Gemeinden in Polen 1555-1939: Eine Parochialgeschichte in Einzeldarstellungen**. Vierkierchen: published by the author, n.d. 358p.

A short, general account of the development of the Evangelical Church of the Augsburg Confession in Poland is followed by a history dealing with particular dioceses and parishes. Interesting illustrations round off the exhaustive work, which leaves an excellent impression of the religious, cultural, and national life of the generally German parishes. The book was written with a scrupulous exactitude not by a historian but by a churchman.

299. Wagner, Oskar. "Staat und Evangelische Kirche in Polen 1918-1921." *Jahrbuch der Albertus-Universität zu Königsberg/Preussen* 10 (1959): 114-67.

The Evangelical Church of the Augsburg denomination represented over 500,000 Germans living in Poland. This essay concentrates on its place and role during the first four years in the newly created Polish state.

Militarism, World War II, Espionage

300. Aurich, Peter. **Der deutsch-polnische September 1939: Eine Volksgruppe zwischen den Fronten**. Politische Studien, Band 10. Munich: Günter Olzog, 1969. 147p. Illus.

Based on available first-hand accounts, this is a detailed reconstruction of the fate of members of the German minority in Poland during the first hectic weeks of World War II, including large-scale arrests, forced marches, and (for approximately 4,000 of them) death at the hands of Polish soldiers and civilians. The author sees some of this as premeditated but attributes most of it to general hysteria and includes examples of humanitarianism on the part of individual Poles.

301. Cygański, Miroslaw. **Hitlerowskie organizacje dywersyjne w województwie śląskim 1931-1936** (Hitlerite Subversive Organizations in the Silesian Voivodship, 1931-1936). Katowice: "Śląsk," 1971. 215p. (Summaries in Russian, English, and German).

Based on captured German documents, this study offers an in-depth account of the Nazi-oriented German organizations in Upper Silesia.

302. Cygański, Miroslaw. **Mniejszość niemiecka w Polsce centralnej w latach 1919-1939** (The German Minority in Central Poland in the Years 1919-1939). Lódz: Wydawnictwo Lódzkie, 1962. 186p.

The author makes the case that even those Germans living in areas of Poland that had not belonged to the German empire before 1919 were never really loyal citizens of Poland. He stresses their early Nazi proclivities and fifth-column activities in 1939. The book was written with apparent present-minded motives, defending the Odor-Neisse boundary against West German "revisionism."

303. Cygański, Miroslaw. **Zawsze przeciw Polsce: Kariera Otta Ulitza** (Always against Poland: The Career of Otto Ulitz). Warsaw: Zachodnia Agencja Prasowa, 1966. 303p.

This is a political biography of the long-time head of the German Volksbund in Polish Upper Silesia between the wars. It seeks to discredit Ulitz, who also was prominent in the Upper Silesian "Landsmannschaft" in West Germany after 1945, by focusing on his alleged ideological affinity toward Nazism in the 1930s and his service in the Nazi occupation regime in Poland after 1939.

304. Cygański, Miroslaw. **Z dziejów Volksbundu (1921-1932)** (From the History of the Volksbund, 1921-1932). Opole: Instytut Śląski, 1966. 109p.

This is an anlysis of the activities and prevalent ideology of the Volksbund, the chief political organization of the German minority in Poland, focusing on Polish Upper Silesia and emphasizing this group's ties to and alleged control by the German government. The author believes this organization helped impede the adjustment of Polish Germans in order to keep revisionist hopes alive.

305. Datner, Szymon. "Z dziejów dywersji niemieckiej w czasie kampanii wrześniowej—kontrakcja polska w Bydgoszczy 3.9.1939 r." (From the History of German Diversions during the September Campaign—Polish Counteraction in Bydgoszcz, 9/3/1939). *Wojskowy Przegląd Historyczny* 4 (1959): 148-80.

The author examines in detail the events in Bydgoszcz (Bromberg) during the first days of World War II seeking to counter allegations of a "bloody Sunday" at the expense of German civilians in the city. It is argued that members of the German minority opened fire on retreating Polish troops, which led to reprisals, but only against clearly subversive and armed elements.

306. Grünberg, Karol. **Nazi-Front Schlesien: Niemieckie organizacje polityczne w województwie śląskim w latach 1933-39** (German Political Organizations in the Sialesian Region in the Years 1933-39). Sponsored by Śląski Instytut Naukowy. Katowice: Śląsk, 1963. 231p. (Summary in English).

The work traces the drift of the Volksbund from a comprehensive organization of the German minority in Polish Upper Silesia to an anti-democratic, pro-Nazi body under growing Reich influence. Based on archival research, it treats the German minority not as a monolithic subversive group but stresses internal differences and anti-Nazi factions as well, though fear of Russia kept the Polish government from dealing with subversive Germans as forcefully as it should have.

307. Kuhn, Walter. "Das Deutschtum in Polen und sein Schicksal in Kriegs- und Nachkriegszeit." In **Osteuropa-Handbuch Polen**, edited by Werner Markert, pp. 138-64. Cologne: Böhlau Verlag, 1959.

Based on secondary sources and aimed at a general audience, this survey focuses on a period that has received relatively little attention: the 1939-1945 era, when the German population of western Poland was supplemented by new settlers from farther east who replaced the many expelled Poles, only to be expelled themselves at war's end.

308. Makowski, Edmund. "Wplyw zwycięstwa hitleryzmu w Niemczech na mniejszość niemiecką w Wielkopolsce" (The Influence of the Victory of Hitlerism in Germany upon the German Minority in Poznania). In **Rola Wielkopolski w dziejach narodu polskiego**, edited by S. Kubiak and L. Trzeciakowski, pp. 345-56. Seria Historia, 83. Poznan: Mickiewicz Uniw., 1979.

This essay focuses on the struggle for dominance within the German minority between the traditional Deutsche Vereinigung (DV) and the pro-Nazi Jungdeutsche Partei (JDP), 1933-1935. It concludes that a clear majority of Germans in Poznania adhered to Nazism earlier even than in the Reich and that their professions of loyalty to Poland in the 1930s were insincere.

309. Osinski, Seweryn. **5ta kolumna na Pomorzu gdańskim** (The Fifth Column in Gdansk Pomerania). Warsaw: Książka i Wiedza, 1965. 317p.

This investigation of the German minority in Pomerania focuses on the 1930s and on the role of Gdansk (Danzig) as a forward base for official German irredentist agitation. It contends that most Germans in this region were not loyal to Poland and that many were involved in the intricate intelligence networks and sabotage plans detailed here.

310. Pospieszalski, Karol Marian. **Sprawa 58,000 "Volksdeutschów"; Sprostowanie hitlerowskich oszczerstw w sprawie strat niemieckiej mniejszości w Polsce w ostatnich miesiącach przed wybuchem wojny i w toku kampanii wrześniowej** (The Case of 58,000 Ethnic Germans: Denial of Hitlerist Accusations Concerning Losses of the German Minority in Poland in the Months Preceding the Outburst of the Coming War and during the September Campaign). Poznan: Instytut Zachodni, 1959. 218p.

The book attempts to deny the mass execution of 58,000 ethnic Germans (*Volksdeutsche*) in Poland shortly before the war and during the September Campaign of 1939. The mass executions took place in the Polish city of Torun (Thorn). Several original German documents and a summary in English are provided.

311. Szefer, Andrzej. **Mniejszość niemiecka w Polsce i w Czechoslowacji w latach 1933-1938** (The German Minority in Poland and in Czechoslovakia in the years 1933-1938). Katowice: Śląski Instytut Naukowy, 1967. 241p. (Summaries in English, German, and Russian).

This is a comparative treatment of German minority attitudes and activities in the two countries, emphasizing the similarities between the two ethnic groups, the leading role of pro-Nazi elements in each case (JDP in Poland, SDHF in Czechoslovakia), and the role these minority populations played as instruments of German foreign policy in the 1930s.

Lithuanians

312.   Chase, Thomas G. **The Story of Lithuania**. New York: Stratford House, 1946. 392p.
   The early history before union with Poland is described in part I of this scholarly outline. The third part, "Lithuania in the Late Middle Ages," includes considerable information on Polish problems. The following history of the Polish-Lithuanian Republic is chiefly a history of Lithuanian separatism, mutual distrust, and an almost complete lack of harmony between Lithuania and Poland.

313.   Gorzuchowski, S. "Ludność litewska na kresach Państwa Polskiego" (The Lithuanian People in the Borderlands of the Polish State). *Sprawy Narodowościowe* 1 (1929): 15-35.
   This essay outlines the problem of the Lithuanian minority within the Polish state.

314.   Jurgela, Constantine. **History of the Lithuanian Nation**. New York: Lithuanian Cultural Institute, 1948. 544p.
   This general survey of Lithuanian history contains an extensive treatment of Polish-Lithuanian relations during the interwar period and the treatment of the Lithuanian minority in Poland. The selected bibliography can be useful for further research.

315.   Kantautas, Adam, and Kantautas, Filomena, comps. **A Lithuanian Bibliography: A Check-list of Books and Articles Held by the Major Libraries of Canada and the United States**. Edmonton, Alberta: The University of Alberta Press, 1975. 725p.

   Kantautas, Adam, and Kantautas, Filomena. **Supplement to a Lithuanian Bibliography**. Edmonton, Alberta: The University of Alberta Press, 1979. 316p.
   Included in this valuable reference tool are 10,168 entries that describe and locate an extensive list of books, journals, pamphlets, articles, and other items in 43 Canadian libraries, 458 American institutions, and 11 depositories in Europe. The items are listed under various topical headings. The *Supplement* lists over 4,000 items.

316.   **Lietuviu Enciklopedija** (Lithuanian Encyclopedia). 36 vols. Boston: Lietuviu Enciklopedijos Leidykla, 1953-1969.

   Lietuviskoji Tarybiné Enciklopedija (Lithuanian Soviet Encyclopedia). 8 vols. Vilnius: Leidykla "Mosklas," 1976-1981. (Vol. 8: Letters M-P).
   Both encylcopedias are in the Lithuanian language and contain much information on the Lithuanians in Poland during 1920-1939.

317. Senn, Alfred Erich. **The Emergence of Modern Lithuania**. New York: Columbia University Press, 1959. Reprint. Westport, CT: Greenwood Press, 1975, 272p.

The author begins by sketching out the growing nationalist concern among Lithuanians which developed out of their burial by Poland. He then notes how each of the major powers figured Lithuania into their plans; material on Poland is the fullest. The work provides a uniquely complete account of events, particularly as they concerned disputes among Lithuanian factions and personalities, the diplomacy of the Entente, and the background to the Vilna question, which became such a stumbling block to the achievement of Lithuanian-Polish accord.

3 _____ National Minorities in Czechoslovakia, 1919-1980

Josef Kalvoda,
with the assistance of David Crowe (Jews)

HISTORICAL SUMMARY

The Czechoslovak Republic came into being in the years 1918 and 1919 by the amalgamation of two groups of territories: Bohemia and Moravia-Silesia, known as the Czech or historical lands, which up until then had formed a part of old Austria; and Slovakia and Ruthenia, which had hitherto been part of the old Hungarian kingdom. After its establishment, Czechoslovakia, a country in the heart of Europe, had an area of 140,484 square kilometers (approximately 55,000 square miles) and, according to the census of 1930, a population of 14,729,536.

A glance at the map of Europe shows the mountain quadrangle of Bohemia and the mountain ellipse of Slovakia. The western part of the country had "natural boundaries" and the Carpathian mountains provided such a boundary in the north of Slovakia and Ruthenia, but there was nothing in the south that would separate the country from Hungary and the eastern part of Austria.

The Czechs and Slovaks had a long history before Czechoslovakia appeared on the map of Europe. Their Slavic ancestors had lived in the area since the seventh century and possibly even earlier. In the ninth century Bohemia became a part of the Frankish empire and subsequently of the Holy

Roman Empire. In the twelfth century the prince of Bohemia became king and eventually one of the electors of the Holy Roman Empire.

For a time the Czechs, Slovaks, and other western Slavic tribes were unified into the Great Moravian Empire. The Magyar invasion (903-907), however, brought the end of the Great Moravian Empire, and the Slovaks became subjects of the Hungarian (St. Stephen) Crown. Thus, after the eleventh century the Czechs and Slovaks were separated and their history evolved along different lines.

The medieval kingdom of Bohemia, ruling also some adjacent provinces (at one time stretching from the Baltic to the Mediterranean), had natural frontiers by a string of mountains and was the westernmost Slavic bastion amidst principalities inhabited by German-speaking peoples. Thus, the Czech national state existed long before Germany, Italy, France, and Spain became united. In the fourteenth century the kingdom had its "golden age" under the rule of Charles IV (I), who was also the Holy Roman emperor. The fifteenth-century Hussite Wars had long-range repercussions. On the one hand, they served as a basis for a variety of interpretations, usually emphasizing the Czech self-image as a small but stubborn nation that was able to defy all of Europe. On the other hand, the country became devastated by the religious wars, isolated and politically weakened, internally and externally. The extremely destructive Thirty Years' War (1618-1648) completed the process, reducing Bohemia's population to about one-fifth of its prewar size. The outcome of the war assured the rule of Habsburgs over the kingdom, which remained a part of their domain until 1918.

In the fourteenth and fifteenth centuries, the Czech (Bohemian) kings called German craftsmen and miners to settle in Bohemia and Moravia to develop industries and crafts. After this, the Czechs and Germans lived side by side in the Czech lands. The Germans were concentrated largely in the border regions of the historical lands and in some of the larger cities. The Habsburgs' policies, notably in the eighteenth century, resulted in considerable Germanization of populations, especially in the cities and the border regions. The Czech language, however, was maintained by the peasants living in the countryside.

The national reawakening in the nineteenth century and Pan-Slav agitation were manifest among both the Czechs and the Slovaks. Although there were some contacts between the Czechs and the Slovaks over the centuries of their separation, Slovak history, mentality, and culture evolved along different lines than those of the Czechs. In the nineteenth century Slovak written language was adopted by the educated Slovaks. The Slovak Catholics used in their schools one of the dialects as literary language, but through L'udovít Štúr's efforts, a central Slovak dialect gradually gained general acceptance among the Slovaks as the Slovak literary language. The language reform, Štúr's political leadership, and his emphasis on separate Slovak national identity had a lasting impact which created a permanent chism between the Slovaks and the Czechs. A small group of educated Slovaks, the *Hlasists*, promoted the idea of Czech-Slovak national unity before World War I, establishing the basis for the concept of a "Czechoslovak" nation adopted by most Czechs (and some Slovaks) during the existence of the first Czechoslovak Republic (1918-1938).

The Czech national reawakening or renascence in the nineteenth century reinstilled the sense of national identity and national pride among the Czechs. Thus, before World War I the hard-working Czechs were well organized in political parties that reflected the whole spectrum of economic and ideological interests. Their schools produced capable intelligentsia, political leaders, and technically skilled persons who built and developed the Czech economic and financial institutions. The growing middle class was prosperous, and cultural life in the historical lands was flourishing. The Czechs, however, had valid political, national, and economic grievances, and their representatives in the Vienna parliament and the provincial diets did not hesitate to voice them. In particular, the bulk of the prewar Czech political parties demanded the restoration of the historical "state rights" of the Bohemian Crown, that is, a tripartite arrangement in the Austro-Hungarian Empire in which the St. Wenceslas (Bohemian) Crown would have a similar position as that of St. Stephen (Hungary). The Social Democrats and Thomas Garrigue Masaryk, the only deputy of the "Realist" party in the Vienna *Reichsrat*, advocated autonomy for national groups on the basis of "natural right." (There were 107 Czech deputies in the *Reichsrat*.) Only the small Czech Progressive State Rights party demanded before World War I the independence of the Bohemian kingdom. But the war created a new situation in which the larger demands of the Czech resistance at home and abroad were realized and the Czecho-Slovak state was established.

According to the Austro-Hungarian census of 1900, some 6 million Czechs and 2 million Slovaks lived in the empire. It may be noted that, in contrast to the Czechs, whose national survival in the Habsburg Empire was not in doubt on the eve of the war, the number of politically and nationally conscious Slovaks was sharply reduced through the consciously pursued policy of Magyarization applied to some one thousand families. The bulk of the Slovak nation consisted of peasants living in the mountainous regions of "Upper Hungary," who were deeply religious, apolitical, and resigned to their fate. While the Czechs had a full range of well-organized political parties reflecting class and ideological divisions in the nation, the Slovak National party was a loose political organization of leaders without a mass following. The party's representation in the Budapest parliament consisted of three deputies before World War I, and it shrunk to just one after the declaration of war (one deputy was called to military service and the other one resigned). Although the policy of Magyarization affected all the national minorities living in Hungary, the nationally and politically conscious Slovaks were on the verge of extinction when the war began.

In May 1918 the leaders of the Slovak National party decided to cooperate with the Czechs, as did the Slovaks in the United States; and, eventually, on October 30, 1918, political leaders of all political factions, assembled at Turčiansky Sv. Martin, formally established the Slovak National Council and issued a declaration demanding the right of national self-determination. Two days earlier, on October 28, 1918, the Czech National Committee, formed in the summer of 1918, proclaimed Czechoslovak independence in Prague. The delegates from the Slovak National Council despatched to Prague cooperated with the Czechs in the efforts to gain control over the area that became known as Slovakia.

The Czecho-Slovak National Council in Paris, an exile group led by Thomas G. Masaryk, Eduard Beneš, and Milan R. Štefánik, issued a declaration of independence on October 18, 1918, and announced the formation of an exile government. The Czech National Committee proclaimed independence on October 28 and, in cooperation with the exiles, became the de facto government in the Czech lands. Its first task was to secure the borderlands of the historical lands inhabited predominantly by Germans and to occupy Slovakia. The Germans, however, were opposed to the establishment of the Czech rule, which would make them a minority in the newly proclaimed state. But the Czechs crushed their resistance and by military force occupied the borderlands during November and December 1918. The governments established by the Germans in several districts were unable to enforce their authority.

The attitude of the new government on the question of German minority in Czechoslovakia was reflected in the inaugural address of President Masaryk on December 22, 1918, in which he categorically stated: "I repeat, *we* have created this state and thus determine the constitutional position of our Germans who originally entered the country as immigrants and colonists. We are fully entitled to the wealth of our land which is necessary to our and the Germans' industry.... We are convinced that considerations of their own economic advantage will draw the Germans over to us.... By building up a really democratic system of self-government we shall have the best means for a solution of the problem of nationalities. A clear-cut frontier is not feasible because of the widespread intermingling...." The Germans resented being called immigrants and colonists, even though the president took a more accommodating attitude when he spoke of full equality of all nationalities in Czechoslovakia when he visited the Prague German Theatre the next day.

The Germans living in the Czech lands were not politically united and differed in their views of the ethnic question in Austria-Hungary. While the German Nationalists considered the Germans to be the master nation in the Austrian part of the empire and propagated the legal concept of a "state language" by which they wanted to perpetuate the ascendancy of German, the Social Democrats called for the creation, as far as possible, of homogeneous, autonomous areas along national lines to solve the nationality question plaguing the country. But after the collapse of Austria-Hungary, all German political parties in the Czech lands formed a temporary coalition and demanded the right of self-determination for the Germans. On October 21, 1918, the German deputies elected in Austria in 1911 proclaimed the "independent German-Austrian State," and following the declaration of independence by the Czech National Committee in Prague on October 28, the German deputies in the Czech lands declared themselves to be the "Provisional Provincial Diet" of German Bohemia that was to be "an autonomous province of the German-Austrian state." The governments of the four administrative areas that were established for the Germans were shortlived, however. The Czech National Committee in Prague, which had become the provisional government of Czechoslovakia, sent Czech troops to the borderlands, an area that became known as Sudetenland, and destroyed the German resistance.

The occupation of Slovakia posed a greater problem to the Czech government in Prague. Responding to the request of the Slovak National Committee established in Turčiansky Sv. Martin, small Czech military units entered Slovakia in November 1918. When they were largely beaten back by the Hungarian troops, the Czechoslovak government spokesman in Paris, Eduard Beneš, secured French support for Czech policy in Slovakia. Czech troops returning from France and Italy and some Czech volunteers, with the assistance of French military officers despatched to Slovakia, successfully occupied the area during the months of December 1918 and January 1919. The Czech presence in Slovakia and the attempt to extend the Czechoslovak state boundaries at the expense of Hungary as well as the boundaries of the other successor states, Yugoslavia and Romania, led to the collapse of the "liberal" government of Count Korolyi, the assumption of power by the Communist regime of Béla Kun and the war between the latter and the successor states. The failure to win military victory on the battlefield brought the end of Communist rule in Hungary. The boundaries of Hungary were delimited by the victorious powers assembled at the Paris Peace Conference on June 12, 1919, assigning a Hungarian minority to Czechoslovakia. When Ruthenia was added to the new state, the size of its national minorities increased further.

The establishment of Czech rule in the Czech historical lands was justified on the basis of historical state rights and economic and military considerations. Slovakia was attached to the new state on the basis of the right of self-determination. When the Paris Peace Conference came to deal with the question of boundaries, the new state already existed by *fait accompli*. It possessed all the major attributes of statehood: it had definite boundaries (at least in the Czech part of the country), population, and a government exercising effective control. International recognition of the government had been achieved by the exile group even before the boundary issue came up at the Paris Peace Conference. Since the Czechs were among the victors and were represented at the conference, and the vanquished nations, the Germans and Hungarians, were denied access to it, the Czech representatives were able to secure international recognition of the boundaries within which lived considerable numbers of non-Czech nationalities.

As noted, the Paris Peace Conference of 1919 was confronted with a *fait accompli*. The Czechoslovak case was well prepared and defended by the delegation headed by the Prime Minister Karel Kramář and its principal spokesman, Eduard Beneš, the country's minister of foreign affairs. The Czechoslovak *aide memoires* were an excellent piece of propaganda. They contained maximum demands, such as the corridor joining the country with Yugoslavia, the adding of Sorb Lusatia and other frontier changes at the expense of Germany, and the extending of the Slovak borders to the disadvantage of Hungary, all of which was never seriously considered by the peace conference.

The *Aide Memoire III*, entitled "The Problem of the Germans in Bohemia," submitted by Beneš to the peace conference, exaggerated the strength of the Czech minorities living in the borderlands of Bohemia. It maintained that the Austrian census of 1910 overestimated the number of Germans in Bohemia by 800,000 to 1,000,000. However, as the Czechoslovak census of 1921 shows, the number of people incorrectly listed as Germans in the 1910 census was nearer to a half million. This Czech exaggeration was called by some a "deliberate deception" in the 1930s, when the issue of the justice of the peace settlement came under sharp criticism. Czechoslovakia's critiques also seized on another point made in the *memoire*: the promise that Czechoslovakia would be a "second Switzerland," a promise that was not kept.

At the Paris Peace Conference the Czechoslovak Commission considered the cession of some border areas inhabited almost exclusively by Germans (including Cheb-Eger) to Germany. The American delegates in the commission wanted to give Cheb to Germany, but the chief French delegate and the commission's secretary, Georges Clemenceau, came out against it, believing that the proposal for border rectification amounted to territorial concessions to Germany. The French wanted to weaken Germany and therefore supported the Czech claim to historical boundaries of the Czech lands.

Although in his memorandum of May 20, 1919, Beneš described "the intention of the Czecho-Slovak Government to create the organization of the State by accepting as a basis of national rights the principles applied in the constitution of the Swiss Republic," Czechoslovakia did not become "a sort of Switzerland." A qualifying sentence suggesting that in the process "the special conditions in Bohemia" would be taken into consideration was used as an escape clause when in 1937 Beneš interpreted the "creation of a new Switzerland" as meaning liberal treatment and liberal attitudes toward national minorities.

Since Slovakia had no historical boundaries and had been an integral part of Hungary since the eleventh century, the Czechoslovak delegates at the Paris Peace Conference invoked the right of self-determination of the Slovaks, claiming that the latter were a branch of the "Czechoslovak nation." When the boundary issue came up for discussion, the Czechs insisted on the new border being drawn far enough south to insure access to the Danube River and to give the new state control over the adjacent rich plains. Thus, in addition to the right of self-determination, economic and strategic interests were invoked by the government. Although the peace conference did not assign all the territories claimed by the Czechs at the expense of Hungary to Czechoslovakia, most of the demands were met and 700,000 Hungarians together with the Slovaks, were incorporated into the republic.

Hungary never accepted the loss of "Upper Hungary" and strove for revision of the Slovak boundary. During the interwar years the Hungarian minority in Czechoslovakia was vocal in its demands for "return to Hungary." However, the Hungarian revisionism was contained by the establishment of the Little Entente. The three members of the entente, Czechoslovakia, Romania, and Yugoslavia, received, at the expense of Hungary, territories with sizable Hungarian minorities and therefore had a vested interest in preventing Hungarian attempts to revise the Treaty of Trianon (1920), by which Hungary lost two-thirds of its original territory to the succession states.

The small Teschen territory, a corner of Austrian Silesia which had belonged to the Bohemian Crown since the fourteenth century, was important to the Czechs for its coal industry and its transportation network. It had high-quality coal reserves, and the railroad going from the Czech lands to Slovakia and on to Ruthenia and Romania passed through. Thus, the Czechs based their claim on historical, economic, and strategic considerations. The Poles, on the other hand, had ethnographic claims to it. Since the delegations of great powers assembled in Paris accepted the Polish position, the Czechs attempted to create a *fait accompli* by sudden occupation of the Teschen area in January 1919. The Poles resisted with military force, and the Teschen issue subsequently was a source of embarrassment for the Czech delegation in Paris. But in July 1920 the Czechs took advantage of the Poles' desperate situation when the Soviet armies were advancing on Warsaw. Thus, Poland had to give up the area, and its railroad junction and coal mines were assigned by the Allies to Czechoslovakia. The Poles considered this loss an injustice, blackmail at the moment of grave crisis, and the dispute over the Teschen district poisoned the relations between the two west Slavic countries for the next twenty years. At the time of the Munich crisis, the Poles took advantage of the situation and occupied the disputed territory.

The easternmost province of Czechoslovakia, Subcarpathian Ruthenia or the Carpatho-Ukraine, was an integral part of Hungary for nine centuries. Approximately 600,000 people, over half of them illiterate, lived in the area at the outbreak of World War I. About two-thirds of the inhabitants were peasants and mountaineers speaking Ukrainian dialect, while the rest were Hungarian officials and landowners, Jewish merchants and innkeepers, Germans, Romanians, and Slovaks. When in 1918 the leader of the Ruthenians in the United States, Grigory Zatkovic, met with Masaryk, an agreement was worked out to affiliate Ruthenia with Czechoslovakia as an autonomous province. The agreement was approved by Ruthenians living in the United States and the Central National Council in Užhorod (Ungvar). Following the shortlived regime of Béla Kun in Hungary, the support that existed for the area's continued association with Hungary as an autonomous province withered away and the Great Powers assigned Ruthenia to Czechoslovakia on September 10, 1919, stipulating that the province be granted autonomy. The promise of autonomy was not kept by the Czechs, however, despite the fact that it was a legal commitment and was incorporated into the Czechoslovak constitution of February 29, 1920.

Ruthenia had a strategic significance for the new state, providing a link with Romania, the Little Entente ally of Czechoslovakia during the interwar period. The population of the province, however, was heterogeneous, and most of the political parties representing it adopted a critical attitude toward the Czech-dominated state. The complaints were political, religious-cultural, and economic in nature. The Czechoslovak government apparently did not understand the psychology of the Ruthenians, their religious outlook, their cultural habits, and their unhappiness with widespread poverty and the unfulfilled promise of political autonomy. Results of parliamentary elections in which the "Czechoslovak" political parties polled a minority of the vote demonstrate the extent of the protest vote in Ruthenia. In the 1935 election, the last before the collapse of the republic, the Communist party polled 25.6% of the vote, though it received merely about 10% of the vote statewide and held 10% of the seats in the National Assembly. The Autonomist bloc received 14.9%, the Hungarian Christian Social and Hungarian National party 11%, and the Catholic party 2.8% of the vote.

The Czechoslovak constitution of February 29, 1920, drafted and adopted by an appointed National Assembly long after the peace treaties had been signed, provided for a centralized state administration. The Slovaks were underrepresented in the National (Constituent) Assembly, most of their delegates were handpicked by the Czechs, and other national minorities had no representation at all. Subsequently, the Slovak autonomists and the national minorities did not approve of the fundamental law of the state and demanded its revision. Yet the constitution was characteristically "liberal." It was based on the principle of civic equality "without consideration of race, language and religion" and guaranteed to all citizens fundamental civil rights, including political freedom. The system of proportional representation was used in parliamentary elections, the vote was universal, equal, direct, and secret, the free use of national language was guaranteed to everyone, schools for national minorities were to provide instructions in their mother tongue, and appropriate subsidies were designated for cultural and other purposes. The constitution prohibited "every kind of forcible denationalization," though the latter was never followed up by legislation. Persons of all religious faiths and languages could be admitted to the public service and could practice any trade or profession.

A special language law was enacted together with the constitution that gave the Czech and Slovak languages a privileged position. Courts and other authorities had to accept written or oral submissions in the minority language where (in the administrative units and judicial districts) more than 20% of the population were of German, Hungarian, or Polish origin. Judgments and other official responses had to be given bilingually, in Czech (or Slovak) and the respective minority language. This, of course, did not apply to the Czechs and the Slovaks, who could always use their language wherever they lived, even if their number in the given community was miniscule. Thus, the Germans and the Hungarians felt themselves discriminated against, though the percentage of their nationals who did not have "language right" did not exceed 10%.

Although the German political parties objected to being denied access to the Paris Peace Conference and the minority status of Germans in Czecho-slovakia, eventually the vast majority of Germans accepted the republic, as the results of the postwar elections indicate. In 1926 the German Christian Social party and the German Agrarian party entered the coalition government of Czechoslovakia, as did the German Social Democratic party in 1929. These political parties, called "activists," were prepared to cooperate with the Czechs on the basis of the existing constitution. They received between 74 and 83% of the German vote in the 1920, 1925, and 1929 elections. The German National and the German National Socialist parties, however, were consistently opposed to the republic, insisting that the latter was "an artificial state," and denounced the injustice of the peace settlement of 1919. Yet, until the 1935 election, the vast majority of the (Sudeten) Germans did not reject the state, even though they did not accept it uncritically.

The world economic crisis also had repercussions in Czechoslovakia and affected the industrial area inhabited by Germans more than the rest of the country. Unemployment here was higher and the need for government relief more pressing. The economic crisis and the rise of Nazism in Germany strengthened the forces of discontent among the Germans and accelerated their demand for cultural autonomy. In the 1935 election, the Sudeten German party, led by Konrad Henlein, received more votes than any other political party. However, due to the intricacy of the electoral system, the party's representation in the National Assembly was slightly smaller than that of the largest Czechoslovak Republican party (44 to 45). The "activist" political parties were decimated. In March of the critical year 1938, the German Agrarian party left the government coalition and joined, as a whole, the

Sudeten German party. The Christian Social party deputies also joined Henlein's party, with the exception of one deputy who resigned from the government. This was a prelude to the dramatic events in the summer and fall of 1938, culminating in the Munich Conference (September 30) and the cession of the border regions of the Czech historical lands to Germany. The Vienna Award (October 1938) assigned the Teschen territory to Poland, and parts of Slovakia and Ruthenia to Hungary. Thus, in October 1938, Czechoslovakia lost territories inhabited by about 5 million people to Germany, Poland, and Hungary.

In the rump Czecho-Slovakia (also known as the Second Republic), Slovakia and Ruthenia had autonomous status. The hyphenation of the name of the state (existing also in all documents submitted to the Paris Peace Conference) reflected the recognition of the Slovak separate national identity and administrative dualism. The Second Republic came to an end in March 1939, when Slovakia, with Germany's support, declared its independence. The rump Czech lands were occupied by Germany and became known as the "Protectorate of Bohemia and Moravia."

Between March 15, 1939 and the end of the war, the Protectorate had a Czech government, dominated by Nazi Germany. The Slovak State government was headed by Dr. Jozef Tiso, its policies subject to German approval. Ruthenia was occupied by Hungary in March 1939 and remained under its control until the arrival of Soviet troops in 1944. With the exception of Ruthenia, which became a part of the Ukrainian Soviet Socialist Republic, Czechoslovakia was restored to its pre-Munich boundaries in 1945.

The following data, pages 117-20, indicate the ethnic structure of Czechoslovakia after its establishment in 1919, the changes resulting from the events in the fall of 1938 and the spring of 1939, the consequences of the population transfer after World War II, and the developments in the ethnic composition of the country during the years 1950-1980.

Number of Czechoslovak State Citizens in Czechoslovakia
and Slovakia in 1920-1921 and 1930.*

Nationality	Czechoslovakia				Slovakia			
	1920-1921		1930		1920-1921		1930	
	Number	%	Number	%	Number	%	Number	%
Czech	6,796,343	65.53	7,406,493	66.91	71,733	68.12	120,926	72.09
Slovak	1,967,870		2,282,277		1,941,942		2,224,983	
German	3,123,624	23.36	3,231,688	23.32	139,880	4.73	147,501	4.53
Hungarian	744,621	5.57	691,923	4.78	634,827	21.48	571,988	17.58
Ruthenian	461,449	3.45	549,169	3.79	85,628	2.90	91,079	2.80
Jewish	180,504	1.35	186,642	1.29	70,522	2.39	65,385	2.01
Polish	75,987	0.57	81,737	0.57	2,499	0.08	933	0.03
Other	23,065	0.17	49,636	0.34	8,967	0.30	31,394	0.96
Totals	13,373,463	100	14,479,565	100	2,955,993	100	3,254,189	100

* *Československá statistika*. Census of Dec. 1, 1930, vol. 98, part I. Prague, 1934. pp. 46-47. The above data are incomplete; it is necessary to add to them inhabitants holding foreign citizenship and whose citizenship was unidentified. Their number in Czechoslovakia was 238,961 in 1920 and 248,971 in 1930. The respective number of those inhabitants in Slovakia was 42,246 in 1921 and 75,604 in 1930, 20,349 of whom reported Hungarian nationality in 1930. Ibid., p. 68, part containing tables.

TABLE I

National Groups in Czechoslovakia — The Census of February 15, 1921

Czechoslovaks 8,760,937

Ruthenians 461,849

Poles 75,853

Germans 3,123,568

Magyars 745,431

Jews 180,855

Others 25,871

Note: There were 238,808 foreigners in the country in 1921.

TABLE II

Distribution of the Population by Religion in Czechoslovakia (1921)

Roman Catholics............................. 10,384,833

Uniate and Armenian Catholics................. 535,543

Protestants (All Denominations)............... 990,319

Czechoslovak Church......................... 525,333

Russian Orthodox............................ 73,097

Old Catholics............................... 20,255

Jews.. 354,342

Unaffiliated................................. 724,507

Other Confessions........................... 2,824

Unknown..................................... 2,119

Source: Official publications of the State Statistical Office of the Czechoslovak Republic, quoted in *Czechoslovakia: A Survey of Economic and Social Conditions*. Edited by Josef Gruber. New York, The Macmillan Co., 1924. pp. 9-11.

Survey of the Consequences of the Munich Settlement and the
Vienna Arbitration—October-November 1938

Territory and Population

	Population		Territory in sq. km.	
German seizure	3,817,865	25.9%	28,291	20.1%
Polish seizure	227,399	1.5%	805	0.6%
Hungarian seizure	972,092	6.6%	11,833	8.4%
Remaining territory	9,712,180	66.0%	99,579	70.9%
Former Czechoslovakia	14,729,536	100.0%	140,508	100.0%

Source: *Mnichov v dokumentech* (Munich in Documents). Vol. II. Prague, 1958. 355p.

Population of Carpatho-Ukraine
According to Its Nationality Affiliations
in the Years of 1910, 1921, 1930 and 1938

Nationality of Citizens	Absolute numbers of inhabitants			
	1910	1921	1930	1938*
Ukrainians............	319,361	372,500	446,916	413,481
Magyars..............	169,434	103,690	109,472	25,894
Jews	———	79,715	91,225	65,828
Czechs and Slovaks	4,057	19,775	33,961	17,495
Germans	62,187	10,326	13,249	8,715
Rumanians	15,387	10,810	12,641	12,641
Gypsies	———	———	1,357	———
Poles	———	298	159	78
Yugoslavs	———	———	69	———
Other	1,062	617	50	627
Total of citizens	571,488	597,731	709,129	544,759
Foreigners	———	6,862	16,228	———
Total of inhabitants ...	571,488	604,593	725,357	544,759

Sources: L'Office de Statistique de la République Tchécoslovaque. *Recensement de la population dans la République Tchécoslovaque le 15 février, 1921*. Prague, 1925. II, pp. 362-63; Statistisches Staatsamt. *Statistisches Jahrbuch der Cechoslovakischen Republik*. Prague, 1934. p. 11.

* Estimates after cession of territory in 1938.

Ethnic Structure of the Population in Czechoslovakia, Czechia (CSR) and Slovakia (SSR), 1961-1980.

Nationality	Czechoslovakia			CSR			SSR		
	1961	1970	1980	1961	1970	1980	1961	1970	1980
				Population					
Czech.........	9,060,222	9,318,019	9,818,618	9,023,501	9,270,617	9,763,384	45,721	47,402	55,234
Slovak........	3,836,213	4,199,902	4,664,460	275,997	320,998	343,321	3,560,216	3,878,904	4,321,139
Ukrainian.....	[1] 54,984	48,754	47,554	[1] 19,549	9,794	10,375	[1] 35,435	38,960	37,179
Russian.......		9,897	7,630		6,619	5,051		3,278	2,579
Polish........	67,552	65,132	67,923	66,540	64,074	65,432	1,012	1,058	2,491
Hungarian.....	533,934	570,478	579,617	15,152	18,472	19,816	518,782	552,006	559,801
German........	140,402	85,663	61,917	134,143	80,903	56,796	6,259	4,760	5,121
Others and unidentified ..	43,270	47,142	29,080	36,649	36,220	24,771	6,621	10,922	4,309

[1] In 1961, Ukrainian and Russian nationalities were listed together.

Source: *Statistická ročenka Československé socialistické republiky 1981* (Statistical Yearbook of the Czechoslovak Socialist Republic 1981). Prague, 1981. p. 92.

According to the Austro-Hungarian census of 1900, about 6 million Czechs, 2 million Slovaks, and over 300,000 Ruthenians lived in the Danubian monarchy. The Czechs lived mostly in the Austrian part of the empire (Cistleithania) and the Slovaks and Ruthenians in the Hungarian kingdom. Statistics on population were compiled by the Austro-Hungarian authorities and were subject to criticism, since they favored the German and Hungarian nationalities. During the period 1880 to 1910, the ethnic structure of the population in the Czech lands had been ascertained in an indirect way, that is, by questions regarding the "language of communication." As a consequence the number of Czechs had been reduced somewhat, as many inhabitants were bilingual and use of the German language brought certain advantages to them. Thus, the number of Germans (and Poles in the Ostrava region of Austrian Silesia) was larger, since it was possible to influence people living in areas with ethnically mixed population not to list themselves as Czechs.

As in the Czech lands, the basis for nationality affiliation in the kingdom of Hungary was the "language of communication," which brought about the reduction of numbers of the Slovaks and Ruthenians. In addition, the Hungarian census put the Jews into the Hungarian or German nationalities according to "maternal language." Nationality of Jews and Gypsies was not recognized.

The Czechoslovak statistics on the ethnic structure of the population during the period between the two wars were fairly accurate, though it was more opportune for some individuals to declare themselves members of the "Czechoslovak" nation. The Czechoslovak censuses of 1921 and 1930 placed Czechs and Slovaks into the same category, listing them as "Czechoslovaks." They added Russians and Ukrainians to the Ruthenian category and made a distinction between Jewish religion and nationality.

According to the census of February 15, 1921, Czechoslovakia had a population of 13,613,172, of whom 8,760,937 were "Czechoslovaks" (6,796,343 Czechs and 1,967,870 Slovaks), 3,123,568 Germans (their number was reduced by some 600,000 in comparison with the census of 1910), 745,431 Hungarians (according to the 1910 census, their number on the territory of the Czechoslovak Republic was 1,070,854), 461,849 Ruthenians (Ukrainians and Russians were included in this number), 180,855 Jews (this contrasts with 354,342 people who were of the Jewish faith), 75,853 Poles (their number in 1910 was listed as 169,641), 25,871 "others" (these included Gypsies and Romanians), and 238,808 foreigners, that is, people holding citizenships of foreign countries or whose citizenship or nationality was unknown.

In the provinces, the population was distributed as follows: Of the 6,670,582 people in Bohemia, two-thirds were Czechs and one-third Germans; of the 2,662,884 people living in Moravia, four-fifths were Czechs and one-fifth Germans; of the 672,268 people in Silesia, 47.6% were Czechs, 40.5% were Germans, and 11.2% of the population were Poles. Of the 3,000,870 inhabitants in Slovakia, 71,733 were Czechs and 1,941,942 Slovaks. Together the "Czechoslovaks" represented 68.1% of the population living in Slovakia. In addition, there were 139,880 Germans (4.7%), 634,827 Hungarians (21.5%), 85,628 Ukrainians (2.9%), 70,522 Jews (2.4%), about 2,500 Poles, and almost 9,000 "others." Of the 606,568 people living in Ruthenia, 372,500 were Ruthenians, Ukrainians, and Russians (62.3%), 103,690 Hungarians (17.34%), 79,715 Jews (13.34%), 19,775 Czechs and Slovaks (3.3%), 10,326

Germans (1.7%), 10,810 Romanians (1.8%), a few hundred Poles and "others," and 6,862 foreigners (these included citizens of Hungary, Poland, Romania, Yugoslavia, and several other countries). The preceding statistics indicate that the number of Ruthenians increased since the census of 1910, when their numbers were given as slightly over 319,000, and the number of Hungarians declined since the same census when their number was 169,434, including most of the Jews living in the province. Also, the number of Germans declined since 1910 from 62,187 to slightly over 10,000, also due in part to some Jews listing themselves as Germans in 1910 and reporting another nationality in 1921.

The census of 1930 showed an increase of the whole population to 14,479,565. The "Czechoslovaks" increased their percentage from 65.5 to 66.9%, the Hungarians declined from 5.57 to 4.78% (their absolute numbers decreased to 691,923 in 1930), and the other nationalities held their own, showing a normal natural increase in absolute figures.

Before World War I, the population in the Czech lands was religiously homogeneous, with merely 2.44% of the Czechs belonging to other than the Roman Catholic Church. Although some Czechs were religious skeptics, anti-clerical, or religiously indifferent, the bulk of the population was religious. The Czech culture was Catholic. It was manifested in the veneration of national and Slavic saints, the Marian cult, pilgrimages, celebration of name days rather than birth days, as well as the use of baptismal certificates rather than birth certificates. After the proclamation of Czechoslovak independence, as a consequence of the anti-Catholic agitation, about 1.25 million Czechs left the Catholic Church, of whom about one-half remained unaffiliated, two-fifths organized an independent Czechoslovak Church, and the remainder joined the several evangelical (Protestant) churches, which included the Methodists, Unity of Czech Brethren, Baptists, Unity of Brethren, Reformed Church, Lutherans (several groups), and Czech Brethren. According to the 1921 census, there were 10,384,833 Roman Catholics, 535,543 Greek and Armenian Catholics (recognizing the Roman pope), and 990,319 Protestants of all denominations. Another 525,333 belonged to the Czechoslovak Church, 73,097 to the Russian Orthodox, 20,255 to the Old Catholic, 354,342 were Jews, 724,507 were unaffiliated, and a few thousand people belonged to other confessions or their religion was unknown. The Ruthenians were, for the most part, Greek Catholics (Catholics of the Byzantine Rite), as were about 100,000 Slovaks. The number of Jews was small in Bohemia (1.2%), in Slovakia somewhat larger (4.5%), and in Ruthenia almost one-sixth of the population.

In October 1938, as a consequence of the Munich settlement and the Vienna Arbitration Award, Czechoslovakia lost to Germany 3,817,865 inhabitants (25.9% of its total population) and 28,291 square kilometers (0.6%), to Hungary 972,092 inhabitants (6.6%) and 11,833 square kilometers (8.4%). Thus, in the remaining territory of the Second Republic, amounting to 70.9% of its former size, lived 9,712,180 inhabitants, of whom 8,807,072 (90.6%) were Czechs, Slovaks, and Ruthenians, 444,280 (4.5%) Germans, 5,507 (0.5%) Poles, 167,737 (1.6%) Hungarians, and 287,584 (2.8%) "others." Together with their nationals, Germany took 962,379 Czechs, Slovaks, and Ruthenians (mostly Czechs), Poland 120,639, and Hungary 347,849 Czechs, Slovaks, and Ruthenians (mostly Slovaks). In the territory occupied by Poland lived only 76,230 Poles (33.5%), 17,182 Germans (7.6%), and 120,639 (53.0%) Czechs and Slovaks.

The Protectorate Bohemia and Moravia and the Slovak Republic were ethnically more homogeneous than was Czechoslovakia before the Munich settlement in 1938. Yet, during the years 1938-1945, due to political events, war, and the front moving across Czechoslovakia, considerable numbers of people were displaced or dislocated. During and immediately after World War II, the country underwent the greatest change in its ethnic structure. In 1948 Czechoslovakia became ethnically much more homogeneous than it had been ten years earlier.

First of all, as a consequence of the Nazi racial policy and the migration of many of the surviving Jews to Israel and other countries, the Jewish minority virtually disappeared. While in 1930, 356,830 persons were of Jewish religion in Czechoslovakia and of this number 186,642 declared themselves of Jewish nationality, the number of Jews living in the country was estimated at some 18,000 in the mid-1960s and their number further declined to some 5,000 in 1980. This was due both to low fertility (the Jews who chose to remain in Czechoslovakia were of advanced age) and migration of Jews to the western countries.

The official cession of Ruthenia to the Soviet Union (incorporated into the Ukrainian SSR) occurred on June 29, 1945, though it had been under virtual control by the Soviets ever since the Soviet troops occupied the province in 1944. This reduced the state's area inhabited predominantly by Ruthenians (Ukrainians), as noted above.

Invoking the principle of "collective guilt," the decrees of President Eduard Beneš, issued in 1945, deprived the Germans and the Hungarians of Czechoslovak citizenship, called for the confiscation of their property, and announced their expulsion. Exempted were only those persons who could prove their innocence, that is, their anti-Nazi orientation or activity. In the Potsdam Agreement of July 1945, the Allies officially consented to transfer Germans from Czechoslovakia to the occupied zones of Germany. The estimated German population in Czechoslovakia in May 1945 was about 3,391,000. It has to be pointed out that the estimates on the number of expellees vary according to sources and that the German statistics are always higher. Between 373,000 to 750,000 Germans fled the country in the "wild expulsion" in 1945, and before the end of 1946 some 2,256,000 Germans were deported in an organized fashion to Germany (of these, 792,000 to the Soviet and 1,464,000 to the American zones). A considerable number of Germans perished during the revolutionary period, and others left the country voluntarily (legally) or escaped. As a result of the great exodus, and the expulsion and annihilation of Germans, their number was reduced to 165,117 persons, according to the 1950 census. In 1930 the Germans accounted for 22.3% of the population of Czechoslovakia; twenty years later their numbers were reduced to 1.3% of the population.

The transfer of the Hungarian minority was also envisaged in the National Front government program of 1945, but its implementation proved to be impractical. Hungary became a part of the Soviet sphere of influence and control, and the Hungarian government was unwilling to resettle those Hungarians, estimated at some 700,000 persons in 1946. In the negotiations about the transfer, the Hungarian side was willing to accept the idea of an exchange but categorically refused to approve any expulsion. Thus, the attempt to liquidate the Hungarian minority was unsuccessful. Only about 92,000 Hungarians left Czechoslovakia during the years 1945-1947, and an additional 68,000 persons in the spring of 1948. Then further transfer stopped because in Hungary the Communist party became a leading force and had the backing of the Soviet authorities.

In addition to the exchange of population and the moderate expulsion of Hungarians, two actions were devised by the Czechoslovak authorities. One, re-Slovakization of those Hungarians who were believed to be of Slovak origin, and, two, resettlement of ethnic Hungarians who did not want to leave for Hungary to the Czech borderlands formerly inhabited by Germans. In the first action, 327,000 Hungarians under pressure declared themselves to be Slovaks, and in the second action about 44,000 persons were transferred to the Czech borderlands, most of them forcibly. As a consequence of these actions, the number of Hungarians in Slovakia was supposedly reduced to about 190,000 in 1948. However, in June 1948 the exchange of population with Hungary was stopped, and, after May 1, 1948, Hungarians who had been forcibly settled in the Czech borderlands were allowed to return (some 24,000 persons took the opportunity). (It should be noted that in February 1948 the Communist party of Czechoslovakia staged a *coup d'etat* and seized power.) In the following years, re-Slovakization was abandoned and all persons were allowed to decide their nationality. As a consequence of the new policy, the number of Hungarians in the country increased to 367,733 in 1950 and further to 533,934 in 1961. This represented a 42.2% increase, indicating that more than 100,000 Hungarians reported a different nationality in 1950, mostly Slovak.

The number of Hungarians further increased in 1970 to 570,478 and in 1980 to 579,617, of whom 559,801 lived in Slovakia. The Hungarian minority in Slovakia represented 12.4% of the population in 1961 and 11.2% of the population in 1980. In all of Czechoslovakia, however, the Hungarians amounted to only 3.9% of the population in 1961, 4.0% in 1970, and 3.8% in 1980. The Hungarian minority in Slovakia has become nationally self-confident and has been pressing for recognition of its legal rights. It has been supported by the fellow-nationals in Hungary and has become an important factor of heterogeneity in Slovakia. The latter province (since 1968 a separate republic within the Czechoslovak federation), in contrast to the Czech lands (Czechia, since 1968), has considerable national minorities and is plagued with the ethnic problem.

According to the census of 1980, Slovakia was populated by 55,234 Czechs (1.1% of the population in contrast to 1930 when they represented 3.7% of the population), 37,179 Ukrainians (0.7%), 2,579 Russians (0.1%), 2,491 Poles (0.1%), 5,121 Germans (0.1%), "others" (1.1%), the above mentioned Hungarians (11.2%), in addition to the 4,321,139 Slovaks (86.6%).

The first post-World War II census in Czechoslovakia held in 1950 was subject to criticism, since it was deficient in the methods of ascertaining nationality. It definitely favored the Czechs and Slovaks. The census of 1961 was more accurate, yet the definition of nationality was not very exact. In the instructions on how to fill in the census form, nationality was understood to mean "...appartenance to the nation with whose cultural and working community the object of the census is innerly linked and which he or she claims as his/her own...." In actual practice, the main criterion in the census was language. In the censuses of 1970 and 1980, mother tongue was ascertained in addition to nationality.

Although in theory all nationalities living in today's Czechoslovakia enjoy the same legal rights as the Czechs and Slovaks, in practice the small number of other ethnics living in the country does not make it possible for them to enjoy the same opportunities for overall development as the two dominant nationalities. Charges of discrimination have been made, particularly by the Hungarians, whose numbers make them a credible political force. The other national minorities' grievances are real, but their small numbers make the redress of these grievances impractical since their voices are not heard by the policymakers. Officially, the status of nationalities and their rights are derived from the appropriate law of the Czechoslovak Socialist Republic No. 144, which is based on the fundamental Czechoslovak Federation Act No. 143 of 1968.

In Czechoslovakia there are two republics — the Czech Socialist Republic (ČSR) and the Slovak Socialist Republic (SSR). The former constitutes an ethnically unified geographical and political entity with small and insignificant numbers of other nationalities. This contrasts with the situation in Slovakia, discussed above. The Slovaks, whose numbers here surpass those of the Germans, the Poles, and "others," are very close to the Czechs in language. In 1950 Czech majority was 93.8%, and since then it has increased slightly. In all the ethnic groups, the percentage of mixed marriages is high. Since the 1961 census, members of Slovak, German, Polish, Hungarian, Ukrainian, and Russian nationalities have often contracted marriages with Czechs. Even the Slovaks, whose numbers in the Czech Socialist Republic are relatively high (320,998 in 1980, representing 3.3% of the population, in contrast to 1930 when they represented merely 0.4% of the population in the Czech lands), and who live together for the most part, often marry Czechs. In 1970, 16.6% of the Slovaks claimed the Czech language as their mother tongue and subsequently their number increased.

The Germans in ČSR have registered the heaviest losses among the minority nationalities since the first postwar census in 1950, in both the absolute and relative sense. In 1950 their total number in Czechoslovakia was slightly over 165,000; in 1961, 140,402; in 1970, 85,663; and in 1980, 61,917, of whom 56,796 lived in ČSR, representing there 0.6% of the population (0.4% in the whole country). The negative balance between natality and mortality rates and assimilation accounts for part of the change. The decline in the numbers of Germans in the ČSR over the past thirty years has been due primarily to migration abroad, mostly to the German Federal Republic and Austria, although a smaller number of Germans went to the German Democratic Republic (East Germany). The decline in the German population has brought about their greater dispersal, and the great majority of them live in communities where they represent but a very small minority. In 1970 more than three-quarters of them lived in communities where they accounted for less than 10% of the population so it was difficult to provide them the right to language, education, culture, and association guaranteed by the constitution of 1968. In addition, over 13% of the Germans claimed Czech as their mother tongue. Continuing migration and the large number of persons of German nationality in the high age brackets (and the consequent low birth rate) indicate a further decline of Germans in the ČSR in the years to come.

There was a slight drop in the number of Poles between 1950 and 1970 and a slight increase in 1980. As many as 72,624 of them were counted in the census of 1950, while in 1961 only 67,552 were registered as Poles (of whom 66,540 lived in the ČSR). In 1970 their number was 65,132 (64,074 in the ČSR), and in 1980 their number increased to 67,923 (65,432 in the ČSR). The losses were due largely to assimilation and to migration. Poles show a higher natural increase than the Czechs, and this accounts for the slight increase of their numbers in 1980. (The number of Poles living in Slovakia was slightly over 1,000 in 1961 and 1970; their number sharply increased to 2,491 in 1980.)

The number of Hungarians in the ČSR steadily increased between 1961 and 1980. The 1970 census showed that their number was higher than the number of Ukrainians and Russians. The increase from 15,152 in 1961 to 19,816 in 1980 was due to a higher birth rate among the Hungarians. Further, Hungarian nationality is claimed by some Gypsy-Romany people who emigrated from the SSR. The Hungarians are widely dispersed among the Czechs, and in 1970 every seventh Hungarian in the ČSR reported Czech, and not Hungarian, as his or her tongue.

Russians registered a consistent decline of their numbers between the 1961 and 1980 censuses. The 1961 census listed the Ukrainian and Russian nationality jointly at 19,549. In 1970 the number of Ukrainians was slightly under 10,000 and Russians slightly over 6,600. According to the census of 1980, the number of Ukrainians increased to 10,375 and the number of Russians dropped to 5,051. Both the Russians and the Ukrainians are widely dispersed, and marriages concluded by them are commonly ethnically mixed, with one of the partners generally being of Czech nationality. About 65.3% of the Ukrainians claimed Ukrainian as their mother language, while 84.45% of Russians claimed Russian as their mother language.

Large numbers of Gypsies died during World War II as they were, like the Jews, victims of "the final solution" pursued by the Nazis. After World War II the Gypsy nationality was no longer recognized in Czechoslovakia, although records have been kept on them. They have caused some problems for the authorities and the people among whom they live, due to their unique cultural customs. The government has sought a solution to these problems with a mixed record of success. Due to the high birth rate among the Gypsies-Romanies, their numbers are increasing. A family counts five to six members on an average, and though in small numbers, they are found in every fifth community. Also, 48% of the Gypsies-Romanies fall into the 0 to 14 age group, indicating that a further growth of their numbers is to be expected in the future. The majority of them are integrated into the society, while some tend to remain different from the rest of the population and lag behind in both education and hygiene. Since the Gypsy-Romany nationality is not listed as such, they register themselves as Czechs, Slovaks, or Hungarians.

In 1919, after its establishment, Czechoslovakia was a nationally heterogeneous state. The large number of minorities represented one of its principal weaknesses. In addition, the officially proclaimed "Czechoslovak" nationality and the insistence that Slovak language is merely a Czech dialect were resented by the Slovaks. As a consequence of the changes in its ethnic composition and the recognition of a separate Slovak nationality after World

War II, the country has become ethnically more homogeneous, with the Czechs and Slovaks accounting for about 95% of its population. The official recognition of the Slovak separate national identity and the establishment of a federal state in 1968 were very significant developments. The percentage of Slovaks in the total population has consistently increased. In 1921 the Slovaks represented 15.1% of the country's population; in 1931, 16.4%; in 1950, 26.3%; in 1970, 29.3%; and in 1980, 30.5%. In absolute figures, the number of Slovaks increased from 1,967,870 in 1921 to 4,664,460 in 1980. Since the Slovaks have a considerably higher birth rate than the Czechs, their numbers are very likely to increase in both absolute and relative figures in the foreseeable future. Slovak political influence in Czechoslovakia has increased dramatically, and with it the tensions between the Slovaks and the Czechs.

Jews

Jewish life in Czechoslovakia differed according to the developmental patterns of the nation's distinct ethnic areas. In the Westernized provinces of Bohemia, Moravia, and Silesia, which had a third of Czechoslovakia's 356,830 Jews in 1931, Jews enjoyed a high degree of ethnic and professional integration, which enabled them to play an important role in these regions' economic and cultural life. On the other hand, their status in Slovakia, with 136,737 Jews, and Carpathian Ruthenia (Rus'), with 102,542, was much more limited.[1]

Legally, Czechoslovakia's Jews enjoyed a unique status afforded few of their counterparts in other east European communities. Jewish leaders, in league with Thomas G. Masaryk, acquired considerable religious and ethnic freedom in the 1920 constitution. Furthermore, Czechoslovakian leaders allowed Jews to choose religion or language as the basis for their national identity in the Czech censuses of 1921 and 1930. Consequently, particularly in the western provinces, these statistics show strong assimilationist trends that had been going on in these areas since the nineteenth century. In Bohemia, 46.4% chose Czech as their nationality, 31.1% German, and 20.2% Jewish. On the other hand, over 50% of the Jews in Slovakia, with their less-integrated Yiddish traditions, chose Jewish as their nationality, and 32% chose Czech. A much smaller number selected German as their ethnic choice. In Ruthenia, 93% chose Jewish as their nationality in the 1930 census.[2]

Jewish communal and religious activities in Czechoslovakia were further affected by the urban-rural balance in Czechoslovakia's major ethnic regions. In Bohemia, Moravia, and Silesia, for example, over 80% of the Jewish population lived in towns over 5,000, and 60% of the population in cities larger than 50,000. The reverse was true in Ruthenia, where 65% lived in villages.[3]

As in many east European countries, Zionists stimulated efforts to reorganize Jewish community activities in the new Czechslovakian state. Although Zionist leaders tried to create a new national Jewish organizational structure, they often found it difficult to transcend the regional and historical boundaries of the country. Zionists had strong roots in the westernized states, Bohemia, Moravia, and Silesia, where many Jews had belonged to the West Austria Zionist Organization. On the other hand, the opposite was true in Slovakia and Ruthenia, where many had belonged to the Hungarian Zionist

Organization. Furthermore, Zionists from the West Austria Zionist group took the first steps to organize a Czechoslovakian national Jewish organization at the end of 1918 with the creation of the Jewish National Council.[4] Unfortunately, a decline in interest in formal religious practice, particularly in western Czechoslovakia, as well as ideological, language, and regional differences, kept the National Council from becoming the national representative body for Czechoslovakia's Jews. Initially, what emerged were separate Jewish community organizations that oversaw educational, cultural, and religious activities of Czechoslovakia's Jews in the country's major regions and cities. During the early days of Czech independence, separate federations of Moravian and Silesian Jewish congregations emerged, while in Bohemia united organizations emerged in Prague for German or Czech-speaking Jewish congregations. Since most Jews in these areas attended government schools, Jewish community activities emphasized growth in other areas, though there were Jewish schools in Prague and Brno. In Slovakia and Ruthenia, orthodoxy predominated, and the leaders followed organizational patterns established in Hungary centuries earlier. The National Federation of Slovak Jews (Svaz Židov na Slovensku), founded in 1919, oversaw recovery activities in Slovakia after World War I and represented its Jewish population politically. The religious community was divided among the Orthodox, with 107 congregations, and the Jeshurun, with 60. Jewish political divisions in Slovakia often followed these patterns as well.[5]

Educationally, Slovak Jews attended Jewish primary schools with instruction first in Magyar, though later Slovak became predominant. Zionist groups played an important role, as they did in other parts of eastern Europe, in stimulating interest among Slovak Jews in Jewish culture.[6]

Education and cultural life among Carpathian Jews were more traditional, since many of them had recently come to the district from Russia, Romania, and Galicia. Almost two-thirds of them lived in poor conditions in rural areas, though they made up 15.4% of the total population. Initially, there were few Hebrew schools in Ruthenia, and most Jewish parents, for economic and sociological reasons, chose to send their children to Ruthenian schools, where Jews made up 72% of the student bodies in 1920-1921 and instruction was in Czech and Magyar. At Zionist instigation, however, Hebrew elementary schools were founded, and soon a Hebrew gymnasium. The Czech government modestly invested in these schools. Unfortunately, Orthodox Jews and those who supported broader integration into Czechoslovakian society opposed these efforts, and *heder* and *yeshivah* schools remained important to the Orthodox and Hasidic communities. One of the accusations against the Jews in Ruthenia in the days before World War II was that their children had "filled the Czech state schools in the region."[7]

Culturally, Czechoslovakian Jews contributed significantly to literature and areas of broad intellectual endeavor. They were prominent in Czech, German, and Magyar literature, and some significant works with Jewish themes were published in Czechoslovakia. Franz Kafka's role in Czech German literature is unique, as is that of Max Brod.[8]

Jews also played an impressive role in Czech journalism, where they held important positions as writers and editors. They published a number of newspapers in Czechoslovakia in German, Czech, Magyar, and Yiddish. Zionists used the press as an important part of their campaign to win converts to their movement, though there were also an equal number of non-Zionist papers published by other Jewish political and religious factions.[9]

Jews had an important role in the Czechoslovakian economy, particularly in the banking, textile, food, and paper industries. In the 1930s it "was estimated that 30-40% of the total capital invested in Czechoslovakian industry ... was Jewish-owned."[10] According to 1921 statistics, 41.15% of the Jewish population, 145,814, were engaged in banking and commerce; 43,261 or 12.21% in agriculture and the fishing industry. The same census figures show that 53.74% owned their own businesses or homes, and nearly 20% held some type of private or public official position. In the context of Czechoslovakia's total population, these figures are less impressive, since 1930 census statistics show that of the total population Jews made up 4.21% of the country's property owners and 4.93% of its officials.[11]

The positive status of Jews in Czechoslovakian life had little impact on their fate in the aftermath of the Munich agreement in 1938. Cession of the Sudetenland to Germany at the Munich conference in the fall of 1938 stimulated a significant exodus of 17,000 Jews into the remainder of Czechoslovakia, Palestine, and elsewhere in Europe, Latin America, and the United States.[12]

Slovakian Jewry suffered when a pro-Nazi Slovakian state emerged and, as a result of the Vienna Accord, turned over portions of its territory and Ruthenia to Hungary. Budapest acquired about 42,000 of the regions' Jews.[13] Hitler's seizure of the remainder of Czechoslovakia in March 1939 saw Slovakia become a puppet state of Germany, while Germans created the Protectorate of Bohemia and Moravia to deal with other sections of its new satellite. Ruthenia became an integral part of Hungary.[14]

Each region now began to deal differently with its Jewish populations, and anti-Semitic policies were uneven and disorganized. In the summer of 1940, a more rigid pro-Nazi regime in Slovakia introduced a number of measures designed to eliminate Jews from Slovakian economic life. A Central Office for Economy (UHÚ — Ustredny Hospodársky Úrad), aided by a Center for Jews (Ústredňa Židov) or Judenrat, began to oversee the seizure of Jewish property. Simultaneously, plans were begun to deport Jews to labor camps, and later to death camps. Once the Slovak government completed its "Aryanization" program, it moved in early 1942 to try to cleanse Slovakia of its Jewish population. Despite protests by the Jewish community and the Vatican, the Slovakian government shipped 50,000 Jews to Auschwitz and Lublin, and by September 1942, according to official Slovak statistics, the Jewish population had dropped from 89,000 to 23,451.[15] Those who remained in Slovakia were shipped to labor camps at Sered, Novaky, and Vyhnia. Deportations to Poland and escape to Hungary slowly diminished this number, and on the eve of the Slovak uprising in August 1944, it is estimated that only 13,500 Jews were left in Slovakia. As a result of the uprising, German authorities began a new wave of deportations and persecutions that resulted in the death of thousands of Slovak Jews. In the end, almost 100,000 Slovakian Jews died in the Holocaust.[16]

Approximately 120,000 Jews lived in Bohemia and Moravia at the time of their German occupation in March 1939. This population, which had grown since the Munich and Vienna divisions of that country earlier, began to shrink as Jews began to flee to other parts of Europe to avoid Nazi persecution.

Consequently, by the end of 1939, only about 98,000 Jews remained in the Protectorate.[17] Initially, German leaders used the Czech government as its front for anti-Semitic laws. In time, however, anti-Jewish legislation came to mirror that of the Reich. Between June 1939 and the spring of 1940, German authorities introduced a number of laws that eliminated Jews from any role in the Protectorate's economic, professional, and social life, overseen by a Central Office for Jewish Emigration (Zentralstelle für jüdische Auswanderung). By the fall of 1939, Nazi officials began to deport Protectorate Jews in small numbers to Poland, and in the fall of 1941, 7,000 were shipped to the east in a new deportation program.[18]

German-Czech officials, however, sent most Protectorate Jews to a new concentration camp in northern Bohemia, Terezín (Theresienstadt). Over a three-and-a-half-year period, it is estimated that almost 80,000 went to Terezín, though it served principally as a transfer point to Auschwitz and other death camps. While it is difficult to be accurate, Jewish survivors in Bohemia and Moravia, including almost 8,500 Jews from Ruthenia, numbered about 24,000.[19]

Hungary obtained Ruthenia in two divisions — the southern portion, along with southeastern Slovakia, in the Vienna Award of November 2, 1938 and on March 15, 1939. The Hungarian census of 1941 stated that there were 78,087 Jews in its portions of Ruthenia. Hungary's move into World War II in 1941 coincided with efforts by pro-Nazi factions to adopt stringent tactics against the country's Jewish population. Consequently, the government implemented a program to send thousands of Jews to German camps in Galicia. Between 30,000 and 35,000 were arrested, many of them from Ruthenia and Slovakia, and about 18,000 were sent to Kamenets-Podolsk, where they were massacred on August 27-28, 1941. Others died in labor battalions on the eastern front.[20] Most Ruthenian Jews, however, survived until the spring of 1944, when German forces occupied Hungary and began to ship them to death camps in Poland. An estimated 8,500 to 15,000 Carpathian Jews survived the Holocaust.[21]

It is difficult to determine precisely the number of Jews in Czechoslovakia who lived through World War II, since in addition to those who acknowledged their ethnicity there were individuals included in statistics whom the Nazis racially classified as Jews and Jews who escaped death by being baptized. Ethnic religious Jews who survived totaled about 44,000, though there were several thousand more from the above classifications who also survived.[22]

At the end of the war, Jewish community reorganization came under the auspices of the Council of Jewish Communities in Bohemia and Moravia, and the Central Union of Jewish Communities in Slovakia. These groups had slowly begun to revive some Jewish communal activities when the Communists seized power in February 1948. Communists began to dominate most Jewish organizations, despite Zionist resistance. This, in conjunction with Israeli independence, prompted a mass migration of Czechoslovakian Jews that decimated the post-Holocaust population. Almost 26,000 Jews left the country within two years of the Communist takeover, after which the government halted these moves. Another 2,000 to 3,000 left in 1965, followed by 3,400 in late 1968. At that time, about 12,000 Jews remained scattered throughout Czechoslovakia.[23]

Notes

[1]Peter Meyer, "Czechoslovakia," in *The Jews in the Soviet Satellites*, ed. Peter Meyer, et al. (Syracuse, NY: Syracuse University Press, 1953), p. 49; *Hitler's Ten Year War against the Jews* (New York: Institute of Jewish Affairs of the American Jewish Congress/World Jewish Congress, 1943), p. 52.

[2]Malbone W. Graham, Jr., *New Governments of Central Europe* (New York: Henry Holt and Company, 1926), pp. 295-97; Václav L. Beneš, "Czechoslovak Democracy and Its Problems, 1918-1920, in *A History of the Czechoslovak Republic, 1918-1948*, ed. Victor S. Mamatey and Radomír Luža (Princeton, NJ: Princeton University Press, 1973), pp. 40-41; Bruno Blau, "Nationality among Czechoslovak Jewry," *Historia Judaica* X:2 (October 1948): 149-51; Egon Hostovsky, "The Czech-Jewish Movement," in *The Jews of Czechoslovakia*, Vol. II (New York and Philadelphia: Society for the History of Czechoslovak Jews and the Jewish Publication Society of America, 1971), pp. 148-54 (offers an interesting view of assimilationism among Czech Jewry). Similar assimilationist tendencies are discussed in Michael Anthony Riff's "Assimilation and Conversion in Bohemia: Secession from the Jewish Community in Prague, 1868-1917," Leo Baeck Institute, *Year Book*, XXVI (London: Secker & Warburg for the Leo Baeck Institute, 1981), pp. 73-87 passim; Meyer, "Czechoslovakia," p. 53.

[3]"Czechoslovakia," *Encyclopedia Judaica*, Vol. 5 (New York: The Macmillan Company, 1971), pp. 1188-89.

[4]Oskar K. Rabinowicz, "Czechoslovak Zionism: Analecta to a History," *Jews of Czechoslovakia*, Vol. II, pp. 19-20; Gustav Fleischmann, "The Religious Congregation, 1918-1938," Ibid., Vol. I, p. 269.

[5]Ibid., pp. 267-69, 295-99, 303-8; Hugo Stransky, "The Religious Life in Slovakia and Subcarpathian Ruthenia," *Jews of Czechoslovakia*, II, pp. 351-55; Livia Rothkirchen, "Slovakia, II: 1918-1938," *Jews of Czechoslovakia*, p. 103.

[6]*Hitler's Ten Year War against the Jews*, pp. 53-54; Blau, pp. 152-54; Stransky, pp. 355-56.

[7]Livia Rothkirchen, "Deep-Rooted Yet Alien: Some Aspects of the History of the Jews in Subcarpathian Ruthenia," *Yad Vashem Studies* XII (January 1977): 149-51, 161-63, 167; Aryeh Sole, "Subcarpathian Ruthenia: 1918-1938," *Jews of Czechoslovakia*, I, pp. 142-45; Stransky, pp. 366, 371, 374-75; Aryeh Sole, "Modern Hebrew Education in Subcarpathian Ruthenia," *Jews of Czechoslovakia*, II, pp. 401-39 passim. While this article provides some valuable facts on the evolution of Hebrew education in Ruthenia, it has no footnotes and takes something of an unscholarly approach to the question.

[8]Egon Hostovsky, "Participation in Modern Czech Literature," *Jews of Czechoslovakia*, I, pp. 441-48; Harry Zohn, "Participation in German Literature," *Jews of Czechoslovakia*, I, pp. 468-522 passim.

[9]Avigoor Dagan, "The Press," *Jews of Czechoslovakia*, I, p. 523.

[10]Joseph C. Pick, "The Economy," *Jews of Czechoslovakia*, II, pp. 359-438 passim. Pick goes into great detail discussing the role of Jews in every major industrial undertaking in interwar Czechoslovakia. His work is based on extensive research cited in his detailed bibliography at the end of his study; "Czechoslovakia," *Encyclopedia Judaica*, Vol. 5, pp. 1192.

[11]Meyer, "Czechoslovakia," *Jews in Soviet Satellites*, pp. 55-56.

[12]Kurt R. Grossman, "Refugees to and from Czechoslovakia," *Jews of Czechoslovakia*, II, pp. 571-74. Other articles in this volume on various aspects of Jewish emigration to and from Czechoslovakia during the Holocaust include Manfred George's "Refugees in Prague, 1933-1938," Ibid., pp. 582-88; Fini Brada, "Emigration to Palestine," Ibid., pp. 589-98; and Aaron Zwergbaum, "From Internment in Bratislava and Detention in Mauritius to Freedom," Ibid., pp. 599-654.

[13]Grossman, Ibid., pp. 577-78; Nora Levin, *The Holocaust: The Destruction of European Jewry, 1933-1945* (New York: Schocken Books, 1975), p. 529.

[14]Jorg K. Hoensch, "The Slovak Republic, 1939-1945," in Mamatey and Luža, pp. 275-76; Gotthold Rhode, "The Protectorate of Bohemia and Moravia, 1939-1945," Ibid., pp. 296-97.

[15]Livia Rothkirchen, "Vatican Policy and the 'Jewish Problem' in 'Independent Slovakia (1939-1945),' " *Yad Vashem Studies*, VI (Jerusalem, 1967), pp. 36-42; Meyer, "Czechoslovakia," p. 63.

[16]*Hitler's Ten Year War against the Jews*, pp. 64-65; Rothkirchen, "Vatican Policy," p. 51; Meyer, "Czechoslovakia," pp. 63-64. Two excellent accounts on Slovakian Jewry during the Holocaust are Yeshayahu Jelinek's "The 'Final Solution' — the Slovak Version," *East European Quarterly* IV:4 (January 1971): 431-41; and Ludovit Holotik's "The 'Jewish Problem' in Slovakia," *East European Quarterly* I:1 (March 1967): 31-37.

[17]Meyer, "Czechoslovakia," p. 61.

[18]*Hitler's Ten Year War against the Jews*, pp. 55-59; Meyer, "Czechoslovakia," pp. 61-62; Moses Moskowitz, "The Jewish Situation in the Protectorate of Bohemia-Moravia," *Jewish Social Studies* IV:1 (January 1942): 18-20, 23-28.

[19]Franz Hobler, "History and Sociology of the Terezin Ghetto," in *Historica Judaica*, ed. Guido Kisch (New York: Historica Judaica, n.d.), pp. 68-69.

[20]Randolph L. Braham, *The Politics of Genocide: The Holocaust in Hungary*, Vol. I (New York: Columbia University Press, 1981), pp. 145, 199, 204.

[21]Meyer, "Czechoslovakia," p. 64; Eugene Duschinsky, "Hungary," *Jews in Soviet Satellites*, p. 397; Rothkirchen, "Jews in Subcarpathian Ruthenia," pp. 178-79; "Subcarpathian Ruthenia," *Encyclopedia Judaica*, Vol. 15 (Jerusalem: Encyclopedia Judaica, 1971), p. 471; Randolph L. Braham, "The Kamenets Podolsk and Delvidek Massacres: Prelude to the Holocaust in Hungary," *Yad Vashem Studies*, IX (Jerusalem, 1973), p. 139.

[22]"Czechoslovakia," *Encyclopedia Judaica*, pp. 1199-1200; Meyer, "Czechoslovakia," pp. 66-68.

[23]"Czechoslovakia," *Encyclopedia Judaica*, pp. 1200-1201; Meyer, "Czechoslovakia," pp. 145-51.

BIBLIOGRAPHY

General Reference Works and Sources

318. Boháč, Antonín. **Obyvatelstvo v Československé Republice** (Population in the Czechoslovak Republic). Prague: (Čs. vlastivěda, II. r Národopis, 1), 1936. 96p.
This handbook contains basic facts and figures on the population in the Czechoslovak Republic after the census of 1930.

319. Boháč, Antonín. **Studie o populaci v Československé Republice** (A Study about Population in Czechoslavakia). I. Rok 1927 (The Year 1927). Population de la République Tchécoslovaque, études demographiques — I. Annes 1927. Prague: State Statistical Office; printed by Melantrich, 1928. 111p. 22 cartograms.
The author provides detailed information on demography in Czechoslovakia, including a large number of statistics, tables and maps. On pages 29-30 are data on birthrates of the individual nationalities in the country.

320. Czechoslovak Republic. Ministry of Foreign Affairs. **Les Minorités dans la République Tchécoslovaque: Notes concernant le "Memoire que les députés et sénateurs Allemands, elus le 18 et le 25 avril 1920 et faisant partie de l'union parlementaire Allemande de l'association des nationalités Tschécoslovaques ont présenté a la Ligue des Nations et qui traite de la violation des règlements sur la protection des minorités établis par le Traité Conclu le 10 septembre 1919 a Saint-Germain en Laye entre les puissances Alliées et Associées et la République Tchécoslovague."** Paris: Bureau d'Informations Politiques et Économiques du Ministère des Affaires Étrangères, 1921. 72p.
This is the Czechoslovak government's presentation of the constitutional and legal protection of minorities in Czechoslovakia. It is a direct response to criticism of Czechoslovak policies toward minorities, documenting that the country complies with international conventions concerning the treatment of national minorities.

321. **Nationality Policy in Czechoslovakia: Speeches by Dr. Hodža, the Premier, and Cabinet Ministers Messrs. Franke, Nečas, and Dérer in the Czechoslovak Parliament.** Czechoslovak Sources and Documents, no. 22. Prague: Orbis, 1938. 96p.
On November 17, 1937, Prime Minister Milan Hodža delivered a speech "On Nationality Policy" before the budgetary committee of the Chamber of Deputies. Three cabinet ministers presented the government's position on the nationality issue — Emil Franke on education, Jaromir Nečas on social relief, and Ivan Dérer on the Czechoslovak system of justice. This is the government's response to charges of discrimination made by the minorities.

322. Häufler, Vlastislav. **The Ethnographic Map of the Czech Lands, 1880-1970.** Prague: NČSAV, 1973. 100p. Maps.
This volume outlines ethnographic conditions based on statistical evidence and maps, ethnographic population changes between 1880 and 1930, revolutionary demographic changes during the years 1938-1947, and the demographic development up to 1970 and its perspectives. Included are a nationalities map of the Czech lands for 1880-1970 and a bibliography.

323.   Mazur, Arnošt. **Národnostní vývoj na území ČSSR se zvláštním zaměřením na Slezko a ostravskou průmyslovou oblast: Výběrová bibliografie** (The Evolution of Nationalities on the Territory of the Czechoslovak Socialist Republic with Special Focus on Silesia and the Ostrava Industrial Region: Selected Bibliography). Ostrava: profil, rozmn. MTZ, Opava, 1969. 649p.

With more than 6,000 entries related to nationalities living in Czechoslovakia (and Lusatian Sorbs in Germany) this selected bibliography has been intended as a heuristical aid to those who do research on the nationality problems and demographic and sociological research on the industrialized regions of the country. Most articles and books are annotated; other items are self-explanatory.

324.   Sobota, Emil. **Das tschechoslovakische Nationalitätenrecht**. Ins Deutsche übersetzt von Dr. J. Kalfus. Tschechoslovakische Quellen und Documente, no. 7. Prague: Orbis, 1931. 462p.

This is volume 7 of Czechoslovak sources and documents which present the government's official position on the legal status of nationalities in Czechoslovakia. It includes a lengthy analysis and a collection of documents on the status of nationalities and language rights in Czechoslovakia (pp. 179-461).

General Monographs and Articles

325.   Bosl, Karl. **Die Erste Tschechoslowakische Republik als multinationaler Parteienstaat**. Munich: R. Oldenbourg Verlag, 1979. 580p.

Containing papers presented at the 1977 and 1978 meetings of the Collegium Carolinum, this large and professionally significant book deals with basic problems of the party system, with the historical development of the parties, and with their ideological and national foundations. The problem of the Germans receives special attention. Tables presenting the composition of the Czechoslovak governments and election results round off this volume, which is not matched by any work of Czechoslovak historians.

326.   Brynda, Alois. **Protektorátní příslušnost a domovské právo podle vlád. nařízení ze dne 11. ledna 1940 Sbírky a norem recipovaných** (Protectorate Citizenship and Domicile Rights According to the Decree of January 11, 1940 Collection and Norms. Collection of Legal Discourses, vol. 35). Prague: Linhart, 1940. 100p.

This is an analysis of laws pertaining to the citizenship of people living in the Protectorate Bohemia and Moravia, their domicile rights and obligations. Also considered are the Slovak domicile rights and German and Hungarian citizenship.

327.   Chmelař, Josef. **Politické rozvrstvení Československa** (Political Divisions in Czechoslovakia). Časové otázky (Current Questions), vol. 4. Prague: Orbis, 1926. 89p. Also in German *Die politische Gliederung der Tschechoslowakei*.

This is a brief discussion of the origins and development of political parties and minorities in Czechoslovakia. It contains basic data, including information on the strength of all political parties representing the various nationalities in Czechoslovakia.

328.   Fischer, Rudolf. **Národnostní vývoj na severní Moravě od roku 1848** (The Evolution of Nationalities in Northern Moravia since 1848). Olomouc: published by the author, 1932. 102p.

Northern Moravia, inhabited by a mixed population, is the subject of this study, which traces the changes in the number of Czech-, German-, and Polish-speaking people in the area.

329. Hájek, M., and Staňková, O. **Národnostní otázka v lidově demokratickém Československu** (The Nationality Question in People's Democratic Czechoslovakia). Prague: Státní nakladatelství politické literatury, 1956. 71p.

This is a Marxist analysis of the nationality question in Czechoslovakia under Communist rule, It treats the developments affecting national minorities in the country since the end of World War II.

330. Krofta, Kamil. **Narodnostní vývoj zemí československých** (The Ethnic Development in the Czechoslovak Lands). Prague: Orbis, 1934. 104p.

This is the fourth volume in the series on nationality questions published by the Czechoslovak Society for the Study of Nationality Questions. The work presents a "Czechoslovak" point of view on the evolution of relations among the ethnic groups in the historical lands—Slovakia and Ruthenia.

331. Mamatey, Victor S., and Luža, Radomír, eds. **A History of the Czechoslovak Republic, 1918-1948**. Princeton, NJ: Princeton University Press, 1973. xi, 534p.

Although several of the essays in this work discuss national minorities in Czechoslovakia, the contribution by Ludvík Němec deals specifically with the "Solution of the Minority Problem" (pp. 416-27). There are statistics and other data pertaining to national minorities and their post-World War II treatment, as well as an extensive bibliography.

332. Perman, Dagmar. **The Shaping of the Czechoslovak State: Diplomatic History of the Boundaries of Czechoslovakia, 1914-1920**. Leiden: E. J. Brill, 1962. v, 339p.

A detailed study of the formation of the Czechoslovak Republic, the work is largely based on archival materials and documents. It is a pioneering effort on the subject of incorporation of national minorities into the state. The book includes a bibliography, two maps, and an index.

333. Peška, Zdeněk. **Kulturní samospráva národních menšin. S předmluvou Dr. Kamila Krofty** (Cultural Self-Government of National Minorities. With an Introduction by Dr. Kamil Krofta). Prague: Orbis, 1933. 76p.

Published as the first volume on "Nationality Questions" by the Czechoslovak Society for the Study of Minority Questions, this work by a Czech jurist discusses the principles of nationalities' self-government before and after World War I. It describes and analyzes political and cultural self-government of national minorities in Czechoslovakia.

334. Peška, Zdeněk. **Národnostní menšiny a Československo** (National Minorities and Czechoslovakia). Bratislava: Komenského Universita, 1932. 233p.

This is a Czech viewpoint on the status of national minorities in Czechoslovakia during the first decade of the state's existence. it contains statistical data and their interpretation. Published as volume 35 of the Library of the Law College, Comenius University, Bratislava.

335. Raschhofer, Hermann, and Wierer, Rudolf. "Die nationale Frage in der Tschechoslowakei seit 1918." *Der Donauraum* 7:2-3 (1962): 82-99.

The nationality question in Czechoslovakia after the adoption of the constituion of 1960 is discussed by two legal scholars. The article points to discrimination of national minorities — specifically Germans — in Czechoslovakia. The second essay concerns itself with the political and legal analysis of the status of national minorities in Czechoslovakia since 1918 and how the nationalities problem affected politics of the country before and after World War II.

336. Sándor, László, ed. **Ez volt a Sarló: Tanulmányok, emlékezések, dokumentumok** This Was the Sarló: Studies, Reminiscences, Documents). Budapest: Kossuth Publishers, 1978. 431p.

Sixteen authors analyze various aspects of the Sarló movement in interwar Czechoslovakia, starting from preoccupation with folksongs ("regölés") between 1925 and 1928, through preaching interdependence and cooperation of east Europeans (1928-1931), to collaboration with the Czechoslovakian radical Left (1931-1934). They claim that two major problems had been left unresolved by the Hungarian War of Independence, 1848-1849 — land reform and the nationalities.

337. Sobota, Emil. **Státní příslušnost, národnost, rasa** (State Nationality, Nationality, Race). Edited and with introduction and notes by Emil Sobota. Library of Legal Actualities of Czech-Moravian Kompas, vol. 31. Prague: Kompas, 1939. viii, 88p.

The Nazi occupation of Bohemia and Moravia in March 1939 created a new legal situation for the Czechs and the Germans. This work points out the difference between nationality, state citizenship, and race under German law and how it affected the inhabitants of the Protectorate Bohemia and Moravia.

338. Sobota, Emil. **Co to byl Protektorát?** (What Was the Protectorate?). Prague: Kvasnička & Hampl, 1946. 163p.

A colloquium of essays examines the language law, the solution of the nationality and racial question, and anti-Semitism during the existence of the Protectorate Bohemia and Moravia (1939-1945). The Czechs were subjects but not citizens of the Third Reich, and Jews were deported.

339. Sobota, Emil. **Národnostní právo československé** (Czechoslovak Nationalities Law). Collection of Works on Law and National Economy, vol. 34. Brno: Barvič a Novotný, 1927. 215p.

A Czechoslovak legal expert discusses the extent of the law relating to nationalities, its historical development, and how it was applied in Czechoslovakia in the 1920s. The book gives an overview of legal sources.

340. Sobota, Emil. **Národnostní autonomie v Československu?** (Autonomy for Nationalities in Czechoslovakia?). Prague: Orbis, 1938. xi, 124p.

This represents volume 11 of publications on the nationality questions published by the Czechoslovak Society for the Study of Nationality Questions in Prague. It compares and contrasts the nationality question in Austria-Hungary and Czechoslovakia, discusses the legal status of the German minority in Czechoslovakia, and rejects the proposals of the latter for an autonomy within the existing state on the grounds that it is a "national" and not a "nationalities" state according to its constitution.

Germans

General Reference Material

341. **Die Deutschen in der Tschechoslowakei 1933-1947: Dokumentensammlung.** Ed. by Václav Král. Prague: Československá akademie věd, 1964. 663p.

A documentary collection on the activities of Germans in Czechoslovakia during the years 1933-1947. Proceeding from the "collective guilt" theory, these materials have been published as part of the government's policy toward Germany and justification for the expulsion of the Sudeten Germans after World War II. The editor is a well-known Communist historican who follows the Soviet line.

342. **Dokumentation der Vertreibung der Deutschen aus Ost-Mitteleuropa.** Bundesrepublik Deutschland. Bundesministerium für Vertriebene, Flüchtlinge und Kriegsgeschädigte.Edited by Theodor Schieder. Vol. IV, 1-2: **Die Vertreibung der deutschen Bevölkerung aus der Tschechoslowakei. 2. Beiheft: Ein Tagebuch aus Prag 1945-46** by Margarete Schell. Bonn, 1957. 279p.

This is a very perceptive and persuasive presentation of events affecting the Germans in Bohemia after the arrival of the Czechoslovak government in May 1945. It is a well-documented German viewpoint and includes several illustrations.

343. **Mnichov v dokumentech** (Munich in Documents). 2 vols. Prague: Státní nakladatelství politické literatury, 1958. Vol. I, 350p.; Vol. II, 433p.

An extremely valuable collection of documents related to the Munich conference and the settlement of the Sudeten question in 1938. The sources of documents are identified, and those of non-Czechoslovak origin (British, French, German, and others) are in Czech translation. Notes provide background history and/or additional information.

344. Nittner, Ernst, ed. **Dokumente zur Sudetendeutschen Frage 1916-1967.** Überarbeitete und ergänzte Neuauflage der "Dokumente zur Sudetendeutschen Frage 1918-1959." 2nd rev. ed. Munich: Ackermann-Gemeinde, 1967. 383p.

This chronological collection of documents—speeches, declarations, reports, and statements—pertains to the status of the German minority in Czechoslovakia. The work was sponsored by the Ackermann-Gemeinde, an organization of the Sudeten Germans expelled from Czechoslovakia, whose representative, D. Hans Schütz, wrote the foreword to this collection.

345. Sigl, Christian. **Quellen und Dokumente: Ein Tatsachenbericht über die Lage im sudetendeutschen Gebiet und über die Entwicklung der tschechoslowakischen Innenpolitik in der Zeit vom 24. April bis zum 12. Juni 1938.** Vienna and Leipzig: Wilhelm Braumüller, 1938. 85p.

Expressing pro-Nazi sympathies and presenting the case of the Sudeten German party, this publication documents the culmination of the nationality problem in Czechoslovakia in the fateful year 1938.

346. Turnwald, Wilhelm K., comp. **Documents on the Expulsion of the Sudeten Germans.** Translated by Gerda Johannsen. Edited by the Association for the Protection of Sudeten German Interests. Foreword to the English Edition by F. A. Voigt. Munich:

Munich University Press, 1953. xxix, 308p. Originally published in German: *Dokumente zur Austreibung der Sudeten-deutschen*. Einleitung und Bearbeitung bei Dr. Wilhelm Turnwald. n.p.: Im Selbstverlag der Arbeitsgemeinschaft zur Wahrung Sudetendeutscher Interessen, 1952. 590p.

In this compilation of documents, events are described by eyewitnesses or persons directly involved. These reports give a general view of what happened in the Sudeten German areas after May 1945. The expulsion of the Sudeten German national group and the theory of "collective guilt" are rejected, and the recognition of the right to a homeland of the expellees and the punishment of the culprits are demanded. The compiler's introductory essay discusses the history of Czech-German relations in Czechoslovakia. The documents include the texts of the "Kaschau Statute" of April 5, 1945, and the Decree of the President of Czechoslovakia of June 21, 1945, concerning the confiscation of the private property of the Sudeten Germans.

History and General Studies

347. Brosz, Paul. **Die Karpaten-Deutschen in der Slowakei 1918-1945**. Stuttgart: Arbeitsgemeinschaft der Karpatendeutschen aus der Slowakei, 1972. 72p. Illus. Maps.

Within the framework of Slovak history, this volume narrates the story of the Germans living in the province and later the Slovak state. The Germans maintained their own cultural, religious, and political organizations and were involved in the historical events of Slovakia. Included are bibliographical references.

348. Brügel, Johann Wolfgang. **Czechoslovakia before Munich: The German Minority Problem and British Appeasement Policy**. Cambridge, MA: Cambridge University Press, 1973. xiii, 334p.

A shortened version of *Tschechen und Deutsche 1918-1938*, the book examines two decades of Czech-German relations, from 1918 until the Munich agreement. It describes and anlyzes both domestic and foreign policy developments regarding Czechoslovakia in general and the German minority in particular. Although pointing out mistakes made by the Czechoslovak government in its attitude toward the German minority, the author blames the Sudeten Germans and the British appeasement policy for the collapse of the Czechoslovak state. A bibliography and an index are included.

349. Campbell, Gregory F. **Confrontation in Central Europe: Weimar Germany and Czechoslovakia**. Chicago: The University of Chicago Press, 1957. xvi, 383p.

Within the broader context of Czechoslovak-German relations, the book examines the status of the Czechs and Slovaks before World War I and the attitudes of Sudeten Germans toward the Czechoslovak state during the years 1918-1933. The work is based on extensive use of documentary materials and secondary sources. Notes, a bibliographical essay, and an index allow further study of the problem of the German minority in interwar Czechoslovakia.

350. **Ein Leben, drei Epochen**. Festschrift für Hans Schütz zum 70. Geburtstag. Im Auftrag der Ackermann-Gemeinde herausgegeben und eingeleitet von Horst Glassl und Otfrid Pustejovsky. Munich: Ackermann-Gemeinde, 1971. 767p.

To commemorate the seventieth birthday of Hans Schütz, one of the leaders of the Sudeten German Christian Democrats (expellees living in the Federal Republic of Germany), this volume presents addresses, essays, and lectures by some 38 scholars and public personalities dealing with geography, history, politics, culture, religion, and other aspects of life of the Germans in Czechoslovakia.

351. Götz, Wolfgang, ed. **Die Sudetendeutsche Frage: Entstehung, Entwicklung und Lösungsversuch 1918-1973. Analysen und Dokumente**. Mainz: Hase & Köhler Verlag, 1974. 230p.

This publication contains essays by Hans Jürgen Wünschel, Erich Röper, Hartmut Soell, and Eugen Lemberg discussing relations between the Czechs, the Slovaks, and the Sudeten Germans in Bohemia and Moravia, the events leading to Munich and the consequence of the latter, the stand taken by the German Social Democratic party on the Sudeten German question, and the history of the Sudeten Germans before and after their expulsion from Czechoslovakia. Several documents, a map, statistical data, and a bibliography are included in the book.

352. Jahn, Egbert K. **Die Deutschen in der Slowakei in den Jahren 1918-1929: Ein Beitrag zur Nationalitätenproblematik**. Veröffentlichungen des Collegium Carolinum, vol. 25. Munich: Oldenbourg Verlag, 1971. 186p.

The political attitude of the German population in Slovakia towards the Hungarian and the Czechoslovak state is described, and particular attention is paid to the encounter between German nationalism and Czechoslovak patriotism. The antagonism of nationalities is considered and interpreted from various points of view, touching on sociological, socioeconomic, and sociopolitical questions. The work is well annotated and based on comprehensive archive studies.

353. Jaksch, Wenzel. **Europe's Road to Potsdam**. Translated and edited by Kurt Glaser. New York and London: praeger, 1963. xxiv, 468p.

This work by the leader of the Sudeten German Social Democratic party, originally published in German (*Europas Weg nach Potsdam*, 1958. 522p.), takes a long-range view on the history of Central Europe—an area of intermingled nationalities. Analyzing the Czechoslovak government policies with respect to national minorities, most specifically Sudeten Germans, the author shows how the road to Munich was followed by the road to Potsdam. Jaksch takes a critical view of the expulsion of Germans from Czechoslovakia. This edition contains valuable explanations by the translator and editor in addition to notes, photographs, maps, documents, and an index.

354. Jung, Rudolf. **Die Tschechen: Tausend Jahre deutsch-tschechischer Kampf**. Berlin: Verlag Volk und Reich, 1937. 246p.

Rudolf Jung, a Sudeten German Nazi, discusses the thousand-year-old struggle between the Czechs and the Germans in central Europe. The principal focus is on the politics and politicians of the Czechoslovak Republic and the German proposals for the solution of the Czech-German problem in Czechoslovakia. There are tables, statistical data, maps, and illustrations in the book.

355. Kozauer, Nikolaus J. "The Carpatho-Ukraine between the Two World Wars; with Special Emphasis on the German Population." Ph.D. dissertation, Rutgers University, 1964. 429p. Illus.

The general situation in Ruthenia and the German minority in particular are described and analyzed in this thesis. It contains data on politics and economics in the province.

356. Lembers, Eugen, and Rhode, Gotthold, eds. **Das deutsch-tschechische Verhältnis seit 1918**. Stuttgart, Berlin, Cologne, Mainz: W. Kohlhammer, 1969. 139p.

These are revised papers of a conference sponsored by the Deutsche Gesellschaft für Osteuropakunde in 1968. The articles on Czech-German relations since the establishment of Czechoslovakia in 1918 are of uneven quality. A bibliography is appended.

357. Luža, Radomír. **The Transfer of the Sudeten Germans: A Study of Czech-German Relations, 1933-1962**. New York: New York University Press, 1964. xxv, 365p.

Written from a Czechoslovak nationalist point of view and accepting the "collective guilt" theory, this book describes and analyzes the Czechoslovak-German relations since Hitler's rise to power. Using Czechoslovak statistics and other data, it provides details on the transfer of the Sudeten Germans from Czechoslovakia after World War II. An extensive bibliography is attached.

358. Molisch, Paul. **Die sudetendeutsche Freiheitsbewegung in den Jahren 1918-1919**. Vienna and Leipzig: Wilhelm Braumüller, 1932. vii, 191p.

Paul Molisch, librarian at the University of Vienna, presents a detailed history of the Sudeten Germans' independence movement in the years 1918-1919 and how it was suppressed by the Czechs. This is a standard work from the German nationalist viewpoint. It also contains a name index.

359. Mühlberger, Josef. **Zwei Völker in Böhmen: Beitrag zu einer nationalen, historischen und geistesgeschichtlichen Strukturanalyse**. Munich: Bogen-Verlag, 1973. 300p.

This history of the Czechs and Germans in Bohemia focuses on the national, spiritual, and cultural trends among the Czechs and Germans in the province from the arrival of the latter until their expulsion after World War II. The work shows cultural similarities and mutual influences of the two nationalities as well as the effect of movements such as humanism, reformation, renaissance, and nationalism, and international events.

360. **Německá otázka a Československo (1938-1961): Sborník statí** (The German Question and Czechoslovakia [1938-1961]: A Colloquium). Bratislava: Vydavatelstvo Slovenskej Akadémie Vied, 1962. 291p. (Summaries in German and English).

This symposium of essays was written by Czech and Slovak Communist historians and published by the Slovak Academy of Sciences in Slovak. It deals with the various aspects of the German question during the years 1938-1961. Among the topics are the transfer of Germans from Czechoslovakia, their activity in West Germany, and their alleged "revanchism." A name index is included.

361. Pozorny, Reinhard. **Deutsche Schutzarbeit im Sudetenland: Die Tätigkeit des Deutschen Kulturverbandes 1918-1938**. Vienna: Österreichische Landsmannschaft, 1974. iv, 51p.

This small volume describes the many and various activities of German cultural organizations and the German intellectual life in Czechoslovakia during the interwar years.

362. Preidel, Helmut, ed. **Die Deutschen in Böhmen und Mähren: Ein historischer Rückblick**. Gräfelfing, Bavaria: E. Ganz, 1952. 392p.

This is a symposium of articles reflecting the Sudeten German viewpoint on the history of the Germans in the Czech lands. The quality of the account varies. Bibliography.

363. Rabl, Kurt. **Das Ringen um das sudetendeutsche Selbstbestimmungsrecht 1918/19: Materialien und Dokumente.** Munich: Verlag Robert Lerche, 1958. 245p.

This is the third volume of the historical-philological works published under the sponsorship of the Munich-based Collegium Carolinum, a research institute for Sudeten German questions. It is a collection of materials and documents relating to the denial of the right of self-determination of the Sudeten Germans in the Czech lands in 1918-1919. This is an excellent source of information on the subject, including an extensive bibliography and a name index.

364. Turnwald, Wilhelm K. **Renascence or Decline of Central Europe: The Sudeten German-Czech Problem.** Translated by Gerda Johannsen. Munich: University Press Dr. C. Wolf & Sohn, 1954. 89p.

A study by a Sudeten German historian of the phases of German-Czech coexistence during the centuries, the national problem in Austria-Hungary, the Paris peace accord that become a source of discord, deceit by Eduard Beneš, causes and consequences of the Munich settlement, Beneš's eastern orientation, and the expulsion of Sudeten Germans. Statistics and footnotes.

365. Winter, Eduard. **Tausend Jahre Geisteskampf im Sudetenraum.** 2nd ed. Salzburg and Leipzig: Otto Müller Verlag, 1938. 442p.

The author, a Sudeten German historian and theologian, concentrates on the historical and religious developments in Bohemia and Moravia from the arrival of Christianity up to the 1930s. This scholarly study points out the conflicts and cooperation between the Czechs and the Germans, their ideologies, traditions, and political movements. It shows the similarities of their cultures and documents that new radical religious and political movements emerged among the Czechs earlier than among the Germans. An extensive bibliography is included.

366. Wiskemann, Elizabeth. **Czechs and Germans: A Study of the Struggle in the Historic Provinces of Bohemia and Moravia.** London and New York: Oxford University Press, 1938; 2nd ed., 1967. viii, 299p. Maps.

This is a documented study of the 1919 settlement concerning Czechoslovakia and the ensuing problems and conflicts between the Czechs and the Germans living in the historic provinces (Bohemia, Moravia, and Austrian Silesia). It presents a historical background for the establishment of the Czechoslovak Republic and the cultural developments among the two nations living in the heart of Europe.

Politics, Government, Law

367. Brügel, Johann W., ed. **Ludwig Czech. Arbeitsführer und Staatsmann.** Mit Beiträgen von Angelica Balabanoff [et al.]. Vienna: Verlag der Wiener Volksbuchhandlung, 1960. 200p.

A biographical account of Ludwig Czech (1870-1942), the leader of the Sudeten German Social Democratic party in Czechoslovakia until 1938, by a Sudeten German living in the United Kingdom. A party member himself, the author describes the "activist" policy of the political party in Czechoslovakia.

368. César, Jaroslav, and Černý, Bohumil. **Politika německých buržoasních stran v Československu v letech 1918 až 1938** (The Politics of the German Bourgeois Parties in Czechoslovakia during the Years 1918-1938). 2 vols. Prague: NČSAV, 1962. Vol. I, 512p.; vol. II, 584p.

A Marxist analysis of the activities, strengths, and orientation of the Sudeten German middle-class political parties in Czechoslovakia during the existence of the First Republic (1918-1938).

369. Chmelař, Josef. **The German Problem in Czechoslovakia**. Czechoslovak Sources and Documents, no. 14. Prague: Orbis, 1936. 96p.

This is an official presentation of the Czechoslovak government's position on the status of the German minority and its demands in Czechoslovakia. The work was translated from German and was also published in French in 1936.

370. Fischer, Josef; Patzak, Vaclay; and Perth, Vincent. **Ihr Kampf; die wahren Ziele der Sudetendeutschen Partei**. Karlsbad: Verlagsanstalt "Graphia," 1937. 139p.

An account of the clandestine activities of the leaders of the Sudeten German party during the years 1933-1937 by their opponents. It reflects the turmoil in the Sudeten area of Czechoslovakia prior to the culmination of the crisis.

371. Goldmann, Rüdiger. **Die sudetendeutsche Frage auf der Pariser Friedenskonferenz**. Publication of the Sudeten German Archive in Munich. Munich: Fides Verlagsgesellschaft, 1971. 140p.

Based on a wide selection of sources, this work shows the two tracks of Czech policy concerning the Germans in Czechoslovakia. The author links the Bohemian question in the Austrian monarchy with the Sudeten German question in Czechoslovakia, revealing the hyposcrisy of Czechoslovak policy. Following an account of the prehistory of the problem, in which the Allies' attitudes are dealt with, is an analysis of the peace conference in which it is shown that St. Germain "was no basis for the future."

372. Hilf, Rudolf. **Deutsche und Tschechen: Bedeutung und Wandlungen einer Nachbarschaft in Mitteleuropa**. Opladen: Leske, 1973. 138p.

Hilf, one of the leaders of the expelled Sudeten Germans, analyzes the relationships between the Czechs and the Germans in their historical setting, beginning with the pre-World War I situation and ending with the status, ambitions, and views held by the expellees living outside Czechoslovakia. This is one of the moderate voices calling for reconciliation between the two nations. A bibliography is included.

373. Lodgman von Auen, Rudolph, ed. **Deutschböhmen**. Berlin: Ullstein Verlag, 1919. 290p.

The editor of this symposium was the leader of the Germans living in Bohemia who established their own governments in areas inhabited by Germans. He left for Germany, where he led an unsuccessful fight for the Sudeten German cause based on the claim to national self-determination.

374. Paul, Ernst, and Werner, Emil. **Was nicht in den Geschichtsbüchern steht: Ruhm und Tragik der sudetendeutschen Arbeiter-Bewegung**. 3 vols. Munich: Verlag "Die Brücke," 1972.

This work, consisting of three slim volumes, comes mostly from the pen of Ernst Paul, a Sudeten and Federal German Social Democrat. Emil Werner contributed only to the first volume. These volumes depict the national, political, and social struggle of the Sudeten German working-class movement in the Austrian monarchy and in Czechoslovakia. The manifold connections with Czechs, Jews, and Poles become visible, pointing to the interlocking of organizations and problems. The book shows the engagement of the Sudeten German working-class movement and its leaders for the cause of German nationality and social justice.

375. Peters, Gustav. **Der neue Herr von Böhmen, eine Untersuchung der politischen Zukunft der Tschechoslowakei**. Berlin: Deutsche Rundschau, G.m.b.H., 1927. 134p.

A well-written, critical study on the new power relationship between Czechs and Germans in the Czech lands from the German viewpoint. The former ruling nation has become a national majority.

376. Prinz, Friedrich. **Beneš, Jaksch und die Sudetendeutschen**. Stuttgart: Seliger-Archiv, 1975. 76p.

Following a brief historical background of the Sudeten question, the author examines the plans by the Czechoslovak government-in-exile, headed by Eduard Beneš (1940-1945), and the latter's protracted negotiations with the leader of the Sudeten German Social Democrats-in-exile, Wenzel Jaksch, which ended in a complete breakdown of communications. Political and ideological aspects are analyzed, and the notes are extremely valuable.

377. Raschhofer, Hermann. **Die Sudetenfrage: Ihre völkerrechtliche Entwicklung vom ersten Weltkrieg bis zur Gegenwart**. Munich: Isar Verlag, 1953. 310p.

This is an analysis of the events influencing the status of Sudeten Germans in 1918, 1938, and 1945 from the legal and nationalist German point of view by an expellee from Czechoslovakia. Biographical footnotes are included.

378. Schaumann, Werner. **Die gewaltsame Vertschechung des deutschen Igellandes**. Vienna and Leipzig: Wilhelm Braumüller Verlag, 1938. x, 127p. 4 maps.

This is one of the Nazi propaganda publications published under the editorship of Karl Hermann Frank. It is designed to prove the Czechization of the Sudeten Germans by the Czechoslovak government. The pamphlet appeared in January of the critical year 1938 and contains seven statistical tables.

379. Schmid, Karin. **Staatsangehörigkeitsprobleme der Tschechoslowakei: Eine Untersuchung sowie Dokumente zur Staatsangehörigkeit der dortigen Volkszugehörigen**. Berlin: Berlin-Verlag, 1979. 133p.

Schmid deals with the acquisition and loss of citizenship in Czechoslovakia, the German minority in that country, its legal status, and the laws related to it. A comparison is made with the situation in the Federal Republic of Germany. A bibliography is appended.

380. Smelser, Ronald M. **The Sudeten Problem 1933-1938: Volkstumspolitik and the Formulation of Nazi Foreign Policy**. Middletown, CT: Wesleyan University Press; Folkstone, England: Dawson, 1975. x, 324p.

Complete with extensive documentation and a bibliography, this is a scholarly study of the role played by Sudeten Germans in the formulation of Nazi foreign policy during the years 1933-1938. It disputes some of the misconceptions about the Sudeten Germans' struggle for autonomy.

381. **Die Sudetenfrage in europäischer Sicht: Bericht über die Vorträge und Ausprachen der wissenschaftlichen Fachtagung des Collegium Carolinum in München-Grünwald am 1.-3. Juni 1959.** Munich: Verlag Robert Lerche, 1962. 281p.

Written by members of several different nationalities, this symposium of papers examines the various aspects of the Sudeten German question in European politics, past and present. All the contributors express viewpoints sympathetic to the expelled national minority.

382. Vorbach, Kurt. **200,000 Sudetendeutsche zuviel! Der tschechische Vernichtungskampf gegen 3.5 Millionen Sudetendeutsche und seine volkspolitischen Auswirkungen.** Munich: Deutscher Volksverlag, 1936. 384p.

This is a German nationalist propaganda directed against the Czechoslovak Republic and its treatment of the German national minority both in Sudetenland and in Slovakia. Several tables with statistical data are attached to the narrative, which tries to prove discrimination against the minority and the policy of "Czechization" pursued by the government of Czechoslovakia. Attached is a short bibliography of publications dealing with the incorporation of the Sudeten Germans into Czechoslovakia and Czech-German relations.

Religion, Culture, Education

383. Donat, Heinrich. **Die deutschen Katholiken in der tschechoslowakischen Republik: Eine Sammlung von Beiträgen zur geistigen und religiösen Lage des Katholizismus und des Deutschtums.** Munich: Aufstieg Verlag, 1970. 360p.

This is a reprint edition of a work published originally in 1934, in which a whole series of articles gives expert information on the German Catholics in prewar Czechoslovakia, their church, charitable, cultural, and national activities, as well as the attitude of the host country toward them. This new edition was necessary because the original had become very rare and is witness to the real status of the Germans in Czechoslovakia, correcting many of the biased pronouncements of the postwar period.

384. Hudak, Adalbert. **Die Karpatendeutschen: Das deutsche Schulwesen und die Tätigkeit des Deutschen Kulturverbandes in der Slowakei 1918 bis 1945.** Vienna: Österreichische Landsmannschaft, 1975. 52p. Maps.

An account of the German educational system and the German cultural society in Slovakia during the itnerwar and war period. The activities of the Kulturverband in Prague are discussed, and maps show the location of the Carpatho-German centers. Bibliography.

385. Hudak, Adalbert, and Guzsak, Ladislaus. **Karpatendeutsche Lebensbilder: Der karpatendeutsche Beitrag zum europäischen Geistesleben.** Erlangen: A. Hudak im Selbstverlag, 1971. 114p.

This biography of Germans who used to live in the Carpathian Mountains and in Slovakia shows their contribution to the development and culture of the areas they inhabited and their intellectual-cultural life. Bibliography.

386. Steinhübl, Josef. **Mein leben: Kampf eines katholischen Pfarrers für den Glauben und das Deutschtum in the Slowakei.** Stuttgart: Hilfsbund karpatendeutscher Katholiken, 1975. 160p.

Within the framework of historical and political developments in Slovakia during the years 1918-1955, a Catholic priest tells of his personal experiences that were affected by the many political changes, including several years in a prison camp. The book contains 47 photographs, several documents, and two maps.

387. **Sudetenland: Böhmen, Mähren, Schlesien: ein Bildband der Heimat mit 217 Fotographien/kultur- und kunstgeschichtlich.** Einleitung von Viktor Aschenbrenner. Frankfurt: Weidlich; Umschau-Verlag (in Kommision), 1976. 23p., (120)p. Illus. Map.

Description and pictures of places that used to be inhabited by Germans in the Czech lands of Czechoslovakia. The photographs show the art and culture of the people who lived in the area.

Hungarians

388. Arató, Endre. **Political Differentiation in the Hungarian Population of Czechoslovakia in the post-World War I Years.** Studia Historica, no. 122. Budapest: Akadémiai Kiadó, 1975. 31p.

A Hungarian historian's analysis of the political differentiation of Hungarians living in Czechoslovakia after World War I. The author emphasizes the activity of the Marxist groups in Slovakia as well as the role of Hungarians in the foundation of the unified Communist party of Czechoslovakia in 1921.

389. Arató, Entre. **A magyar—cseh—slovak viszony ötven éve** (Hungarians in Czechoslovakia). Budapest: Kossuth Könyvkiado, 1969. 141p.

This study deals with the history of the dismemberment of the Austro-Hungarian monarchy and the incorporation of a Hungarian minority into Czechoslovakia, with emphasis on the status of the Hungarians in the latter country since World War II. It is based largely on Hungarian and Czech secondary sources listed in the attached bibliography.

390. Czanda, Sandor. **V spoločnej vlasti: študie o politickom, spoločenskom, kultúrnom a hospodárskom živote občanov madiarskej národnosti v Československu** (In Common Fatherland: Study of Political, Social, Cultural and Economic Life of Citizens of Hungarian Nationality in Czechoslovakia). Translated by helena Szászová and Valeria Hamzová. Bratislava: Pravda, 1975. 318p.

This study on the political, social, cultural, and economic aspects of life of the Hungarian minority in Czechoslovakia was translated into Slovak from the Hungarian original, *Közös hazában* (Bratislava: Pravda, 1972). It reflects official government views and policies.

391. Hoensch, Jörg K. **Der ungarische Revisionismus und die Zerschlagung der Tschechoslowakei.** Tübingen: J.C.B. Mohr (Paul Siebeck), 1967. xiv, 323p.

A documented study of the Hungarian revisionist movement following the signing of the Treaty of Trianon (1920). Regarding Czechoslovakia, the Vienna Award (1938) represented a success of Hungarian foreign policy and was followed by the seizure of Ruthenia in March 1939. There are two maps, sources, and an index.

392. Houdek, Fedor. **Vznik Hranic Slovenska** (Genesis of the Boundaries of Slovakia). Bratislava: Prudy, 1931. 412p. Maps.

Houdek provides a detailed study on the establishment of the boundaries between Slovakia and Hungary and, thus, on the incorporation of national minorities into the eastern part of the Czechoslovak state. Sources are listed.

393. **Hungarians in Czechoslovakia.** New York: Research Institute for Minority Studies on Hungarians Attached to Czechoslovakia and Carpatho-Ruthenia, 1959. 166p.

This work examines the legal status and political, economic, social, cultural, and religious conditions of the Hungarian minority in Czechoslovakia. It reports on the treatment of Hungarians in Czechoslovakia after World War II and on irredentist tendencies among them.

394. Janics, Kalman. **Czechoslovak Policy and the Hungarian Minority, 1945-1948.** Introduction by Byula Illyes. An English version adapted from the Hungarian by Stephen Borsody. War and Society in East Central Europe: The Effects of World War II, vol. IX. New York: Social Science Monographs, 1982. 240p. Distributed by Columbia University Press.

This is an English translation of a work written in Hungarian by a medical doctor and sociologist living in retirement in one of Slovakia's still predominantly Hungarian regions. It is the most exhaustive study, written from the point of view of the Hungarian minority living in Czechoslovakia, about the treatment accorded to the group during the years 1945-1948. Additional data are given in the "Epilogue" as is information on the status of the Hungarian minority in Czechoslovakia up to 1980.

395. Kovacs, Endre, and Novotný, J. **Madǎři a my; z dějin madǎrsko-československých vztahů** (Hungarians and We; from the History of Hungarian-Czechoslovak Relations). Prague: Státní nakladatelství politiké literatury, 1959. 313p.

This is a revised translation from the Hungarian *Magyar-csech történelmi kapcsolatok* (Kozoktasugyi Kiadovallalat, 1952). It is a Marxist interpretation of Hungarian-Czechoslovak relations and history, with illustrated text.

396. Kramer, Juraj. **Iredenta a separatizmus v slovenskej politike, 1919-1938** (Irredentism and Separatism in Slovak Politics, 1919-1938). Bratislava, 1957. 248p.

A Communist analysis of the role of Hungarian revisionist propaganda and its Slovak collaborators in Slovak politics during the interwar years.

397. Krofta, Kamil. **The Substance of Hungarian Revisionism.** Prague: Orbis, 1934. 30p.

Krofta offers a Czechoslovak description and analysis of the nature of Hungarian revisionism and how it affected Czechoslovakia. The pamphlet was designed to counteract the Hungarian revisionist propaganda in English-speaking countries by the Czechoslovak Ministry of Foreign Affairs.

398. Purgat, Juraj. **Od Trianonu po Košice: K madǎrskej otázke v Československu** (From Trianon to Košice: On the Hungarian Question in Czechoslovakia). Bratislava: Epocha, t. Pravda, Žilina, 1970. 323p.

This is a history of the Hungarian minority in Czechoslovakia between the end of World War I and the arrival of the National Front government to Košice (Slovakia) in April 1945. Tables, statistics, a chronology of important events, a bibliography, and an index are included.

399. Révész, László. "Die magyarische Minderheit in der Tschechoslowakei." *Der Donauraum* 19: 1-2 (1974): 25-46.

The essay analyzes the conditions in which the Hungarian minority lives in Czechoslovakia. It provides statistical data and historical background and surveys the legal status of the ethnic group.

400. Steier, Lajos. **Ungarns Vergewaltigung: Oberungarn unter tschechischer Herrschaft.** Zürich, Leipzig, Vienna: Amalthen-Verlag, [c. 1929]. xxxii, 1007p. 87 plates, Ports, 8 maps.

Written by a Hungarian nationalist, this mammoth work explores the consequences of World War I on the fate of the Hungarians settled in "Upper Hungary" (Slovakia). It describes and analyzes religious and cultural trends among the Hungarians in Slovakia, the political and legal status of the Hungarian minority in Czechoslovakia, its aspirations and grievances, and the autonomist movement in Slovakia. This is the most extensive treatment in German of the Hungarian question in Czechoslovakia in the 1920s.

401. Varsik, Bronislav. **Narodnostná Hranice Slovensko-Madǎrská** (The Ethnographic Slovak-Hungarian Boundary). Opera eruditae societatis slovacae I tomus. Bratislava, 1940. 89p. Maps.

This Slovak publication focuses on the ethnographic boundary and the number of national minorities, especially Hungarians, living in Slovakia and Slovaks living in Hungary.

402. Williams, R. E. Vaughan, ed. **The Hungarian Question in the British Parliament: Speeches, Questions and Answers Thereto in the House of Lords and the House of Commons from 1919 to 1930.** Introduction by Roland E. J. Vaughan Williams. London: G. Richards, 1933. 459p.

These are the views expressed by members of the British parliament and the British government on the Hungarian question and the Hungarian minorities living in neighboring countries, including Czechoslovakia.

403. Zimák, Jozef, ed. **Vpád madǎrských bolǎevikov na Slovensko v roku 1919** (The Invasion of the Hungarian Bolsheviks into Slovakia in the Year 1919). 2nd corrected ed. Bratislava, J. Zimák, 1938. 260p.

This publication contains some 35 essays written by participants in the Czechoslovak-Hungarian war of 1919. The war over Slovakia was lost by the Hungarian government of Bela Kun, and the area, with its large Hungarian minority, became part of Czechoslovakia. Included is an essay by Lt. Col. Karel Vondráček of the Czechoslovak general staff, summarizing the struggle for Slovakia during 1918-1919.

404. **Zpráva o rozhodnutí Nejyyǎǎí Rady Spojenců ze dne 12. června 1919 o úpravě hranic mezi Uherskem a Státem Ceskoslovenským** (Report on the Decision of the Allied Supreme Council of June 12, 1919 on the Delimitation of Boundaries between Hungary and the Czechoslovak State). Zasedání Národního shromǎǎdění československého roku 1919. Příloha k tisku 1630. no. 5. Prague, 1919. 9p.

The report was published as an annex to the official publication of the Czechoslovak National Assembly for 1919. It contains detailed description of the boundaries and, by implication, determines how many Hungarians would become Czechoslovak subjects.

405. Zvara, Juraj. "K problematike postavenia maďárskej národnostnej skupiny v ČSR v období boja za upevnenie ľudovej demokracie a rozšířenie moci robotnickej triedy 1945-1948" ("On the Problems of the Situation of the Hungarian National Group in Czechoslovakia during the Period of the Struggle for the strengthening of the People's Democracy and the Expanding of the Power of the Working Class, 1945-1948"). *Historický časopis* XII (1964): 28-49.

A Slovak historian analyzes the status and role of the Hungarian minority in Czechoslovakia during the years 1945-1948.

406. Zvara, Juraj. **Maďárská menšina na Slovensku po roku 1945** (The Hungarian Minority in Slovakia after 1945). Bratislava: Epocha, t. Pravda, 1969. 221p.

Zvara, a Slovak historian, discusses the status of the Hungarian minority in Slovakia since 1945. He divides the relations between the Hungarians and the Slovaks into two periods — 1938-1945 and 1945-1948 — and traces the development of the status of the Hungarians in Czechoslovakia since 1948. Footnotes and a bibliography are included.

Ukrainians

407. Dami, Aldo. **La Ruthénie subcarpathique**. Genève-Annemasse: Éditions du Mont-Blanc s.a., [1944]. vii, 375p., 31 fold. col. map.

This is a general history of the people living in Ruthenia up to 1944. Bibliography, pp. 363-75.

408. Hatalák, Petr. **Jak vznikla myšlenka připojit Podkarpatskou Rus k Československu** (The Genesis of the Idea to Annex Carpatho-Ruthenia to Czechoslovakia). Uzhorod: Zvláštni otisk z *Podkarpatských Hlasů*, č. 192/203, 1935. 38p.

This is a reprint of an article originally published in the Czech language in *Podkarpatské Hlasy*, No. 192/203, on the origin of the idea of attaching Ruthenia to Czechoslovakia. It deals with the economic, ethnic, and cultural conditions in the province.

409. Hora, Alois. **Podkarpatská Rus** (Carpatho-Ruthenia). Prague: Československý cizinecký úřad, 1919. 34p. Map.

This publication of the Czechoslovak Office for Foreign Nationals deal with the ethnic conditions in Ruthenia. The analysis is based in part on church records and on rather inflated data on the number of Rusins living in the province.

410. Lacko, Michael. **Unio Uzhorodensis Ruthenorum Carpaticorum cum Ecclesia Catholica**. Rome: Ponti Institutum Orientalium Studiorum, 1955. xviii, 276p. 2 maps.

The history of the Church (Byzantine Rite) in Ruthenia is explored in this extensive doctoral dissertation by Rev. Lacko, S.J. It gives details on the reunion of the Orthodox Christians in the province with the Catholic Church. The Uniate Church (Catholic of the Byzantine Rite) was the largest religious denomination in Ruthenia during the years preceding that province's incorporation into the Soviet Union. The work contains some documents, a chronology of events relating to the Church, tables, and an index.

411. Lev, Vojtěch. **Brána na východ (Karpatská Rus)** (Gateway to the East: Carpatho-Ruthenia). Prague: Československá sociálně demokratická strana, 1920. 55p.

This Czechoslovak Social Democratic party publication deals with the strategic importance of Ruthenia. It describes the ethnic structure of the population, the province's economy, and its natural resources.

412. Lewandowski, Krzysztof. **Sprawa ukraińska w polityce zagranicznej Czecho-slowacji w latach 1918-1932** (The Ukrainian Problem in the Foreign Policy of Czecho-slovakia during 1918-1932). Wroclaw: Polish Academy of Science, 1974. 336p.

Although the book is not a complete and systematic exposition of the Ukrainian problem, it does provide a great deal of useful material on Ukrainian-Czech and Ukrainian-Polish relations. The author admits that after World War I the Czechs helped Ukrainians more than any other country did, especially by supporting the Ukrainian Free University in Prague and the Ukrainian Husbandry Academy in Poděbrady. He believes that Czech pro-Ukrainian politics were guided by the desire to establish a common border with Ukraine and subsequently with Russia.

413. Magocsi, Paul R. "The Ruthenian Decision to Unite with Czechoslovakia." *Slavic Review* XXXIV:2 (1975): 360-81.

The author focuses on the role of the Ruthenians in the United States in the decision of the Paris Peace Conference and the people living in the province to join Czechoslovakia in 1919. This scholarly treatment of the events also provides extensive notes containing bibliographical data.

414. Magocsi, Paul Robert. **The Shaping of a National Identity: Subcarpathian Rus',** **1848-1948**. Cambridge, MA: Harvard University Press, 1978. 640p.

The theme of the book is that Subcarpathian Rusyns failed to develop into an independent nationality because their intelligentsia suffered from a sense of inferiority *vis-à-vis* other closely related nationalities. The author divides his discussion into three sections: the historical background up to 1919; the cultural setting; and political development to 1948. Magocsi's own Rosyn-Magyar background and his anti-Ukrainian bias prevented him from seeing the Carpatho-Rusyn linkage to the Ukrainian nation. Otherwise, the study contributes to the understanding of the national development of people who for centuries have lived under foreign domination.

415. Marcus, Vasyl. **L'incorporation de l'Ukraine subcarpathique à l'Ukraine soviétique, 1944-1945**. Preface by Andre Pierre. Louvain: Centre ukrainien d'études en Belgique, 1956. 144p. Map.

In this account of Ruthenian politics during the process of the Communist seizure of power and the province's incorporation into the Soviet Union (Ukrainian Soviet Socialist Republic), the author compares the methods used with those employed by the Soviets in 1940 when the Baltic republics were annexed by the Soviet Union. After the province was de facto a part of the Soviet state, the Czechoslovak government formally recognized the cession of it by an act of parliament adopted in June 1945. Attached are a list of documents and a bibliography.

416. Martell, Rene. **La Ruthenie Subcarpatique**. Paris: Paul Hartmann, 1935. 138p.

This work provides information about the general situation in Ruthenia, including data on its population.

417. Mousset, Jean. **Les villes de la Russie Subcarpatique (1919-1938): L'effort Tchecoslovaque.** Paris: Librairie Droz, 1938. 139p. Map.

Beginning with the pre-history of the region, the author traces the history of migrations and invasions affecting Ruthenia. He gives data on demography and emigration, sociology of the region, the development of industries and urban centers, and the role of the Czechoslovak Republic in the province. In addition, he explores the political problems stemming from the presence of several nationalities and interests of the neighboring countries. There are tables, statistics on nationalities and religion in Ruthenia, and a bibliography.

418. Němec, František, and Moudrý, Vladimír. **The Soviet Seizure of Subcarpathian Ruthenia.** Toronto: W. B. Anderson, 1955. ix, 375p.

František Němec, a delegate of the Czechoslovak government-in-exile in London sent to represent that government and exercise its authority in Ruthenia (which was part of Czechoslovakia), was unable to perform the task of governing and tells the story of the Communist seizure of power and the province's incorporation into the Soviet Union from his pro-Czech perspective. Personal observations and published materials are the basis for this work. A selected bibliography is included.

419. Pazhur, Olena, comp. **Ukraintsi Chekhoslovachchyny 1962-1964rr.: Bibliohrafiia knyh, zhurnalnykh ta hazetnyth stattei** (Ukrainians in Czechoslovakia 1962-1964: Bibliography of Books, Periodicals and Newspaper Articles). Priashiv: Derzh. nauk. biblioteka, 1967. xv, 257p.

This bibliography includes 3,951 entries covering various subjects pertaining to Ukrainians in Czechoslovakia. Geographical and name indexes are provided.

420. Revay, Julian. "The March to Liberation of Carpatho-Ukraine." *Ukrainian Quarterly* X (1954): 227-34.

Mr. Revay, a minister in the short-lived Ukrainian government under the presidency of Augustin Voloshin, disputes the Hungarian and Czechoslovakian claims to Carpatho-Ukraine.

421. Shandor, Vincent. "Carpatho-Ukraine in the International Bargaining of 1918-1939." *Ukrainian Quarterly* X (1954): 235-46.

This is an informative account of international diplomacy regarding the fate of Carpatho-Ukraine. It focuses on the efforts of the governments in Berlin and Budapest that led to Hungary's annexation of the country.

422. Shtefan, Avhustyn. **Avhustyn Voloshyn, prezydent Karpats'koi Ukrainy. Spomyny** (Avhustyn Voloshyn, President of Carpatho-Ukraine: Memoirs). Toronto: published by Free Press for the Carpathian Research Center, 1977. 210p.

The author was the close friend and co-activist of the late president of Carpatho-Ukraine, Msgr. Dr. Augustin Voloshyn. The book is a detailed biography of Voloshyn, richly illustrated, with maps and an extensive bibliography. The author expands his coverage to other personalities active in Carpatho-Ukrainian politics, making his memoir an important contribution to the literature on the history of that region. This work covers the period from the early 1900s to 1945.

423. Stercho, Peter George. **Diplomacy of Double Morality. Europe's Crossroads in Carpatho-Ukraine 1919-1939.** New York: Carpathian Research Center, [1971]. xxii, 495p.

This extensive study of Carpatho-Ukraine comes complete with illustrations, maps, and statistical tables. Stercho traces the development of the Trans-Carpathian region of Ukraine from the end of the nineteenth century until the time the province was incorporated into Hungary in 1939. The study, based on published material as well as many unpublished documents, looks into the background of the province's annexation to Czechoslovakia, the abuses of power by the Prague government, and the latter's denial of the right of Ruthenian self-determination. It deals with the short-lived independence of Ruthenia in March 1939 and provides relevant documents, an extensive bibliography, indexes of geographic place names and personal names, and a chronology of events.

424. Stercho, Petro (Peter G.). **Karpato-ukrains'ka derzhava: do istorii vyzvolnoi borot'by karpats'kykh ukraintsiv u 1919-1939 rokakh** (The Carpatho-Ukrainian Republic: A Contribution to the History of the Carpatho-Ukrainian Struggle for Freedom, 1919-1939). Toronto: Shevchenko Scientific Society, 1965. 288p. Maps. Photos.

The book offers a detailed and documented account of the Carpatho-Ruthenian drive toward self-determination beginning with the first attempts in 1919 to achieve autonomy within the Czecho-Slovak Republic. The author discusses the status of the region within the republic, the birth of a briefly independent Carpatho-Ukrainian state in March 1939, and the invasion by Hungarian troops, concluding with a survey of Nazi German policy regarding the region.

425. Voloshin, Augustin. "Carpathian Ruthenia." *Slavonic and East European Review* XIII (Januaryh 1935): 372-78.

This essay compares the conditions in Carpatho-Ruthenia under Czechoslovak rule, which brought many improvements, with those under Hugnarian rule prior to 1919.

426. Warzeski, Walter C. **Byzantine Rite Rusins in Carpatho-Ruthenia and America.** Pittsburgh: Byzantine Seminary Press, 1971. x, 332p.

Warzeski covers a long span of history of the Uniate Church in Ruthenia and America. He discusses the Union of Užhorod, the roots of Ruthenian national consciousness, the birth of Carpatho-Ruthenia and its incorporation into Czechoslovakia, its autonomy in 1938-1939, "independence," return of the province to Hungary, and, lastly, its becoming a part of the Soviet Union in 1944-45. The study includes statistics, several documents, a map, and an index.

427. Winch, Michael. **Republic for a Day: An Eyewitness Account of the Carpatho-Ukraine Incident.** London: R. Hale, 1939. 286p.

Winch, a British correspondent, details the history of the short-lived independence of Carpatho-Ukraine before it was overrun by Hungarian troops. He also provides a lively description of the country and its people.

428. Zatloukal, Jaroslav, ed. **Podkarpatská Rus. Sborník hospodářského, kulturního a politického poznání Podkarpatské Rusi** (Carpatho-Ruthenia: Symposium of Economic, Political and Cultural Information about Carpatho-Ruthenia). Bratislava: Klub přátel Podkarpatské Rusi, 1936. 330p.

This is a collection of addresses, lectures, and essays on how Ruthenia became part of Czechoslovakia, the Czech attitude toward Ruthenians, and political, economic, and social conditions prevalent in the province as seen from the Czechoslovak point of view. With illustrations and portraits.

Poles

429.   Chmelař, Josef. **Polská menšina v Československu** (The Polish Minority in Czechoslovakia). Prague: Orbis, 1935. 107p. Also published in French under the title *La minorité polonaise en Tchécoslovaquie*. Prague: Orbis, 1935. 127p.

This is the sixth volume in the series on nationality questions published by the Czechoslovak Society for the Study of Nationality Questions. Since the Polish minority was a cause of discord between Czechoslovakia and Poland, the Czechoslovak governing circles saw to it that their views would be available to the international forum as well; hence the French edition. The work surveys the status of the Polish minority in Czechoslovakia and presents the Czech point of view on the number of people speaking the Polish language in the disputed Teschen district—a bone of contention between the two countries during the interwar period.

430.   Grappin, Henry. **Polonais et Tchèques; la question de la Silésie de Teschen**. Paris: M. Flinikowski, 1919. 67p. Map.

This piece of propaganda deals with the Teschen territory, which was claimed by both Czechoslovakia and Poland at the Paris Peace Conference. The data on the nationalities of people living in the district were used to support the Polish position.

431.   Hejret, Jan. **Těšínsko** (The District of Teschen). Prague: E. Solc, 1919. 76p.

Hejret's pamphlet analyzes the ethnic composition in the disputed Teschen district from the Czechoslovak point of view. It shows the strategic and economic importance of the area for Czechoslovakia.

432.   Káňa, Otakar, and Pavelka, R. **Těšínsko v Polsko-Československých vztazích 1918-1939** (Teschen in Polish-Czechoslovak Relations, 1918-1939). Ostrava: Profil, 1970. 366p. (Summaries in Russian, German, and French).

This is the most extensive examination of the situation in the district of Teschen (and the Polish minority therein), which was a bone of contention between Czechoslovakia and Poland during the interwar period. The book contains detailed information on the composition of the population, tables, statistics, and results of parliamentary elections in 1925 and 1929 showing the strengths of individual national minorities. The bibliography is very extensive; there is also an index.

433.   Kozusznik, Boguslav. **The Problem of Cieszyn, Silesia**. London: n.p., 1943. iv, 122p.

The author, a Polish exile in London, presents the Polish viewpoint in this history of the disputed territory of Teschen.

434.   Krčmář, Jan. **Javorina před stálým dvorem mezinárodní spravedlnosti v Haagu a před radou Společnosti národů v Paříži** (Javorina before the Permanent Court of International Justice in the Hague and before the Council of the League of Nations in Paris). Zvláštní otisk ze *Zahraniční Politiky*. Prague: Orbis, 1924. 52p.

This is a reprint of an article from the semi-official Czechoslovak government periodical *Zahraniční Politika* on the settlement of the dispute between Poland and Czechoslovakia over the district of Javorina, located in northern Slovakia.

435. Pelc, Ferdinand. **O Tĕšínsko. Vzpomínky a úvahy** (For Teschen: Recollections and Reflections). Slezská Ostrava: Nakladem Slezské Matice Osvĕty Lidové, 1928. 227p.

A Czech nationalist reflects upon the struggle for the Teschen area. He gives the Czech rationale for the incorporation of the district into Czechoslovakia.

436. **Les Polonais en Tchécoslovaquie a la lumière des faits et des chiffres; memoire de la Commission d'études sur les relations polono-tchèques.** Warsaw: Polski Instytut Współpracy z Zagranicą, 1935. 142p. Map.

This publication presents the Polish point of view on the status of the Polish minority in Czechoslovakia and on the disputed district of Teschen. Some of the data provided here differ from those given by the Czechs. The book also appeared in Polish: *Polacy w Czechoslowacji w świetle faktów i liczb* (Warsaw, 1935. 126p.).

437. **Ročenka o československo-polské spolupráci 1938. K jubileu dvacetileté samostatnosti ČSR sestavil Alois Režucha** (Yearbook of Czechoslovak-Polish Cooperation 1938. On the Twentieth Anniversary of the Czechoslovak Independence Compiled by Alois Režucha). Prague: Československo-polská společnost, 1938. 101p.

The yearbook contains a symposium of articles on cultural and economic contacts between the Czechs and Poles, national minorities (Polish in Czechoslovakia and Czech and Slovak in Poland), and activities of Czechoslovak-Polish organizations in Czechoslovakia and Poland. This publication was designed to promote Czechoslovak-Polish cooperation. With illustrations and tables in the text.

438. Roy, James Alexander. **Pole and Czech in Silesia.** London: John Lane, 1921. iv, 212p.

A British view on the conflict between the Czech and Polish nationalities in the province of Silesia. The author surveys the history of the area of mixed nationalities.

439. Semkowicz, Wladyslaw. **Materjaly źródlowe do dziejów osadnictwa Górnej Oravy** (Original Sources to the History of the Settlement in Upper Orava). 2 vols. Zakopané: Muzeum Tatrżańskie, 1932.

A collection of materials concerning the population in the Upper Orava region. The area was claimed by both Poland and Czechoslovakia.

440. Sworakowski, Witold. **Polacy na Śląsku za Olzą** (The Poles in the Trans-Olza). Warsaw: Instytut badań spraw narodowościowych, 1937. 289p.

The Polish case in the dispute over the Teschen district between Czechoslovakia and Poland is the subject of this publication. The work contains a survey of the press, cultural arrangements, organizations, schools, and the conditions under which the nationalities of the area live. Illustrations, tables, and a map are in the text. Translated into German under the title *Die Polen in Schlesien hinter der Olsa* (Berlin Publication Bureau, 1938) in the series Polacy za granicą.

441. Sworakowski, Witold. "Polacy w Czechoslowacju w swietle wyborow" (The Poles in Czechoslovakia in the Light of Elections). *Sprawy Narodowościowe* 1-2: (1935): 93-100.

The Polish author argues that the Czechoslovak statistics on the Polish national minority in Czechoslovakia are inaccurate and that the actual number of Poles is much larger. He presents the Polish version relative to the dispute over the territory, which was inhabited, according to the Austrian census, largely by Poles prior to the end of World War I.

442. Szymiczek, Franciszek. **Walka o Śląsk Cieszyński w latach 1914-1920** (The Struggle for Silesian Teschen 1914-1920). Katowice: Instytut Śląski, 1938. 212p.

The Silesian Institute in Katowice, Poland published this study to argue its viewpoint on the problem of the Teschen district and its political orientation. The work surveys the organizations of the "Silesians" and their political outlook and presents statistics and other data on the population of the area.

443. Tapie, Victor. **Le Pays de Teschen et les Rapports entre la Pologne et la Tchecoslovaquie**. Centre d'études de politique étrangère, Section d'information, Publication no. 3. Paris: Paul Hartmann, 1936. 80p. Map.

A French study on the situation in the Teschen district and the claims to it by Czechoslovakia and Poland.

444. Uhlíř, František. **Těšínské Slezsko** (The Teschen Silesia). Ostrava and Prague: J. Lukašík, 1946. 364p.

This is a history and description of ethnic conditions in the Teschen district of Silesia, claimed by Czechoslovakia on historical grounds and by Poland on ethnic grounds following World War I. The dispute between the two countries poisoned their relations for twenty years, and the problem was solved only after World War II.

445. Witt, Kurt. **Die Teschener Frage**. Berlin: Verlag Volk und Reich, 1935. 291p.

A German writer analyzes the Teschen question, taking a critical view of the Czechoslovak position.

Jews

General Reference Material

446. **Jahrbuch der Gesellschaft für Geschichte der Juden in der tschechoslowakischen Republik**. Neunte Ausgabe von Prof. Sammuel Steinherz. Prague: Jahrbuch, 1929-1938.

The articles in this yearbook reflect Czech Jewish interest in their past, though most articles deal with pre-twentieth-century topics. The work was revived as *Judaica bohemiae* in 1965. Its Czech counterpart was *Ročenka Společnosti pro Dějiny židů v Československé Republice*.

447. **Judaica bohemiae**. Prague: Státní židovské muzeum. Vol. I (1965); Vol. II (1966).

A revived journal once issued before World War II in Czech and German is published in Russian, French, English, and Czech. Although most of its articles deal with pre-twentieth-century Czechoslovakia, its reviews and other commentaries are often valuable for those interested in modern Czechoslovakian studies.

448. Muneles, Otto. **Bibliographical Survey of Jewish Prague: The Jewish State Museum of Prague**. Prague: Orbis, 1952. 562p.
This bibliography surveys principally the holdings of the Jewish Library of Prague. It also appeared in Czech as *Bibliografický přehled židovské Prahy* (1952). The work discusses a variety of publications in many languages published over the past four centuries on the history of the Jewish community in Prague.

449. **Rat der jüdischen Gemeinden in Böhmen und Mähren, und Zentralverband der jüdischen Gemeinden in der Slowakei**. Informationsbulletin. 1956.
Appearing in Czech as *Věstník židovských náboženských obcí v Československu*, this quarterly journal is the official publication of the Assocation for Jewish Communities in Czechoslovakia.

450. Svatuška, Ladislav. **Židovské předpisy v Protektorátu Čechy a Morava a vývoj rasového práva v Říši** (Rules Pertaining to Jews in the Protectorate Bohemia and Moravia and the Evolution of Racial Law in the Reich). Prague: Právnické knihkupectví a nakladatelství V. Lenhart, 1940. 152p.
This collection of legal documents traces the evolution of the Jewish question and Nazi policies *vis-à-vis* the Jews in the Protectorate Bohemia and Moravia up to 1940. The author was commissioner of political administration in the Protectorate's Ministry of the Interior. He states the then official position on the Jewish question. The work begins with a bibliography listing relevant German and Czech publications.

451. **Zeitschrift für die Geschichte der Juden in der Tschechoslowakei, 1930-1939**. Brno: Jüdischer Buch- und Kunstverlag, 1930-1939.
Published throughout the 1930s in German, this quarterly journal contains a number of valuable articles on the history of Czechoslovakian Jewry.

452. **Židovská ročenka 5715** (Jewish yearbook 5715). Prague: Rada židovských nabeženských Obcí, 1955-1970.
This journal covers various topics in Czechoslovakian Jewish history, though there is little on the Holocaust period.

Articles and Monographs

453. Adler, Hans G. **Theresienstadt, 1941-1945; das Antlitz einer Zwangsgemeinschaft, Geschichte, Soziologie, Psychologie**. 2nd rev. ed. Tübingen: J. C. B. Mohr, 1960. 892p. Map.
The most important study of Czech Jewry during the Holocaust. It provides an introduction on the Protectorate period of 1939 to 1941 and an extensive bibliography on all aspects of the Holocaust.

454. **Die Ausschaltung der Juden aus der Wirtschaft des Protektorats Böhmen und Mähren**. Prague: Böhmisch-Mährische Verlags- und Druckerei-Gesellschaft, 1941. 132p.
This is a history of the evolution of anti-Semitic laws and statutes aimed at excluding Jews from the economic sector in the Protectorate of Bohemia and Moravia.

455. Černý, Bohumil. **Most k novému životu. Německá emigrace v ČSR v letech 1933-1939** (Bridge to New Life: German Emigration in the Czechoslovak Republic in the Years 1933-1939). Prague: Lidová Demokracie, 1967. 188p.

Černý deals with Jewish emigration and Czechoslovakia in the years prior to the Munich Pact. He documents the evolution of Nazi anti-Semitic theories and its impact on Czechoslovakia during this period. The volume is valuable for its information on Czechoslovakian Jewry during this time and the influence of Nazism on some Czechoslovakians before Munich. It has a valuable bibliography and an excellent collection of photographs and illustrations.

456. Friedmann, František. **Pražští židé. Studie statistická** (Prague Jews: Statistical Study). Prague: n.p., 1929. 63p.

An excellent statistical study of Jews in Czechoslovakia from the late eighteenth through the early twentieth century. It covers Jewish migration to and from Czechoslovakia, Jewish population trends, university enrollment, and professional development.

457. Gold, Hugo, ed. **Die Juden und die Judengemeinde Bratislava in Vergangenheit und Gegenwart**. Brünn: Jüdischer Buchverlag, 1932. 192p.

This is a history of Jews in Bratislava, an important urban area in Slovakia.

458. Gold, Hugo, ed. **Die Juden und Judengemeinden Mährens in Vergangenheit und Gegenwart**. Brünn: Jüdischer Buch- und Kunstverlag, 1929. 623p.

This is an excellent, in-depth study of the history of the Jewish community in Moravia. It covers each area separately, and one portion of the book is devoted to a statistical survey of each community. A similar book, also edited by H. Gold, is *Die Juden und Judengemeinden Böhmens in Vergangenheit und Gegenwart*, vol. 1 (Brünn: Jüdischer Buch- und Kunstverlag, 1934. 735p.).

This work deals with 342 Bohemian Jewish communities excluding Prague, which was intended to be the subject of a second volume that was never published.

459. **Heroes and Victims**. London: Czechoslovakian Ministry of Foreign Affairs Information Service, 1945. n.p.

This volume, with an introduction by Jan Masaryk, was issued to commemorate the Jews who died at the hands of the Germans during World War II. It contains details about major German atrocities and lists those known officially to have died because of their political activities against the Germans.

460. Iggers, Wilma A. "The Flexible National Identities of Bohemian Jewry." *East Central Europe* VII:1 (1930-1939): 39-48.

Although the Republic of Czechoslovakia (1918-1938) recognized a separate Jewish nationality, the vast majority of Jews in Bohemia and Moravia declared as their own either German or Czech nationality, depending on the area in which they lived. Prior to the establishment of the republic, the overwhelming majority of the Jews, including those living in Prague, registered themselves as Germans.

461. Jacoby, Gerhard. **Racial State, the German Nationalities Policy in the Protectorate of Bohemia-Moravia**. New York: Institute of Jewish Affairs of the American Jewish Congress and World Jewish Congress, 1944. xii, 355p.

This is a history of German policy in this rum portion of Czechoslovakia through most of World War II. Based on what primary source material was available on the Holocaust during this period, it approaches the question of German racial policies in Bohemia and Moravia and theoretical questions centering around Nazi racial philosophy current at the time. Bibliographical references in footnotes and bibliography.

462. **The Jews of Czechoslovakia: Historical Studies and Surveys.** 2 vols. Comp. by The Jewish Publication Society of America, Philadelphia. New York: Society for the History of Czechoslovak Jews. Vol. I, 1968. xxiii, 583p.; Vol. II, 1971. xxii, 707p.

Volume 1 offers essays dealing with the history of the jews in the Czech historical lands, Slovakia, and Ruthenia before and after the establishment of the Czechoslovak state, their legal position, organizational life, religion, welfare, education, art, and emigration, with a name and subject index. The collection of essays in volume 2 is devoted to past leaders of the Jewish movement in Czechoslovakia, Zionism, religious life and organization, the economy, literature, the press, publishing houses, and music of Jews in Czechoslovakia.

463. Kulka, Erich. **Židé v Československé Svobodově armádě** (Jews in the Czechoslovak Svoboda Army). Toronto: Sixty-Eight Publishers, 1979. 293p.

This account, dealing with the role of Jews in Svoboda's army, is part of an ongoing project to write the history of Czechoslovakian Jewry's struggle against the Germans during World War II. The study includes bibliographical references.

464. Laor, Eran. **Vergangen und ausgelöscht: Erinnerungen an das slowakisch-ungarische Judentum.** Stuttgart: Deutsche Verlagsanstalt, 1972. 276p.

Sponsored by the Leo Baeck Institute, this history focuses on Slovakian-Hungarian Jews from 1700 through 1920. About two-thirds of the book deals with the period 1900-1920. The work treats all aspects of Jewish life from a personal perspective. No footnotes or bibliography.

465. Lederer, Zdenko. **Ghetto Theresienstadt.** London: Edward Goldston & Son, 1953. 275p.

A very balanced, scholarly history of this unique concentration camp from its opening in late 1941 until it was closed in May 1945. German officials used it to convince international figures that rumors of anti-Semitic excesses were a fabrication, yet of the 140,000 Jews sent there, only 17,320 survived. The author goes into great detail on daily camp life and the governing Jewish social structure, and provides ample statistics to document his arguments.

466. Lion, Jindrich. **The Prague Ghetto.** Translated by Jean Layton. London: Spring Books, 1959. 96p.

This volume, a history of the 1,000-year-old Prague ghetto, appeared in German as *Das Prager Ghetto* (1959). It is a good, brief account of this important segment of Bohemian Jewish history.

467. Lipscher, Ladislav. **Die Juden im slowakischen Staat, 1939-1945.** Munich and Vienna: R. Oldenbourg, 1980. 210p.

This is a very valuable, well-documented study of German policy towards the Jews of Slovakia during World War II. The author begins with the creation of the autonomous Slovak republic on October 6, 1938, and traces the evolution of anti-Semitic policy through Slovakia's checkered history as a Nazi satellite. Lipscher goes into some depth on the deportation of Slovakian Jews to death camps in the east. He ends his study with the aftermath of the Holocaust through the spring of 1945.

468. Neumann, Oskar. **Im Schatten des Todes: Ein Tatsachenbericht vom Schicksals-kampf des slowakischen Judentums.** Tel Aviv: Edition "Olamenu," 1956. 299p.

Neumann's account details the history of the Holocaust in Slovakia, and centers on the ghettoization and ultimate destruction of that area's Jewish population during World War II.

469. Rat der jüdischen Gemeinden in Böhmen und Mähren, and Zentralverband der jüdischen Gemeinden in der Slowakei. **Die aussäen unter Tränen mit Jubel werden sie ernten (Psalm 126): Die jüdischen Gemeinden in der Tschecoslowakischen Republik nach dem Zweiten Weltkrieg.** Prague: Zentral-Kirchenverlag, 1959. 215p. Illus.

This publication by the organ of the federations of Jewish communities in Czechoslovakia surveys the situation of Czechoslovakia's remaining Jews twenty years after the Holocaust. It goes into some detail on the status of each community, and illustrations of synagogues, ritual objects, gravestones, etc., accompany the text.

470. Rothkirchen, Livia. **Hurban Yahadut Slovakia** (The Destruction of Slovakian Jewry). Jerusalem: Yad Washem Martyrs' and heroes' Memorial Authority, 1961. 257p.

Written in Hebrew but with a 75-page introduction in English, this volume contains an excellent selection of documents that is used by the author to trace the history of the Holocaust in Slovakia. Attached are indexes of persons and names.

471. Rychnovsky, Ernst, ed. **Masaryk und das Judentum**. Prague: Mars-Verlags-gesellschaft, 1931. 362p.

Also issued in Czech as *Masaryk a židovství*, this collection of articles underlines the positive role of Thomas G. Masaryk towards this nation's Jewish population.

472. **Der slowakische Judenkodex**. Translated and with an introduction by Ludwig A. Dostal. Pressburg: Roland-Verlag, 1941. 90p.

An excellent study of early anti-Semitic legislation in Slovakia between 1938 and 1940.

473. **The Use of Anti-Semitism against Czechoslovakia: Facts, Documents, Press Reports**. London: Institute of Jewish Affairs, in association with the World Jewish Congress, 1968. 24p.

This smallish book, deals with the official use of anti-Semitism in Czechoslovakia in the aftermath of the Soviet invasion of that country in August 1968. According to the authors, the Soviets and their Czech supporters depicted Jews and Zionists as being the backbone of the "Czech spring" phenomenon. Texts from radio broadcasts, newspaper articles, and other items document the theme.

474. Volavková, Hana. **Zmizlé pražské ghetto** (Prague's Vanished Ghetto). Prague: Sportovní a turistické nakládatelstvi, 1961. 63p. (Summaries in Russian, German, and English).

An interesting collection of photographs, documents, and illustrations is included in this brief history of the Prague ghetto through the end of the Second World War.

Gypsies

475. **Cikánské obyvatelstvo k 31. 12. 1968** (The Gypsy Population as of December 31, 1968). Prague: Federální statistický úřad, 1969. 45p.

This official Czechoslovak government publication contains statistics on Gypsies in Czechoslovakia, their concentration or dispersion, family size, and work habits as of 1968.

476. Koudelka, Josef. **Gypsies: Photographs**. Millerton, NY: Aperture, 1975. 135p.

A collection of photographs and commentaries on the life of Gypsies in eastern Slovakia.

477. Nečas, Ctibor. **Nad osudem českých a slovenských cikánů v letech 1939-1945** (On the Fate of Czech and Slovak Gypsies during the years 1939-1945). [Brno]: Univerzita J. E. Purkyně v Brně, 1981. 180p.

The Gypsies, as well as the Jews, fell victim to the "final solution" during the Nazi occupation. Published by the pedagogical faculty of the University of J. E. Purkyně, this is one of the few sources on the fate of Czech and Slovak Gypsies during World War II.

478. Srb, Vladimír, and Vomáčková, O. "Cikáni v Československu v roce 1968" (Gypsies in Czechoslovakia in 1968). *Demografie* 11:3 (1969): 221-30.

Although not recognized as a separate nationality, Gypsies in Czechoslovakia form a distinct ethnic group and subculture. Their number and movements are closely monitored by the authorities.

4 _____ National Minorities in Hungary, 1919-1980

Martin L. Kovacs
with the assistance of David Crowe (Jews)

HISTORICAL SUMMARY

In 1919, Hungary's boundaries were largely marked by the Carpathian Mountains. However, much of her territory was occupied by Romania and the recently created states of Czechoslovakia and Yugoslavia, the mother nations of most national minorities in Hungary. A year later, the area known as "Burgenland" was ceded in the Treaty of Trianon (June 1920). As a result, Hungary retained less than one-third of her former area, that is, about 93,000 square kilometers, constituting the central portion of the drainage basin of her principal river, the Danube.[1]

Until the 1870s, Hungary had been an agricultural country, prosperous due to the fertility of her plains and the hard work of her peasant population. Although she lost most of her mines, mineral resources, and forests in 1920, significant production of electric energy, as well as the exploitation of coal and, more recently, natural gas, oil, uranium, and bauxite deposits, contributed to the growth of industrialization, particularly in the Budapest region.

Budapest, the capital, is the principal industrial, commercial, and financial center of Hungary and, at the same time, accommodates the headquarters of most important organizations, including state enterprises. As in

160

the case of Paris, France, most railway lines and roads radiate like spokes from the capital city, a metropolis of over 2 million.

Little recent information is available outside Hungary concerning the minority populations in that country, and still less in the English language. Therefore, in the present study, stress has been placed on the collection of related literature. Since most of that literature is in Hungarian, selection has been directed — wherever possible — towards the most recent of those publications. Where the opportunity arose, studies reflecting such varied facets of the minority culture as literature, history, and ethnography were chosen.

In an effort to resolve the need for both brevity and informativeness, preference was given to the requirements of researchers to the extent of equipping them with knowledge of primary and secondary sources. The first step involved the selection of those libraries likely to contain a store of Hungariana and which specialized in studies on national minorities. On this continent, libraries that met this requirement were those at Columbia and Stanford Universities (with particular reference to the Hoover Library at Stanford), the Library of Congress, and the New York Public Library in the United States; and in Canada, those at the University of Toronto, the University of Ottawa, the University of Alberta, and the University of Regina.

Libraries in Hungary that provided useful information for the present study were the National Széchenyi Library, the Library of the National Archives, and the Library of the Eötvös Lóránt University, all in Budapest. Furthermore, helpful publications, particularly in German, were located in the Nationalbibliothek, Vienna, Austria.

Post-Trianon Hungary

The successive waves of nationalities settling in Hungary left behind various elements that had to merge into a viable community. After two, three, or more generations, depending on the numbers and the proportions of ethnocultural groups, often a distinct nationality community emerged, adopting the language, customs, and traditions prevailing in the village or town. The outcome of this process of fusion usually was decided locally and spontaneously. An important factor was differences in fecundity among the communal groups. Such differences frequently depended on external factors illustrated by the correlation between fertility and church membership.

In the case of groupings of nationalities, an ethnocultural boundary came into existence beyond which all ethnocultural elements were submerged into the Magyar majority; on the other side of the boundary, the scattered Magyars were assimilated. A study of the Ruthenian (Carpatho-Ukrainian) settlements in Hungary clearly shows this process. The one-time existence of Ruthenian groups in about fifty villages[2] is indicated by the recollections and folklore among the current Magyars describing the settlements concerned. The Ruthenians were also known as Ruszins, Rusznyáks, and Kisoroszes. In many instances, assimilation occurred between Carpatho-Ukrainians and Slovaks, which made it difficult to establish the ethnic descent of the few scattered Szotáks. No statistical data concerning Carpatho-Ukrainians in Hungary have been found.

The South Slavs in Hungary include 95,000 Croats, the largest grouping. The subgroups of the Croats are the Bunyevaci (in Bács), the Sokaci (in Bácska, in Mohács, in the "villages," and along the Drava), the Bosnians (in Baranya), the Croats[3] proper (along the Mura and in West Hungary), and the Raic-Croats.

The number of Serbs has declined, owing to territorial changes, to 7,000 in the 1970s, from more than half a million in 1910, and about 165,000 in 1941. The Serbs are settled around Mohács and Budapest, and in the counties Békés and Csongrád.

The Slovenes, numbering about 6,000, live in the city of Szentgotthárd, and mostly in seven villages of the county of Vas. Despite their relatively small population, these villages in Vas are significant, as they are among the few nationality settlements in Hungary that form a majority population. Since the land around these villages is second rate, many families have moved to Szentgotthárd, forming an urban island. The Vas County Council has come up with several measures to promote the survival of the Slovene ethnocultural group, such as the furnishing of facilities at the teacher-training college in Szombathely for the training of primary and secondary school teachers of the Slovenian language, with five primary schools and one secondary school in 1979.[4]

Romanians

The ancestors of the Romanians in present-day Hungary arrived after the end of the Turkish wars. The Romanians in the counties Hajdú-Bihar and Békés belong to the Bihar ethnolinguistic group, while the ones in Csongrád speak Banat Romanian. The 30,000 Romanians, according to the 1920 census, increased to over a million for a few years after 1940, only to drop to about 12,600 in the 1970 census because of territorial changes. The latter census included an additional 25,000 as being in various stages of assimilation. The Romanians in Hungary have their own kindergartens, schools, teachers, schoolbooks, publications, clubs, and libraries, just as other nationalities do, and their museum, folklore collections, and dancing and theatrical groups are described as being very active.[5]

Slovaks

The Slovaks constituted one of the very few ethnocultural groups that had settled in their mountainous homeland prior to the arrival there of the Magyars. Owing to the physiography of the area of their original settlement, they not only survived the onslaughts of the Turkish armies between 1526 and 1715, but in fact greatly increased in numbers. Because of this rapid increase in numbers as well as the unavailability of fertile land at home, a steady stream of surplus labor came—at first to the vast areas of land depopulated of its original settlers, mainly in the south, but also in other parts of Hungary. Another factor could have been religious persecution by landlords of Lutheran Slovaks. In most cases, Austrian aristocrats or other persons close to the Court wanted to utilize, as much as possible, grants of large tracts of land by procuring settlers for them. Thus, a major characteristic of Slovak settlements is their island-like nature, whether in Békés County or in Yugoslavia and

Romania. An example of this tendency is the Bácska village of about 1,300 whose population came from 55 places in nine counties. In this case, as in that of Medja in the Banat, where 219 Slovak families had come from 10 counties and 49 villages, the settlement was made up of a number of minute ethno-cultural islands. An extreme occurrence, in this respect, is Békéscsaba, which incorporates settlers from 128 villages in 20 counties. The movement of the original settlers had been directed by agents of such large landlords as Johann Georg Harruckern of Vienna.[6] There was a tendency for such settlers to settle not only in the same village, but also in the same street. It is revealing that in no instance did Slovak immigrants of different church memberships settle together. In many cases, in some other streets, families of German, Romanian, or other ethnocultural backgrounds formed communities. In addition to the settlements in Békés-Csongrád counties, numerous Slovak groupings found opportunities for settlement in the eighteenth century and later.

Not all Slovak settlers were farmers, even at the beginning of the migra-tional movement. Increasing numbers of later generations of Slovaks became urbanized by moving into larger towns or to Budapest. One important point raised in related literature is the question of the falling numbers of Slovaks in Hungarian census. The gist of the debate is the extent to which the diminution of Slovak population figures indicates planned Magyarization or merely a natural process of assimilation.

Some of the reasons mentioned in the present context include the repatriation of Slovak workers and ex-soldiers in 1918 and the inability of formerly numerous Slovak seasonal workers to enter Trianon Hungary and be counted at census-time as Slovaks. Another disadvantageous factor for the survival of the Slovak element in Hungary is that they do not form bloc settlements. Their networks of settlements are situated in the counties Komárom and Veszprém, Nógrád and Pest, Békés and Csanád, as well as Borsod-Abaúj-Zemplén and Szabolcs. It is relevant that each of the three complexes of Slovak villagers originally was mixed linguistically. But, no doubt as a result of continuous and internal linguistic assimilation, the villagers had finally become speakers of three distinct idioms, after the linguistic pattern in Slovakia—the western, central, and eastern Slovak dialects.[7]

Since 1945 the Slovaks in Hungary have been exposed to the same socio-economic forces as the rest of the population and have gone through similar stages of development. A striking departure from the trend was instanced by the population exchange project between Hungary and Czechoslovakia that resulted in the loss of some 73,000 identity-conscious Slovaks. Thus, the 1970 census in Hungary could not list more than about 21,000 Slovaks, as well as 110,000 such persons at some stage of assimilation. Not unlike the other nationality groups in Hungary, the Slovaks have had their own national organizations, schools, and activities, but have encountered, at times, serious difficulties because of the Slovak intellectuals' departure, almost in their entirety, to Slovakia in 1946-1947.[8]

Germans

One of the problems for the student of nationalities in Hungary has been the striking decrease in the number of Hungarian Germans between 1880 and 1910, that is, from 13.6 to 10.4% of the total population. The number of Hungarian Germans suffered a further loss with the Treaty of Trianon. Not only did the number change from more than 2 million (1910) to about 550,000 (1920), but their contact with Austria was lost. However, the figure increased again to over 700,000 with the return to Hungary, between 1938 and 1941, of some of the territories lost in the Treaty of Trianon. Although some sizable immigration, affecting the German element, was taking place in the interwar era as well, undeniably there must have been losses of population owing to the scattered nature of the settlements. First of all, such settlements did not form a large bloc with well-defined sociocultural boundaries. The oldest of the German-Hungarian areas along the western border of the country had had the advantage of continual contact with the Austro-Bavarian population. On the other hand, the majority of German villages originated between 1690 and 1790, owing to a great extent to the enterprise of Joseph II's state and to the colonizing efforts of landowners. The settlement area most resembling the bloc type, with relatively well-defined boundaries, was in the Danube-Drava corner next to the Danube and half surrounding the city of Pécs; it included parts of the counties of Baranya, Tolna, and Somogy. Portions of the Bácska and Banat that remained within the Hungarian area comprised only a small fraction of those territories, with their main portion having been allotted to Yugoslavia, and contained only a sparse population.

Much more significant German populations were situated in the Budapest area, sufficiently far from the metropolis not to be unduly affected by its assimilative influences yet close enough to find a market for produce and fruits. Few of the German settlements in Hungary possessed homogeneous communities because the "in-between" non-German elements found themselves in a process of reinforcement on the score of what has been described as a consistent Magyarization policy.

On the other hand, urban elements of German background were, by far, more exposed to Magyarization. In urban surroundings, ethnocultural segregation is very superficial and boundaries are subject to continual changes. Thus, it was hardly surprising to find the cities and towns resembling, to an inordinate extent, the proverbial "melting-pots" of cosmopolitan populations. Of course, the most highly urbanized elements of previous eras, the Germans and the Jews, proved the most susceptible to the Magyarizing influence of the huge Magyar influx into cities and towns which resulted from the liberation of the serfs in Hungary at the middle of the century and the subsequent collapse of the socioeconomic status of the small and middle nobility.[9] The great socioeconomic changes were signified by the development of the sleepy little cities of Buda and Pest into the metropolis of Budapest half a century after the compromise with Austria in 1867. There had been little connection between the Germans in the cities, the commercial and trade middle classes, and the "Swabian" peasants of the villages. The ambitions of the urban Germans did not grow proportionately with the rate of urbanization, and most of them retired or withdrew from commerce and enterprise, preferring to avoid commercial risk by investing in landed property, particularly in large apartment buildings. Their sons found their way into government administration alongside the offspring of the ruined gentry. In a short time, officials of German extraction were adopting the gentry outlook, the gentry values and mannerisms, together with the Hungarian language and culture.[10]

It is not generally known abroad that a strong opposition existed in Hungary among the followers of Kossuth, after 1867, to the Compromise and cooperation with Austria. Mihály Károlyi, the head of this party just before and during the First World War, was fighting not only for a Kossuthist program, but also for social reforms. Some of his more hot-headed followers were making statements as late as 1914 about the possibility of taking up arms against "Austrian tyranny." So it was not at all unexpected that Károlyi should take over the government when the dissolution of the monarchy began after the military collapse.

The Hungarian governments between August 1, 1919, the end of the Soviet regime, and June 4, 1920 (the Treaty of Trianon) were optimistic about the forthcoming peace treaty, and a new nationality policy was formulated accordingly, with Jacob Bleyer, a representative of the Germans in Hungary, acting as Minister for Nationalities. The Treaty of Trianon turned out to be harsher than even the pessimists among Hungarian politicians had expected, and all the initiatives for innovation in nationality matters disappeared together with the Ministry for Nationalities. An irate Hungarian public pinpointed concessions to the nationalities as the major cause for the Trianon Treaty and the country's dismemberment.[11]

The nationality decree of the Bethlen government provided for the full equality of all Hungarian citizens, irrespective of language, religion, or descent. The native tongue was permitted as the language of instruction in the schools. The Klebelsberg decree saw to the setting up of three types (ABC) of schools: the first with the language of instruction of the nationalities, with Hungarian as a compulsory subject; the second with nationality and Hungarian languages of instruction; and the third in which Magyar was the language employed, along with the compulsory teaching of a nationality language.[12]

The next major reform in nationality instruction was introduced by the Gömbös government. The "ABC" system of schools was replaced by unitary schools with nationality-Magyar (mixed) languages of instruction. The signing of the Vienna Protocol (August 30, 1940) involved not only the return to Hungary of northern Transylvania, together with the land of the Székelys, but also the acceptance by the Hungarian government of the German "nationality group" principle. A further consequence was the incorporation into Hungary of about a million Romanians and a significant number of Germans.

Another result of Bleyer's efforts was visits to German villages in Hungary by specially trained groups to promote German national consciousness there. On the other hand, numerous scholarships in Germany, obtained by Bleyer, enabled young Germans from Hungary to receive training as leaders of the German nationality movement in Hungary.

National Socialist organizers began to spread a new terminology for the interpretation of nationalities' relations, and the words "minority" and "nationality" were replaced with the term "*Volksgruppe*" (its members became *Volksdeutsche*, individuals of German descent, but without German citizenship, living outside Germany). The names in themselves would not have meant much had there not been the potential threat of the autonomy of the *Volksgruppe* behind them. Then, in the fall of 1938, the *Volksbund der Deutschen in Ungarn* was permitted by Hungarian authorities as a bid for the loyalty of Germans in Hungary.

With the passage of time, the *Volksbund* became the bridge between the National Socialist leadership of Germany and a portion of the Germans in Hungary as well as between the German political leadership and the Hungarian National Socialist groups. Perhaps the most important role of the *Volksbund*, from the standpoint of National Socialist Germany, was its repeated efforts to draft recruits for the German SS from among the German population of Hungary. These efforts yielded about 140,000 recruits. The *Volksbund*ists also provided strong support for the six-month regime of the Szálasi-Arrow Cross government from October 1944 onwards.

Nevertheless, the participation of the Hungarian Germans in loyalty movements for Hungary should not be forgotten. The greatest strength of the *Volksbund*, 300,000, or about 41% of the total Hungarian German population, occurred in the fall of 1942.

In 1945, in the tragic process of sorting out the question of responsibility for the occupation of the country by the Germans, the blame was levied against Germans or Hungary as a whole. The anti-expulsion side attempted to blame the government, some organizations, and anti-German biases in and outside Hungary. The Hungarian side, on the other hand, pointed to pro-Nazi activities of *Volksbund*ists and to the prolongation of the War through their support of recruiting campaigns and similar activities. The actual expulsion began in January 1946 and lasted through 1948. Those expelled numbered around 250,000, which would leave a 1948 German population of 220,000 in Hungary, regarded, to a great extent, as second-rate citizens.

The rehabilitation of Hungarian Germans to have equal rights with other Hungarian citizens took place as a result of a government ordinance of March 25, 1950. The makeup of post-1945 German settlements in Hungary has changed considerably. For instance, 90% of the German population of Zsámbék has been replaced by Magyar settlers from 28 villages.[13]

Jews

There have been Jews in Hungary from that country's beginning. The new arrivals from Russia after the pogroms there in the 1880s turned up, for the most part, poor in assets but rich in commercial and communal experience that had been handed down from one generation to another over the centuries. Those with some means or skills and education tended to move at once into urban communities or to Budapest itself. Many more settled in counties in the north and the northeast that had Ruthenian and Slovak populations, with whom they could make themselves understood.[14]

In lifestyle and by inclination an urban population, the Jews quickly adjusted themselves to the economic and sociocultural conditions of Hungary. Thus, a self-Magyarization society arose, which carried out its work among non-Hungarian-speaking Jews. Its members included the soon-to-be chief of Kossuth's press, as well as Kossuth's private secretary during the revolution. The first yearbook of the society glowed with "pro-Magyar patriotism." While other nationalities made efforts to retain their national identities, the Jews went out of their way not to be a nationality but to be accepted as Magyars. The Magyar "hyperpatriotism" of the Jews partly derived from fear of anti-Semitism, which would affect their economic leadership. In this manner, they became natural allies, or even part, of the Hungarian leadership, attempting to spread (or at least maintain) its language, literature, and historical traditions. Apart from all this, the Jews appreciably contributed to the Magyar percentages in successive censuses.[15]

Then, in a relatively short time, the Jews achieved a high representation among the owners, but even more so among the tenants, of large landed estates. Their visibility in trade, commerce, finance, and industry is attributed in part to their pre-emancipation exclusion from other than finance-related activities. In these vocations, they could be found in all manner of positions, whether as owners, managers, or employees. And since the Jews were at home in such high-profile ventures as theatre and newspaper and book publishing, they also became shapers and arbiters of public opinion and taste.

Although a large portion of the Jews remained in the lower strata of society, many of them, owing to the reasons discussed above, eventually held leading positions in their respective fields. Thus, Jewish factory hands would quickly emerge as trade union leaders to demand social justice from factory owners. Jewish proletarians and intellectuals also stood against Jewish capitalists and businessmen to provide a large part of the leadership of the 1919 Soviet Republic in Hungary, which aimed to nationalize Jewish assets as well. There was a positive relationship, even in the late 1930s, between the Jews and the Magyars because of their "complementary" qualities.

According to 1910 statistics, Hungary's Jews numbered 911,227, or 5% of the population. Furthermore, they made up 55-60% of the country's merchants, 45% of its lawyers, and 49% of its physicians.

Many Hungarians felt that the Jews had played a major role in Béla Kun's Communist government, which collapsed in 1919. Consequently, many Jews died in a post-Kun "White Terror" that engulfed Hungary. Postwar Hungary was no longer a heterogeneous society in which the percentage of Magyarized Jews (6%) maintained Magyar statistical majority over the ethnic minorities. Parliament passed its first anti-Semitic legislation, which restricted the number of Jews who could attend Hungary's universities. Although anti-Semitism remained visible, its political impact was moderated under István Bethlen, with a resultant lifting of some of the legal restrictions against the Jews.

The First Anti-Jewish Law, 1938, which attempted to reduce by 20% the number of Jews in various professions and in business and economic concerns that had more than ten employees, affected some 50,000 Jews. The Second Anti-Jewish Law, 1939, placed much more severe economic, professional, and racial restrictions on the Jews. During 1938-1941, Hungary's Jewish population, with the return of former parts of the country, rose from 480,000 to 825,000. The Third Anti-Jewish Law, 1941, was in part "the expression of Hungary's indebtedness to the Reich for the re-occupation of Northern Transylvania and of the Délvidék." The losses of Jewish labor battalions, set up in 1939 and sent to the front in 1941, amounted to about 42,000 by the end of the war. A major atrocity was the massacre of 18,000 Slovak, Ruthenian, and Galician Jews by German forces at Kemenets-Podolsk on August 27-28, 1941. The government of Miklós Kállay refused to agree to the deportation of

Hungary's Jews to certain death elsewhere, which ensured their safety until the German occupation of 1944.[16]

Kállay's pro-Allied drift and his refusal to aid completely the German war effort and to adopt a Nazi deportation program for the Jews were among the factors that contributed to Hitler's decision to occupy Hungary on May 19, 1944. In mid-May the deportations began, mainly to Auschwitz, with the resultant transfer and death of 437,000 to 450,000 Hungarian Jews over a two-month period. Horthy, however, stopped the removal of Budapest's Jewish ghetto population early in July.

Horthy's futile attempt to conclude an armistice with the approaching Soviet forces on October 15, 1944 was followed by a new wave of deportations with the assistance of the new Arrow-Cross (Nazi) government. Despite efforts to save them, 85,453 Jews died. Soviet forces took Budapest and occupied all of the country by early April 1945.

In spite of the loss, by the end of the war, of 564,507 out of 825,000, Hungary still had one of Europe's largest Jewish communities—255,500. Because of Hungary's severe postwar economic crisis and the presence of Soviet occupation forces, any return of Jewish property was, as a rule, handled personally. Besides, new anti-Semitic outbursts attempted to lay the blame on the Jews for many of the country's difficulties.[17]

Despite this atmosphere, a workable Jewish community life was revived. Zionists began to play an important role and were able to re-establish a network of Jewish schools from the elementary through the gymnasium level that attracted 4,642 students by 1947. The radical socialization of Hungary in 1948, however, drastically affected the economic, cultural, and religious life of Hungarian Jews. Hungary's Zionist organization was disbanded, and its leaders were tried and imprisoned. The anti-Jewish climate in Hungary changed after the death of Stalin in 1953, and many deportees returned to their homes. The 1956 uprising prompted over 20,000 Jews to emigrate to the West, although by the late 1950s Hungary's Jews were able to revive some of their community activities. Hungary's Jewish community, centered principally in Budapest, had shrunk, according to 1967 statistics, to between 80,000 and 90,000, although there were still a number of synagogues, a gymnasium, and a rabbinical seminary in operation.

Post-World War II Development

Hungarian schools changed drastically in 1945 with regard to language of instruction. The schools with nationality language of instruction were obliged to provide classes in Hungarian language and literature, while the rest of the subjects were taught in nationality tongues. A second type, the language-instruction school, was available, offering tuition in Hungarian, with the minority languages as compulsory subjects.

Until 1952, standard Croatian-Serbian, Slovene, Slovakian, and Romanian constituted the subjects or the languages of instruction in these schools. Primary teachers' colleges, with Croatian-Serbian, Slovakian, and Romanian languages of teaching, were set up between 1946 and 1953. For the German nationality, primary schools were not established until 1952, and teachers' colleges not until 1956. Teacher training for nationalities at the advanced level and for kindergarten teachers was introduced in 1959. However, nationality kindergartens had begun to function in 1953. In fact, most elementary nationality education took place at language-instruction schools and—from 1960 on—the schools with nationality-language of instruction were transformed into bilingual schools in which the science subjects were taught in Hungarian and the humanities subjects in the native languages of the students.

As a result of the impact of the human rights movement and the increasing awareness of ethnic studies, the grip of automatism in Hungary was weakening. This was reflected in a measure of 1968 providing for an inquiry into the efficiency of nationality education as a whole and for the elimination of the shortcomings. Consequently, the revitalized Nationalities Department in the Ministry for Culture was to be supported by a newly established Nationalities Chair at the National Institute for Pedagogy. In 1970, a network of nationality inspectors for the counties was set up. At the same time, seven nationality gymnasia were in existence, subordinated directly to the Nationalities Department.

The increasing importance of the nationalities was shown, from 1969 on, by the 5 to 10% special increment for teachers at nationality schools, by the reduction of the minimum from 25 to 15 children required for organizing nationality kindergartens, and by the directive in December 1972 of the Ministry for Culture which—among other things—specified objectives for nationality education. Among these goals was to secure the following for nationality students: background instruction in their native tongues; up-to-date basic education in their native languages and literatures so as to enable them to carry on unaided; inclination towards and facility for the efficient application of both the mother tongue and Hungarian; and appreciation of the native language and culture.

Both the structuring and the network of the nationality schools seem to have reached completion by 1961. That year witnessed the peak in the number of nationality students, with about 2,200 attending kindergarten, 2,500 attending schools with nationality-language as the language of instruction, and about 26,500 attending schools with the mother tongue taught as a subject. The years 1962 through 1968 composed a period of regression, however, with, for example, a decline of 53% in the number of Slovakian students.

An important characteristic of nationality policies in Hungary is that changes originate with the organs of the ruling party (HSWP, the Hungarian Socialist Workers' Party) or the appropriate department or division of the Ministry for Culture. It was a sign of the rejection of automatism that the working-out of systematic nationality syllabi fell to the National Institute for Pedagogy, which prepared and published them in nationality languages between 1969 and 1972.

These and other reform measures soon brought an end to the decline, and in the years between 1968 and 1979 the number of kindergarten pupils rose from 1,340 to 9,463; the corresponding figures concerning the students of schools with the mother tongue taught as a subject were about 18,200 in 1968, and almost 31,000 eleven years later. However, the case was different with the bilingual primary schools and the nationality gymnasia; in both instances, there occurred hardly any growth in the enrollment during the same period of time.

Advanced teacher training for secondary, primary, and kindergarten teachers has been provided for nationalities in nine different colleges situated in as many cities, other than Budapest. While the total number of nationality students at higher teacher-training institutions was 136 in 1968, in 1979 it rose to 446.

Until the end of the 1960s, not even the nationality associations could achieve much with respect to folk-cultural activities. More recently, these associations have taken it upon themselves to initiate and participate in cultural activities and coordinate them nationally. The nationality institutions regularly have been supported by, or have functioned within, the local council cooperative and other enterprises. As to the nationality associations, they supply the local nationality folk-cultural groups with program material and advise them on the level of form and content and on proper ideology.

The number of nationality ensembles varied greatly according to changes in outside opinion. In the 1960s, it was often charged that the only activities they were capable of were dancing and singing. The greater esteem derived from the upgrading of the activities favorably influenced the ensembles' efforts to foster tradition. As a result, more such ensembles are now active, and their artistic expression has greatly improved. Indeed, the number of these ensembles was growing at such a rate that there were almost 500 groups touring in 1977. The number of specific folk-dance ensembles of the nationalities grew from 63 in 1968 to 145 in 1977. During the same period, the number of nationality folk orchestras almost doubled, to 106. The development of folk theatre societies was less consistent. An important component of nationality-cultural work has become the cultural tour. The arrival of a touring nationality ensemble would be particularly effective in settlements with only scatterings of nationalities.

Clubs set up for the cultivation of nationality languages, with adaptable rules and programs, were suitable for the circumstances of small nationality islands in the midst of Magyar populations. Such clubs were organized in larger cities as well, including Budapest. Their number grew to 43 by 1975, and in another two years reached 68.

An effective and well-organized network of nationality libraries did not come into being until 1969. Before the introduction of book exchanges with the neighboring countries (that is, the mother nations of the nationalities), the libraries of the minority areas stocked as few as 17,000 books. By the end of 1974, 60 community libraries contained about 30,000 Croatian-Serbian books, 160 contained 37,000 German books, 97 had 31,000 books in Slovakian, 14 had 11,600 Romanian books, and 9 community libraries had almost 7,000 volumes in the Slovenian language. The total number of nationality books had risen to about 185,000 by the end of 1977. Base libraries were organized within the general library network in cities close to areas with scattered nationality groups, which in turn served the library needs of 361 communal libraries of the nationalities. Quantities of related books were loaned from the base library to the communal libraries, where they could be kept for as long as interest was shown by readers.

Owing to the application of a similar method to the collection and safeguarding of the artifacts and ethnographically significant traditions of the nationalities, four base museums were set up: one in Mohács for the Southern Slavs, one in Tata for the Germans, and two in Békéscsaba for the Slovaks and

Romanians, respectively. In addition, 22 smaller collections were organized—6 with German, 6 with Southern Slav, and 10 with Slovak artifacts.

The researchers of the nationality section of the Hungarian Ethnographical Society maintain contact with the nationalities, publicize the importance of the latter, and explain, in books and articles, aspects of nationality folklore. Several recent international ethnographical conferences on nationalities in Hungary resulted in scholarly papers and publications and in the exchange of observations and ideas on the conditions of nationalities.

It is possible for nationality groups to publish books in nationality languages. During the period 1970-1980, the publication of 54 nationality books in 175,000 copies was approved. By the end of 1980, 80 of these were actually published. The volumes thus published included ethnographical volumes written in the nationality languages. The publication of 157 nationality books has been envisaged for the years 1981-1985. Finally, it should be noted that the educational system of present-day Hungary reflects the Marxist-Leninist principle "national in form, socialist in content," which suggests that the promotion of cultural and administrative self-determination for the nationalities constitutes only a developmental stage on the road to a "single consciousness."

In the twenty years after 1949, official thinking was colored by automatism, the expectation of the automatic elimination of the problem of nationalities through the erection of socialism. During this almost "millenarian" stage, work on practical problems, research on the clarification of principles, and the preparation of plans for action concerning such pragmatic tasks as education and promotion of cultural advancement in the midst of nationalities came to a halt.

The 1956 upheaval led to the reassessment of the conditions of the nationality groups as well. The Hungarian Socialist Workers' Party directed on October 7, 1958 that workers of nationality background, including university graduates, should be employed in areas inhabited by the same native speakers. From 1968 on, interest in nationality problems was resuscitated, as illustrated by the HSWP program declaration in 1975 which emphasized, in addition to general civic rights, the freedom of contact and cultural exchange with the nationalities' mother nations. According to the Twelfth Congress of the HSWP in March 1980, a new approach to the problem of nationalities was needed.

The first new and striking point was the recognition of the definite relationship between the nationalities in Hungary and the Magyars, who form, in their turn, nationalities in the neighboring countries. Then the "free development of bilingual and bicultural citizenry on either side of the border" was stressed as a means towards "the international solution of the nationality problem." The request that appears to lie below the surface of the statement is a very moderate one compared with demands voiced during the interwar period. Mention of the "free development of bilingual and bicultural citizenry" reveals the anxiety that, in one or some of the neighboring countries, the official objective may be the production of unilingual and unicultural citizens, to the detriment of the native background of the Magyar citizens of those countries. In any case, the nationality question (or rather, its satisfactory solution) is presented as a condition "to the deepening friendship and coopera-tion" among the peoples of the area.[18]

Notes

[1]See Charles L. Mee, Jr., *The End of Order: Versailles 1919* (New York: E. P. Dutton, 1980). Also see Edward Chaszar, "The Problem of National Minorities before and after the Paris Peace Treaties of 1947," in *Nationalities Papers* 9 (Fall 1981); Ernest Flachbarth, *Histoire des minorités nationales en Hongrie* (Paris and Clermont-Ferrand: Hachette et Cie, 1944); Béla K. Király, Peter Pastor, and Ivan Sanders, eds., *War and Society in East Central Europe*. Vol. VI: *Essays on World War I: Total War and Peace-making. A Case Study on Trianon*; and item 491 in bibliography below.

[2]Attila Paládi-Kovács, in his "Ukrán szórványok a 18-19 században a mai Magyarország északkeleti részen" (Scatter-Settlements of Ukrainians in the Eighteenth and Nineteenth Centuries in the Northeastern Part of Present-Day Hungary), in Gyula Ortutay, editor-in-chief, *Népi Kultura—Népi Társadalom: A Magyar Tudományos Akadémia Néprajzi Kutató Csoportjának Évkönyve VII* (Folk Culture—Folk Society: Yearbook VII, the Ethnographical Research Group of the Hungarian Academy of Sciences) (Budapest: Akadémia, 1973), establishes that by the mid-1800s, the Ruthenian (Ukrainian) scatter-settlements were in a state of bilingualism in about 50 villages and that the number of such Ruthenians was at that stage between 35,000 and 40,000. According to Paládi-Kovács, the whole process of language switch among them, as a rule, took from 150 to 200 years (see, in particular, p. 346).

[3]See György Sarosácz, "Magyarország délszláv nemzetiségei" (The Southern Slav Nationalities in Hungary), in Gyula Ortutay, pp. 369-90. The related data are on pp. 369-70.

[4]Ibid., *Népi Kultura*, pp. 370-71. See also László Kövágó, *Nemzetiségek a mai Magyarországon* (Nationalities in Present-Day Hungary) (Budapest: Kossuth, 1981), pp. 144-45.

[5]István Tálasi, "Néprajzi csoportok Békésben a XVIII-XX században" (Ethno-cultural Groups in [the county of] Békés in the 18th-20th Centuries), in Ernö Eperjessy and András Krupa, eds., *A II Békéscsabai nemzetközi néprajzi nemzetiségkutató konferencia elöadásai* (The Papers Read at the Second International Ethnographical, Nationality-Research Conference at Békéscsaba) 3 vols. (Budapest and Békéscsaba: The Self-Contained Nationality Department, Ministry of Culture, 1981), vol. 1., pp. 51-68. See also Kövágó, *Nemzetiségek*, pp. 25 and 49.

[6]János Manga, "Magyarországi szlovákok" (The Slovaks in Hungary), in Gyula Ortutay, pp. 211-49. See also Tálasi, *Népi Kultura*, "Néprajzi csoportok."

[7]Ján Botík, "Az alföldi szlovákság etnokulturális továbbélésének folyamatai és tényezöi" (The Processes and Factors of the Ethnocultural Continuation of the Slovaks in the Alföld), in Eperjessy and Krupa, *Békéscsabai*, vol. 3, pp. 69-78.

[8]See Sándor Balogh, "Jelenkori népvándorlás: Kitelepités és lakosságcsere Magyarországon a felszabadulás után" (A Present-Day Migration of Peoples: Eviction and Population Exchange in Hungary after the Liberation), in *História* (Hungary: No. 3, 1981), pp. 24-26. The resultant conflict among the Slovaks in Hungary is discussed in György Lázár, "A népek barátságáért, a reakció és a sovinizmus ellen" (For the Friendship of Peoples: Against Reaction and Chauvinism), in *Tiszatáj* (Hungary: No. 11, 1981), pp. 24-30. Also see, for Slovak organizations, schools, etc., in Hungary, Kővágó, *Nemzetiségek*, pp. 60-66, 142-47.

[9]Of the substantial related literature on Germans in Hungary, see, for instance, Miklós Hutterer, "A magyarországi német népcsoport" (The German Nationality Group in Hungary), in Ortutay, *Népi Kultúra*, pp. 93-117; and Béla Bellér, *A Magyarországi németek rövid története* (A Short History of Germans in Hungary) (Badapest: Magvető, 1981), about the first 100 pages.

[10]Bellér, *Magyarországi*, pp. 102-22. After the compromise between Austria and Hungary in 1867, great economic developments followed, particularly shown by the growth of industrialization and modernization in Budapest. This reflected itself in the changing role and assimilation of the Germans of the capital.

[11]See note 1 above.

[12]Thomas Spira, *German-Hungarian Relations and the Swabian Problem: From Károlyi to Gömbös 1919-1926* (Boulder, CO: *East European Quarterly*, 1977). See also Bellér, *Magyarországi*, pp. 136-61; and Anthony Komjathy and Rebecca Stockwell, *German Minorities and the Third Reich: Ethnic Germans of East Central Europe between the Wars* (New York and London: Holmes and Meier, 1980).

[13]Lóránt Tilkovszky, *Ungarn und die deutsche "Volksgruppenpolitik" 1938-1945* (Budapest: Kossuth, 1978). Also Johann Weidlein, *Schuld des Volksbundes an der Vertreibung der Ungardeutschen: Kritische Unterschungen ungarischer Anschuldigungen* (Schorndorf, West Germany: published by the author, 1967); Lóránt Tilkovszky, *SS toborzás Magyarországon* (SS Recruiting in Hungary) (Budapest: Kossuth, 1974); Bellér, *Magyarországi*, pp. 160-91; Budainé, Erzsébet Hajdu and Péter Ullmann, "Zsámbéki német népdalok" (German Folksongs of Zsámbeék), in Eperjessy and Krupa, vol. 3, pp. 526-32.

[14]For a short but very helpful account of the history and basic data of the Hungarian Jewry, see Sándor Scheiber, "Zsidók" (Jews), in *Magyar Néprajzi Lexikon*, 5 vols. (Budapest: Akadémia, 1982), vol. 5, pp. 632-33.

[15]In Braham's opinion as well, the Jews' role in Magyarization was most important. Their contribution to the propagation of the Hungarian language and to the spreading of Magyar patriotism from about the mid-1840s appears significant. See Randolph L. Braham, *The Politics of Genocide: The Holocaust in Hungary*, 2 vols. (New York: Columbia University Press, 1981), vol. I, pp. 7-11.

[16]See Randolph L. Braham, *The Hungarian Labor Service System 1939-1945* (Boulder, CO: *East European Quarterly*, 1977), as well as chapter 10 of his *The Politics of Genocide*, vol. I, pp. 285-361.

[17]It is difficult to compute the exact number of Jewish survivors in Hungary in 1946, partly because converts and members of other churches, but of Jewish origin, could not be reached easily at the time. Besides, there were Hungarian Jews who, having been deported during the war, took advantage of resettlement facilities offered by the UNRRA instead of returning to Hungary. Compare figures provided by Braham on pp. 1143 and 1146 of *The Politics of Genocide*, vol. 2, respectively.

[18]This section, on cultural and educational developments, is largely based on Kővágó's *Nemzetiségek a mai Magyarországon*, which seems to present the latest available information on the subject.

BIBLIOGRAPHY

General Reference Works

479.   Bako, Elemer. **Guides to Hungarian Studies.** 2 vols. Stanford: Hoover Institution Press, 1973. Vol. 1. 636p.; vol. 2. pp. 639-1218.

The guide provides information from Magyar and Western language sources on Hungary, its society, culture, history, and economics up to the late 1960s. There are sporadic references to nationalities. The data listed derive not only from books and periodicals but also from maps and music.

480.   Erdei, Ferenc, ed. **Information Hungary.** Countries of the World Information Series, vol. 2. Oxford: Pergamon Press, 1968. 1,144p.

The contributors are all prominent Hungarian scholars, literati, and public officials. This reference book is divided into 11 major sections covering such topics as the country's geography, history, governmental apparatus, economy, health, education, science, literature, the fine arts, and international activities. It contains maps and illustrations of Hungarian paintings and folk art. Much of the information is presented here for the first time in English.

481.   Kabdebo, Thomas, comp. **Hungary.** World Bibliography Series, vol. 15. Santa Barbara, CA: American Bibliography Centre—ABC-Clio Press, 1980. lvi, 281p. Map.

This volume has 1,094 annotated entries on the most important Hungarian works dealing with the geography, history, economy, and politics of Hungary, and with Hungarian cultural and social organizations. The titles are 96% English, 3% other Western languages, and 1% Hungarian. A 53-page-long introduction attempts to sketch a highly condensed cultural-historical background of Hungary. The main body of the volume is topically organized, and is followed by a composite index of authors, titles, and subjects.

482.   **Kisebbségi Körlevél** (Minority Circular). 1937-1944. Pécs. Bimonthly.

Issued by the Research Institute of Minorities at the University of Pécs, the circular focuses on the problems of national minorities in the Danubian Basin, with emphasis on east central Europe. It contains book reviews, maps, statistics, surveys, laws, decrees, statutory provisions, and published texts.

483.   **A magyarországi nemzeti kisebbségekre vonatkozó programmok, törvény-javaslatok, törvények és rendeletek, 1827-1920** (Programs, Bills, Acts of Parliaments, and Ordinances on National Minorities in Hungary, 1827-1920). Budapest: Hungarian Society for Foreign Affairs, 1922. 43p.

The items published in the booklet constitute some of the most significant source material on the study of nationalities in Hungary between 1827 and 1920. Of the 18 texts presented, three are relevant in the present context: The Nationality Ordinances of the Hungarian People's Republic 1918-1919; The Language Ordinance of 1919, dated August 21, 1919; and The Provisions of the Peace Treaty of Trianon, June 4, 1920.

484.   Pécsi, Márton, and Sárfalvi, Béla. **The Geography of Hungary.** London: Collets, 1964. 299p. Maps. Photographs. (Originally printed in Hungary. Budapest: Corvina Press, 1964.)

This study contains 81 very useful black-and-white maps, 2 folded color maps, and 61 photographs. Its 12 chapters discuss such topics as the evolution and present aspects of the relief, mineral resources, climate, soils, population and settlement, industry, agriculture, and forestry. Most valuable is the excellent regional discussion called "Landscape Units of Hungary." Also presented are changes in the demographic and economic development of Hungary.

485. Telek, Joseph. **History of Hungary and Hungarians, 1848-1977: A Select Bibliography.** 2 vols. Hungarian Historicals Studies, nos. 1 and 3. Toronto: published by the author. Vol. 1, 1972 (1980). vi, 346p.; vol. 2, 1978 (1981). xvi, 963p.

The bibliography lists mainly monographs available in the University of Toronto Library, with references to titles in the Library of Congress and the British Museum. Volume 1 contains: Historical Periods; General References; General History; Hungarian Civilization and Culture. Volume 2 includes: Historical and Other Connected References; Prelude to the European War of 1914-1918 and Background Studies; European War, 1914-1918, and the Peace Settlement; Inter-War Period, 1919-1939; World War, 1939-1945, and the Peace Settlement with the Lesser Allies; After World War II; Foreign Relations and General Relations; Geographical and Other Related References.

National Minorities — General Works

486. Ats, Erika, comp. **In mehreren Sprachen, mit gemeinsamen Willen: Nationalitäten in der ungarischen Volksrepublik.** Budapest: The Propaganda Bureau for Popular Culture on Behalf of the Nationalities Department of the Ministry for Culture, 1977. 120p. Photos. Map.

The volume constitutes an official description and evaluation of the nationalities in Hungary in the 1970s. The publication states that 170,000 German Hungarians were expelled from Hungary as a result of the Potsdam Agreement and that about 73,000 Slovaks left Hungary in the framework of a population exchange with Czechoslovakia between 1946 and 1948, thus reducing the two largest nationalities of post-1945 Hungary. Another section of the book presents and illustrates the nationality policies of the Hungarian state.

487. Diószegi, Vilmos, ed. **Népi Kultúra-Népi Társadalom: A Magyar Tudományos Akadémia Néprajzi Kutató Csoportjának Évkönyve VII** (Folk Culture-Folk Society: Yearbook VII, the Ethnographical Research Group of the Hungarian Academy of Sciences). Budapest: Akadémia, 1973. 413p.

One of the most scholarly and most important publications on the subject, this volume deals not only with the ethnographical and folkloric aspects of the nationalities in Hungary, but also covers historical and socioeconomic aspects. Some of the studies are listed under the names of the contributors.

488. Eperjessy, Ernö, and Krupa, András, eds. **A II Békéscsabai nemzetközi néprajzi nemzetiségkutató konferencia elöadásai** (The Papers Read at the Second International Ethnographical, Nationality-Research Conference at Békéscsaba). 3 vols. Budapest and Békéscsaba: The Self-Contained Nationality Department, Ministry of Culture, 1981.

The conference took place on September 30 through October 2, 1980. Volume 1 contains the opening address by the parliamentary representative of the County of

Békés, who emphasized the importance attached to the education of the children in the nationality groups in Hungary and provided statistics of attendance from kindergarten to the university level. He also gave details of the "communal houses of culture," the nationality clubs, and nationality base-centers.

489.   Herczeg, Ferenc. **Az MSzMP nemzetiségi politikája** (The Nationality Policies of the Hungarian Socialist Workers' Party). Budapest: Kossuth, 1976. 87p.

The ruling party of Hungary, the MSzMP, possesses authority as regards the formulation of nationality policies. The roots of these policies go back to the Hungarian Communist party's program declaration of October 2, 1944, which promised major improvements in the field of nationality relations. Important decisions affecting principles and practice in nationality work were made in 1958. It was 10 years later that this work was significantly broadened and made more active.

490.   Junghann, Otto. **National Minorities in Europe**. New York: Covici-Friede Publishers, 1932. 121p.

The provisions of the Treaty of Trianon, 1920, secured protection for Hungary's minorities, which comprised at that time, in descending order, Germans, Jews, Slovaks, Croats, Romanians, and Serbs. Although measures were passed in 1919 and 1923, they were reported by the author as not having been carried out by 1930. The German minority had no schools with German as the language of instruction.

491.   Király, Béla K., Pastor, Peter, and Sanders, Ivan, eds. **War and Society in East Central Europe**. Vol. VI: **Essays on World War I: Total War and Peacemaking. A Case Study on Trianon**. Social Science Monographs. Brooklyn, NY: Brooklyn College Press, 1982. ix, 678p. Distributed by Columbia University Press.

Several of the 32 essays, written by different authors from different perspectives, present and analyze statistical and other data on national minorities in Hungary and the successor states before and after the signing of the Treaty of Trianon in 1920. The volume contains a bibliographical index, a gazetteer, a list of maps and charts, and a list of contributors.

492.   Kósa, László. "Thirty Years of Ethnographic Research among the Minority Groups Living in Hungary (1945-1974)." *Acta Ethnographica Scientarum Hungaricae* 24:3-4 (1975): 231-46.

While before 1920 only about one-half of Hungary's population was Hungarian, truncated Hungary emerging after World War I was an overwhelmingly national state surrounded by other new multinational states. After 1945 the situation changed significantly. The expulsion, in accordance with the Potsdam Agreement, of a large segment of the German population of the country, the exchange of Slovaks for Magyars in Slovakia, and the deterioration of the relationship with Yugoslavia resulted in distrust and uncertainty. In due course, however, complete political, cultural, and national equality for the remaining national minorities was incorporated into the constitution. National minority departments set up in the Hungarian Ethnographic Society and later in the Ministry of Culture and Education served to emphasize the importance of minorities.

493. Kovács, Ágnes. "Idegen nyelvü sztereotipiák, mondóka- és dalbetétek anyanyelvi prózai népköltési szövegekben" (Foreign Language Stereotypes, Speech- and Song-Insertions in Native-Language Texts of Folk Poetry). In **Népi Kultúra-Népi Társadalom: A Magyar Tudományos Akadémia Néprajzi Kutató Csoportjának Évkönyve VII** (Folk Culture-Folk Society: Yearbook VII. The Ethnographical Research Group of the Hungarian Academy of Sciences), edited by Vilmos Diószegi. Budapest: Akadémia, 1973. 413p.

There are many village communities in Hungary that are bilingual and trilingual. In their oral poetry, and in other forms of expression, including song, texts often occur in the language or languages of the foreign-speaking population elements. In the author's opinion, local folk poetry and folk songs, instead of degenerating, will be enriched with many "stylistic instruments." An appendix of some four pages contains texts with foreign-language insertions.

494. Kovács, Endre. **Szemben a történelemmel: A nemzetiségi kérdés a régi Magyaroroszágon** (Facing History: The Nationality Problem in Hungary of Old). Budapest: Magvető, 1977. 555p.

This is one of the best studies on the subject. While the larger portion of the book treats topics of nationality history in pre-1918 Hungary, it incorporates valuable discussions on such aspects as "the concept of nation," "the emergence of national consciousness," "national character, national belonging," and "Hungarian illusions." Most valuable are the chapters "Nationalities and Assimilation" and "The Balance."

495. Kővágó, László. **Kisebbség-nemzetiséq** (Minority-Nationalities). Budapest: Kossuth, 1977. 157p.

The international usage of the terms "minority" and "nationality" and such related matters as the processes of the socialization of minorities are utilized to explain the huge decline in the numbers of minority populations in Hungary and the neighboring countries. The "minority-nationality" designation is extended by the author to cover immigrants and those who are referred to in English-speaking countries as "ethnic groups." A short survey of the nationalities in Hungary in 1970 and of their legal and cultural circumstances is appended.

496. Kővágó, László. "Nationalitätenfrage und Nationalitätenpolitik in Ungarn." *Der Donauraum* 25:3 (1980): 92-104.

The study deals with the impact of such developments as the expulsion of certain categories of Germans from Hungary (1946-1949) and the population exchange between Hungary and Czechoslovakia in the late 1940s. Impressive data are provided on nationality schooling, libraries, museums, and culture.

497. Kővágó, László. **Nemzetiségek a mai Magyarországon** (Nationalities in Today's Hungary). Budapest: Kossuth, 1981. 189p.

A categorization of the various nationalities of the country shows their areas, origins, densities of population, and relationships to the successive Hungarian governments. Further topics discussed include the formation of socialist nationality policies, laws and regulations into action, their socioeconomic circumstances, the nationality languages and cultures, and the apparent clash between the legal expectation and the objective fact that nationalities are very strongly tied to another state through their blood relationship, language, culture, and past. The appendix includes 13 statistical tables and the text of a statement of the Cultural Ministry (1972) defining the education objectives for nationality instruction.

498. Macartney, C. A. **Hungary and Her Successors: The Treaty of Trianon and Its Consequences 1919-1937.** London: Oxford University Press, 1968 (1937). 504p.

The main objective of the volume was the consideration of the problems of the treaty's revision. Besides the heavy emphasis on the discussion of national minorities in the Burgenland, Slovakia, Ruthenia, Transylvania, Croatia, the Vojvodina, Fiume, and Hungary, each country, or area, is considered from the viewpoint of its geography, population, history, economy, culture, and education, as well as political conditions.

499. Mándics, Mihály. "A nemzeti kongresszusok után (After the Nationality Conventions). *Pedagogical Review* 4 (1979): 353-58.

Discussions at the conventions, in November 1978, of the associations of the German, Slovak, south-Slav, and Romanian nationalities in Hungary included the fostering of nationality appreciation of the native tongues and their traditions. The associations were keen to assist in fulfilling the respective plans of the Instruction and Culture ministries with explanatory work in their nationality areas. The training of German, Croatian, Serbian, Slovene, Slovak, and Romanian teachers was proceeding with the help of the neighboring socialist states.

500. Volgyes, Ivan. "Legitimacy and Modernization: Nationality and Nationalism in Hungary and Transylvania." In **The Politics of Ethnicity in Eastern Europe**, edited by George Klein and Milan J. Reban, pp. 127-46. East European Monographs, 93; ASN Series in Issue Studies, 2. Boulder, CO: East European Monographs, 1981. Distributed by Columbia University Press.

Volgyes attempts to provide an example for the crystallization of satisfactory definitions for "nation," "nationality," and "nationalism" based on the examination of major catastrophes in Hungary's past which were followed by sweeping ethnocultural changes. The latest such event, the Second World War, entailed the reduction of Hungary's minority population by 170,000 ethnic Germans and 73,273 Slovaks. Hungary's minority policies guaranteed primary instruction in nationality langues; some 400 primary schools listed the nationality mother tongue as a school subject, with the rest of the instruction in Hungarian. Several secondary schools, opportunities for kindergarten, nursery school, and primary teachers, and university training were available.

Germans

501. Bellér, Béla. **A magyarországi németek rövid története** (A Short History of Germans in Hungary). Budapest: Magvető, 1981. 212p.

After a discussion of the settling of Germans in Hungary and their contributions, four chapters are allotted to the 1840s. It was not until 1918 that a large movement (Brandsch) was formed for full autonomy, which was indeed granted by the Berinkey government in January 1919. After the collapse of the republic, Jakob Bleyer, the head of the German group, was appointed minister for national minorities. While the discussion ends with 1945, a short "Prospects" refers to development thereafter.

502.   Frey, Katherine Stenger. **The Danube Swabians: A People with Portable Roots**. Belleville, Ont.: Mika Publishing Company, 1982. 172p.

A short account of the Swabian migration is followed by historical surveys of the settling, lifestyles, and post-1945 decline of Swabian settlements in Romania and Yugoslavia. The traditional attitude of Magyar-Swabianism in Hungary gave way in the late 1930s to the pro-Nazi movement among younger Swabians. More than half of Hungary's Swabians were expelled.

503.   Hajdú, János, and Tóth, Béla C. **Der Volksbund in Ungarn**. Budapest: Pannonia, 1962. 83p.

The booklet sets out to show how the *Volksbund* of Germans in Hungary gradually became an agency of national-socialist Germany with the task of channelling the minority's human and economic resources towards the waging of total war.

504.   Hutterer, Miklós. "A magyarországi német népcsoport" (The German Nationality Group in Hungary). In **Népi Kultúra-Népi Társadalom: A Magyar Tudományos Akadémia Néprajzi Kutató Csoportjának Evkönyve VII** (Folk Culture-Folk Society: Yearbook VII, the Ethnographical Research Group of Hungarian Academy of Sciences), edited by Vilmos Diószegi, pp. 93-117. Budapest: Akadémia, 1973. 413p.

In this well-documented study, the author discusses his subject from three different, yet connected viewpoints. The treatment of the history of the three stages of the "Great Swabian Immigration" in the eighteenth century is followed by the crystallization of the successive levels in the gradual fusion of the various German tribal elements, first into ethnic communities, then into regional groupings. In the part "Settlement Geography," the scatter- and bloc-settlements of the German population in Hungary are located and discussed. The final segment of the study records the landmarks in the progress of the nationality in recent years.

505.   Manherz, Károly. "A nyelvi váltás folyamata a nyugat-magyarországi németeknél" (The Process of Language Switching among Germans in Western Hungary). In **Nemzetközi néprajzi nemzetiségkutató konferencia** (International Ethnographical Conference on Nationality Studies), pp. 212-25. Békéscsaba, October 28-31, 1975. Budapest: Hungarian Ethnographical Society, 1976.

The examination of speech development in three German nationality groupings in western Hungary shows three successive stages in the process potentially leading towards a switch in favor of Hungarian. In the first instance, only words referring to things novel or unknown to the speakers were taken over from the Hungarian. At the next stage (during the nineteenth century) Hungarian was substituting German as the literary language in the urban areas. In more recent years, rural areas as well have been penetrated by Hungarian, not excepting the common idiom either.

506.   Manherz, Karl. **Sprachgeographie und Sprachsoziologie der deutschen Mundarten in Westungarn**. Budapest: Akadémia, 1977. 189p. 90 language-geographical maps + 3 illus.

In the years since the Second World War, much work has been done in the field of language-geography. Part of this effort has been the mapping of the German dialects in three western counties of Hungary as well as the study of their historical voice-geographies and the peculiarities of their word-geographies. Finally, the language-sociological part shows the differences between the contrasting developments of the language provinces used by such social layers as peasants, tradesmen, and the literati.

507.   Mrnić, Josip. **Nemci u bačkoj u drugom svetskom ratu** (The Germans of Bácska during the Second World War). Novi Sad: Institut za izučavanje istorije Vojvodine (Research Institute for the History of Vojvodina), 1974. 385p.

The author's source material in German, Serbian, and Hungarian, collected in the archives of Yugoslavia, Hungary, and West Germany, forms a broad basis for the thorough understanding of the history of the Bácska Germans during the Second World War.

508.   Paikert, G. C. **The Danube Swabians: German Populations in Hungary, Rumania and Yugoslavia and Hitler's Impact on Their Patterns.** Studies in Social Life, X, edited by Günther Beyer. The Hague: Martinus Nijhoff, 1967. 324p.

The author makes a point of stating that the Swabians in the Danube Basin had always been constructive and that only in the decade starting in 1935 did they adopt "a negative position toward the state in which they lived; and an enthusiastic, unscrupulous support of Nazism." The Swabian leaders, almost as a group, had vested interest in the success of the Reich.

509.   Paikert, G. C. **The German Exodus: A Selective Study on the Post-World-War-II Expulsion of German Populations and Its Effects.** Publications of the Research Group for European Migration Problems, XII. The Hague: Martinus Nijhoff, 1962. 97p.

This is a study about the motives for and the circumstances of the expulsion of Germans from east central Europe, including Hungary.

510.   Schieder, Theodor, ed. **The Fate of Germans in Hungary: A Selection and Translation. Dokumentation der Vertreibung der Deutschen aus Ost-Mitteleuropa,** Band II. Bonn: Federal Ministry for Expellees, Refugees and War Victims, 1961. 214p.

The work consists of an introductory description and documents. Detailed consideration is given to the expulsion and the fate of Germans in Hungary. Nineteen eyewitness accounts and recollections illustrate the sufferings of Hungarian Germans and the changes in their lives towards and after the end of the Second World War.

511.   Schmalstieg, William R., and Magner, Thomas F., eds. **Sociolinguistic Problems in Czechoslovakia, Hungary, Romania and Yugoslavia.** Columbus, OH: Slavica Publishers, 1978. 503p. Maps. Tables.

The contributions of Conrad C. Reining and Bela C. Maday are of interest to Hungarianists. Based on a year-long field work project in a German-speaking village in south-central Hungary, Reining approaches the problem of ethnic identity on the microlevel. Maday states that "it is widely believed that the principle of *one ethnic group, one language* or *one nation*, reinforces cohesion, while multilingualism weakens attachment, loyalty, and conformity." The basic effort of most east European governments is toward assimilating their minorities into a cohesive, monocultural, and monolingual nation-state.

512.   Spira, Thomas. **German-Hungarian Relations and the Swabian Problem: From Károlyi to Gömbös 1919-1926.** East European Monographs, no. 25. Boulder, CO: East European Quarterly, 1977. 382p. Distributed by Columbia University press.

The author provides more in this book than the title indicates, since the three introductory chapters cover "Hungary's Minority Policy before World War I," "Minorities 'Conciliated'—Education and Cultural Policy 1918-1919," and "The Early

Horthy Era: Swabians, Austrians and Germans—The Seeds of a Dilemma (1919-1922)."
The remaining chapters deal with historical surveys of the difficulties between the
Magyars and the Swabians, the latter being the largest and most vocal minority
remaining in Trianon Hungary.

513.   Tilkovszky, Lóránt. **Ez volt a Volksbund: A német népscsoportpolitika és
Magyaroroszág 1938-1945** (Such Was the Volksbund: The German People's Group
Politics and Hungary 1938-1945). Budapest: Kossuth, 1978. 424p. German edition:
Ungarn und die deutsche "Volksgruppenpolitik" 1938-1945. Cologne and Vienna:
Böhlau Verlag, 1981. 370p.

By the mid-1930s, a trend had developed in Germany which referred to Germans
living in countries other than Germany as *Volksdeutsche,* who formed *Volksgruppen*
rather than national minorities and were entitled to *Volksgruppenautonomie.* By the
fall of 1938, the Swabians in Hungary succeeded in establishing the *Volksbund.* Almost
one-fourth of the Swabian population in Hungary in 1942-1943 were members of the
Volksbund, and large numbers joined the SS either as draftees or as volunteers.

514.   Tilkovszky, Lóránt. **SS toborzás Magyarországon** (SS Recruiting in Hungary).
Budapest: Kossuth, 1974. 193p.

The SS, having been set up as the defensive organization of the National Socialist
party, became a second army in Germany. The consequence for the German nationality
groups in Hungary of their closer association with the Reich was the possibility for the
SS to carry on recruiting in three successive waves among the German minority, yielding
20,000 recruits.

515.   Weidlein, Johann. **Schicksalsjahre der Ungardeutschen: Die ungarische
Wendung.** Ostdeutsche Beiträge aus dem Göttinger Arbeitskreis, Band II. Würzburg:
Holzner Verlag, 1957. 164p.

This is an early version of the author's perspective of the historical developments in
Hungary, ending in the expulsion of a great many Germans. Interest centers on the
causes and legal preparation for the expulsion of Germans from Hungary. Weidlein
argues that the reference to Hungarian Germans in the Potsdam Agreement was
inserted "at the request of Budapest."

516.   Weidlein, Johann. **Geschichte der Ungardeutschen in Dokumenten 1930-1950.**
Schorndorf, West Germany: published by the author, 1959. 408p.

Of the 42 items of the documentation, 8 refer to the final struggles of Jakob Bleyer;
17 pieces illustrate the fight for the "annihilation" of the Germans in Hungary. Another
8 items document the conflict after the establishment of the *Volksbund,* the question of
Magyarization, and the impact of Stalingrad on the Germans in Hungary. Nine of the
documents are connected with the actual expulsion.

517.   Weidlein, Johann. **Schuld des Volksbundes an der Vertreibung der
Ungardeutschen: Kritische Untersuchungen ungarischer Anschuldigungen.** Schorndorf,
West Germany: published by the author, 1967. 100p.

In an effort to rectify or refute the findings of Hungarian authors concerning the
causes and circumstances of the expulsion of Hungarian Germans between 1946 and
1948, Weidlein presents his own perspectives not only on the subject matter but on
writers, scholars, and politicians who were actually involved.

518.   Weidlein, Johann. **Jüdisches und deutsches Schicksal in Ungarn unter dem gleichen Unstern.** Schorndorf, West Germany: published by the author, 1969. 84p.

Weidlein attempts to prove that Hungarian politics were, particularly from 1919 on, directed by a Turanian movement whose "Asiatic" racialism was actually responsible for the destruction of both the Jews and the Germans in Hungary.

519.   Weidlein, Johann. **Der madjarische Rassennationalismus: Dokumente zur ungarischen Geistesgeschichte im 20. Jahrhundert.** Schorndorf, West Germany: published by the author, 1961. 132p.

The hypothesis, for the testing of which "evidence" is provided by the author, is that not only the tragedies of the Jews and the Germans in Hungary towards and after the end of the Second World War, but also the devastation and collapse of the country itself, were due to linguistic and racial nationalism on the part of the Magyars.

520.   Weidlein, Johann. **Pannonica: Ausgewählte Abhandlungen und Aufsätze zur Sprach- und Geschichtsforschung der Donauschwaben und der Madjaren.** Schorndorf, West Germany: published by the author, 1979. viii, 428p.

This volume contains 40 papers that were previously published in books and periodicals. Six of these deal with the earlier history of Hungary and the Germans in Hungary. Seventeen discuss the linguistic dialects of Danube Swabians. Thirteen are about the impact of Magyar nationalism on Germans in Hungary, and the remaining four treat German education in Hungary and the image of Germans presented in Magyar schools.

Jews

General Reference Material and Sources

521.   Braham, Randolph L., ed. **The Destruction of Hungarian Jewry: A Documentary Account.** 2 vols. New York: Pro Arte for the World Federation of Hungarian Jews, 1963. Vol. I, 416p.; vol. II, 555p.

This extensive documentary collection has reproduced exact copies of German and other records dealing with the Holocaust in Hungary. The first volume deals with the period from September 1940 through March 19, 1944, when the Germans officially occupied Hungary, while the second volume covers the period through April 4, 1945. It was during this latter period that most Hungarian Jews lost their lives.

522.   Braham, Randolph L. **The Hungarian Jewish Catastrophe: A Selected and Annotated Bibliography.** Yad Washem Martyrs' and Heroes' Memorial Authority, Jerusalem, and YIVO Institute for Jewish Research, New York. Joint Documentary Projects. Bibliographical Series no. 4. New York, 1962. 86p.

The publication lists 732 items—pamphlets, books, articles—in various languages dealing with the Holocaust, its background, and the aftermath. This source may be supplemented by the author's *Destruction of Hungarian Jewry.*

523.   **Monumenta Hungariae-Judaica.** Budapestini, 1903- .

This is an important collection of documents from public and private archives illustrating the history of the Jews in Hungary—their legal status, relations with the non-Jewish population and authorities, economic activities, etc. Nine volumes, covering the period 1092 to 1760, appeared before 1966. Between 1903 and 1938, the work was published by the Hungarian Jewish Literary Society (Izraelita magyar irodalmi társulat), and from 1959 by the Central Board of the Jewish Communities in Hungary (Magyar izraeliták országos képviselete) under the editorship of Alexander Scheiber. Hungarian title: Magyar-zsidó oklevéltár.

524. **Uj élet: a magyar izraeliták lapja** (New Life: The Journal of Hungarian Jewry). 1945- . Budapest. Fortnightly.

This is the organ of the Central Board of Jewish Communities, and the only Jewish periodical published in postwar Hungary.

525. **Vádirat a Nácismus Ellen: Dokumentumok a Magyarországi Zsidóüldözés Történetéhez** (Indictment against Nazism: Documents to the History of the Persecution of Jews in Hungary). Vol. I. **1944 március 19-1944 május 15. A német megszállástól a deportálás megkezdéséig**. Edited by Ilona Benoschofsky and Elek Karsai. Budapest: A Magyar Izraeliták Országos Képviselete Kiadása, 1958. 379p.

This is a collection of documents drawn from German and Hungarian sources on the development and implementation of the Nazi program to deport Hungary's Jewish population to concentration camps. The 170 documents deal with the period from March 19 to May 15, 1944.

Monographs

526. Braham, Randolph L., ed. **Hungarian-Jewish Studies**. 2 vols. New York: World Federation of Hungarian Jews, 1966.

A collection of studies by experts on Hungary dealing with the history of the Jews in Hungary, their extermination during the last years of the Second World War, and the present situation of the survivors. Bibliography.

527. Braham, Randolph L. **The Politics of Genocide: The Holocaust in Hungary**. 2 vols. New York: Columbia University Press, 1981. Vol. 1: xiii, 594p.; vol. 2: xii, 674p. Figures. Maps. Photographs.

At the time of the German occupation of Hungary on March 19, 1944, 825,000 Jews lived there. Within four months, a relatively small band of Germans had manipulated the Hungarian police and state administration into shipping almost half a million Jews to Auschwitz, where most were promptly killed. A quarter of a million Budapest Jews were saved from deportation by Regent Horthy early in July 1944, but after his replacement by a Fascist regime on October 15, Hungarian Nazi terrorists slaughtered about 60,000 more Jews, mainly in the capital. By the end of the war, 564,507 Hungarian Jews had been murdered.

528. Braham, Randolph L. **The Hungarian Labor Service System, 1939-1945**. East European Monographs, no. 31. Boulder, CO: East European Quarterly, 1977. x, 159p. Distributed by Columbia University Press.

This is a detailed history of the auxiliary labor service into which Hungarian Jews were compelled during the Second World War. Hungary's treatment of Jews throughout the war was as contradictory as the entire participation of Hungary in World War II. Braham demonstrates conclusively that non-Jewish Hungarians, at least, cannot completely escape a measure of blame for the catastrophe which befell their

Jewish compatriots. At the same time, he points out that at least some conscience-stricken Hungarian military officers and democratic-minded politicians did try, however feebly and unsuccessfully, to alleviate the lot of the Jewish labor servicemen.

529. Handler, Andrew, ed. and trans. **The Holocaust in Hungary: An Anthology of Jewish Response**. University, AL: University of Alabama Press, 1982. 162p.

This is a collection of memoir accounts and essays by Hungarian Jews who survived the Holocaust. Most of the accounts were written originally in Magyar, and provide a valuable personal insight into the catastrophe in that nation. The book contains a good historical overview of the Holocaust there, and has an excellent segment of bibliographical notes.

530. **The Jews of Hungary: Survey of Their History and Postwar Situation**. New York: Institute of Jewish Affairs, World Jewish Congress, 1952. 22p.

A brief outline of the Jews' situation in Hungary during the period of liberation (1945-1948) and the consolidation of the Communist regime (1948-1952). It deals with the effect of political changes on Jewish life and is based on information from the Hungarian Jewish periodical *Uj élet* (New Life) and from Western periodicals.

531. Katzburg, Nathaniel. **Hungary and the Jews: Policy and Legislation, 1920-1943**. Ramat-Gan: Bar-Ilan University Press, 1981. 299p.

This is a history of Hungary's Jewish minority and its altered status after the Treaty of Trianon. Beginning with the White Terror that followed Bela Kun's brief reign, the author traces growing pressure by right-wing forces in Hungary, particularly after 1933, to find legal ways to eliminate Jews from a prominent role in Hungary's economic and social life. The work covers the implementation of the first two Jewish laws, and discusses other anti-Semitic legislation between 1939 and 1943. A collection of documents is appended.

532. Lambert, Gilles. **Operation Hazalah**. Translated by Robert Bullen and Rosette Letellier. Indianapolis and New York: Bobbs-Merrill Co., 1974. xi, 235p.

This book relates the story of the courageous and desperate Jewish resistance movement, organized in Budapest, Hungary in 1944 by young Zionists, which helped save tens of thousands of Jewish lives in the face of the awesome and efficient death machine commanded by Adolf Eichmann. With forged documents, members of the resistance released condemned Jews from prison or from trains heading for death camps and guided escapees over borders.

533. Lévai, Jenö. **Eichmann in Hungary: Documents**. Budapest: Pannonia Press, 1961. 294p.

This is an extensive historical and documentary study of the role of Adolf Eichmann in the scheme to deport Hungary's Jews to death camps elsewhere in Europe. It covers German plans for the "Final Solution" and the place of Hungary in this scheme. It also discusses the implementation of these policies as well as Eichmann's efforts to trade Jewish lives for war materials. The latter third of the volume is a documentary appendix.

534. Lévai, Jenö. **Fekete könyv a Magyar Zsidóság Szenvedéseiröl** (Black Book of the Suffering of Hungarian Jews). Budapest: Officina, 1946. 319p.

An excellent official history of Hungarian Jewry from 1933 to 1945. It investigates the impact of growing anti-Semitism in Europe and Hungary on the Jewish community after 1933. The core of the work, however, deals with the period after March 1944, when German forces occupied Hungary and began to implement a deportation scheme designed to eradicate the nation's Jewish population.

535. Lévai, Jenö. **Zsidósors Magyarországon** (The Fate of Jews in Hungary). Budapest: Magyar Téka, 1948. 479p.

This study contains a detailed history of the Hungarian Jewish community from 1933 to 1945, with emphasis on the later years. The documents are drawn from German, Hungarian, and Jewish sources.

536. Moskovits, Áron. **Jewish Education in Hungary (1848-1948)**. New York: Bloch Publishing Company, n.d. 351p.

This survey traces the continual struggle to maintain a separate Jewish educational system and to keep Jewish religious and cultural traditions alive. The author concludes that it was the divisions between the Orthodox and other Jewish groups that destroyed Hungarian Jewry's educational system. An excellent bibliography is appended.

537. Patai, József. **Harc a zsidó kultúráért** (Struggle for Jewish Culture). Budapest: Mult és Jövö Jubileumi Kiadás, 1936. 317p.

The subject of this study is Jewish culture and religion in Hungary in relation to assimilation and Magyarization over the past century. It also deals with Hungarian anti-Semitic reaction to the growing economic strength of Hungary's Jews.

538. Schickert, Klaus. **Die Judenfrage in Ungarn**. Essen: Essener Verlagsanstalt, 1937. 194p.

The study focuses on Jewish assimilation and anti-Semitism in Hungary over the past century. It traces the early history of Hungarian Jewry, and studies the impact of Jewish emancipation on the economic and social status of the Jewish community *vis-à-vis* Hungary's ruling class. The book ends with a look at Hungarian anti-Semitism. Bibliography.

Romanians

539. Kovács, Ágnes. "A magyarországi román mesemondók" (Romanian Storytellers in Hungary). In Eperjessy and Krupa, eds. See entry 488. Vol. 3, pp. 579-89.

In order to assist members of the Romanian minority in keeping their native culture, teachers and researchers with Romanian backgrounds are trained at the high school in Gyula, the Teachers' Training College in Szeged, and the universities of Budapest and Debrecen. The weekly *Foaia Noastra* makes its contribution to the same purpose by keeping its readers abreast of Romanian-related news.

540. Turza, Maria. **A Vásárhelyi Találkozó** (The Meeting at Vásárhely). Bucharest: Political Publishers, 1977. 259p.

Not unlike the celebration of the Ides of March, 1937, in Budapest, the meeting at Vásárhely, in Transylvania (now Romania), on October 2-4 of the same year signified the gathering together of opposition to national socialism. Most of the leaders and intellectuals of the Magyar minority were present, and they were eager to join forces in the spirit of a "Popular Front." Their *Hitvallás* (Declaration of Adherence) called for cooperation of the nationalities, with particular reference to the Romanians and the Magyars. The author of the book suggests that early representatives of the radical Left were in attendance at Vásárhely.

Slovaks

541. Chmelař, Josef. **National Minorities in Central Europe**. Prague: Orbis, 1937. 106p. Map.

The chapter on Hungary (pp. 56-64) criticizes the government for aiming at denationalization, which caused a steep decline between 1920 and 1930 in the number of nationalities, and for its treating minorities as "groups of citizens speaking another language ... from whom Magyar patriotism is demanded." The schools available, particularly to the Slovak minority, are described as insufficient.

542. Gyivicsán, Anna. "Activities of the Democratic Association of Slovaks in Hungary, 1956-1968." In **Spoločný osud—splpoločna cesta: účast príslušníkov slovenskej národnosti v robotníckych a rol'nickych hnutiach 19. a 20. storouči na území mad'arska (štúdie)** (Common Destiny—Common Approach: The Participation of Slovaks of Hungary in National Labor and Peasant Movements during the Nineteenth and Twentieth Centuries. Studies), edited by Imre Polányi. Budapest: School Textboook Publishers, 1980. 186p.

The author covers not only the period 1956-1968, but also the years after 1948. She draws attention to the fact that the association in the 1950s was almost completely restricted to cultural matters and not active to any important social or political extent, even if that would have been of great momentum in the socialist reorganization of agriculture. The author also reveals noncompliance with several party decisions after 1957 concerning the strengthening of the nationality associations' political and social activities, and their expansion within the framework of the Patriotic People's Front.

543. Polányi, Imre, ed. **Spoločný osud—spoločna cesta: účast príslušníkov slovenskej národnosti v robotníckych a rol'nickych hnutiach 19. a 20. storouči na území mad'arska (štúdie)** (Common Destiny—Common Approach: The Participation of Slovaks of Hungary in National Labor and Peasant Movements during the Nineteenth and Twentieth Centuries. Studies). Budapest: School Textbook Publishers, 1980. 186p.

The volume is the first of a series published on behalf of the Slovak Democratic Association in Hungary and constitutes the result of a very useful initiative. The association wishes to recount the story of the Magyars' and Slovaks' centuries-long coexistence and common struggles. The six studies follow in chronological sequence of their respective subject matter, covering the period from about 1830 until modern times. Summaries in Hungarian and German are included.

544. Swetoň, Ján. **Die Slowaken in Ungarn: Beitrag zur Frage des statistischen Madjarizieren**. Bratislava: Verlag Slowakische Rundschau, 1943. 208p.

Swetoň, a researcher in the Slovak Foreign Studies Institute, Bratislava, contends on the basis of comparative statistical studies of several censuses that the number of Slovaks in Hungary was actually much greater than reported in official Hungarian publications.

545.   Tilkovszky, Lóránt. **Juzné Slovensko v rokoch 1938-1945** (Southern Slovakia, 1938-1945). Bratislava: Vydavatel'stvo Slovenskej Akadémie Vied, 1972. 219p. (Summaries in Russian and German).

This Hungarian socialist interpretation of the seven-year history of southern Slovakia under Hungarian rule first points out how Germany could take advantage of the less-than-satisfactory state of Czechoslovakia's minority affairs in turning the parties to the conflict into satellites. Other chapters deal with the unfavorable effects of prevailing socioeconomic conditions and negative governmental attitudes toward reform.

Ukrainians

546.   Magocsi, Paul Robert. **The Shaping of a National Identity: Subcarpathian Rus', 1848-1948**. Cambridge, MA: Harvard University Press, 1978. xiii, 640p.

See entry 414 for annotation. The author also discusses Hungary's policy in Carpatho-Ukraine during the years 1849-1944.

547.   Markus, Vasyl. "Carpatho-Ukraine under Hungarian Occupation." *Ukrainian Quarterly* X:2 (Summer 1956): 252-56.

The author details the policy of Magyarization by the Hungarian government in the Carpatho-Ukraine during the period 1939-1944.

South Slavs

548.   Buzási, János. **Az Újvidéki "Razzia"** (The Raid at Újvidék). Budapest: Kossuth Publishers, 1963. 125p.

One of the actions connected with the "pacification" of territories restored to Hungary during the Second World War was the "raid" at Újvidék. In January 1942, when an armed group of 30-40 opened fire on Hungarian soldiers and gendarmes, not only was the group wiped out, but many of the population of the area who had failed to report the group and had provided them with food were killed. In the course of anti-partisan raids, everyone's identity was checked and those found to be suspect were shot. The official enquiry into the deaths of more than 3,000 persons failed to result in the punishment of the guilty officers.

549.   Maučec, Jože, and Novak, Vilko. **Slovensko Porabje** (Slovene Porabje). Ljubljana: Slovenski knjizni zavod OF, 1945. 31p. Map.

The booklet covers the geography, history, language, and customs of Porabje, the Slovene-inhabited area along the Raba River in Hungary. It includes data by townships from Hungarian censuses of 1890, 1900, 1910, and 1921. The Slovene minority in the Radkersburg/Radgona area in the Austrian province of Styria is also treated.

550.   Miklavc, Janja, and Olas, Ludvik. "Socialnogeografska analiza slovenskega Porabja na Madzarskem" (A Socio-geographic Analysis of the Slovene Porabje in Hungary). *Razprave in gradivo* 9-10 (1979): 137-48.

The essay analyzes demographic growth as well as the industrial and educational structure of the population in the Slovene-inhabited Porabje area of Hungary. Due to isolation from main transportation arteries, the area has not participated in the overall economic development, with resulting depopulation, population aging, and poor educational structure.

551. Mukicsné, Kozar Mária. "A magyarországi szlovének néprajzi vizsgálatána mai helyzete és eredményeinek összegezése (The Present-Day Position of the Ethnographical Examination of Slovenes in Hungary and the Summation of Findings). In Eperjessy and Krupa, eds. See entry 488. Vol. 3, pp. 559-65.

Of the Yugoslav nationalities in Hungary, numbering about 100,000, 90% are Croats and 5% each are Serbs and Slovenes. The first Slovene settlements came about in the twelfth century. The larger portion of the Vend area became part of the kingdom of the Serbs, Croats, and Slovenes in 1920 as a consequence of the Trianon Treaty. Only 10 Slovene settlements of the Vend area stayed within the Hungarian borders.

552. Sarosácz, György. "Magyarország délszláv nemzetiségei" (The South-Slav Nationalities in Hungary). In Diószegi, ed. See entry 486. Pp. 369-90.

A substantial portion of the study examines the historical and geographical aspects of the settling of the south-Slav nationality groups over the centuries. The most numerous grouping among the South Slavs in Hungary is the Croats; their number was estimated in the early 1970s at 94,700, while those of the Serbs and Slovenes were estimated at 7,000 and 5,500, respectively.

553. Slavič, M. **Prekmurje**. Ljubljana: Slovenska krsčanskosocialna zvea, 1921. 131p.

The study treats the Slovene minority in Hungary, including the period of Hungarian Bolshevik administration in the spring of 1919. At that time, the Hungarian rule extended to Prekmurje, later ceded to Yugoslavia. This is an eyewitness account of the negotiations for the Yugoslav-Hungarian boundaries at the Paris Peace Conference in 1919.

5   National Minorities in Romania, 1919-1980

Stephen Fischer-Galati

HISTORICAL SUMMARY

The national minorities question in Romania has been one of crises and polemics. This is due, in part, to the fact that Greater Romania, established at the end of World War I, brought the incorporation into the body politic and social of the Old Romanian Kingdom, itself relatively free of minority problems, territories inhabited largely by national minorities. Thus, the population of Transylvania and the Banat, both of which had been constituent provinces of the defunct Austro-Hungarian Monarchy, included large numbers of Hungarians and Germans, while Bessarabia, a province of the Russian empire, included large numbers of Jews. While the Hungarian (Szeklers and Magyars), German (Saxons and Swabians), and Jewish minorities were the largest and most difficult to integrate into Greater Romania, other national minorities such as the Bulgarians, Russians, Ukrainians, Tatars, Serbians, Turks, and Gypsies also posed problems to the rulers of Greater Romania during the interwar period and, in some cases, even after World War II.

It is fair to say that those national minorities which could and did become focal points in international disputes and whose status in Romania became internationalized in one form or another or at one time or another since World

War I, were singled out for special treatment by Romania's rulers. This affected the course of their own history and of that of the Romanian state during the last sixty years or so. These were the Hungarian, the German, and the Jewish.

The national minorities problem cannot be taken out of the general context of Romanian history and politics, as has been done with such polemical energy ever since the question itself was first formulated a century ago, as it is intertwined with the entire historic and political evolution of independent Greater Romania. At the heart of the question is Romanian nationalism and the role that the political leaders of the Old Kingdom were to play in the enlarged Romanian state established after 1918. Since the legitimacy of Greater Romania was based on the historic claim of Romanian numerical and cultural predominance in all provinces incorporated into the Old Kingdom, and since the constituent provinces of the Old Kingdom were the Romanian principalities of Wallachia and Moldavia, both regarded as the core of Romanianism in the multinational Greater Romanian state, the political leaders of the Old Kingdom sought at all times to secure power in the enlarged Romanian state. However, as the provinces which were united with the Old Kingdom were more populous and larger in area than the Old Kingdom and also had different historic and cultural traditions, the primary goal of the leaders of the Old Kingdom was to prevent the more modern, better educated, and wealthier inhabitants of the newly incorporated provinces from reshaping the old Romanian political ways.

This is an important consideration in any assessment of the true nature of the nationality question in Romania since the policies of the rulers in Bucharest were directed not only toward containment of the political rights of the "advanced" nationalities such as the Hungarians, the Germans, and the Jews but also against those Romanians from outside the Old Kingdom whose expectations and plans were often a function of their own historic experience. The one common experience shared by all inhabitants of Greater Romania, whether Romanians or members of national minorities other than the Jews, was anti-Semitism. Consequently, the Jewish question assumed immediate importance at the end of World War I. Next in significance was the Hungarian question, since the historic and political experiences of the Romanians of Transylvania were inexorably linked with the history of Hungary and the Hungarians. Third was the German question, as the Germans of Transylvania (Saxons) and of the Banat (Swabians) retained a civilization of their own, distinct from that of other nationalities, and their allegiance to the Romanian cause was often questioned by the ruling class in Bucharest.

Of the three minority questions that assumed preeminence in interwar Romania, the Jewish one was the most significant. Its significance lies in the perception by the inhabitants of Greater Romania, particularly by the Romanians of Moldavia, Bessarabia, Bukovina, and certain parts of Transylvania and Wallachia, that the Jews were an alien and unassimilable element and in the exploitation of these prejudices by nationalist Romanian politicians. The Jewish question reached its first crisis during the Great Peasant Revolt of 1907, in Moldavia and Wallachia, when the disgruntled masses identified the Jewish estate managers of absentee landlords as ruthless exploiters of the Christian peasant. That crisis lent justification to the traditional policies of pre-World War I Romanian governments of denying civil rights and citizenship to Jews.

The incorporation of Bessarabia and of Bukovina after World War I, provinces with large, unassimilated, and non-Romanian speaking Jewish populations, exacerbated the Romanians' anti-Semitic feelings, especially as the Bessarabian Jews were considered, or at least branded, by political leaders as agents of Bolshevism if not Bolsheviks as such. Thus, the theory of a Judaeo-Communist conspiracy added fuel to the innate hostility of Romanian students, intellectuals, workers, and peasants toward Jews. The insistence by the Allied and Associated Powers to secure citizenship rights for the Jews as a prerequisite for recognizing Greater Romania further aggravated the Jewish question. In fact the Powers had little concern for the Jews of Romania, and from the enactment of the constitution of 1923 until the closing stages of World War II the Jewish question became almost entirely an internal Romanian problem. As such, however, it assumed ever greater political importance as the radical right, first headed by the Moldavian-based League of National Christian Defense and later by the Christian populist and virulently anti-Semitic Iron Guard, committed itself to establishing a Romanian Orthodox Christian state which would solve the Jewish question. Hitler's advent to power facilitated anti-Semitic actions and agitation in the 1930s and culminated eventually in the establishment of the so-called National Legionary State, led by General Ion Antonescu, in 1940, shortly before Romania joined Nazi Germany in the war against the Soviet Union.

It is noteworthy, however, that specific anti-Semitic legislation was not enacted before 1940 and that, in comparison with other east European countries under Nazi occupation or allied with Hitler's Germany, the Jews of Romania fared relatively well during World War II. In fact, Hitler's "final solution" was resisted by the Antonescu regime, and the vast majority of Romania's Jews suffered from nothing more than restrictive humiliations during the war. Yet, the sparing of the Jews was not reflective of the absence of anti-Semitic sentiments and actions in Romania. What was ultimately responsible for a different resolution of the Jewish question in Romania than elsewhere in Nazi-occupied eastern Europe was the Romanian rulers' realization, from perhaps as early as 1942, that Nazi Germany would not be able to defeat the Russians and that a Russian takeover of Romania was likely at the end of the war. To avoid that fate, or at least to make it more palatable, the Romanian leadership adhered to a policy of relative toleration toward Jews, hoping that it would provide flexibility in negotiations with the western anti-Fascist allies and a certain degree of maneuverability in the military and diplomatic moves that would determine the postwar status of Romania. It was indeed those considerations and not the drastic reduction in the size of the Jewish population after the involuntary cession of Northern Transylvania to Hungary and of Bessarabia and Northern Bukovina to the Soviet Union in 1940 that accounted for Romanian policies toward the Jewish minority.

Statistical data on Romania's Jews are generally misleading. Figures based on nationality differ considerably from those based on religion, since many Jewish inhabitants of Romania considered themselves Jewish Romanians rather than Jews in Romania. Thus, the number of Jewish inhabitants of Romania before World War II has been variously recorded as between 750,000 and 1,500,000. The most widely accepted figure, as of 1939, is slightly over

1,000,000, which would represent approximately 6% of the entire population of Romania. That would also rank the Jewish population as the second largest national minority after the Hungarians, whose number is placed at approximately 1,500,000. Data on Jewish schools, occupational patterns, and other standard statistical categories are also inconclusive. One of the main difficulties in these respects lies in the quality of pre-World War II Romanian statistical methods and the fact that, legally, the Jews did not represent a national minority but a religious one. Statistical data are equally questionable for the period following World War II.

In the absence of censuses, estimates have varied. On the basis of credible evidence, the number of Jews in Romania in 1945 was 385,000, the decline in the size of the Jewish population being attributed to the loss of Bessarabia and Northern Bukovina and to the extermination of a significant number of Jews of Northern Transylvania during the war. By 1949, following the beginning of emigration to Israel, the number was placed at 256,000. By the end of 1955, some 175,000 Jews were still living in Romania. The continuing emigration to Israel depleted the ranks of the Jewish population over the ensuing twenty-five years, and, according to the best current estimates, the number of Jews living in Romania in 1982 is placed at approximately 40,000.

Despite this drastic alteration in the size of the Jewish minority, the Jewish question did not go away under Communist rule and, if anything, has gained in importance for a variety of reasons. In the immediate postwar period, the Kremlin found it expedient to rely on the "victims of fascism" for the pursuit of its policies in Romania, and entrusted key positions in the Romanian government to "anti-Fascist" Jews such as Ana Pauker, Gheorghe Stoica, Leonte Răutu, and a large number of lesser "democratic" Romanian Jews. The encouragement of "socialist patriotism" in the early 1950s resulted in the gradual elimination of Jews from primary and secondary posts in the government and the Communist party and the unleashing of the pent-up anti-Semitic sentiments of the anti-Communist Romanian masses. As a consequence, emigration to Israel was encouraged. As the Romanian leadership reacted to Khrushchev's plans for Romania and sought contacts with the United States in the early 1960s, the Jewish question assumed new significance. American insistence on an unrestricted emigration policy for Romania's Jews and the linking of that position with the granting of economic and political concessions to Romania expedited emigration. Moreover, as the policy of "independence" from the Soviet Union required the creation of an international image and relations which would provide optimum options and flexibility for Romania, the rulers of Romania, especially after the advent to power of Nicolae Ceauşescu in 1965, maintained and promoted friendly relations with Israel. That policy, in conjunction with expanded economic and political relations with the United States and western European states, resulted in the de facto elimination of the Jewish question through rapid emigration by all Jews who wished to lave Romania.

The few Jews still in Romania are now regarded not as a national minority, not even as a "coinhabiting nationality," but as Jewish Romanians with a historic culture of their own. Romania's Jews are entitled to maintain their own religious and cultural organizations, including Jewish theatres, but are legally Romanians and treated as such. However, as long as any Jews continue to live in Romania, the Jewish question will continue to exist because it is activated by external groups which regard the Romanian Jews as a weather-vane of Romania's attitudes toward national minorities, human rights, and emigration. In purely internal terms, however, the Jewish question has ceased to exist except to the extent to which Romanian nationalism, even in its socialist garb, is fundamentally incompatible with Judaism. As such, opportunities for total Jewish assimilation or integration into the Romanian body politic and social are well nigh impossible, and latent anti-Semitism — one of the principal ingredients of Romanian nationalism — has persisted even into the 1980s.

In some ways more serious, and certainly more vexatious, than the Jewish question have been the problems related to the Hungarian national minority in Greater Romania. The Hungarians, whether Magyars or Szeklers, were incorporated into the Romanian body politic when Transylvania became part of Romania at the end of World War I. At that time, according to what may be regarded as reliable statistics, approximately one-third of the total population of that province consisted of Hungarians, whose actual number was around 1,500,000. More than one-half of Transylvania's population was Romanian (approximately 2,850,000), while the balance of the inhabitants consisted primarily of Germans (about 550,000) and lesser national minority groups. The size of the Hungarian population, fairly constant during the interwar years, was markedly reduced between 1940 and 1945 because of the temporary reannexation of Northern Transylvania by Hungary in 1940, but since World War II the Hungarian population has maintained itself at approximately the prewar levels. All in all, the Hungarian population of Romania has represented approximately 8% of the total population of Greater Romania.

While that percentage is not inordinately high for any state with an overwhelmingly dominant ethnic population, the Hungarian national minority has been the subject of both special treatment and special discrimination. The special treatment was the result of the Great Powers' insistence that Romanian governments respect the provisions of the minority treaties enacted at the end of World War I. By virtue of the rights granted to national minorities in Romania, all cultural, religious, social, political, and economic activities of the Hungarians were to be guaranteed and protected by the Romanian state. In theory, the Romanians adhered to the letter of the treaties, as schools, publications, political organizations, and social clubs controlled by the Hungarian minority and conducted in the Hungarian language were allowed to function during the interwar years. In practice, however, the Hungarian population of Transylvania was discriminated against to the extent that the political and economic power base of the ruling classes and urban and rural bourgeoisie were in fact destroyed. The massive agrarian reform carried out after World War I virtually eradicated the Hungarian peasantry in the villages, while the massive Romanianization of the civil service and of urban centers deprived the Hungarians of their preeminence in Transylvania. Although the actions of the Romanian governments were understandable in terms of the determination of Bucharest to control all of Romania and thus eliminate those elements of the Transylvanian historic tradition which could interfere with the attainment of its goals, it is clear that the Hungarians were singled out for greater discrimination than Hungarianized Romanians if for no other reason than that the Hungarians were depicted as agents of Hungarian revisionism. And indeed, that element in interwar Romanian-Hungarian relations, both in Transylvania and internationally, gave the Hungarian question its greatest visibility and acrimony.

It is probable that had it not been for the constant confrontation and polemic between the governments of Hungary and Romania, which brought seemingly endless litigation and disputes before the League of Nations and other international forums and which embittered Romanian-Hungarian relations during the interwar years, a modus vivendi could have been established after the initial Romanianization of the early 1920s. However, as Hungarian revisionism secured the support of Italy, Germany, and the Soviet Union in the 1930s, the discrimination against and "oppression" of the Hungarians of Transylvania became a focal point of Hungary's foreign policy. The participation of the Hungarians of Transylvania in Budapest's efforts to reincorporate Transylvania was generally restrained. Restrained, too, was the reaction of the Romanian governments of the 1930s, which were more concerned with the political issues of fascism and communism. It was only after Hungary joined the Axis powers and the ensuing intensification of Hungarian revisionist propaganda and demands connected with Transylvania that an exacerbation of internal Romanian-Hungarian relations took place. Yet even during phases of internecine hostilities the Romanian governments did not abrogate the minority rights of the Hungarians, nor did they enact explicit disciminatory legislation against Romania's Hungarian subjects.

The loss to Hungary of Northern Transylvania, with its largely Hungarian population, through the Vienna Diktat of 1940 had dire consequences for Hungarian-Romanian relations in Transylvania. Systematic persecution of the Romanian population in Northern Transylvania and of the Hungarian population of Southern Transylvania, which allegedly involved much brutality, made national reconciliation difficult after the restitution of Northern Transylvania to Romania in 1945. For that reason and because of the "fraternal ties" established between the ruling Romanian and Hungarian Communist parties and states after World War II, the so-called Magyar Autonomous Region was created in 1952 and unusually extensive rights and privileges were granted to the Hungarian population of Romania. Self-governance, within the limits imposed and tolerated by the very nature of Communist political systems, was granted to the Hungarians; "the most favored nationality" treatment was extended to the Hungarian minority until the later 1950s — schools, publications, freedom of worship, unrestricted utilization of the Hungarian language in official matters, and extensive political representation at all levels of the party and state.

The de facto isolation of the Hungarian community of Transylvania from the Romanian majority did not, however, lead to meaningful coexistence between the two nationalities, partly because of the wartime experiences and partly because of the large representation of Hungarian Communists in official posts. As a nationalist Romanian trend became apparent both in internal party affairs and in Romania's relations with the Soviet Union and Hungary after Stalin's death, the Romanian leadership undertook, especially after the Hungarian Revolution of 1956, to systematically curtail the special privileges enjoyed by the Hungarians. The autonomy of the Magyar Autonomous Region was severely restricted by 1960, the Hungarian Bolyai

University was merged into the Romanian Babeş University, and the process of Romanianizing urban centers was accelerated.

Whether these actions were related to the sympathy expressed by Hungarian students and intellectuals for the Hungarian Revolution or whether the revolution was used as justification for consolidating the power of the Romanian Communists who regarded both Khrushchev and Kadar as anti-Stalinists and, as such, dangerous for the survival of the Stalinist Romanian regime, the measures taken by Gheorghe Georghiu-Dej were reflective of the evolution of a "Romanian road to socialism" in which national minorities were subordinated to the Romanian majority. And, as the rift between Stalinists and Khrushchevites widened both internally and externally, the Romanian leadership pursued its national communism with increasingly greater vigor and efficiency. In the process, the position of national minorities deteriorated as more and more Romanians became dominant in the party and state apparatus and Romanianization was carried out in the educational, cultural, and socioeconomic fields as well. By the mid-sixties, as Nicolae Ceauşescu replaced Gheorghe Gheorghiu-Dej, the position of national minorities, especially of the Hungarians, was redefined to the disadvantage of the minorities.

In general, the national minorities were considered "coinhabiting nationalities" whose rights and privileges remained legally intact but whose representation in the political and socioeconomic order was limited to the proportion that individual coinhabiting nationalities bore to the total Romanian population. Moreover, whereas instruction in Hungarian in both Hungarian language and bilingual schools in Transylvania continued, a knowledge of Romanian became indispensable for promotion in all ranks of the state and party bureaucracy, as in the country's political and economic life. Although assimilation did not legally become a prerequisite for advancement or for construction of socialist Romania, the policies and actions of the rulers of Romania since the mid-1960s have clearly moved in that direction. Another discriminatory act was the Romanianizing of Transylvania through the mass transfer of Wallachian and Moldavian Romanians into that province. The aim of those population transfers has not necessarily been the diminution of the percentage of Hungarians in Transylvania. The aim, in fact, appears to be the destruction of Hungarian cultural and social values historically identified with Transylvania. The corollary movement of Hungarians from Transylvania to other parts of Romania, largely young men and women engaged in non-agricultural pursuits, is steadily diluting the Hungarian civilization and "bourgeois-intellectual" values of historic Transylvania.

Assimilation of the Hungarian nationality, direct and indirect, is justified by the Romanian regime in terms of the obligatory commitment of Romanians and coinhabiting nationalities alike to the common effort of constructing the Communist homeland. In fact, however, most of the ostensibly discriminatory policies directed against the Hungarian nationality are rooted in causes unrelated to the Transylvanian Hungarians per se. One of these causes is the exploitation of the Hungarian nationality question in Transylvania by the Soviet Union and Hungary for anti-Romanian purposes. The Soviet Union, faithful to the policy of divide-and-conquer and anxious to restrain and control the so-called "Romanian independent course," has used the Hungarian nationality question as an instrument for containing Ceauşescu's regime. The veiled threat of seeking a just resolution of nationality questions through a potential readjustment of the territorial boundaries of Transylvania in favor of Hungary has resulted in renewal of Hungarian revisionism in the name of protection of conationals against abuse by the contemporary Romanian regime. These actions have, on the one hand, strengthened the Romanians' determination to Romanianize Transylvania and, on the other, led to renewal of violent polemics, conducted largely by Hungarian revisionists outside of Hungary. The revisionists, with clear support from Moscow and Budapest, denounce Romanian persecution of its national minorities and violations of human rights, all designed to seek restitution of Transylvania to Hungary. A corollary factor which renders the problems of the Hungarian nationality important is the striking difference between the standards of living and political freedom in contemporary Hungary and Romania. The Hungarians of Transylvania, keenly aware of the advantages provided by Hungarian communism over Romanian communism, would prefer to be subject to Budapest rather than to Bucharest.

The position of the Hungarian national minority in Romania is therefore turbulent. The Romanian rulers, anxious to defuse the Hungarian question, view it as a potential instrument for external interference in Romania's internal affairs and as a potential magnet for demands by other inhabitants of Transylvania for a better existence. Yet, they are caught in the dilemma of how to realize their commitment to a Romanian road to communism, ostensibly rooted in the historic experience and aspirations of Romanians, while adopting policies identified with the economically successful Communists of Hungary. The attitude and policies of the Romanian Communist rulers toward the Hungarians of Romania tend to be conciliatory, but the presence of Kadar's Hungary at the borders of Transylvania and the inability and unwillingness of Ceauşescu's regime to provide comparable advantages to the inhabitants of Romania make resolution of the Hungarian nationality problem in Romania unlikely in the foreseeable future.

The third largest minority group in Romania is German. The overwhelming majority of the members of that nationality were incorporated into Romania at the end of World War I. Of the total of some 750,000 Germans living in Greater Romania between the two world wars, approximately one-third were Transylvanian Saxons, another third Swabians from the Banat, and the rest were dispersed in Bukovina, Bessarabia, and the Old Kingdom. The German minority consisted primarily of small businessmen and artisans living in historic towns such as Sibiu, Braşov, Mediaş, and Timişoara, and of rather well-educated and prosperous peasants. The German community was tightly knit and generally isolated from neighboring Romanian or Hungarian villages. The Germans had their own schools, publications, social and cultural societies, and even political organizations. Until the later 1930s, they were isolated from the mainstream of the politics of their ancestral homeland.

The Romanian government regarded the Germans as a politically neutral national minority and, consequently, adhered to the provisions of the minority treaties applicable to Romania. Hitler's interest in the German minorities of eastern Europe led to the emergence of pro-Nazi political leaders from the German communities in Romania who, by the late thirties, sought to secure the status of a state within a state for Romania's Germans. During World War II the Germans of Romania tried to maintain a separate identity from both Germany and Romania, although numerous young members of the German minority considered themselves Germans rather than Romanian Germans and fought with the German armies on the Russian front.

The position of the German minority became precarious as Romania joined the anti-German coalition in August 1944 and declared war on Nazi Germany. The postwar Romanian governments, Communist-dominated or actually Communist, sought to destroy the homogeneity of what was perceived as bourgeois, "Fascist" German enclaves often through repatriation or resettlement. Officially, nevertheless, Germans were granted the same privileges as other national minorities, including the use of the German language in official transactions and in educational and cultural activities. In the 1960s and 1970s, the Romanian Communist regime allowed and even encouraged emigration to West Germany, primarily for economic reasons related to Romania's need for hard currency and trade with West Germany. The emigration of those years, combined with wartime casualties and earlier emigration and resettlement, led to a drastic reduction of the size of the German population in Romania. By 1966 the German minority was about one-half of the size it had been in 1940, totalling only some 375,000 people. By 1977 the number of Germans in Romania declined by another 25,000.

The steady departure of Romania's Germans, when taken in conjunction with intensification of the present Romanian rulers' determination to Romanianize Transylvania and the Banat and bring about the integration of all coinhabiting nationalities into the total effort of building a Communist homeland, has eroded the homogeneity and cultural and social values of the German communities. The German towns are becoming more and more Romanian in population structure, language, culture, and attitudes. Minority rights, however, are respected, and deliberate efforts at maintaining the facade of separate and well-defined characteristics of coinhabiting nationalities are made by the Romanian government. The reality is, however, somewhat different in that assimilation and integration of the German minority is progressing at a rapid pace.

Among the other national minorities in Romania, only the Gypsies continue to be of historic significance. This is because most of the larger minority groups of interwar Greater Romania, such as Ukrainians, Russians, Bulgarians, Turks, Tatars, Serbians, and Găgăuți, whose total number was approximately 1,800,000, or 10% of Romania's population, were either inhabiting Bessarabia, Bukovina, or Southern Dobrudja and, as such, ceased to be part of Romania's population after World War II, or, as in the case of the Turks left in Northern Dobrudja, emigrated to their ancestral lands. By 1980, the total number of members of national minorities other than Hungarians, Germans, Jews, and Gypsies reached only some 250,000, or less than 1.5% of the total population. These groups are allowed to maintain their own educational, cultural, and social organizations, although for practical purposes they are being assimilated and integrated into the Romanian socialist construction.

This is even true of the Gypsies, who traditionally have been regarded as an undesirable ethnic group. The number of Gypsies in Romania has remained fairly constant since World War I, fluctuating between 220,000 and 250,000. The status of the Gypsies has been historically more comparable to that of the Jews than that of other national minorities since they were regarded as Romanians and as a migratory people without a homeland. The traditional antipathy of all inhabitants of Romania toward Gypsies has only recently been somewhat altered as the Romanian Communist regime has attempted to settle Gypsies into sedentary occupations. Whereas these efforts have not been altogether successful, it is evident that the younger generation of Gypsies is being integrated into the socialist construction process. Assimilation and social integration have remained illusory, however, despite the enhanced economic, cultural, and educational opportunities afforded to the Gypsies of Romania.

The problems related to national minorities in Romania—except for the Hungarians—are in the process of simplification. In general, Romanian minority policies have not been harsher than those practiced in other societies with significant ethnic minorities. In fact, in some instances the Romanian policies have been more tolerant than those enacted in neighboring countries. For instance, with the exception of anti-Semitic manifestations, there has been unusual toleration toward the religious organizations of national minorities. Catholics, Protestants, Mohammedans, and even members of the Mozaic faith have never been denied the right to worship; nor has there been any wanton destruction of places of worship. In addition, there has been a remarkable degree of toleration of the cultural and educational activities of national minorities. Such anti-minority measures as were taken, overtly or covertly, were largely motivated by political interests, as were, for that matter, many of the pro-minority policies.

It is fair to say, however, that Romanian political nationalism, whenever practiced or advocated, is incompatible with the goals and aspirations of most national minorities. Historically, the Jews and the Hungarians have been most affected by nationalist discrimination. But it is also fair to say that traditional Romanian caution and political intelligence and moderation have mitigated against extreme intolerance and actions against national minorities and that, all in all, the position of national minorities in Romania, while less protected from a constitutional and legal standpoint than that of minorities of other multinational countries, has been much better than depicted by polemicists and detractors.

Were it possible to examine actual records and archival materials relative to national minority problems in Romania, it would be easier to ascertain the validity of the polemics and contradictions which have enveloped the pertinent issues. For obvious reasons, however, objective data and information are difficult to locate and consult. Romanian sources, other than printed materials, are generally unavailable because, officially, the nationality question has been solved in Romania. Similarly, relevant materials cannot be located in Hungary largely because of the Hungarian government's unwillingness to admit to any official interest in the problems of the conationals in Romania. But even for earlier periods, most of the information consisted of denunciations, diatribes, and enumerations of statistical data which were questionable at best and likely fabricated for political purposes. Nor are there any meaningful or accessible collections available for the study of problems pertinent to the status of other national minorities except for the Germans. During the last thirty years, both Swabian and Saxon cultural societies established in West Germany, such as the *Arbeitskreis für Siebenbürgische Landeskunde*, have been extremely active in collecting records, establishing archives, and publishing valuable collections or primary sources and monographic studies on the German minority in Romania since the end of World War I. Still, as the following annotated bibliography of national minorities in Romania reveals, most of the literature on those minorities is confined to simple factual data and arguments and, frequently, to polemics.

BIBLIOGRAPHY

General Reference Works and Sources

554. Beck, Erich. **Bibliographie zur Landeskunde der Bukowina. Literatur bis zum Jahre 1965.** Munich: Verlag des Südostdeutschen Kulturwerkes, 1966. 378p.

This invaluable, extensive bibliography, with 7,371 entries comprising all nationalities populating Bukovina, is divided into the following chapters: Bibliographies, The Land, Places, Peoples, Sociology, Anthropology, Education, Art and Culture, Churches, Law and Administration, Economy, Biographies, Genealogy, and Miscellany. It lists books and articles in all European languages.

555. Demeter, János; Eisenburger, Eduard; and Lipatti, Valentin. **Romania and the National Question: Facts and Figures.** Bucharest: Meridiane, 1972. 94p.

Statistical data abound in this survey of the nationality problems in contemporary Romania. The publication is designed to show the wisdom of Romanian policies toward coinhabiting nationalities.

556. Fischer-Galati, Stephen A. **Rumania: A Bibliographic Guide.** Washington, DC: U.S. Government Printing Office, 1963. 75p.

A useful bibliographic guide which contains references to the national minority problems.

557. **Le nouveau régime légal des nationalités en Roumanie.** Bucharest: Imprimeria de stat, 1946. 51p.

This publication contains legislative enactments and a basic discussion of the nationality policies of the immediate post-World War II political regimes in Romania.

Monographs and Articles

558. Baerlein, Henri. **Bessarabia and Beyond.** London: Methuen, 1935. 276p.

This is a rather superficial discussion of issues affecting interwar Bessarabia. The author sheds light on Romanian minority policies in Bessarabia, which he regards as generally adequate for the needs of an underdeveloped province threatened by Soviet revisionism.

559. Bányai, Ladislau. "Aportul tovarăşului Nicolae Ceauşescu la intărirea unităţii frăţeşti dintre poporul român si naţionalităţile conlocuitoare" (The Contribution of Comrade Nicolae Ceauşescu to the Strengthening of the Fraternal Unity of the Romanian People and the Coinhabiting Nationalities). *Revista de istorie* 31:1 (1978): 83-93.

The study eulogizes the nationality policy of President Nicolae Ceauşescu as a great solution to historic and contemporary nationality issues in Romania.

560. Bolinder, Gustaf. **Rumänska problem, den transsylvanska och den bessarabiska fragan.** Stockholm: Natur och kultur, 1944. 97p.

An unusual volume, prepared by a Swedish scholar, which raises interesting issues related to Romanian rights and claims to Transylvania and Bessarabia, and analyzes, albeit briefly, Romanian nationality policies in both provinces.

561.   Boteni, Viorica. **Les minorités en Transylvanie**. Paris: Pedone, 1938. 272p.

This is an extensive account of the history and status of the national minorities of Transylvania with a distinct pro-Romanian bias.

562.   Cornish, Louis Craig, comp. **The Religious Minorities in Transylvania**. Boston: Beacon Press, 1925. 174p.

An essentially descriptive account of the religious minorities in Transylvania and of religious life in that province.

563.   Dima, Nicholas. **Bessarabia and Bukovina: The Soviet-Romanian Territorial Dispute**. East European Monographs, no. 110. Boulder, CO: East European Monographs, 1982. 179p. Distributed by Columbia University Press.

A thorough study of historical and contemporary problems, which includes important data on the national minority problems of interwar Romania. The author also presents the historical evolution of this territorial conflict and illuminates the political, socioeconomic, and ethnodemographical changes that have occurred in the area between 1944 and 1980.

564.   Dragomir, Sylvius. **The Ethnical Minorities in Transylvania**. Geneva: Sonor Printing Co., 1927. 129p. Map. Tables.

A basic Romanian presentation by one of the leading Romanian students of Transylvanian affairs, claiming that Romania has not only scrupulously respected the obligations imposed upon her by the additional Treaty of December 9, 1919, regarding her ethnical and religious minorities, but has also protected their cultural and social consolidation. Statistical data and tables on various aspects of non-Romanians living in Transylvania are useful, especially on educational and religious matters.

565.   Dragomir, Silviu. **La Transylvanie roumaine et ses minorités ethniques**. Bucharest: Imprimerie Nationale, 1934. 281p.

This is a pro-Romanian survey of the nationality problems of Transylvania supportive of Romanian policies.

566.   Gall, Erno. **Dimensiunile conviețuirii: Studii despre națiune și naționalitate** (The Dimensions of Coexistence: Studies on Nation and Nationality). Bucharest: Kriterion, 1978. 450p.

This is a standard survey of national minority problems and policies pursued by the Romanian Communist regime. The predictable conclusion is that the policies of President Nicolae Ceaușescu have resolved all problems.

567.   Ghibu, Onisifor. **Politica religioasă și minoritară a României** (The Religious and Minority Policy of Romania). Cluj: Ardealul, 1940. 107p.

Ghibu's brief study was designed to prove that the policies of the Romanian rulers affecting the national minorities have been fair and non-discriminatory.

568. Gilberg, Trond. "Ethnic Minorities in Romania under Socialism." *East European Quarterly* VII:4 (1974): 435-58.
   An important and objective analysis of contemporary nationality policies in Romania.

569. Gold, Jack. "Bessarabia: The Thorny 'Non-Existent' Problem." *East European Quarterly* XIII:1 (1979): 47-74.
   The author presents an exceptionally detailed and perceptive study stressing the Russification of Bessarabia. He compares and contrasts Russian and Romanian policies toward national minorities in Bessarabia.

570. Gündisch, Gustav; Klein, Albert; and Krasser, Harald, eds. **Studien zur siebenbürgischen Kunstgeschichte**. Bukarest: Kriterion, 1976. 319p.
   The volume represents a valuable survey of the contribution of Transylvania's various nationalities to the art history of Transylvania.

571. Hartl, Hans. **Nationalitätenprobleme im heutigen Südosteuropa**. Munich: Oldenbourg Verlag, 1973. 159p.
   This survey of nationality problems in southeastern Europe is an important contribution to the study of the minorities. It contains useful references to the national minority question in contemporary Romania.

572. Illyes, Elemer. **National Minorities in Romania: Change in Transylvania**. East European Monographs, 112. Boulder, CO: East European Monographs, 1982. 360p. Distributed by Columbia University Press.
   This is a fundamental study of the historic and contemporary problems related to the position of all national minorities in Transylvania. The work contains an excellent bibliography in addition to statistical tables on population for the years 1910 to 1956. The author discusses the process of forceful Romanianization of non-Romanians living in Transylvania and uses little-known Romanian and Hungarian sources. This volume is an updated version of the author's *Nationale Minderheiten in Rumänien: Siebenbürgen im Wandel* (Vienna: Braumüller Verlag, 1981. 348p.), focusing on the development after 1945.

573. Makkai, László. **Histoire de Transylvanie**. Paris: Presses universitaires de France, 1946. 382p.
   This excellent study treats the minority problems in Transylvania in an open-minded manner.

574. Nagy, Lajos. **A kisebbségek alkotmányjogi helyzete nagyromániában** (The Constitutional Position of the Minorities in Greater Romania). Kolozsvar: Minerva, 1944. 551p.
   A pro-Hungarian treatise designed to condemn discriminatory Romanian policies and practices.

575. Popovici, Andrei. **The Political Status of Bessarabia**. Washington, DC: Randsell, 1931. 299p.
   Although this book is primarily concerned with the validity of Romania's claims to Bessarabia, it contains important data on Romanian policies toward national minorities in the province.

576.   Reiter, Wilhelm. "Die nationalitätenpolitik der rumänischen Volksrepublik im Spiegel der Statistik." *Osteuropa* 11 (1961): 189-97.

A brief but comprehensive survey of contemporary nationality policies in Romania from the perspective of statistical analysis.

577.   Roucek, Joseph S. **Contemporary Roumania and Her Problems: A Study in Modern Nationalism.** Stanford, CA: Stanford University Press, 1932. 437p.

This book contains important and objective information on the status of national minorities and of governmental minority policies in the early 1930s.

578.   **Roumania Ten Years After.** Boston: Beacon Press, 1928. 152p.

An interesting survey of the status of national minorities in Romania conducted and prepared by an American group of laymen.

579.   Satmarescu, G. D. "The Changing Demographic Structure of the Population of Transylvania." *East European Quarterly* VIII:4 (1975): 425-40.

A demographic study, rich in data, which questions the validity of Romanian data and claims on the demographic structure of Transylvania.

580.   Szaz, Z. Michael. "Contemporary Educational Policies in Transylvania." *East European Quarterly* XI:4 (1978): 493-501.

A valuable and informative contribution, essentially favorable to contemporary Romanian policies, by a critic of the Romanian regime. The essays contain important statistical data.

581.   Tibal, Andre, ed. **Le problème des minorités.** Paris: Publications de la Conciliation Internationale, 1929. 114p.

This volume contains a discussion of the minority problems in Romania. It is of interest mainly because of the author's pacifism and idealism.

582.   Weber, Hermann. **Die Bukowina im Zweiten Weltkrieg: Völkerrechtliche Aspekte der Lage der Bukowina im Spannungsfeld zwischen Rumänien, der Sowjetunion und Deutschland.** Darstellungen zur Auswärtigen Politik, vol. 11. Hamburg: Alfred Metzner Verlag, in Kommission, 1972. 86p.

Two aspects of the Bukovina problem — the 1940 cession of Northern Bukovina to the Soviet Union and the later reunification with Romania — are presented within their historical and legal framework. Reproductions of documents add to the presentation. In a larger historical context, the problems of Romanian sovereignty during this period are also analyzed, as are the problems of the persecution of Jews.

Germans

General Reference Material and Sources

583.   Hienz, Hermann. **Bücherkunde zur Volks- und Heimatforschung der Siebenbürger Sachsen.** Munich: Oldenbourg Verlag, 1960. xx, 579p.

This is an important bibliographic-historiographic collection. Many of the references are trivial, but altogether this is an indispensable guide.

584. Wagner, Ernst, comp. **Quellen zur Geschichte der Siebenbürger Sachsen 1191-1975.** Cologne: Böhlau Verlag, 1976. 443p.

Excerpts from diverse source materials show the history of the Transylvania Germans from 1191 to 1975. Historical introductions preceding the documentary chapters, statistical data, and tables add to the volume's value. The book is an important presentation of the history of southeast Europe, of relations between Germany and southeast Europe, as well as of Romanian history.

Monographs and Articles

585. Barcan, Monica, and Millitz, Adalbert. **Naţionalitatea germană din România** (The German Nationality in Romania). Bucharest: Kriterion, 1977. 144p.

A descriptive account of the rights and privileges of the German minority in Romania. The authors echo the official Romanian position, according to which the Communist regime has resolved all outstanding problems related to national minorities in contemporary Romania.

586. Barth, Fredrick H. **A Transylvanian Legacy: The Life of a Transylvanian Saxon.** Salt Lake City: Transylvania, 1979. 309p.

An important autobiography by a Transylvanian Saxon. The author describes village life in pre-World War I Transylvania, Saxon life in interwar Romania, and problems related to adaptation of the Saxons to Romanian rule before World War II.

587. Binder, Ludwig, and Scheerer, Josef. **Die Bischöfe der evangelischen Kirche A. B. in Siebenbürgen: II. Teil: Die Bischöfe der Jahre 1867-1969.** Cologne: Böhlau Verlag, 1980. 252p.

An important contribution to the literature on Saxon civilization, culture, and religious organization and life in Transylvania, this work details the history of the bishops of the German Protestant church in Transylvania from 1867 to 1969.

588. **Bukowina, Heimat von gestern.** Karlsruhe: Verlag "Arbeitskreis Bukowina Heimatbuch," 1956. 408p.

A sentimental but informative compendium which sheds much light on the life of the German minority of Bukovina.

589. Connert, Hans. **Geschichte des Hermannstaedter Maennergesangvereines von 1885-1935.** Sibiu: Heiser, 1935. 138p.

This is a delightful and informative account of the choral society of the Germans of Hermannstadt (Sibiu) in Transylvania.

590. Eckhart, Franz G., and Broszat, Martin, eds. **Das Schicksal der Deutschen in Rumänien.** Bonn: Bundesministerium für Vertriebene, Flüchtlinge und Kriegsgeschädigte, 1957. 426p.

A major collection of studies on the German minority in Romania written by an important congregation of scholars. Invaluable for the study of the Germans in Romania and of Romanian nationality policies.

591. Grentrup, Theodore. **Das Deutschtum an der mittleren Donau, in Rumänien und Jugoslawien unter besonderer Berücksichtigung seiner kulturellen Lebensbedingungen.** Münster: Aschendorff, 1930. 336p.

This volume contains a comprehensive report on German cultural and educational institutions and activities in Romania, and to a lesser degree in Yugoslavia. There is a wealth of statistical data available, together with references to sources and secondary literature.

592. Hartl, Hans. **Das Schicksal des Deutschtums in Rumänien, 1938-1945.** Würzburg: Holzner Verlag, 1958. 117p.

An important and objective account of the activities and status of the German minority in Romania during the critical period 1938-1945.

593. Hermann, Albert. **Die deutschen Bauern des Burzenlandes.** Jena: G. Fischer, 1937. 136p.

A descriptive but important study of the German peasants of Ţara Bârsei (Burzenland) written at a time of growing German concern with conationals in Romania.

594. Horváth, Jenö. **Die Geschichte Siebenbürgens.** Budapest: Danubia, 1943. 216p.

This basic polemical study sets out to prove the historic rights of Hungary to Transylvania.

595. Keintzel-Schön, Fritz. **Die siebenbürgisch-sächsischen Familiennamen.** Cologne: Böhlau Verlag, 1976. 373p.

This contribution traces the history of Transylvanian Saxons through their surnames to show their historic ties with other German-speaking lands.

596. Klein, Karl Kurt. **Transsylvanica: Gesammelte Abhandlungen und Aufsätze zur Sprach- und Siedlungsforschung der Deutschen in Siebenbürgen.** Munich: Oldenbourg Verlag, 1963. 374p.

An important collection of essays focusing on the language and settlement culture of the German minority of Transylvania. The compendium includes valuable data on Saxon attitudes toward Romanian rule.

597. Lang, Franz, ed. **Buchenland: 150 Jahre Deutschtum in der Bukowina.** Munich: Südostdeutsches Kulturwerk, 1961. 527p.

This collection of several major studies on various aspects of the history of the Germans of Bukovina is the most comprehensive and scholarly work on the subject.

598. Lukinich, Imre, ed. **Die siebenbürgische Frage; Studien aus der Vergangenheit und Gegenwart Siebenbürgens.** Budapest: Verlag des Osteuropa-Instituts an der Budapester Peter Pazmany-Universität, 1940. 398p.

A collection of studies on Transylvania, the volume is primarily designed to show the primacy of the Hungarians and, to a lesser extent, of the Germans in Transylvania.

599. Maenner-Weinheim, Emil. **Guttenbrunn: Das Odenwälder Dorf im rumänischen Banat.** Munich: Südostdeutsches Kulturwerk, 1958. 96p.

This is an important socioeconomic and political study of a German village in the Banat. Although not in conformity with the latest principles of social history, it is of great value to students of the German minority in Romania.

600.   Mammel, A. **Das Bild der Heimat: Beiträge zur Geschichte der Kolonie Klöstitz in Bessarabien.** Wasseralfingen, Germany: Koch, 1962. 177p.
   An essential study for students of minority problems in Bessarabia. The emphasis is on the German minority, although much information can be gathered with respect to other coinhabiting nationalities in Bessarabia.

601.   Müller, Friedrich. **Die Geschichte der Deutschen in Rumänien.** Hermannstadt: Kraft & Drotleff, [194-?]. 194p.
   The work contains a standard survey of the hsitory of the German minority in Romania. It is a brief but informative account. Other titles from this author: *Die Geschichte unseres Volkes: Bilder aus Vergangenheit und Gegenwart der Deutschen in Rumänien.* Hermannstadt: W. Kraft, 1926. 185p.; *Die Siebenbürger Sachsen und Ihr Land.* 4th ed. Stuttgart: Heimat und Welt Verlag, 1932. 164p.

602.   Petri, Hans. **Geschichte der deutschen Siedlungen in der Dobrudscha.** Munich: Südostdeutsches Kulturwerk, 1956. 112p.
   This represents the only objective study on the Germans of the Dobrudja by a German scholar. The survey is, however, more of an outline than a major monographic contribution to the subject.

603.   Philippi, Paul, ed. **Neue Beiträge zur siebenbürgischen Geschichte und Landeskunde.** Cologne: Böhlau Verlag, 1962. 231p.
   The editor is the leading Saxon scholar on Romanian problems. He has brought together an important collection of studies on various aspects of Transylvanian history and related problems, with special emphasis on the German minority.

604.   Philippi, Paul, ed. **Studien zur Geschichtsschreibung im 19. und 20. Jahrhundert.** Cologne: Böhlau Verlag, 1967. 244p.
   An important contribution to the cultural and intellectual historiography of the German minority in Transylvania during the last two centuries. The several contributions are all informative and intelligent.

605.   Philippi, Paul, ed. **Zur Rechts- und Siedlungsgeschichte der siebenbürgen Sachsen.** Cologne: Böhlau Verlag, 1971. 300p.
   This collection of studies, edited by a leading Saxon scholar, focuses on the legal aspects and settlement history of the Saxons in Transylvania.

606.   Schubert, Hans Achim. **Nachbarschaft und Modernisierung: Eine historische Soziologie traditionaler Lokalgruppen am Beispiel Siebenbürgens.** Cologne: Böhlau Verlag, 1980. 226p.
   This work is an outstanding contribution to the literature on the social history and sociology of the Transylvanian Germans.

607.   Schuster, Oskar, comp. **Siebenbürger Sachsen gestern und heute.** Düsseldorf: Wegweiser Verlag, 1961. 103p.
   A brief but informative and intelligent survey of the history of the Saxons of Transylvania.

608.   Teutsch, Friedrich. **Kirche und Schule der Siebenbürger Sachsen in Vergangenheit und Gegenwart.** Hermannstadt: W. Krafft, 1923. 328p.

The volume comprises a sound historic survey of the religious and cultural life of the Transylvanian Saxons. The author envisages retention of traditional rights and privileges under Romanian rule after World War I.

609. Teutsch, Friedrich. **Die Siebenbürger Sachsen in Vergangenheit und Gegenwart.** Hermannstadt: W. Krafft, 1924. 367p.

This is an important historical survey of the history of the Transylvanian Saxons by the leading scholar of the period. The work is totally free of controversy and polemics.

610. Wagner, Ernst. **Geschichte der Siebenbürger Sachsen: Ein Überblick.** Innsbruck: Wort und Welt Verlag, 1981. 108p.

An expatriated Saxon has written an intelligent though brief survey of the history of the Transylvanian Saxons. The work is prudent, but all major political and socio-economic issues are addressed.

611. Wagner, Ernst. **Historisch-statistisches Ortsnamenbuch für Siebenbürgen.** Cologne: Böhlau Verlag, 1977. 535p.

This volume represents an important contribution to the literature related to the history of the Germans in Transylvania and to their civilization, as it provides a survey of the names of settlements with statistical analysis.

612. Weber, Georg. **Beharrung und Einfügung: Eine empirische-soziologische Analyse dreier Siedlungen.** Cologne: Böhlau Verlag, 1968. 470p.

A splendid sociological treatise by a leading German sociologist. The author, a Transylvanian Saxon by birth, provides important data and personal observations on the German Saxon community using the example of three settlements.

613. Welisch, Sophie A. "The Bukovina-Germans in the Interwar Period." *East European Quarterly* XIV:4 (1981): 423-37.

A thoughtful and well-documented study of the German minority in interwar Bukovina.

614. Wittstock, Oskar. **Die Siebenbürger Sachsen und der gesamtdeutsche Gedanke.** Brünn: R. M. Rohrer, 1943. 251p.

The author attempts to demonstrate the validity of Pangermanism by claiming close identity between the German minority in Transylvania and the Germans of the Third Reich. Although the main thesis and evidence are questionable, some data related to the pro-Nazi Germany positions of the Saxons are valuable.

Hungarians

General Reference Material and Sources

615. **Agrarian Reform in Roumania and the Case of the Hungarian Optants in Transylvania before the League of Nations.** Paris: Imprimerie du Palais, 1927. 320p.

This publication contains a collection of statements and documents related to one of the most vexing problems affecting Hungarian-Romanian relations in the immediate post-World War I years. The reader is to draw his own conclusions.

616. Bako, Elemer, and Solyom-Fekete, William, comps. **Hungarians in Rumania and Transylvania: A Bibliographical List of Publications in Hungarian and West European Languages Compiled from the Holdings of the Library of Congress.** Washington, DC: U.S. Government Printing Office, 1969. 192p.

There are 2,065 entries divided into 13 subjects such as General Reference Works, Geography, The People, History, Government and Politics, Economy, Religion, Intellectual Life, Literature, and Press and Publishing. Most of the chapters are subdivided as follows: Special Reference Works, Periodicals and Serials, Monographs, and Minor Publications.

617. Horváth, Jenö. **The Hungarian Question: A Bibliography on Hungary and Central Europe.** Budapest: Sarkany, 1938. 20p.

A bibliographic guide designed to provide data for Hungarian revisionist demands, especially *vis-à-vis* Romania.

618. Tezla, Albert. **An Introductory Bibliography to the Study of Hungarian Literature.** Cambridge, MA: Harvard University Press, 1964. 290p.

This major bibliographic guide includes references to Hungarian literature in Transylvania.

Monographs and Articles

619. Balázs, Sándor. **Szociológía és nemzetségi önismeret. A Gusti iskola és a romániai magyar szociográfia** (Sociology and Nationality-Identity. The Gusti School and the Hungarian Sociography in Romania). Bucharest: Politikai Publishers, 1979. 263p.

Of the social sciences between the two world wars, sociography prevailed in Romania. Sociographical research had a significant role to play in the crystallization of the new identity of the Hungarian nationality there. This research received some of its techniques and objectives from Dimitrie Gusti's monographical school, and was also influenced by the neo-populistic movements of the 1930s. Accounts are given of organizations engaged in nationality research and of village explorers and their intellectual backgrounds.

620. Balogh, Edgar. **Szolgálatban: Emlékirat, 1935-1944** (Serving: Reminiscences, 1935-1944). Bucharest: Kriterion Publishers, 1978. 382p.

The author, a member of the radical Left in Czechoslovakia, was expelled from that country in the mid-thirties and then continued his work in Transylvania in connection with the promotion of Hungarian culture and the literary and social conditions of the Magyar minority prior to 1944. This autobiographical writing contains details as well of the efforts of the Left—after the return of a large portion of Transylvania to Hungary—to achieve that country's withdrawal from the war. The author also favored reconciliation with the Romanians and contact with minority groups.

621. Bányai, L. **Pe făgaşul tradiţiilor frăţeşti** (On the Path of Fraternal Traditions). Bucharest: Institutul de studii istorice şi social-politice de pe lîngă C.C. al P.C.R., 1971. 286p.

This rather propagandistic study outlines the community of Hungarian and Romanian interests in the construction of socialism in Romania.

622. Benkö, Samu. **A helyzettudat változásai** (Knowledge of the Situation). Bucharest: Kriterion Publishers, 1977. 447p.

The apparent lack of studies written by members of the Hungarian minority in Transylvania dealing with their present-day conditions in Romania seems to be compensated for by shorter or longer studies going back to their past. This publication is an example of that trend, in which strength is derived from the cultural past to enable over 2 million people to endure the vicissitudes of the present. By means of plentiful notes and 11 book reviews, the reader is informed of other scholarly and literary endeavors.

623. Biro, Jozsef. **Erdélyi kastélyok** (Transylvanian Castles). Budapest: Új Idök Irodalmi Intézet, 1940. 209p.

This writing is an important contribution to the literature on Hungarian civilization in Transylvania.

624. Biro, Jozsef. **Erdélyi müvészete** (Arts in Transylvania). Budapest: Király Magyar Egyetemi Nyomda, 1941. 304p.

An interesting volume, the purpose of which is to show the artistic achievements of the Hungarians in Transylvania and to minimize those of the Romanians.

625. Bólyai Tudományegyetem. **A kolozsvári Bólyai Tudományegyetem, 1945-1955** (The Bolyai University at Kolozsvar, 1945-1955). Cluj: Állami Tanügyi és Pedagógiai Könyvkiadó, 1956. 642p.

This is a historic survey of the Bolyai Unviersity of Cluj, the most important center of Hungarian academic activities in Transylvania.

626. Borbély, Andor, and Fall, Endre. **Román uralom Erdélyben** (Romanian Rule in Transylvania). Budapest: Magyar Reviziós Liga, 1936. 170p.

A typical anti-Romanian account of persecution of national minorities in Transylvania by exponents of the positions of militant Hungarian revisionists.

627. Buday, György. **Székely népballadák** (Szekler Folk Ballads). Budapest: Király Magyar Egyetemi Nyomda, 1948. 277p.

This contribution focuses on the cultural life of the Szeklers in Transylvania through an anlysis of their folk ballads.

628. Cabot, John M. **The Racial Conflict in Transylvania**. Boston: Beacon Press, 1926. 206p.

This work contains a descriptive but perceptive account of the national minority problems in Transylvania, with special emphasis on Hungarian-Romanian controversies and confrontations.

629. Cernea, Radu. **La Roumanie et le revisionisme**. Paris: A.R.I.S., 1935. 103p.

A standard Romanian contribution to the polemics related to the alleged mistreatment of Hungarians in Transylvania by the rulers of interwar Romania. The author rejects all anti-Romanian allegations and accuses the Hungarians of stirring up trouble through revisionistic actions.

630. Codarcea, Cornelius. **Le litige roumano-hongrois.** Bucharest: Universul, 1937. 185p.

The author reviews the problems resulting from the incorporation of Transylvania into Greater Romania and condemns Hungarian revisionism since, in his view, a peaceful resolution of problems related to the Hungarian minority in Transylvania is possible.

631. Deák, Francis. **The Hungarian-Rumanian Land Dispute: A Study of Hungarian Property Rights in Transylvania under the Treaty of Trianon.** New York: Columbia University Press, 1928. 272p.

This work presents an excellent study of land reform in Transylvania. The author analyzes the political and economic purposes and effects of the reform which worked to the detriment of the historic ruling class in Transylvania.

632. Donald, Sir Robert. **The Tragedy of Trianon: Hungary's Appeal to Humanity.** London: Butterworth, 1928. 348p.

A pro-Hungarian statement which condemns the provisions of the Treaty of Trianon and provides disputable data on Romanian policies toward the Hungarians in Transylvania.

633. Dragomir, Silviu. **La Transylvanie avant et après l'arbitrage de Vienne.** Sibiu: Centrul de studii şi cercetări privitoare la Transilvania, 1943. 52p.

A leading student of Transylvanian problems strongly condemns Hungarian revisionism and rejects Hungarian contentions with respect to mistreatment of the Hungarian minority by the Romanian government.

634. Gartner, Károly. **A sipotei Golgotha; romániai rabmagyarok története** (The Golgotha of Sipote: History of Captured Hungarians in Romania). Budapest: Sárkány, 1932. 260p.

This is a virulent anti-Romanian treatise condemnatory of Romanian inhumanity toward Hungarians.

635. Gyula, David; Marosi, Peter; and Szász, János. **A romániai magyar irodalom története** (A History of the Hungarian Literature in Romania). Bucharest: Editura didactică şi pedagogică, 1977. 331p.

Even though it is designed as a textbook for higher schools, this work can be regarded as a comprehensive study of the history of the Hungarian literature in Transylvania. It provides a systematic structure, particularly for the pre-1944 Transylvanian Magyar literature. Some of the literary works have been subjected to critical evaluation.

636. Horváth, Andor, and Kacsir, Maria, eds. **Haz szülöföld, nemzetiséq. A Hét évkönyve, 1978** (Mother Country, Native Land, Nationality). Bucharest: The Hét Almanac, 1978. 293p.

The almanac for 1978, the Hungarian weekly of the Socialist Cultural and Educational Council in Romania, is a first. Numerous authors, including Romanians, present descriptions of nationality institutions, such as newspapers and cultural and educational establishments, and an expert explanation of the nationality laws in Romania.

637. Jancsó, Benedict de. **The Székelys: A Historical and Ethnographical Essay.** Budapest: Printing Office Victor Hornyánszky, 1921. 46p.

The author, a Székely Hungarian scholar, sets out to provide the gist of the geographical, economic, statistical, and historical background of the Székelys, and the land in which they lived, Transylvania. A large part of the study deals with the origin, institutions, cultural contributions, and folklore of the Székelys.

638. Kántor, Lajos, and Láng, Gusztáv. **A romániai magyar irodalom 1944-1970** (Hungarian Literature in Romania 1944-1970). Bucharest: Kriterion, 1973. 503p.

This survey of Hungarian literature is designed to reinforce Romanian claims regarding the minorities' privileged status in Romania.

639. Knight, George Angus Fulton. **History of the Hungarian Reformed Church.** Washington, DC: Hungarian Reformed Federation of America, 1956. 163p.

A rather pedestrian but useful survey of the history of the Hungarian Reformed Church, including information on the church in Transylvania.

640. Kovács, Ferenc, ed. **Bitay Árpád: "...hogy románok és magyarok jobban megismerjék egymást** (Árpád Bitay: "...Romanian and Hungarian Better Understanding of Each Other). Bucharest: Politikai Könyvkiadó, 1977. 240p.

Árpád Bitay was doing the work of a historian, philologist, linguist, and *litterateur* prior to his death in 1937. He strove to bring about better understanding between Romanians and Magyars by introducing them in some of his publications to the best of their respective literary achievements.

641. Macartney, Carlile Aylmer. **Hungary and Her Successors: The Treaty of Trianon and Its Consequence, 1919-1937.** London: Oxford University Press, 1937. 504p.

This is a classic work by a distinguished British scholar. The author is sympathetic to Hungarian positions, but his analysis of Romanian policies in Transylvania is essentially dispassionate.

642. Mikó, Imre. **Huszonkét év, 1918-1940** (Twenty-Two Years, 1918-1940). Budapest: Studium, 1940. 326p.

The book is a typical revisionist work which attacks the policies of the Romanians toward the Hungarian national minority and justifies Hungarian positions on reincorporation of Transylvania.

643. Mikó, Imre. **A csendes Petöfi utca** (The Quiet Petöfi Street). Kolozsvár-Napoca: Dacia Publishers, 1978. 172p.

Imre Mikó (1911-1977), a historian and sociologist, is also known as a literary writer. His present book, published posthumously, stops with his memoirs in 1940. Particularly interesting are his recollections of his university years, minority organizational activities, and the village exploration at Kolozsborsa.

644. Sanborn, Anne Fay, and Wass de Czege, Géza. **Transylvania and the Hungarian-Rumanian Problem.** Astor, FL: Danubian Press, 1979. 276p.

This very polemical, anti-Romanian work is reflective of contemporary currents regarding Romanian minority policies and the present and future status of Transylvania.

645.   Siculus (pseud.). **A moldvai magyarok östelepülése és mai helyzete** (The Original Settlements of the Hungarians in Moldavia and Their Present Situation). Pécs: Pesti Lloyd Társulat, 1942. 184p.

Although an irredentist study, the work provides data on the *Csángó*-Hungarian population in Moldavia.

646.   Szász, Zsombor. **The Minorities in Rumanian Transylvania.** London: Richards, 1927. 414p.

This factual survey is intended, in part, to demonstrate the importance of the Hungarians in the shaping of the history and civilization of Transylvania.

647.   Váli, Ferenc A. "Transylvania and the Hungarian Minority." *Journal of International Affairs* XX:1 (1966): 32-44.

Relying primarily on secondary sources, the author reviews the historical status of the Hungarian minority in Transylvania.

Jews

648.   Berkowitz, Joseph. **La question des Israelites en Roumanie.** Paris: Jouve, 1923. 798p.

This large volume is one of the few studies on the Jewish question in Romania. The author is concerned primarily with legislative matters and, in general, abstains from polemical comments or direct criticisms of Romanian policies.

649.   Broszat, Martin. "Von der Kulturnation zur Volksgruppe: Die Stellung der Juden in der Bukowina im 19. und 20. Jahrhundert." *Historische Zeitschrift* 200 (1965): 572-605.

An important sociopolitical study of the Jewish question in Bukovina by a German specialist. The article provides valuable insights into the Romanian attitudes toward Jews and non-Jews in Bukovina.

650.   Carp, Matatias. **Cartea neagră: fapte şi documente. Suferinţele evreilor din România 1940-1944** (Black Book: Facts and Documents. The Suffering of the Jews of Rumania 1940-1944). 3 vols. Bucharest: Socec and Co., 1946. Dacia Traiană, 1947-1948.

This multivolume study by the former secretary of the Federation of Jewish Communities discusses in some depth the plight of Romania's Jews during the Holocaust. Volume I covers the period through the Iron Guard rebellion in Bucharest in early 1941; volume II the Jassy massacre the same year; and volume III the Transnistra reservation. The author initiates his account with a historical overview of the Holocaust.

651.   Feinberg, Nathan. **La question des minorities à la Conférence de la Paix de 1919-1920 et l'action juive en faveur de la protection internationale des minorités.** Paris: Rousseau, 1929. 167p.

This writing on the minorities question at the Paris Peace Conference also contains references to the position of the Jews in Romania.

652. Filderman, Wilhelm. **Adevǎrul asupra problemei evreeşti din România, în lumina textelor religioase şi a statisticei** (The Truth Regarding the Jewish Question in Romania, in the Light of Religious Texts and of Statistics). Bucharest: Triumful, 1925. 313p.

In his search for a *modus vivendi* between Jews and non-Jews within the borders of Greater Romania, the president of the Romanian Jewish community tends to minimize the significance of the Jewish problem in post-World War I Romania.

653. Hâciu, Anastase N. **Evreii in ţǎrile Româneşti** (The Jews in Romanian Lands). Bucharest: Cartea Româneascǎ, 1943. 631p.

An extensive survey of the history of the Jews in Romania. Despite the author's anti-Semitism, important data on the Jewish question are provided.

654. Pantelimonescu, V., comp. **Statutul evreilor din România. Legislaţia de la 1918-1941** (The Statute of the Jews in Romania. legislation 1918-1941). Bucharest: Universul, 1941. 192p.

This is essentially a documentary compendium. It is informative and essential for the study of the Jewish question between 1918 and 1941.

655. Schuster, Hans. **Die Judenfrage in Rumänien**. Leipzig: F. Meiner, 1939. 244p.

A surprisingly objective study of the Jewish question in Romania by a German scholar writing in the late 1930s.

656. **Sinai; anuar de studii judaice**. Vol. 1-5 (1928-1933). Bucharest: Institutul de istorie Evreo-Românǎ.

This annual journal was issued by the Societatea de Studii Judaice din România. It published articles in German, Romanian, and other languages on different aspects of Romanian Jewish history, culture, and religion.

657. Solomon-Maaravi, Tony. **Days of Anger: The Chronicle of Jewish Suffering in the Years of 1937 to 1944** (in Hebrew). Tel-Aviv: Ha-menorah, 1968. 407p.

A history of the Romanian Jewish community from 1937 to 1944.

658. Vago, Bela, and Mosse, George L., eds. **Jews and Non-Jews in Eastern Europe 1918-1945**. Jerusalem: Keter, 1974. 352p.

This book presents an important collection of studies on the Jewish minority in eastern Europe. The chapters on the Jews in Romania provide much insight into the Jewish question in interwar and World War II Romania.

659. Vssoskin, Moshe. **Struggle for Survival: A History of Jewish Credit Co-operatives in Bessarabia, Old-Rumania, Bukovina, and Transylvania**. Jerusalem: Jerusalem Academic Press, 1975. 345p.

The author provides a detailed examination of the Jewish credit cooperative movement in the four main regions of Romania. He traces its origin in each region after World War I, then gives a detailed breakdown of each cooperative, its leadership, and its method of operation. Integrated throughout the volume are a large number of charts and ledgers. There is also a lengthy set of appendixes at the end.

Other Minorities

660. Georgiev, Ivan. **Dobrudzha v borbata za svoboda, 1913-1940** (The Dobrudja in the Struggle for Freedom, 1913-1940). Sofia: BKP, 1962. 447p.

Despite its title and propagandistic character, this work on the Dobrudja provides important data on the status of the Bulgarian minority in interwar Romania.

661. Kvitkovsky, Denys; Bryndzan, Theophile; and Zhukovsky, Arkadii, eds. **Bukovyna: ïï mynule i suchasne** (Bukovina: Her Past and Present). Paris, Philadelphia, and Detroit: Vyd-vo "Zelena Bukovyna," 1956. 965p.

This book deals with the history of North Bukovina, the area inhabited by Ukrainians. Information is provided on the national and social composition of its people, political life, literature, newspapers, schools, churches, and youth organizations. Each of the topics is amply documented and equipped with an appropriate bibliography, maps, and photos. This work remains the standard source of information on Ukrainians in Bukovina.

662. Poppov, Joseph V. **La Dobrudja et les relations bulgaro-roumaines**. Liège: Thone, 1935. 195p.

Poppov surveys Bulgarian-Romanian relations and examines the significance of the Dobrudja in determing those relations. The work contains basic data on the Bulgarian population of the Dobrudja.

663. Potra, George. **Contribuţiuni la istoricul ţiganilor din România** (Contributions to the History of the Gypsies in Romania). Bucharest: Fundaţia Regele Carol I, 1939. 376p.

This is the only detailed account related to the history of the Gypsies in Romania. An important and remarkably objective work.

664. Stojanov, Pavle. **Jugoslovenska nacionalna manjina u Rumuniji** (The Yugoslav Ethnic Minority in Romania). Beograd: Kultura, 1953. 193p.

The Yugoslav minority in Romania inhabits the area northwest and south of Timisoara as well as the left shore of the Danube along the Yugoslav border. Of the total number of 55,000, the Serbs account for 43,000 and the Croats for 5,000; the remainder is referred to as *Krašovani*. The book covers the interwar period, including the 1933 agreement on minority schools reached between Romania and Yugoslavia, the minority's role in the wartime guerrilla activities, and the persecution by Romanian authorities following Yugoslavia's expulsion from the Cominform.

665. Tichner, H. **Roumania and Her Religious Minorities**. London: Philot, 1923. 100p.

A brief account of religious policies of postwar Romania. The author is critical of Romanian implementation of provisions of treaties governing the rights of religious minorities.

666. Zaharieff, Malomir. **Les minorités bulgares en Roumanie**. Paris: Domat-Montchrestien, 1940. 99p.

A brief but interesting survey of the history and status of Bulgarians in Romania.

6 _____ National Minorities in Yugoslavia, 1919-1980:
Linguistic Minorities from an Economic Perspective

Toussaint Hočevar,
with the assistance of David Crowe (Jews)

HISTORICAL SUMMARY

In 1918, when Yugoslavia was formed, its official name, the Kingdom of the Serbs, Croats, and Slovenes, reflected the premise that these ethnic groups were the constituent units of the new state. The second Yugoslavia, which emerged after World War II, added to the list of constituent nations the Macedonians and the Montenegrins, both of whom had been formerly subsumed under the Serbian label. Later, the Moslems, defined as an ethnic group, were given the nation status, with Bosnia and Herzegovina being considered as their home republic.

Of the remaining ethnic groups, ten are significant enough to have been recognized as nationalities: Albanians, Bulgarians, Czechs, Hungarians, Italians, Romanians, Ruthenians, Slovaks, Turks, and recently Romanies (Gypsies).[1] Common to all these groups, except Gypsies, is the fact that their ethnic state (*matična država*) happens to be outside of the Yugoslav territory. The related technical distinction between "nations" and "nationalities" is that the principle of national self-management, on which Yugoslavia is based, is recognized for constituent nations but not for nationalities. Thus, according to the current Yugoslav political philosophy, the two autonomous provinces, Kosovo and Vojvodina, which are inhabited by the Albanian and Hungarian nationalities, respectively, lack the attribute of a state.[2]

The Evolution of Linguistic Minorities

Although the historical evolution of Yugoslav ethnic groups with national status is a subject worthy of study, the treatment here is limited to nationalities, those presently recognized as such as well as those who have occupied a similar position during recent history, e.g., Germans and Tsintsars. Since in the Western literature non-state nationalities are usually referred to as minorities, this term is used, even though it generally connotes subordination, which the semantics of "nationality" are designed to avoid.[3] Subordination is a relative concept, defineable not only in political but in sociolinguistic and economic terms as well. Since it is difficult, if not impossible, to draw clear boundaries based on all of these criteria, designations such as minority, nationality, and nation are of necessity somewhat arbitrary. Hence, it appears that no harm is done by adopting the term minority, as long as it is recognized that the degree of subordination or the degree to which sovereignty is approximated may vary for any given group over time as well as between groups.

To provide an analytical framework for the study of ethnic minorities within Yugoslavia and peripheral areas, conceptual lines suggested by economic theory are used here. Although the terms "ethnic minority" and "linguistic minority" are often used interchangeably, the focus here is on linguistic minorities since in economic significance the linguistic attribute generally outweighs other attributes which define ethnic groups. After all, communications involve substantial costs, and it is precisely the distribution of these costs between linguistic groups which gives the minority status an important economic dimension.[4] The subsequent discussion hinges in part on these costs.

In order to treat the historical evolution of linguistic minorities within our purview, two economic paradigms are proposed: 1) the principle of equimarginal returns to factors of production, and 2) the principle of cost minimization as applied to linguistically alternative communication systems. The first of these paradigms helps to explain the making of a minority, and the second her subsequent persistence under conditions of a stationary equilibrium or, alternatively, her evolution away from the minority status. The latter occurs either through assimilation, i.e., linguistic merging with the dominant group, or through emancipation, i.e., assertion of linguistic autonomy, both in conditions of economic development.

The applicability of the first paradigm, that of equimarginal returns, derives from the observation that the emergence of a linguistic minority can generally be traced to the migration between linguistic territories. According to the equimarginal principle, resources are optimally distributed when the marginal physical product of a resource is equalized between firms as well as between regions. If opportunities for interregional trade and associated specialization are limited, then the marginal physical product tends to be equalized interregionally through migration of resources, the population being one such resource.

The second paradigm, developed fully elsewhere by this author,[5] focuses on the alternative investment choices associated with the entry of minority members into functional domains from which the minority language is excluded. Under the first alternative, entrants into excluded domains invest in the learning of the majority language. Under the second alternative, the collectivity invests in resources necessary for the introduction of the minority language into excluded domains. If the aggregate cost incurred by learners of the majority language (first alternative) exceeds the cost of enlarging the functional scope of the minority language through investment in specialized literature, etc. (second alternative), the latter is economically justified. The critical variable is the number of potential minority entrants into excluded domains, which in turn depends not only on the total size of the minority population but on the level of economic development as well; structural changes linked to development require occupational and industrial mobility, implying that an increased number of the minority is drawn into activities which correspond to the domains from which their language is excluded.

In an agricultural environment, external communication requirements are likely to be minimal. Hence the linguistic identity of a rural minority can be preserved as long as conditions of a stationary economy prevail. However, once the process of economic development has begun, laborsaving agricultural technology, coupled with demographic expansion, causes a part of the agricultural labor force to become redundant, forcing it into the growing nonagricultural sector, in which communications tend to be more intense and varied than in the agricultural environment.

If the language used in nonagricultural activities differs from that spoken by the agrarian population, this part of the population is placed in a subordinate position, even though numerically they may represent the majority in a given region. Under such conditions, the need for linguistic adaptation acts as a barrier for the entry of the nondominant language group into occupations within the upper range of the occupational hierarchy, slowing down the occupational mobility. Those unable to assimilate linguistically move to menial occupations in which communication requirements are limited or continue crowding the agricultural sector. The nondominant language group is placed into the position of an underprivileged residual, in all outward appearance impregnable to modernization.

There are nevertheless instances where sufficient transfer of agrarian population into the nonagricultural sector transforms their language into the dominant language, reversing the direction of assimilation. The inflow of rural population into nonagricultural activities accelerates at all occupational levels, speeding up the transformation processes associated with sustained economic development and growth.

Since the minorities of Yugoslavia and adjacent areas generally fit one of the above models, their evolution will be treated under the following topical headings: 1) external migration, i.e., in-migration from outside the linguistic region, within which category the distinction is made between a) land colonization, and b) external migration into the urban sector; and 2) internal migration, specifically the migration of the agrarian population into urban centers. Historically, external migration preceded massive transfer of agrarian population into nonagricultural, urban activities, and therefore it will be treated first.

Land Colonization

The history of settlement of the German minority, the strongest numerically, in interwar Yugoslavia confirms the operation of the equimarginal principle, since the migration was directed toward relatively thinly settled areas, where the marginal productivity of labor appears to have exceeded that prevailing in the more densely settled home areas of the migrants. The systematic settlement of German peasants occurred first during the Middle Ages and then again during the eighteenth and nineteenth centuries.

During the medieval period the region of the eastern Alps, situated roughly between the Danube and the Gulf of Trieste and settled by the proto-Slovene population, acted as a magnet for German colonization: following the inclusion of the Slovene state of Karantania into the Frankish empire around the middle of the eighth century, the Bavarians began to move into the territory of the eastern Alps in a southerly direction. In the area to the north of the Drava River, with the exception of the Klagenfurt Basin, the newcomers succeeded in assimilating the less numerous Slovene population.[6] Farther to the south, German peasants imported by individual feudal landlords over the course of the centuries were readily assimilated by the Slovenes. However, the fourteenth-century settlement of Thuringian and Franconian peasants in the practically uninhabited, forested Kočevje (Gotschee) area was important enough to create a German linguistic enclave, which remained intact until the 1941 resettlement of the Kočevje Germans to the territory which had been annexed by the German Reich following the occupation of Yugoslavia.[7]

During the eighteenth and nineteenth centuries, German settlement occurred father to the east in the largely deserted territory of modern Vojvodina. By that time the Habsburg forces had pushed the border of the Ottoman empire back to Belgrade. In contrast to the earlier settlement of the Austrian side of the Turkish border with military guards recruited from the ranks of Serbian refugees, the eighteenth-century settlement of Vojvodina served primarily economic purposes; the military aspect came into play only indirectly, since the colonists were expected to make deliveries of grain to the army.

The economic motive of colonization had its roots in the Habsburg mercantilist policy referred to as populationism, which aimed at enlarging the existing tax base. The objective was to raise the productivity of underutilized natural resources by combining them with additional labor. At the same time, the productivity of labor was to be increased by promoting improved technology and skills. Both aspects are in evidence in the settlement of Vojvodina. Through the importation of German and other settlers, the area under cultivation was increased. On the other hand, the introduction of the three-field system represented a more productive method of cultivation than the two-field system used in the Turkish areas.

Between 1740 and 1770, the Habsburgs lured 43,000 German immigrants into an area which comprised the present Yugoslav Vojvodina and the adjoining Romainian Banat by offering them free houses and a six-year tax exemption. During the reign of Joseph II (1780-1790), these settlers were joined by another 40,000 immigrants. Eligibility criteria used by the Vienna colonization agency included literacy and skills in farming or in some craft. In addition to Germans, the inflow of settlers included Serbians, Romanians, Croats, and Hungarians, as well as Slovaks. No small wonder that by 1787 the population of the Bačka and Srem each exceeded 20,000 and that of the larger Banat, the northern part of which is now under Romania, approached 300,000, a tenfold increase since the beginning of the century.[8]

Non-German immigrants formerly engaged in livestock raising adopted German grain cultivation techniques of sowing several crops and using an iron plow. In addition to wheat, they planted hemp, flax, and some mulberry trees. The predominant part of the cultivated area had been reclaimed from former swamps through drainage.

Lampe points out that these accomplishments were possible not only because of active Habsburg policies of promoting German colonization, but also because of their efforts of keeping the Hungarian nobility from moving in to make serfs of the assorted immigrants.[9] However, when in 1799 all of Banat and Bačka, with the exception of the military border, came under the Hungarian jurisdiction, the Hungarian nobility succeeded in reasserting old feudal rights on the estates they acquired.

The immigration into Vojvodina continued into the nineteenth century. During this period the immigrants consisted of Hungarians and Germans from Hungary. The Germans introduced artesian wells, which allowed richer, clay soils to be cultivated. (Formerly the cultivation had been limited to poorer alluvial soils along the river banks.) Through four- and five-field systems of cultivation, the fallowing was ultimately eliminated. By the mid-nineteenth century, German immigrants owned more land in the Banat than any other group.

The Western and Eastern Slavic ethnic groups who moved into Vojvodina came from the overpopulated Carpathian region: from the Tatra Mountains Slovak landless peasants were brought in by the Hungarians, while the Ruthenian branch of the Ukrainians moved in from their Trans-Carpathian homeland.[10]

Vojvodina is not the only area where the presence of minorities can be traced back to the availability of land. It appears that the migration of the Albanian Moslems northward into Old Serbia, particularly into the Kosovo area, was induced by a much higher ratio of productive land to the total land area in Kosovo than in Albania. The influx of Albanians gained momentum following the Serbian Great Migration of 1690, and it soon spilled beyond Old Serbia. However, as during the nineteenth century the young Serbian state gradually expanded its southern boundaries, Albanian population was forced back into the Turkish-administered areas, while the Serbian population from these areas moved into the liberated territory. The consequence was a concentration of the Albanian population in Kosovo and adjacent areas.[11]

Migrations elsewhere included the Croat families fleeing the Turkish onslaught. They founded new homes in western Hungary and Lower Austria as early as the end of the fifteenth century. The present Croat minority in the Austrian province of Burgenland owes its origin to these migrations. The Burgenland Croats were settled on depopulated lands owned by Hungarian magnates. According to a recent author, this allowed for "rational cultivation."[12]

In the Somogyi district (*megye*) of Hungary, at the confluence of Mura and Drava, land was leased to a group of settlers from northeastern Slovenia in 1718.[13] Their Slovene-speaking descendants were found there, in 1948.[14] This group should be distinguished from the Slovenes in the Hungarian districts of Vás and Zala, who settled there prior to the arrival of the Hungarians in the Pannonian Basin.

External Migration into the Urban Sector

Minorities typically engaged in nonagricultural pursuits owe their presence in Yugoslavia to two distinct yet somewhat related phenomena, namely, the political rule by outside powers and the high interregional mobility of persons in nonagricultural industries such as trade and crafts. Over the centuries the external political influences ranged from Germanic and Venetian to Turkish, Hungarian, and Italian. On an intra-Balkan level there were periods of Serbian dominance in Kosovo and Serbian or Bulgarian dominance in Macedonia. The salient point for the study of linguistic minorities is that within areas under foreign political influence, the language of the ruling elite became dominant in certain activities, even though the bulk of the population spoke the indigenous language.

In the administrative sector, the nonindigenous languages were propagated by the ruling feudal nobility and later by assorted public officials of the central government recruited from outside the linguistic region. This group was augmented by local natives who had invested in the learning of the dominant language and who in time assimilated with the dominant group. The actual conditions varied between regions. In the Slovene lands, the German language dominated the activities of the upper social strata, even though recent research shows that the role of Slovene outside of the peasant sphere was greater than was previously held.[15] In Croatia and Slavonia, the situation resembled that in Slovenia, although in addition to German, Latin was used to a greater extent. Moreover, the Hungarians were at least partially successful in imposing Hungarian in these areas.[16]

In Serbia and in other areas under Ottoman rule, Turkish was used by the central administration. The Serbs in turn imposed their language as the only official language in the predominantly Albanian-speaking Kosovo and in Macedonia following the Balkan wars. Italian was imposed, after 1918, in the formerly Austrian Coastland, inhabited by Slovenes in the north and by Croats in the south. During World War II, Bulgarian served as the administrative language in Macedonia, while the languages of other occupying powers held a similar status elsewhere.

Besides the implantation of nonindigenous languages by political fiat, in certain urban activities their use was promoted through immigration of traders and craftsmen. Here the adage that trade follows the flag is generally applicable, although in at least one case the sequence was in the opposite direction, namely, the Italian urban settlement preceded the extension of the Venetian rule to towns along the Adriatic Coast. This sequence seems to be confirmed by the fact that even in the city-state of Dubrovnik (Ragusa) Italian held an important place as a language of commerce. In Serbia, Greek was dominant in import and transit trade because traders were either Greeks or Hellenized local Tsintsars who had abandoned the Romance dialect spoken by rural Tsintsars, or Vlachs.[17]

In short, as a result of the dominant role of nonindigenous languages in the urban sector, well into the nineteenth century and in some areas until this century, the indigenous population had to assimilate with the foreign, dominant language group in order to gain entry into various nonagricultural pursuits, especially at the higher occupational levels.

Internal Migration into the Urban Sector

The strengthened role of the indigenous population in the political sphere and/or their accelerated mobility into the urban sector under the impact of economic development caused the gradual replacement of existing dominant languages in urban activities by indigenous regional languages. This reduced the formerly dominant linguistic groups to the position of minorities, reversing the direction of assimilation. The Italian population in Dalmatia and the Hellenized Tsintsars in Serbia are cases in point. With the economic decline of Venice and the acquisition of Venetian territories by Austria, the Italian linguistic influence waned, especially as the proportion of South Slavic population in urban activities at all occupational levels increased. In Serbia, starting in the 1830s, Prince Miloš Obrenović began restricting the commercial privileges, such as trade passports and state orders, of the Greeks. Although the Tsintsars were able to avoid these restrictions by accepting Serbian business partners, this was coupled with the substitution of Serbian for their adopted Greek language, which speeded up the process of Serbianization.[18]

In the Slovene lands, the expansion of indigenous entrepreneurship around the middle of the nineteenth century was followed by the establishment of indigenous financial intermediaries (cooperative and municipal savings banks and later commercial banks). The indigenous business institutions were instrumental in the Slovenization of the business sector. Resisting the process were a few large outside companies, for example, the Southern Railroad, which clung tenaciously to the exclusive use of German until the end of World War I. However, neither the linguistic policy of outside firms nor the organized implantation of German-speaking workers by German nationalists succeeded in tipping the balance in favor of German.

In the administrative domain, Slovenization was linked to the political democratization, which started in 1848. Nevertheless, the relative political power varied considerably between provinces, depending on their ethnic mix: for the Slovenes the most favorable conditions existed in Carniola, and the least favorable in Carinthia. In Carniola, linguistic assimilation in the urban sector was reversed in favor of Slovene before the turn of the century.[19]

The Interwar Period

The period following 1918 can be viewed as one during which the use of the two principal indigenous languages of interwar Yugoslavia, Serbo-Croat and Slovene, was extended to all domains of social activity within their respective territories. Although this process was favored by political conditions which emerged after 1918, the basic rationale for the change is to be sought in the transformation of economic structure and associated modernization. Since the demand for human resources originating in the expanding nonagricultural sector had to be met by the indigenous, rural population, there was a natural tendency for linguistic conformity between that population and the language in urban activities. Because modernization had a longer tradition in the northwestern than in the southeastern regions of Yugoslavia, this economically determined path to linguistic conformity can be traced historically most clearly in Slovenia and in Croatia. In Serbia, which had attained political independence during the nineteenth century, the establishment of an indigenous administrative apparatus appears to have had a determining influence on the linguistic use, rather than economic impulses. Finally, Macedonia and Kosovo lacked both political and economic preconditions for functional expansion of regional languages, which explains why these areas fell prey to Serbian linguistic hegemony.

It seems that within Yugoslavia, as well as within peripheral areas, friction produced by the implantation of nonregional languages varied according to the level of economic development: to the bulk of the largely rural and illiterate Albanian population, the fact that a few officials with whom they came in contact used Serbo-Croat was of limited consequence. On the other hand, in the Slovene coastland, where a large percentage of the population was engaged in nonagricultural activities and literacy was nearly universal, the exclusion of Slovene from schools, the replacement of Slovene administrative personnel by Italians, and the supression of Slovene cooperatives and other institutions gave rise to deep frustration. The cost of linguistic adaptation was high, in that during the decades which preceded the Italian administration the Slovenes had extended the use of their language to most urban activities. Now their investment in indigenous economic and cultural institutions was written off by Italian edict accompanied by brutal repression through Mussolini's black-shirts. No wonder that Slovenes, regardless of their political or ideological orientation, rebelled against fascism before any other group in Europe.[20]

In Austrian Carinthia, Germanizing tendencies were strengthened under the First Austrian Republic, to be followed under the Third Reich by physical terror, which included the deportation of Slovene farm families to the interior of Germany and the carrying-out of death sentences by decapitation.[21]

In other areas bordering on Yugoslavia, the effective pressure on South Slavic minorities appears to have varied in accordance with the level of economic development and the repressiveness of political regimes. The Croats of Burgenland, the Slovenes of Hungary, the Serbs of Romania, and the Macedonians of Bulgaria, Greece, and Albania all come to mind. Each of these deserve separate treatment, a task beyond our purview.

In order to evaluate the minority situation within Yugoslavia, it is instructive to examine the relative numerical strength of the minorities and their geographical distribution as shown in Table 1, page 224.

Table 1. Principal Linguistic Minorities in Yugoslavia, 1921

Banovina (Italics indicate percentages)	German		Hungarian		Albanian		Romanian		Turkish		Czech or Slovak		Ruthenian		Polish		Italian		Other	
Dravska (Slovenia)	40,920	8.1	14,426	3.1	103	0.0	31	0.0	237	0.2	2,932	2.5	34	0.1	336	2.3	701	5.6	752	1.1
Savska (Croatia)	59,953	11.9	51,648	11.0	578	0.1	346	1.1	279	0.2	39,548	34.2	1,995	7.9	2,858	19.4	4,644	37.0	4,432	6.3
Vrbaska (Bosnia and Herz.)	8,396	1.7	880	0.1	109	0.0	802	0.3	70	0.0	2,763	2.4	7,964	31.5	9,708	65.8	1,174	9.4	998	1.4
Primorska (Croatia, Bosnia, and Herz.)	1,241	0.2	105	0.0	96	0.0	74	0.0	60	0.0	540	0.5	12	1.0	196	1.3	3,552	28.3	763	1.1
Drinska (Bosnia and Herz., Serbia)	31,579	6.2	11,033	2.4	493	0.1	2,834	1.2	186	0.1	5,550	4.8	4,472	17.7	975	6.6	663	5.3	10,181	14.6
Zetska (Montenegro)	452	0.1	88	0.0	67,128	15.3	211	0.1	5,232	3.5	334	0.3	18	0.0	74	0.5	1,110	8.8	1,821	2.6
Dunavska (Vojvodina)	344,136	68.0	385,526	82.4	893	0.2	79,621	34.5	291	0.2	60,968	52.8	11,084	43.8	340	2.3	249	2.0	11,752	16.8
Moravska (Serbia)	774	0.2	281	0.1	58,404	13.3	135,998	58.9	2,490	1.7	552	0.5	7	0.0	42	0.3	182	1.4	10,921	15.6
Vardarska (Macedonia, Kosovo)	252	0.0	157	0.0	311,432	70.8	9,451	4.1	140,982	93.8	201	0.2	8	0.0	27	0.2	34	0.3	24,379	34.9
Belgrade	18,047	3.6	3,514	0.8	421	0.1	700	0.3	495	0.3	2,144	1.9	21	0.1	208	1.4	244	1.9	3,879	5.5
Total	505,790	100.0	467,658	100.0	439,657	100.0	230,068	100.0	150,322	100.0	115,532	100.0	25,615	100.0	14,764	100.0	12,553	100.0	69,878	100.0

Source: Kraljevina Jugoslaviju, Opšta državna statistika, Statistički godišnjak, Knjiga 1, 1929, Belgrade, 1932, p. 69.

The German minority, which numbered one-half million, was concentrated in Vojvodina, that is, within the Danube and Sava administrative units, or *banovinas*. The only other localized German community was in the Kočevje area of Slovenia (*Dravska banovina*). The remaining Germans were scattered among the urban population. Their number included the Jews of German language, particularly in Croatia.[22]

The Hungarians were concentrated in the same general area as the Germans, i.e., in the grain-rich Vojvodina, as were the Ruthenians and the Slovaks. (The latter predominate in the statistical rubric "Czech or Slovak," at least as far as the area of Vojvodina is concerned.)

The Albanians and the Turks lived principally in the southeastern *banovinas* of Vardar, Zeta, and Morava. This area remained longest under the Ottoman domination and served as a catch basin for the Islamic population retreating from the areas to the north during more than a century of waning Ottoman power.

The Romanian linguistic group was made up of the population along the Romanian border and of Vlachs living in the interior of Serbia and in Macedonia. Like the Romanians, the Vlachs are believed to have descended from the Romanized population present in the Balkans prior to the arrival of the Slavs. The Romanian rubric may also include some Gypsies (Romanies), whose affinity with the Romanians has been documented.[23]

Finally, some 12,000 Italians lived in towns along the Adriatic Coast, not including Zadar/Zara and Rijeka/Fiume, both under Italian administration during the interwar period.

Under the provisions of the Treaty of Saint-Germain between the Principal Allied Powers and Associated Powers and the Serb-Croat-Slovene state, the linguistic minorities had the right to use their languages in private schools and other social institutions. In towns and districts where a given minority represented a considerable proportion of the population, the government was obligated to provide primary instruction in the minority language and to appropriate an equitable share of public funds for education purposes of the minority. Also, facilities had to be provided for the minority members to use their language, either orally or in writing, before the courts. Similar provisions were contained in the interwar treaties concluded between Italy and Yugoslavia.[24]

Any assessment of the extent to which linguistic usage was affected by Yugoslav interwar policies would have to take into account that several languages which after 1918 emerged as minority languages had previously occupied the dominant position, especially German and Hungarian. The erosion of their functional role must therefore be attributed in part to changes in international political boundaries. Moreover, a substantial number of the administrative personnel who promoted the use of dominant languages returned to their home countries (Austria, Hungary) at the end of World War I, thus reducing the number of speakers of their respective languages, especially in towns.

Although the Yugoslav government failed to take any statutory measures which would have provided for protection of linguistic minorities as groups, no negative laws were promulgated, as was the case in Italy, which banned the use of Slovene in public. Occasional complaints of German and Hungarian groups concerned the use of their language in the educational sector. Also, the

Hungarians complained that in the distribution of lands under the Yugoslav agrarian reform, Serbs were favored over Hungarians.[25] Through the agrarian reform laws of 1919 and 1921, cultivable land in excess of 300 *ha.* for any single holding was expropriated against compensation. The same maximum applied to holdings in Macedonia and Kosovo, while for other regions the maxima were set at lower levels. The discrimination derived from the fact that Serbian war veterans were given preference in the colonization of expropriated lands. In this way Serbian presence was increased not only in Vojvodina,[26] but in Kosovo as well, where it is estimated that nearly 40,000 Serbian families were settled on lands formerly in the public domain.[27]

World War II and Beyond

Occupation of Yugoslavia

In 1941 Yugoslavia was overrun by Axis forces, which had a significant impact upon minorities. In areas which had been occupied by, or attached to, their kin countries, the role of respective minority languages was enhanced. Thus in Kosovo, which had been attached administratively to Albania by the Italians, Albanian was reintroduced as the language of instruction in primary and secondary schools. Hungarian became the official language in parts occupied by Hungary. German gained importance in Banat, which remained attached to the German-occupied Serbia, but was endowed with administrative autonomy within the Danube *banovina*. The autonomous authority, the so-called *Behörde des Vize Banus der Donaubanschaft für das Banat*, had its seat in Petrovgrad and was headed by an ethnic German.

Local minority institutions and minority populations were used by the occupying powers to the latter's economic and military advantage. Initially, Hitler entertained the idea of resettling the Germans of Banat in the Reich,[28] but faced with the exigencies of war, he decided to postpone such plans: Banat was an important granary and the German minority there possessed a network of agricultural cooperatives upon which Germany could rely for a steady supply of foodstuffs. In Kosovo, another area noted for grain production, the Italians reintroduced the feudal *chiftlik* system, which had been abolished under interwar Yugoslavia. They did so not only in order to win the allegiance of local begs, but also because the *chiftlik* system facilitated the collection of grain for the Italian army. Feudal lords regained the right to collect from their tenants one-fifth of the produce. The state tax, which consisted of the tithe and was collected in kind, was leased out in auctions.[29]

During the thirties National Socialists had exploited the ethnic allegiance of the German minority for their political advantage. Now they declared ethnic Germans (*Volksdeutsche*) living in Banat and within the Axis-allied state of Croatia fit for service in the SS divisions. As a result, ethnic Germans subject to draft were recruited almost exclusively into the SS. Later in the war, as the need for military manpower mounted, the Germans mobilized a division of Kosovo Albanians, known as the "SS Skanderbeg." Incidentally, yet another SS division was made up of Yugoslav Moslems. All these units were engaged principally against Yugoslav guerrillas.[30]

Toward the end of the war, a sizable number of ethnic Germans withdrew with the German armed forces. Others were subsequently expelled by Yugoslav authorities. As to the Hungarians, the Central Committee of the Yugoslav Communist party decided that they should not be expelled.[31] On formerly German-occupied land, the authorities settled population from agriculturally poor regions of Montenegro and Lika.

Changes in the Relative Numerical Strength of Minorities

Table 2, page 228, shows changes in the number of persons belonging to principal minorities between 1921 and 1953. Many of these changes came about as a consequence of the war. Thus the postwar departure of ethnic Germans reduced their number by 88%. On the other hand, the substantial increase in the number of ethnic Italians is attributable to the attachment of Rijeka (Fiume) and of the Istrian Peninsula to Yugoslavia. Since interwar data for the Romanian group apparently include the Vlachs (Tsintsars), it can be safely assumed that the decrease of this group occurred because of the assimilation of Vlachs with the Serbs or possibly Macedonians.[32] The increase in the number of Ruthenians (Ukrainians) may be due in part to their having been entered in the Czecho-Slovak or Polish rubric in 1921.

The Albanians, who in 1921 ranked third, emerged by 1953 as the most populous minority. This most likely would have happened even in the absence of the German exodus because the Albanian rate of natural increase exceeded by far that of either the Germans or the Hungarians. The economic implications of the Albanian demographic growth will be covered in the special subsection treating this minority.

From Table 3, page 229, it can be seen that between 1953 and 1981 all minorities, except the Albanians and the Romanies, experienced absolute declines in number. During the same period the population of Yugoslavia as a whole increased by 32%. Although in the case of Turkish, German, and Italian groups emigration had been a contributing factor, for all other groups assimilation should be viewed as the principal cause of the decline. The sharp drop in the number of both Romanies and Vlachs between 1953 and 1961, followed by a rebound in 1971, reveals a negative statistical bias as far as these two groups are concerned.

Regional distribution of minorities is shown in Table 4, page 230. Outside of Kosovo, where Albanian is one of the official languages, the Albanians are represented mainly in western Macedonia. The Hungarians are concentrated in Vojvodina, where they represent 19% of the total population. Among towns where the Hungarian presence is felt are Bačka Topola, Kanjiža, Senta, Subotica, and Temerin.[33] Outside of Vojvodina, smaller Hungarian groups are found in northern Croatia and in northeastern Slovenia around Lendava. Romanies are scattered throughout the country, with concentration in Macedonia, Kosovo, and Serbia proper.

(Text continues on page 231.)

Table 2. Principal Linguistic Minorities in Yugoslavia, 1921-1953

	1921	1931	1953	Percentage change 1953/1921
	(in thousands)			
German	506	500	61	-87.9
Hungarian	468	468	502	7.3
Albanian	440	505	754	71.4
Romanian (including Vlachs)	230	138	97	-58.0
Turkish	150	133	260	73.3
Slovak	} 116	76	} 120	} 3.4
Czech		53		
Ruthenian (Ukrainian)	26	28	37	42.3
Italian	13	n.a.	36	176.9

Sources: For 1921, Kraljevina Jugoslavija, Opšta državna statistika, *Statistički godišnjak, Knjiga 1, 1929*, Belgrade, 1932, p. 69. For 1931, *Gliederung der Bevölkerung des ehemaligen Jugoslawien nach Muttersprache und Konfession, nach den unveröffentlichten Angaben der Zählung von 1931, bearb. u. hrsg. von der Publikationsstelle Wien, 1943*, as quoted in Germany, Federal Republic, *Das Schicksal der Deutschen in Jugoslawien*, Bundesministerium für Vertriebene, 1961, p. 11E. (Dokumentation der Vertreibung der Deutschen aus Ost-Mitteleuropa, Band V.). For 1953, *Statistički godišnjak Jugoslavije* for 1953.

Table 3. Principal Linguistic Minorities in Yugoslavia, 1953-1981

	1953	1961	1971	1981	Percentage change 1981/1953
		(in thousands)			
Albanian	754	915	1,310	1,731	129.5
Hungarian	502	504	477	427	- 15.0
Romany (Gypsies)	84	32	78	168	100.1
Turkish	260	183	128	101	- 60.9
Slovak	85	84	84	80	- 5.5
Romanian	60	61	60	55	- 9.0
Bulgarian	62	63	58	36	- 41.4
Vlach (Tsintsar)	37	9	22	32	- 12.7
Ruthenian	} 37	} 39	25	23	- 3.3
Ukrainian			14	13	
Czech	35	30	25	20	- 43.1
Italian	36	26	22	15	- 57.8
German	61	20	13	9	- 85.6

Sources: Various volumes of *Statistički godišnjak Jugoslavije* and *Saopštenje Saveznog zavoda za statistiku*, 26/112 (April 29, 1982).

Table 4. Regional Distribution of Minorities, 1981
(Percentage of the total population of a given minority)

	Kosovo	Vojvodina	Serbia proper	Macedonia	Montenegro	Bosnia and Herzegovina	Croatia	Slovenia
Albanian	70.9		4.2	21.8	2.2			
Hungarian		90.3					6.0	2.2
Romany	20.3	11.7	34.0	25.7				
Turkish	12.4			85.6				
Slovak		86.5					8.1	
Romanian		86.1	11.6					
Bulgarian		7.0	85.0					
Vlach			79.6	19.9				
Ruthenian		82.9					14.3	
Ukrainian		39.0				35.1	19.6	
Czech		10.3	6.0				76.7	
Italian							77.1	14.5
German		43.7	16.1				25.0	

Sources: Various volumes of *Statistički godišnjak Jugoslavije* and *Saopštenje Saveznog zavoda za statistiku*, 26/112 (April 29, 1982).

The Turks live mostly in Macedonia. Along her eastern border they preserve old traditions and lead a half-nomadic existence. Towns with substantial Turkish populations are Debar, Kruševo, Brod, Valandovo, Gostivar, Ohrid, Skopje, Titov Veles, and Štip. Over the years the migratory flow of Turks to Asia Minor has been substantial, which accounts for their falling numbers.

It should be noted that Turkish sources generally exaggerate the number of Turks in Yugoslavia because they include other Moslems, many of whom are of Slavic stock and language and who are considered as a special ethnic group. Admittedly the line between these two groups may often not be easy to draw, especially since the linguistic assimilation with one or another of the South Slavic groups tends to transform ethnic Turks into ethnic Moslems.

As to the remaining minorities, the Slovaks are settled in Vojvodina, where Bački Petrovac serves as their cultural center. Other locations are Bačka Palanka, Kovačica, Novi Sad, Stara Pazova, and Šid. Also in Vojvodina are the Romanians, particularly around Vršac, Kula, and Bela Crkva. The Bulgarians are found in eastern Serbia, mainly around Pirot, as well as in certain villages of Vojvodina. Ruthenians in Vojvodina continue using their variant of Ukrainian in written form, despite attempts to favor the standard Ukrainian. Finally, the Czechs are found mostly in the town of Daruvar in the Slavonia region of the republic of Croatia.

Ethnic Policy

The Yugoslav postwar constitution of 1946 rested on federalist principles similar to those of the USSR. The territories of five of the six federal republics were drawn along ethnic lines. Only the republic of Bosnia and Herzegovina was constituted as an ethnically mixed unit. Within Serbia, two autonomous units were constituted: the Autonomous Province of Vojvodina, with a strong Hungarian minority, and the Autonomous District of Kosovo and Metohija, or Kosmet, the home of the Albanian minority. The fact that the Albanian minority was accommodated through the establishment of an autonomous district, rather than a province, is to be attributed to the view shared with the USSR that less-developed nationalities and territories were to enjoy a lesser degree of autonomy.[34]

Following the break with the Cominform in 1948, Yugoslavia began to develop a distinct form of socialism, which affected ethnic policy as well. Three phases of this development can be distinguished so far. During the first, the imperative, centralist economic planning was replaced by a system of self-management at the enterprise level, implying a substantial measure of decentralization in economic decision-making, even though the allocation of investment funds remained centralized in Belgrade. In the competition for these funds, certain regional interests crystallized, leading to pressures for a greater measure of self-government at the level of the republics. Such tendencies were at first resisted. However, with the removal of the federal interior minister Aleksander Rankovič and his associates, in 1966, a phase of liberalization set in, culminating in constitutional reforms of 1967 and 1968, which strengthened the de facto autonomy of the republics as well as of the two autonomous provinces. It should be noted that Kosmet had gained the status of province earlier through the constitution adopted in 1963, but at that time the provinces lost their original characteristics of federal units: their representatives in the Federal Assembly became part of the delegation of the Republic of Serbia, and departments of the Supreme Court of Serbia were opened in Vojvodina as well as in Kosmet. Through 1968 amendments of the federal constitution, the provinces regained their role in the federal system. At the same time, the designation Kosovo and Metohija, or Kosmet, was changed to Kosovo.

During the third phase, which followed the removal in the early seventies of liberal leaders in Croatia, Serbia, and Slovenia, there was a strengthening of the influence of the League of Communists. However, the 1974 constitution, currently still in force, retained the basic features of expanded federalism and decentralization.

Although of primary concern to the constituent nations of Yugoslavia, the decentralization process affected the minorities as well. Thus, in 1974 the two provinces attained a constitutional status which for all practical purposes equals that of the republics. The provinces are represented in all federal organs, even though in some organs they have a smaller number of representatives than the republics. The existence of provinces allows for meeting special needs of the minorities in these provinces, such as the use of their languages in schools and public administration. Occasionally voiced demands for giving Kosovo the status of a federal republic have been so far categorically rejected by the Yugoslav spokesmen.

In other territories inhabited by minorities, rights are stipulated in the constitutions of individual republics as well as in the statutes of local political units where minorities have been traditionally present. In such areas their language serves as the second official language, and the education is either bilingual or in their mother tongue. Minority cultural and other institutions receive public support, public information is disseminated in the language of the minority, and their representation in various public bodies is guaranteed along parity principles.[35]

It is worth noting that these requirements do not extend to the business sector. For example, in the labeling of products the minority languages and often even the official language of the republic where the product is sold are ignored. With the passage of a federal law which requires that multilingual instructions for product use be provided, the situation appears to be improving at least in this respect.

The Economics of the Albanian Minority

In the section on the evolution of linguistic minorities, it is shown that interregionally unequal factor ratios, e.g., the population/land ratio, have historically led to migration, which helped in reducing interregional inequalities in factor returns. Today, under conditions of rapid demographic growth observed in less-developed countries, it may not be possible to syphon off the excess agrarian population through migration. Moreover, where employment opportunities in the nonagricultural sector fail to keep up with the growth of the labor force, the pressure against limited nonhuman resources may produce social tension. It appears that such a scenario is *grosso modo* appropriate for describing the situation in Kosovo and that serious disturbances in April of 1981, which caused federal authorities to impose the state of emergency in

Kosovo and to bring in security forces from as far as Slovenia,[36] should be gauged against changes in relevant socioeconomic indicators during the past few decades.

First of these is the phenomenal natural increase of the Albanian population, as reflected in the growth of their number from 754,000 in 1953 to 1,731,000 in 1981, an increase of 130%. During the same period the population of Yugoslavia as a whole increased by only 32%. Even though between 1953 and 1979 in Kosovo the portion of population engaged in agriculture was reduced from 72.4 to 42.2% of the total population, the ratio of agricultural population per *ha.* of cultivable land increased from 1.48 to 1.65. Hence, in 1979, there were 1.54 *ha.* of cultivable land for each person attached to agriculture in Yugoslavia, against the corresponding figure of 0.61 *ha.* in Kosovo.[37]

As reported in the Yugoslav press, in Kosovo the Albanians are eagerly purchasing land owned by Serbs and Montenegrins. Moreover, in some instances intimidation has been used to drive Serbian farm families out of Kosovo.[38] Before placing the exclusive blame for such a turn of events on ethnic intolerance or outside political forces, one should consider that Albanian households are typically larger in size than those of the Serbs, suggesting a more pressing need for land.[39] Also, for the Serbs migrating to Serbia proper or Montenegro, no linguistic or cultural adaptation is required, which contributes to their mobility. An analogous pattern has been observed in the rural-urban migration in Macedonia, where local Albanians tend to occupy homesteads which had been vacated by Macedonians migrating to Skopje and other urban centers in which Macedonian serves as the working language.[40]

As a result of these developments, the countryside is becoming increasingly Albanian. In Kosovo, Albanization is being felt in towns as well, since due to improved educational opportunities Albanians are entering white-collar occupations formerly held mainly by the Serbs. The concomitant phenonemon is that the Albanian is being used in an extended number of functions and by an increasing number of speakers. The causation is actually circular, since Serbs not fluent in the Albanian language are becoming less and less suited for jobs with a heavy communication content and seek employment in areas where their language is dominant. Educated Albanians, on the other hand, are moving from Macedonia and Montenegro to Kosovo. A similar process could be observed in Slovenia during the nineteenth century. With the institutionalization of Slovene in Slovene-controlled Carniola, the employment opportunities there became less and less attractive for German monolinguals, while educated Slovenes from Styria and Carinthia migrated to Carniola, at least as long as the Slovenization of institutions did not extend to Slovene-inhabited parts of Styria as well. Once the initial adjustment had been completed, that is after the German monolinguals had moved out, the migration of intellectual capital between the Slovene and German linguistic regions slowed down considerably.[41] A similar situation may arise in Kosovo after the out-migration of Serbo-Croat monolinguals will have run its course.

The present structure of employment in Kosovo reflects the direction taken by past development efforts. The latter have been financed largely through income transfers from developed regions of Yugoslavia. One channel for such transfers has been a special federal fund fed by contributions from the developed republics and used for subsidizing economic investments in less-developed areas. Given Kosovo's endowment with mineral resources, especially lead ore and coal, these investments have been concentrated in extractive industries, which in 1979 accounted for 21.9% of total employment in manufacturing and mining, as compared with the corresponding figure of 4.4% for all of Yugoslavia.[42]

The second channel for transferring income has been the federal budget, through which public services in Kosovo are being subsidized. A substantial part of employment growth in the nonagricultural sector has been linked to these services, which in 1979 accounted for 26% of the total number of employees, as compared to 17% for Yugoslavia as a whole. Among public services, education occupies first place. Because of Kosovo's youthful demographic profile, one-third of the province's total population is in school or university. The progress achieved in the educational sphere over a little more than one generation can be inferred from the data of school enrollment. In 1939/40, total enrollment in Kosovo's elementary schools was 33,000, of which Albanians accounted for only 36%. In 1979/80, the corresponding figure was 321,000 pupils, of which 81% belonged to the Albanian minority. During 1979/80, enrollment at the new University of Prishtinë/Priština was 34,000. Of this total, 25,000 were full-time students. The faculty of 1,000 was largely Albanian-speaking, including a number of visiting professors from Albania, so that three classes were taught in Albanian for every one in Serbo-Croatian.[43] It should be noted that communications between Albanian speakers have been made easier ever since, in April 1966, a Conference on Language held in Prishtinë/Priština resolved to abandon the literary use of the Geg dialect in favor of the Tosk dialect, which has been the official language of neighboring Albania.

Absorbing an increasing number of entrants into the labor force should be one of the most pressing problems in the near future. Given the relatively low propensity of the Albanian population to migrate to other regions of Yugoslavia, provision of productive employment opportunities appears as the most viable alternative to further social unrest. Existing capital scarcity suggests focusing on labor-intensive industries. But, at least in the short run, some migration of Albanians may be unavoidable. One way of encouraging such migration would be to offer Slovene language courses in Kosovo schools, since Slovenia, where the rate of unemployment is the lowest, has traditionally provided jobs for migrants from less-developed regions.

Notes

[1]Dušan Popovski, "Respect for the Rights of Ethnic Minorities," *Socialist Thought and Practice* 16:1 (1976): 68.

[2]Milija Komatija, "The Policy of the League of Communists of Yugoslavia on Resolving the National Question," *Socialist Thought and Practice* 21:10 (1981): 47-48.

[3]In Yugoslavia the term "national minority" was in official use until the constitutional amendments of 1963, when it was replaced by the term "nationality." Popovski, "Respect for the Rights of Ethnic Minorities," p. 69.

[4]For a survey of literature on the economics of language, see François Vaillancourt, "The Economics of Language and Language Planning," *Cahiers*, 8882, 1982 (Département de sciences économiques et Centre de recherche en développement économique, Université de Montréal).

[5]"Les aspects économiques de la dynamique fonctionelle des langues," *Language Problems and Language Planning* 7:2 (Summer 1983).

[6]Aleš Lokar, "Nemci in Slovenci. Nekaj misli o kompleksnem odnosu skozi stoletja," *Most* 33-34 (1972), esp. p. 55.

[7]For a historical bibliography on Kočevje Germans, see *Gospodarska in družbena zgodovina Slovencev, Zgodovina agrarnih panog, I. zvezek: Agrarno gospodarstvo* (Ljubljana: SAZU—Državna založba Slovenije, 1970), p. 81. For the details on carrying out the 1941 Italian-German resettlement treaty, see Helga H. Harriman. *Slovenia under Nazi Occupation, 1941-1945* (New York: Studia Slovenica, 1971), esp. pp. 40-41. Of the 12,400 Kočevje Germans, 11,756 opted for the Reich.

[8]John R. Lampe and Marvin R. Jackson, *Balkan Economic History, 1550-1950: From Imperial Borderlands to Developing Nations* (Bloomington, IN: Indiana University Press, 1982), pp. 64-65.

[9]Ibid., p. 66.

[10]Ibid., p. 67.

[11]L. M. Kostić, *Nacionalne manjine u srpskim predelima: Demografsko etnografska studija* (Toronto: Srpski kulturni klub "Sv. Sava," 1961), p. 63.

[12]Josef Breu, *Die Kroatensiedlungen in Burgenland und den anschliessenden Gebieten* (Vienna, 1970), p. 15.

[13]M. Slavič, *Prekmurje* (Ljubljana: Slovenska krščansko-socialna zveza, 1921), p. 18.

[14]Vladimir Murko, "O neznanih in pozabljenih Slovencih na Madžarskem," in *Prekmurski Slovenci v zgodovini*, ed. Bogo Grafenauer (Murska Sobota: Pomurska založba, 1961), pp. 90-102.

[15]Particularly important is the recently discovered Slovene correspondence between two countesses published by Pavle Merkù under the title *Slovenska plemiška pisma* (Trieste: Založba tržaškega tiska, 1980).

[16]Before World War I, it was impossible to buy a postage stamp in the post office of Rijeka (Fiume) without requesting it in Hungarian. Cf. A. J. P. Taylor, *The Habsburg Monarchy, 1815-1918: A History of the Austrian Empire and Austria-Hungary* (London: Macmillan and Co., 1942).

[17]D. J. Popović, *O Cincarima: Prilozi pitanju postanka našeg gradjanskog društva* (Belgrade, 1937).

[18]Lampe, *Balkan Economic History*, p. 118.

[19]Toussaint Hočevar, "Economic Determinants in the Development of the Slovene National System," *Papers in Slovene Studies*, vol. 1, 1975. Also, Toussaint Hočevar, *The Structure of the Slovenian Economy, 1848-1963* (New York: Studia Slovenica, 1965).

[20]Tone Ferenc et al., *Slovenci v zamejstvu: Pregled zgodovine 1918-1945* (Ljubljana: Državna založba Slovenije, 1974). Also, Jože Pirjevec, "The Slovenes of the Trieste Area—An Historical Approach," *Nationalities Papers* 11:2 (Fall 1983): 152-61. As early as 1930, four Slovenes were executed following a show-trial in Trieste.

[21]*Koroška v borbi: Spomini na osvobodilno borbo v Slovenski Koroški* (Celovec/Klagenfurt): Zveza bivših partizanov Slovenske Koroške, 1951).

[22]According to the 1931 census, the German group included 10,026 persons of the Jewish religion, while another 18,044 persons, mostly in Bosnia and Herzegovina, declared Jewish as their mother tongue.

[23]When in 1941 the Germans required Gypsies in Serbia to wear identifying badges, the Romanian dictator Antonescu intervened on their behalf, stating that Serbian Gypsies were actually Romanians (Vlachs). The Germans withdrew the order. Kostić, *Nacionalne manjine u srpskim predelima*, p. 74.

[24]For texts and discussion of these treaties, see Pierre Jacquin, *La question des minorités entre l'Italie et la Yougoslavie* (Paris: Recueil Sirey, 1929).

[25]Sir Robert Gower, *The Hungarian Minorities in the Succession States* (London: Grant Richards, 1937).

[26]L. M. Kostić, *Srpska Vojvodina i njene manjine: Demografsko-etnografska studija* (Toronto: Srpski kulturni klub "Sv. Sava," 1962), pp. 55-57. During World War II, the interwar Serbian settlers were expelled from Hungarian-occupied parts of Vojvodina.

[27]Peter R. Prifti, *Socialist Albania since 1944: Domestic and Foreign Developments* (Cambridge, MA: The MIT Press, 1978), p. 228.

[28]Harriman, *Slovenia under Nazi Occupation*, p. 24.

[29]Ali Hadri, "Albanska narodnost u Jugoslaviji od 1918. do 1941. godine i njeno učešće u NOB Jugoslavije," in *Iz istorije Albanaca* (Beograd: Zavod za izdavanje učbenika SR Srbije, 1969), p. 194.

[30]Holm Sundhaussen, "Zur Geschichte der Waffen-SS in Kroatien 1941-1945," *Südost-Forschungen* 30 (1971): 177-96. Also, Prifti, *Socialist Albania*, fn. 19, p. 297.

[31]Milovan Djilas, *Wartime* (New York and London: Harcourt Brace Jovanovich, 1977), pp. 422-24.

[32]The Peace Treaty of Bukarest signed at the conclusion of the Second Balkan War in 1913 failed to mention the Vlach minority. In a subsequent exchange of notes between Romania on the one hand and Greece, Serbia, and Bulgaria on the other, the latter three powers guaranteed a measure of autonomy for Vlach schools and church communities. However, following World War I, these guarantees were not observed. Cf. Max Demeter Peyfuss, *Die Aromunische Frage: Ihre Entwicklung von den Ursprüngen bis zum Frieden von Bukarest (1913) und die Haltung Österreich-Ungarns* (Vienna: Hermann Böhlaus Nachf., 1974).

[33]Information on the distribution of minorities by towns has been drawn from Rudolf Grulich's working paper "Jugoslawien-Albanien-Bulgarien," prepared for the Conference of the International Institute for Nationalities Law and Regionalism, held in Brixen, Italy, Oct. 31-Nov. 3, 1978.

[34]Kurteš Saljiu, "The Development of Autonomy in Yugoslavia," *Socialist Thought and Practice* 22:8 (1982): 35.

[35]Ernest Petrič, "Regionalism in Yugoslavia: Some Constitutional Aspects" (recent unpublished paper).

[36]Dennison I. Rusinow, *Unfinished Business: The Yugoslav "National Question"* (Hanover, NH: American Universities Field Staff, 1981). (Report 1981/No. 35).

[37]Calculated from the *Statistički godišnjak Jugoslavije*, 1980.

[38]*Nedeljski dnevnik*, 12 September 1982.

[39]In the absence of data by ethnic group, household size data for Kosovo can be taken as representative of the Albanian group and those for Serbia proper for the Serbian group. Between 1948 and 1971, household size in Serbia proper decreased from an average of 4.54 to 3.63 persons, while the corresponding figures for Kosovo are 6.36 and 6.61. *Statistički godišnjak Jugoslavije*, 1968 and 1980.

[40]Jean-Pierre Debats, "Nationalités et groupes ethniques en République Socialiste de Macédoine," *Revue geographique de l'Est* 19:1-2 (1979): 67-85.

[41]For an empirical study of the phenomenon discussed here, see Toussaint Hočevar, "Mednarodna mobilnost človeškega kapitala v tradicionalnem in razvijajočem se gospodarstvu: Slovenski primer," *Most* 31-32 (1971): 2-7.

[42]Employment data are from *Statistički godišnjak Jugoslavije*, 1980, pp. 426-27.

[43]Dennison I. Rusinow, *The Other Albania: Kosovo 1979, Part I: Problems and Prospects* (Hanover, NH: American Universities Field Staff, 1980). (Report 1980/No. 5, Europe).

Jews in Yugoslavia

Yugoslavia's Jewish communities developed along the same diverse paths as other Yugoslavian minorities, and many Sephardic communities, particularly in Slovenia and Serbia, traced their origins back for centuries. As a result, they retained their traditional religious and cultural heritage. In contrast, Yugoslavia's Ashkenaz Jews, in the nineteenth century, came into what became Yugoslavia, particularly those portions under Habsburg control, and tended to blend better into local society.[1]

Yugoslavia's Jews, like Poland's, were concentrated in the cities of a predominantly rural country. They numbered only 71,342 in 1938 out of a total population of over 15,000,000, and lived primarily in cities, whereas only 10% of other Yugoslavians lived in urban areas. According to 1931 statistics, 26,168 Sephardic Jews, 39,010 Ashkenzic Jews, and 3,227 Orthodox Jews resided in Yugoslavia.[2]

Yugoslavia's Jewish communities were organized into the Federation of Jewish Religious Communities, the position of which was strengthened by the Law on the Religious Community of Jews set forth in the Kingdom of Yugoslavia in 1929. This law allowed for religious development along Sephardic, Ashkenaz, and Orthodox lines with state subsidies that amounted to 16.5 dinars per Jewish member. This was far more than the amount given to other ethnic minorities, and indicates the positive relationship between the government and its Jewish minority.[3] Within this structure, there were 72 Ashkenazic, 36 Sephardic, and 13 Orthodox Jewish communities in Yugoslavia at that time. Over the years, Zionist influence dominated the federation, and by 1933 most of the delegates at the federation's Fifth Congress "supported a Zionist platform based on Jewish nationality, the primacy of Palestine, and solidarity with all Jewry." Unfortunately, though the Zionist Federation dominated the Yugoslavian Federation throughout the rest of the interwar period, conflicts with Sephardic Jews and Zionist Revisionists severely divided the Jewish community and lessened its ability to handle the severe difficulties it faced after 1939.[4]

Jewish education in the nineteenth-century Yugoslavian territories tended to be strictly religious in nature, and little was done, particularly in predominantly Sephardic areas, to transmit Serbo-Croatian language or Slavic culture. After independence, Zionist influence strengthened and forced the modernization of the Jewish curriculum. Jewish enrollment in these schools, however, steadily declined throughout the interwar period, despite government approval of their curriculum, because of their inferior nonreligious educational standards vis-à-vis public education throughout Yugoslavia.[5] On the other hand, Yugoslavia's Jewish community opened an excellent seminary, the Jewish Middle Theological Seminary, in Sarajevo in 1928, to provide secondary education to their rabbis for work in small synagogues or to prepare them for higher rabbinical education elsewhere. The curriculum of the seminary expanded over the years, and provided strong religious leadership for the country's Ashkenazic and Sephardic communities.[6]

In the fall of 1940, the Yugoslavian government passed numerous clausus legislation that restricted the number of Jewish students in public schools and universities to their percentage of the total population. In addition, non-Yugoslavian Jews could no longer attend public schools. Jews, who made up a far greater portion of the country's students than of the population, were severely affected by this law. A network of Jewish secondary schools cropped up at this point to handle the excluded students, though it did not last long.[7]

Economically and professionally, Jews played an important, but not an overwhelming, role in Yugoslavia's regional economies. The majority of Jews engaged in business and commerce, and to a lesser degree the professions. They were particularly important in the economic and professional life in Croatia, where they held positions as lawyers, doctors, and bankers, whereas in Serbia and even poorer regions of Yugoslavia, their economic and professional stature was less significant.[8]

Organized anti-Semitism was essentially unknown in Yugoslavia for most of the interwar period, in part because of the support of the Karageorgevich royal family, its successive governments, and the Orthodox Church in Serbia.[9] What anti-Semitic feelings did periodically surface, particularly in regions once part of the Austrian empire, tended to be more anti-Habsburg than racial. But with the advent of the Nazi regime in Germany in 1933, some National Socialist propaganda began to appear in German and Serbo-Croatian in Croatia, Slovenia, and Vojvodina.[10]

Yugoslavia's drift towards Germany did not alter the government's tolerant policies towards its Jewish population until after the outbreak of World War II. Then, in response to a growing number of Jewish refugees who had been entering the country since 1933, the government prepared legislation that it never implemented that would have forced foreign Jews to leave the country within a three- to six-month period. By 1940 this tolerant mood changed, and two laws came into force on October 5, 1940 that limited Jewish enrollment in the "wholesale food business or related occupations." Although Jews now had lost their co-equal status in Yugoslavia, the new position did not become dramatically apparent until the German invasion of the country the following spring.[11]

Yugoslavia's adherence to the Tripartite Pact on March 25, 1941 prompted an anti-Axis coup several days later that convinced Hitler and Mussolini to invade the country on April 6, 1941. This was done in alliance with Hungary and Bulgaria. Yugoslavian territory was divided among the four conquering powers, and German satellite governments were created in Serbia and in the independent state of Croatia.[12]

The status of the 12,000 Jews in Serbia degenerated rapidly, particularly in the midst of a growing Serbian partisan movement. Nazi decrees quickly deprived Jews of their economic, social, and civil status, and by the summer of 1941 began a wave of killings, of Jews and Serbs, partially in retaliation for successful partisan activities. Some Jews were used in labor squads; others were transferred to concentration camps outside of Belgrade. Soon, all Jewish males were imprisoned in camps and systematically murdered by the Germans at various sites in Serbia. It is estimated that 4,000 to 5,000 Jews died as a result of these initial exterminations by the Wehrmacht.[13] In the aftermath of these executions, Nazi officials removed the remaining Jewish population, mainly women and children, to a concentration camp at Sajmište (Semlin), where, the following spring, over 6,000 Jews were gassed in special vans. By late summer 1942, one German official boasted in a report that "Serbia [sic] only country in which Jewish question and Gypsy question solved."[14]

The situation in the independent state of Croatia was similar, with initial "Aryanization" programs followed by the creation of several concentration camps. It is estimated that over 20,000 Jews died in these camps, the worst being the one at Jasenovac. By 1942, German officials began to deport Jews, principally to Auschwitz, a process that continued throughout the war and resulted in thousands of deaths. By the end of World War II, only 1,000 Jews lived in Croatia.[15]

The 8,000 Jews under Bulgarian control survived until the spring of 1943, when Bulgarian authorities agreed to ship them to Treblinka.[16] Serbian Jews under Hungarian control suffered a similarly harsh fate. Approximately 1,250 Jews died at the Delvidék and Ujvidék massacres in early 1942, while thousands more were sent to labor camps in Hungary and Ukraine.[17] Those under Italian control fared better until the Italian surrender in 1943, when many Jews came under German control.[18] The total losses for Yugoslavian Jewry during the Holocaust were 55,000-60,000 lives, or 80% of the prewar population.[19]

Approximately 15,000 Yugoslavian Jews survived the Holocaust—12,495 on Yugoslav soil. In 1948, after the creation of the Israeli state, Tito's government allowed them, with the exception of certain needed professionals, to emigrate. Over the next four years, 7,578 Jews left for Israel. A 1952 census showed 6,250 Jews in Yugoslavia, and 6,691 in 1957, most living in larger urban areas. Those who remain work principally in white-collar positions, in the technical, professional, and medical fields.[20]

The Federation of Jewish Communities, revived after World War II, has involved itself in Jewish community activities, while differences between Ashkenazic, Sephardic, Orthodox, and Neologues are no longer dividing each communtiy. The federation publishes a yearbook, *Jevrejski Almanah*, and a journal, *Jevrejski Pregled* (Jewish Review). Under the federation, the larger religious communities have established museums such as the one in Belgrade, and a research center on the history and culture of Yugoslavian Jewry.[21]

On the other hand, there has been a shift away from religious emphasis in the Jewish communities, and many synagogues have been turned into museums or cultural centers. In 1968, Yugoslavia's last rabbi died, and religious services, which center around important Jewish holidays, are now conducted by laymen. Consequently, despite the continued existence of small Jewish communities in the larger cities of Yugoslavia, they are only shadows of what some Jews considered their golden age in Yugoslavia, the interwar years.[22]

Notes

[1]Harriet Pass Freidenreich, *The Jews of Yugoslavia: A Quest for Community* (Philadelphia: The Jewish Publication Society of America, 1979), pp. 5-8.

[2]Ibid., pp. 58, 218.

[3]Ibid., pp. 71-72, 105.

[4]Ibid., pp. 103-4; "Tentative List of Jewish Educational Institutions in Axis-occupied Countries," *Jewish Social Studies* VIII:4 (October 1946): 94.

[5]"Tentative List," p. 95; Freidenreich, *The Jews of Yugoslavia*, pp. 92-95.

[6]Freidenreich, *The Jews of Yugoslavia*, pp. 107-9.

[7]Ibid., pp. 188-89, 95-96; "Tentative List," p. 93.

[8]"Yugoslavia," in *Hitler's Ten-Year War on the Jews* (New York: Institute of Jewish Affairs of the American Jewish Congress/World Jewish Congress, 1943), p. 96; Freidenreich, *The Jews of Yugoslavia*, p. 141.

[9]"Yugoslavia," *Encyclopedia Judaica*, Vol. 16 (Jerusalem: *Encyclopedia Judaica*, 1971), p. 873; Freidenreich, *The Jews of Yugoslavia*, pp. 179-82.

[10]Freidenreich, *The Jews of Yugoslavia*, pp. 183-84; "Yugoslavia," *Encyclopedia Judaica*, p. 873; *Hitler's Ten-Year War*, p. 97.

[11]Freidenreich, *The Jews of Yugoslavia*, pp. 188-89; *The Crimes of the Fascist Occupants and Their Collaborators against Jews in Yugoslavia* (Belgrade: Federation of Jewish Communities of the Federative People's Republic of Yugoslavia, 1957), XIII.

[12]Fredenreich, *The Jews of Yugoslavia*, p. 190.

[13]Nora Levin, *The Holocaust* (New York: Schocken Books, 1975), pp. 511-12; Lucy Dawidowicz, *The War against the Jews: 1933-1945* (New York: Bantam Books, 1976), p. 529; Raul Hilberg, *The Destruction of the European Jews* (New York: Franklin Watts, 1973), pp. 435-41; "Yugoslavia," *Encyclopedia Judaica*, pp. 874-75; Freidenreich, *The Jews of Yugoslavia*, p. 191; *Hitler's Ten-Year War*, pp. 101-2.

[14]Hilberg, *The Destruction of the European Jews*, pp. 439-40.

[15]"Yugoslavia," *Encyclopedia Judaica*, p. 877; Dawidowicz, *The War against the Jews*, pp. 529-30; Levin, *The Holocaust*, pp. 514-17; Hilberg, *The Destruction of the European Jews*, pp. 453-58; *Hitler's Ten-Year War*, pp. 104-8; Freidenreich, *The Jews of Yugoslavia*, pp. 191-92; Charles W. Steckel, *Destruction and Survival* (Los Angeles: Delmar Publishing Co., 1973), pp. 12-15; *Crimes of the Fascist Occupants*, pp. 85-106.

[16]Freidenreich, *The Jews of Yugoslavia*, p. 192; Levin, *The Holocaust*, pp. 553-54; Frederick B. Chary, *The Bulgarian Jews and the Final Solution, 1940-1944* (Pittsburgh: Pittsburgh University Press, 1972), p. 127 (Chary says there were only 7,160 Macedonian Jews involved in these deportations); *Crimes of the Fascist Occupants*, pp. 195-97. An excellent study of the fate of the Macedonian Jews is found in Aleksandr Matkovski, "The Destruction of Macedonian Jewry in 1943," *Yad Vashem Studies* III (Jerusalem, 1959): 208-58 *passim*.

[17]Randolph L. Braham, *The Politics of Genocide: The Holocaust in Hungary*, Vol. I (New York: Columbia University Press, 1981), pp. 204-411; Steckel, *Destruction and Survival*, pp. 37-39; *Crimes of the Fascist Occupants*, pp. 178-88.

[18]Freidenreich, *The Jews of Yugoslavia*, p. 192. For an excellent account of efforts to save Jews in the Italian zone, see Daniel Capri, "The Diplomatic Negotiations over the Transfer of Jewish Children from Croatia to Turkey and Palestine in 1943," *Yad Vashem Studies* XII (January 1977): 109-21.

[19]Freidenreich, *The Jews of Yugoslavia*, p. 192; Levin, *The Holocaust*, pp. 715-18; Hilberg, *The Destruction of the European Jews*, p. 670; Dawidowicz, *The War against the Jews*, p. 530; *Crimes of the Fascist Occupants*, XIII-XIV.

[20]Freidenreich, *The Jews of Yugoslavia*, pp. 193-95; "Yugoslavia," *Encyclopedia Judaica*, p. 882; Steckel, *Destruction and Survival*, pp. 39-40.

[21]"Yugoslavia," *Encyclopedia Judaica*, p. 882.

[22]Freidenreich, *The Jews of Yugoslavia*, pp. 199-201, 210.

BIBLIOGRAPHY

General Works, References, and Sources

667. Bebler, Aleš. "Die Stellung der nationalen Minderheiten in Jugoslawien." *Razprave in gradivo* (Inštitut za narodnostna vprašanja v Ljubljania) 1 (1960): 11-38. (Summary in English).

Text of a lecture held before the Society for Foreign Policy in Vienna, June 1966. The author underlines the Yugoslav adherence to the subjective principle applying to 1) an individual's right to officially declare his nationality, and 2) parental choice of the language of instruction where the latter is provided in more than one language. The English summary contains complete translation of the passage treating general principles. The Slovene version of this paper has been published in pamphlet form under the title *Narodnostne manjšine v Jugoslaviji*.

668. Gasinski, Thaddeus Z. "The National Minority Policy of Today's Yugoslavia." *Nationalities Papers* 8:1 (1980): 29-51.

This is an analysis of the Yugoslav minority policy, touching upon linguistic as well as national defense, foreign affairs, and demographic aspects. The only permanent feature of the Yugoslav nationality policy seems to be its insistence on the principle that only the nations, i.e., Croats, Macedonians, Moslems, Serbs, and Slovenes, have the right to self-determination. Others may be given only cultural autonomy. Included are statistics on publishing in minority languages and on minority population, 1948-1971.

669. **Die Gliederung der Bevölkerung des ehemaligen Jugoslawien nach Muttersprache und Konfession, nach den unveröffentlichten Angaben der Zählung von 1931.** Vienna: Publikationsstelle Wien, 1943. 415p. Map.

This volume contains previously unpublished data of the 1931 Yugoslav census showing the population by mother tongue and religion, by counties. The map includes *banovina* and *obćina* (county) boundaries.

670. Jončić, Koča. **The Relations between Nationalities in Yugoslavia.** Beograd: Medjunarodna štampa—Interpress, 1967. 76p.

The author surveys the political and constitutional principles underlying interethnic relations in Yugoslavia, especially with regard to linguistic minorities. Emphasis is on socioeconomic aspects of these relations, based in part on Lenin's *Critical Notes on the National Question*. The work includes statistical data on the ethnic composition of population by republics and educational data for linguistic minorities.

671. Klopčič, Vera. "Pravni položaj narodnosti v SAP Vojvodini" (The Legal Situation of Nationalities in the Socialist Autonomous Province of Vojvodina). *Razprave in študije* 11-12 (1980): 51-58.

The article deals with the civil rights of minorities in Vojvodina provided for in the 1974 constitution. It focuses on provisions for language use and school instruction in the mother tongue.

672. Komatina, Milija. "The Policy of the League of Communists of Yugoslavia on Resolving the National Question." *Socialist Thought and Practice* 21:10 (1981): 39-57.

During the interwar period, the Yugoslav Communists linked the solution of national tensions to the revolutionary struggle for socialism. In contemporary Yugoslavia, the distinction between nations and nationalities hinges on the principle of national self-management, which is recognized for the former but not for the latter. Consequently, the autonomnous provinces of Kosovo and Vojvodina lack the attributes of a state. To explain the relationship between Yugoslavism and national communities, the author draws upon the theories of Edvard Kardelj.

673. Kostić, L. M. **Nacionalne manjine u srpskim predelima: Demografsko-etnografska studija** (National Minorities in Serbian Lands: A Demographic-Ethnographic Study). Srpski problemi, Serija nacionalnih spisa 1. Toronto: Kulturni klub "Sv. Sava," 1961. 76p.

A discussion of the historical and demographic development of national minorities in Serbian territories. The demographic trends point to a weakening of the share of Serbian population in Kosovo and to a strengthening of its share in Vojvodina.

674. Kostić, L. M. **Srpska Vojvodina i njene manjine: Demografsko-ethnografska studija** (Serbian Vojvodina and Her Minorities: A Demographic-Ethnographic Study). Srpski problemi, Serija nacionalnih spisa 2. Toronto: Kulturni klub "Sv. Sava," 1962. 111p.

The author focuses on the ethnic structure of Vojvodina from a demographic perspective, including such nonlinguistic groups as Bunjevci and Šokci. Since World War II the Serbs have made considerable gains, due largely to in-migration. The 1953 census shows a slight "de-Croatization" of the Bunjevci group.

675. Lalović, Miroslav. "Etničke karakteristike migracija u Vojvodini" (Ethnic Characteristics of the Migrations in Vojvodina). *Statističar* 2:7-8 (1980): 131-36.

The article discusses the land colonization of Vojvodina since the eighteenth century. Statistics on external and internal migration in 1971 are shown by ethnic groups. The established minorities — Hungarians, Ruthenians, Romanians, and Slovaks — show a lower tendency to migrate than do other groups.

676. Markert, Werner, ed. **Jugoslawien. Osteuropa-Handbuch**. Cologne-Graz: Böhlau-Verlag, 1954. 400p. Maps.

This is the most comprehensive handbook on Yugoslavia published in the West. Twelve West German scholars offer a wealth of information on all aspects of Yugoslavia, including geography, population, politics and government, history, foreign relations, and economy, in addition to a list of agreements signed by the government and an extensive bibliography. The chapter "People and Nationalities" (pp. 14-36) provides data on all national minorities for the period 1921-1948, together with an ethnographic map. This is an indispensable guide on Yugoslavia and her peoples.

677. Marković, Jovan Dj. **Karakteristike regionalnog razmeštanja etničkih grupa u Jugoslaviji** (Characteristics of Regional Distribution of Ethnic Groups in Yugoslavia). *Zbornik radova PMF* (Beograd) 18 (1970).

This publication deals with the ethnic composition of Yugoslavia by republics and autonomous regions. It includes statistical tables. Data are for 1961.

678. Popovski, Dušan. "Respect for the Rights of Ethnic Minorities." *Socialist Thought and Practice* 16:12 (December 1976): 58-71.

Following a survey of international norms and standards applicable to ethnic minorities, the author outlines the Yugoslav constitutional provisions and practice concerning nationalities. He provides 1956 census data on the number of Macedonians in Bulgaria (188,000); in Blagoevgrad the school population included 32,000 Macedonian and 3,000 Bulgarian children.

679. Reissmüller, Johann Georg. **Jugoslawien: Vielvölkerstaat zwischen Ost und West.** Düsseldorf: Eugen Ciedericks Verlag, 1971. 240p.

The main theme of this account is the national and cultural differences in Yugoslavia and the resulting dangers for the political development of the country. The latest developments in party, state, and society are related against this background, arranged by regions which are also firm cultural areas. The many-sided stresses and difficulties are presented in this well-balanced work.

680. Sentić, Milica, et al. **Demografska kretanja i karakteristike stanovništva Jugoslavije prema nacionalnoj pripadnosti** (Demographic Changes and Characteristics of the Population of Yugoslavia by Ethnic Affiliation). Beograd: Centar za demografska istraživanja, Institut društvenih nauka, 1978. 160p.

This statistical analysis by ethnic groups provides vital statistics and data on migration and on the structure of individual groups by age, education, and industrial affiliation.

681. Stojković, Ljubiša, and Martić, Miloš. **National Minorities in Yugoslavia.** Beograd: "Jugoslavija," 1952. 226p.

The historical portion of the book includes treatment of the participation of minorities in the Yugoslav partisan movement during World War II. Mentioned are military units composed of individual minorities, such as the Czechoslovak Brigade, the "Sandor Petöfi" Brigade, and the "Ernst Thälmann" Company. The latter was formed in Zvečevo of German national minority partisans in 1943. Other chapters treat the legal status of minorities in general and the cultural life of individual minorities.

682. Zografski, Dancho. "Nationalities in Yugoslavia." *Macedonian Review* 9:2 (1979): 179-83.

This essay outlines the status of nations and nationalities in Yugoslavia since 1945, with particular reference to the republic of Macedonia.

Germans

683. Baš, Franjo. "Kulturbund v Celju med dvema vojnama" (The *Kulturbund* in Celje between the Two Wars). *Časopis za zgodovino in narodopisje, Nova vrsta* 2 (1966): 215-22.

The *Kulturbund*, whose original aim was to protect the interests of ethnic Germans, became increasingly a political instrument of the Reich, engaging in para-military and intelligence activities. The article focuses on the organizational activities in Celje, Slovenia, under the leadership of industrialist Adolf Westen.

684. Engelmann, Nikolau. **Die Banater Schwaben: Auf Vorposten des Abendlandes.** Freilassing, Germany: Pannonia Verlag, 1966. 119p.

The account contains historical, economic, and ethnographic information on the Germans of the Banat region, undocumented, though with numerous illustrations.

685. Harriman, Helga H. **Slovenia under Nazi Occupation, 1941-1945.** Studia Slovenica, XI. New York and Washington: Studia Slovenica, 1977. 94p.

This study covers Germanization policies in the Slovene territory annexed by Germany in 1941. To protect the southern flank of the extended Reich, the Germans resettled in the Sava-Sotla strip around Brežice 13,000 ethnic Germans from the Italian-occupied Kočevje area of Slovenia. The settlers were assigned the homes of Slovenes who had been deported to Serbia. Various original documents are presented in the appendix.

686. Hegedüs-Kovačević, Katalin. "Das Österreichbild dreier Zeitschriften aus der Batschka." *Österreich in Geschichte und Literatur* 22:6 (1978): 350-55.

An examination of the attitudes toward Austria and German Austrian literature of three journals from Bačka (Vojvodina) during the interwar period. The author detects an affinity with the old Austrian spirit due to the historical ties with Vienna.

687. Jankulov, B. **Pregled kolonizacije Vojvodine u XVIII i XIX veku** (A Survey of the Colonization of Vojvodina during the Eighteenth and Nineteenth Centuries). Novi Sad: Matica Srpska, 1961. 117p.

This is a history of the colonization of Vojvodina by Germans, Hungarians, and other nationalities. The author points out the economic aims of colonization. Political aims date back to the centralist philosophy of Karl VI. Accordingly, the intermingling of peoples contributed to the weakening of their cultural and ethnic peculiarities while strengthening them politically and economically. Documents and an index of place names are appended.

688. Lenz, Adolf. **Die deutschen Minderheiten in Slowenien.** Graz: Alpenland Buchhandlung, 1923. 94p.

The author, an expert on international law, discusses the legal aspect of the German-speaking people in Slovenia. Of special importance to the researcher is the bibliography comprising titles not listed anywhere else.

689. Milošević, Slobodan. "Kvislinške snage u Banatu u službi nemačkog okupatora 1941-1944. godine" (Quisling Forces in Banat in the Service of the German Occupiers, 1941-1944). *Vojnoistorijski glasnik* 30:1 (1979): 139-53.

During World War II the Yugoslav Banat was occupied by the Germans. Although it was formally a part of Serbia, all key posts in the regional administration were held by the local ethnic Germans. Efforts of the Serbian Chetniks to gain a foothold in the area were thwarted by the organizations of other, mutually hostile, ethnic groups — Hungarian, Romanian, and Slovak — encouraged by the Germans.

690. **Das Schicksal der Deutschen in Jugoslawien.** Dokumentation der Vertreibung der Deutschen aus Ost-Mitteleuropa, vol. 5. Bonn: Bundesministerium für Vertriebene, Flüchtlinge und Kriegsgeschädigte, 1961. 633p. Maps.

The introductory chapters treat the German minority in Yugoslavia since its creation in 1918. The documentary section contains agreements and statutes pertaining to the German minority which were passed during and after World War II, including the agreement between Italy and Germany for the resettlement of the Kočevje Germans. The largest part of the book consists of statements by eyewitnesses of events since 1941.

691. Senz, Josef Volkmar. **Das Schulwesen der Donauschwaben im Königreich Jugoslawien.** Munich: Verlag des Südostdeutschen Kulturwerks, 1969. 303p.

The description of the situation of the Swabians' schools on the territory of the future Yugoslavia is the opening of this book. The educational policy of the new state, with its nationalistic orientation, resulted in periods of restrictive approaches by the government, followed by more relaxed periods. The author describes also the internal problems of these German schools. Documents help to prove the cultural achievements of the German nationality group in Yugoslavia.

692. Šijački, Ljubica. "O zatvorima, logorima i logorskim radionicama u Banatu 1941-1944. godine" (Prisons, Concentration Camps, and Work Camps in Banat, 1941-1944). *Vojnoistorijski glasnik* 30:1 (1979): 175-90.

The article surveys the penal institutions in Banat set up by the German occupying authorities and points out that most atrocities were committed by the local German minority, aided by the Hungarian sympathizers of the Horty regime and by Serbian quislings. During the period 1941-1944, camps and prisons in Banat processed 10,000 people.

693. Toutenuit, Ludwig. **Setschan: Monographie einer deutschen Gemeinde im Mittleren Banat.** Freilassing, Germany: Pannonia Verlag, 1962. 75p.

A local history of the German settlement Setschan in the vicinity of Veliki Bečkerek (now Zrenjanin), Vojvodina. The account focuses on pre-World War II life in the village and on the events following the arrival of Soviet troops in 1944.

694. Wehler, Hans-Ulrich. **Nationalitätenpolitik in Jugoslawien: Die deutsche Minderheit, 1918-1978.** Göttingen: Vandenhoeck & Ruprecht, 1980. 164p.

Wehler presents a history of the German minority in Yugoslavia, 1918-1978. Emphasis is on the World War II period, including the German-initiated resettlement of ethnic Germans from parts of Slovenia, Bosnia, and Serbia. There are statistics on the number of those who settled in Austria and West Germany during the post-World War II period.

695. Zorn, Tone. "Narodnostna podoba dela kočevskega območja po podatkih italijanskega ljudskega štetja z dne 31. julija 1941" (Ethnic Structure of a Part of the Kočevje Area According to Data of the Italian Census of July 31, 1941). *Zgodovinski časopis* 29:3-4 (1975): 247-53.

This essay consists of an analysis of the ethnic and occupational structure of a part of the Kočevje district for which detailed data are preserved in the archives of Slovenia. According to the summary data for the district, the number of ethnic Germans was 9,145, out of a total population of 40,074.

Jews

696. **Albat Vajs: 1905-1964; Spomenica** (Albat Vajs: 1905-1964; Festschrift). Beograd: Savez Jevrejskih Opština Jugoslavije, 1965. 226p.

A collection of memorial articles on the life and career of one of Yugoslavia's important Jewish leaders.

697. **The Crimes of the Fascist Occupants and Their Collaborators against Jews in Yugoslavia.** Belgrade: Federation of Jewish Communities of the Federative People's Republic of Yugoslavia, 1957. 197p.

This official Yugoslavian Jewish publication discusses the history of the Holocaust in Serbia, Croatia, Slovenia, Bačka, Baranja, and Macedonia. It deals with specific major crimes against these areas' Jewish populations, such as forced labor and executions.

698. Cvetić, Nikola. **Himmlerov pokusni kunić** (Himmler's Guinea Pig). Zagreb: Epoha, 1965. 210p.

This publication examines Nazi anti-Semitic policies in Yugoslavia during World War II and their impact upon Yugoslavia's small Jewish community.

699. Debreceni, Jozef. **Hladni krematorijum** (The Cold Crematorium). Belgrade: Prosveta, 1951. 202p.

A memoir dealing with Yugoslavian Jews at the German concentration camp at Auschwitz.

700. Eventov, Y. **A History of Yugoslav Jews.** Edited by C. Rotem. Tel-Aviv: Copyright Hitahdut Olej Yugoslavija, 1971. 432p.

This is a broad historical account of Yugoslavian Jewry. Eventov studies the Sephardic Jews of Bosnia and Serbia as well as groups in Slovenia and Croatia. There are English and Serbo-Croatian summaries.

701. Freidenreich, Harriet Pass. **The Jews of Yugoslavia: A Quest for Community.** Philadelphia: Jewish Publication Society of America, 1979. xiv, 323p.

Following a brief introduction, this volume is divided into three parts, plus an epilogue. Part 1 traces the development of Jewish life; part 2 examines communal, organizational, and cultural activities, while part 3 deals with problems of national identity and political life and relations. On the whole, Yugoslav nationalism facilitated the acceptance of the Jews as a nationality, but it also made it more difficult for them to integrate into the mainstream of Yugoslav society. Zionism and communism emerged as alternatives. About 80% of Yugoslavia's Jews perished in the Holocaust, and the majority of the survivors emigrated to Israel, leading to the situation where presently the Yugoslav Jewish community gradually is becoming extinct.

702. **Jevrejski Almanah** (Jewish Almanac). Beograd: Savez jevrejskih opština Jugoslavije, 1954-1970.

This almanac is one of the official publications of the Federation of Jewish Communities of Yugoslavia, with articles on various aspects of Yugoslavian Jewish history, culture, and religion.

703. **Jevrejski pregled.** Beograd: Savez jevrejskih opština Jugoslavije, 1950-1982.

Published by the Yugoslavian Jewish communities, this journal presents articles on different aspects of that country's Jewish history, with emphasis on the Holocaust.

704. Kečkemet, Duško. **Židovi u povijesti Splita** (The Jews in the History of Split). Split: Jevrijska opčina, 1971. 252p. (Summary in English).

This is a rather detailed history of the small Jewish community of Split from its inception in Roman times through the Holocaust. Although the core of the book deals with pre-1918 Yugoslavia, it still gives valuable insight into the history and culture of Yugoslav Jewry, and includes a good bibliography.

705.   Kosier, Ljubomir Stefan. **Historija jevreja u Jugoslaviji** (A History of Jews in Yugoslavia). Zagreb: "Bankarstvo," 1929. 44p.

This publication consists of a brief statistical history of the Jewish community in interwar Yugoslavia.

706.   Kosier, Ljubomir Stefan. **Jevreji u Jugoslaviji i Bugarskoj** (Jews in Yugoslavia and Bulgaria). Zagreb: Tipografija, 1930. xx, 406p.

The author offers a statistical study of the Jewish communities in Yugoslavia and Bulgaria, with emphasis on the economic status of Jews in both countries. The book contains an excellent selection of tables and charts and has summaries in English and German. A companion volume, *Statistika Jevreja u Jugoslaviji i Bugarskoj* (Statistics of Jews in Yugoslavia and Bulgaria) (Zagreb: Tipografija, 1930. 58p.), provides charts that compare statistics of Jews in regions of both countries and also their position *vis-à-vis* other European states.

707.   Levi, Moric. **Sefardi u Bosni**. (Prilog istoriji Jevreja na Balkanskom poluostrvu) (Sephardic Jews in Bosnia. [A Contribution to the History of Jews in the Balkan Peninsula]). Beograd: Savez jevrejskih opština Jugoslavije, 1969. 110p.

This is a translation of *Die Sephardim in Bosnien*. It consists of a brief history of the Sephardic Jewish community in Bosnia and Herzegovina.

708.   Löwenthal, Zdenko, ed. **The Crimes of the Fascist Occupants and Their Collaborators against Jews in Yugoslavia**. Belgrade, 1957. xix, 245p.

An official account of the Holocaust in Yugoslavia.

709.   Molho, Michael, and Nehenia, Joseph. **Shoat Yehudei Yavan** (The Destruction of Greek Jewry, 1941-1944). Jerusalem, 1965. x, 266p.

This publication contains an account of the destruction of Macedonian and Thracian Jewry.

710.   Perić, Marko. "Posebno demografsko istraživanje jevrejske zajednice u Jugoslaviji" (The Special Demographic Survey of the Jewish Community in Yugoslavia). *Stanovništvo* 12:3-4 (1974): 169-84.

This article is drawn from a survey conducted by the Federation of Jewish Communities of Yugoslavia of 2,500 Jewish families between 1971 and 1972. It provides an excellent statistical overview of the status of contemporary Jews in that country. Summaries in English, French, and Russian.

711.   **Spomenica. 400 godina od dolaska Jevreja u Bosnu i Hercegovinu, 1566-1966** (In Commemoration of the 400th Anniversary of the Arrival of Jews in Bosnia and Herzegovina, 1566-1966). Umetnička obrada: Ante Martinović. Sarajevo: Jevrejska zajednica, 1967. 364p.

A history of Jews in Bosnia and Herzegovina over the past 400 years. It has summaries in English and French.

712. **Spomenica, 1919-1969** (Memoirs, 1919-1969). Edited by Branko Gostl and others. Belgrade: Savez jevrejskih opština Jugoslavije, 1969. 242p.

This is a historical overview of Yugoslavian Jewry with German summaries. The volume was issued as a memorial publication celebrating the fiftieth anniversary of the Federation of Jewish Communities in Yugoslavia. It contains a bibliography and a summary in English.

713. Steehel, Charles W. **Destruction and Survival**. Los Angeles: Delmar Publishing Co., 1973. 179p.

This is a history of Yugoslavia's, especially Bosnia's, Jews during the Holocaust. The bulk of the study, though, consists of a collection of letters from the commissioners of the Jewish Religious Communities in Sarajevo to various regional communities through 1941.

Italians

714. Jacquin, Pierre. **La question des minorités entre l'Italie et la Jougoslavie**. Paris: Recueil Sirey, 1929. 220p.

This study covers the ethnic situation in the formerly Austro-Hungarian territories claimed by Italy at the end of World War I. The discussion centers on the negotiations leading to the establishment of the interwar Yugoslav-Italian border, accompanied by appropriate maps. The book also covers Italian-Yugoslav treaties containing minorities guarantees. Italy extended such guarantees to Yugoslavs in Rijeka (Fiume) and Zadar (Zara), but not to South Slavic — Slovene and Croat — minorities in the Julian March. The appendix contains texts of the Treaty of Rapallo (1920), the Accord on Fiume (1924), and extracts from the Convention of Santa Margherita (1922), as well as the Accords of Nettuno (1925) and an exchange of letters on educational matters.

715. Opassi, Ennio. "Attività ed esperienze della comunità d'interesse autogestive per l'instruzione e la cultura degli appartenenti alla nazionalità italiana di Capodistria, Isola e Pirano." *Razprave in gradivo* 9-10 (1979): 55-67.

The article deals with the activity of self-managed interest communities of the Italian minority in the counties of Koper (Capodistria), Izola (Isola), and Piran (Pirano). Instituted in 1975 under provisions contained in the constitution of Slovenia and in the communal statutes, these minority interest communities are concerned with cultural and educational problems, including radio and TV programming. They also maintain cultural contacts with Italy.

716. Tollefson, James W. **The Language Situation and Language Policy in Slovenia**. Washington, DC: University Press of America, 1981. 285p.

This sociolinguistic study focuses on the language situation and language policy in Slovenia. The situation in the city of Piran, which includes the Italian minority, is examined in detail.

Vlachs, Romanians

717. Gligorijević, Branislav. "Jugoslovensko-Rumunska konvencija o uredjenju manjinskih škola u Banatu 1933 godine" (The Yugoslav-Romanian Convention on Romanian Minority Schools in Banat, 1933). *Zbornik za istoriju* 7 (1973): 79-103.

An examination of the elementary education provisions extended to the 60,000 Romanians living in Yugoslavia and the educational status of a similar number of Serbs residing in Romania. The negotiations concerning Romanian schools in Banat advanced from the initial agreement in principle (1921), to the Protocol of Timisoara (1923), to the Convention of Bled (1927), and finally to the above convention, though full implementation of the provisions was delayed until 1939. Educational statistics on the affected localities in Yugoslavia are given.

718. Peyfuss, Max Demeter. **Die aromunische Frage: Ihre Entwicklung von Ursprüngen bis zum Frieden von Bukarest (1913) und die Haltung Österreich-Ungarns**. Wiener Archiv für Geschichte des Slawentums und Osteuropa, 7. Vienna: Hermann Böhlaus Nachfolger, 1974. 125p.

The Aromanian (Vlach) question had its beginnings in the Aromanian national movement at the outset of the nineteenth century. It focused on promoting the use of Aromanian in schools and churches. The politicizing of the issue is attributed to Greeks and other opponents. The Peace Treaty of Bukarest at the conclusion of the Second Balkan War (1913) failed to mention the Aromanian minority. In a subsequent exchange of notes between Romania on the one hand, and Greece, Serbia, and Bulgaria on the other, the three Balkan states guaranteed the autonomy of Aromanian schools and churches. Serbia closed the Romanian schools in Macedonia as early as 1918. Today the Aromanians possess no schools, churches, or media in their mother tongue.

719. Popi, Gligor. "Iz političke aktivnosti Rumuna u Banatu posle prvog svetskog rata" (On the Political Activity of Romanians in Banat after World War I). *Zbornik za istoriju* 6 (1972): 173-76.

After World War I, the Banat was divided between Romania and Yugoslavia, with 60,000 Romanians within the Yugoslav part. The essays survey the political and cultural life, including the 1923 congress, at which the Romanian party was founded, and the appearance of the Romanian weekly in the area, *Graiul Românesc*.

720. Popi, Gligor. **Rumuni u jugoslovenskom Banatu izmedju dva rata (1918-1941)** (Romanians in the Yugoslav Banat during the Interwar Period, 1918-1941). Monografije, 16. Novi Sad: Institut za izučavanje istorije Vojvodine, 1976. 178p.

This study deals with the social history of Romanians in the Yugoslav Banat. The Romanian party, organized in 1923, functioned until King Alexander's dictatorship in 1928. Among Romanian grievances were the allocation of land expropriated under the post-World War I agrarian reform, transformation of Romanian church schools in Yugoslavia into state schools, and curtailment of Romanian in elementary schools. The Bled Agreement of 1927 and the Romanian-Yugoslav Belgrade Convention on minority elementary schools (1933) established reciprocity in this domain, since there was also a Serbian minority in the Romanian Banat. The study further covers Romanian publishing in Yugoslavia and the status of the local communities of the Romanian Orthodox Church. An appendix contains the text of the Belgrade Convention and a memorandum outlining Romanian demands for its implementation. A bibliography of archival and other sources and a map of Romanian settlements are included.

Macedonians

721. Debats, Jean-Pierre. "Nationalités et groupes éthniques en République socialiste de Macédoine (Yougoslavie)." *Revue géographique de l'Est* 19:1-2 (1979): 67-85.

The emigration of Turks during the 1950s and the acculturation of Vlachs have reduced the ethnic diversity of Macedonia. Because of an above-average rate of natural increase, the share of Albanians in the total population is increasing. In the countryside they tend to replace the Macedonian population which is moving to the cities.

722. Hristov, Aleksandar T. **KPJ vo rešavanjeto na makedonskoto prašanje (1937-1944)** (The Communist Party of Yugoslavia in the Resolution of the Macedonian National Question, 1937-1944). Skopje: Kultura, 1962. 108p.

This volume contains a detailed but largely uncritical history of the work of the Yugoslav Communists in the formation of the Republic of Macedonia as one of the federated Yugoslav republics, and of the events that transpired.

723. Jiljovski, Kiril. **Makedonskoto prašanje vo nacinalnata program na KPJ (1919-1937)** (The Macedonian Question in the National Program of the Communist Party of Yugoslavia, 1919-1937). Skopje: Kultura, 1962.

This volume, which is one of a whole genre on the subject, discusses the struggles within the Communist party of Yugoslavia during the interwar period over the problem of Macedonia. It is a companion volume to A. T. Hristov's work (see entry 722), which is concerned with the same question during the period from 1937 to 1944.

724. Mitrev, Dimitar. **Pirinska Makedonija vo borba za nacionalno osloboduvanje** (Pirin Macedonia in the Struggle for National Liberation). Skopje: Slavinot odbor na Narodniot front na Makedonija, 1950. 461p.

The author, a Macedonian residing in Yugoslavia, presents the Yugoslav position at the time regarding the Macedonian population of the Bulgarian Pirin area.

725. Palmer, Stephan E., Jr., and King, Robert R. **Yugoslav Communism and the Macedonian Question.** Hamden, CT: Archon Books, 1971. 247p.

This volume offers a political history of post-World War II Yugoslav Macedonia, focusing on the events, factors, and personalities that led to the formation of the Macedonian Republic within the Yugoslav Federation.

Albanians

726. Bakali, Mahmut. "Thirty Years of the Socialist Development in Kosovo." *Socialist Thought and Practice* 16:1 (January 1976): 14-40.

Bakali surveys the socioeconomic development of the Kosovo Autonomous Province since the 1950s. Emphasis is on educational and cultural developments, including radio and television programs in Albanian, Serbo-Croatian, and Turkish emanating from Priština. According to the 1971 census, the Albanian population of the province accounted for 74%. Investment plans call for a 15% annual increase, 80% of which is to be allocated from funds outside the province.

727. Biberaj, Elez. "Albania-Yugoslav Relations and the Question of Kosovë." *East European Quarterly* 26:4 (1982): 485-510.

Discussion centers on Albanian-Yugoslav relations over the treatment of Kosovo Albanians after 1945. Of special interest is the statistical table for Kosovo province indicating demographic changes which have occurred between 1948 and 1981; 1,227,000 Albanians resided in the province in 1981. The article is critical of Yugoslav treatment of Albanians.

728. Hari, Ali. "Albanska narodnost u Yugoslaviji od 1918. do 1941. godine i njeno učešće u NOB Jugoslavije" (The Albanian Nationality in Yugoslavia between 1918 and 1941 and Its Participation in the National Liberation Struggle of Yugoslavia). In **Iz istorije Albanaca: Zbornik predavanja. Priručnik za nastavnike**, pp. 187-210. Belgrade: Zavod za izdavanje učbenika SR Srbije, 1969.

Hari surveys the Albanian-settled areas of Yugoslavia between 1918 and 1945. Serbian policies favoring assimilation included the closing of the few Albanian schools that had been instituted during World War I. There is a detailed discussion of the administration during World War II by Albania, Bulgaria, and Serbia in their respective territories. Albanians, under Italian tutelage, reintroduced the feudal system,which Yugoslavia had abolished during the interwar period. The survey covers the history of the Communist party of Yugoslavia in the area, the partisan movement, and the liberation of Priština by Bulgarian forces and Serbian partisans in 1944.

729. Islami, Hivzi. "La croissance démographique du Kosovo." *Population* 34:4-5 (1979): 915-19.

The article describes the demographic growth in the autonomous province of Kosovo, largely populated by Albanians, since the 1920s, noting the high rates, especially since 1960, and comparing them with Yugoslavia's as a whole and with Albania's.

730. Islami, Hivzi. "Pregled rasprostranjenosti i porasta broja Albanaca u svetu" (A Survey of the Distribution and Growth of the Number of Albanians in the World). *Stanovništvo* 16:1-4 (1978): 188-211.

This is a survey of the history of emigration from Albania. Of the estimated 6 million Albanians throughout the world, 42% live in Albania and 27% in Yugoslavia. The Albanians have a natural rate of increase of between 27 and 34%, which is among the highest in the world. There is no sign that this high rate is diminishing, and in areas with a high concentration of Albanians it may even be increasing.

731. Nusi, Pajazit. "Qualitative Changes in the Cultural Emancipation of the Albanian Nationality in Yugoslavia." *Socialist Thought and Practice* 16:12 (December 1976): 72-87.

The cultural emancipation of the Albanian minority in Yugoslavia is viewed as an expression of the workers' self-management. Contemporary Albanian literature in Yugoslavia, as well as important musical works, derive their inspiration from the ancient wellspring of folk songs and tales. In collaboration with the artists from the ranks of the Serbian and Montenegrin nations, the "Kosovo school of art" is seen as emerging.

732. Perazić, Gavro. "International Aspects of Albanian Interference in Kosovo Events." *Socialist Thought and Practice* 21:10 (1981): 58-72.

The author polemicizes with the Albanian newspaper *Zëri i popullit* concerning the Albanian irredentism *vis-à-vis* the Kosovo province of Yugoslavia. He reviews the 1913

London Agreement and other pertinent international agreements which define the present Yugoslav-Albanian border.

733. "Political Stabilization and Socio-Economic Development in the Socialist Autonomous Province of Kosovo." *Socialist Thought and Practice* 21:11-12 (1981): 81-136.

The article contains the integral text of the "Political Platform for Action by the League of Communists of Yugoslavia in Developing Socialist Self-Management, Brotherhood, Unity and Fellowship in Kosovo." The platform, adopted on November 17, 1981 in Belgrade, was drafted in response to disruptive events in Kosovo, which claimed several lives, during March and April of the same year.

734. Prifti, Peter R. **Socialist Albania since 1944: Domestic and Foreign Developments.** Cambridge, MA: The MIT Press, 1978. 311p.

This study contains a chapter (pp. 222-41) on the Albanian minority in Yugoslavia. It surveys the history of, and current situation in, Kosovo and adjoining areas.

735. Reuter, Jens. **Die Albaner in Jugoslawien.** "Untersuchungen zur Gegenwartskunde Südosteuropas," Südost-Institut Müchen, vol. 20. Munich: R. Oldenbourg Verlag, 1982. 140p.

This is a condensed, yet the most objective, study in a Western language on the Albanians in the Kosovo province. Against a historical background, the author discusses the fate of the Yugoslav Albanians since their incorporation into the Yugoslav state. Numerous tables and several maps help illuminate the problem. Appendixes include documents covering various subjects on Yugoslav-Kosovo-Albanian aspects and an updated bibliography.

736. Rusinow, Dennison I. **Unfinished Business: The Yugoslav "National Question."** Reports, 1981, no. 35 Europe. Hanover, NH: American Universities Field Staff, 1981. 13p.

The report surveys the disturbances which broke out in the largely Albanian-inhabited Socialist Autonomous Province of Kosovo in April 1981, as a result of which a state of emergency had to be imposed. The main body of the report analyzes Yugoslav ethnic policy since World War II.

737. Rusinow, Dennison I. **The Other Albania: Kosovo 1979. Part I: Problems and Prospects.** Part II: **The Village, the Factory, and the Kosovars.** Reports, 1980, nos. 5 and 6. Hanover, NH: American Universities Field Staff, 1980. 17p.; 11p.

This two-part report is based on visits to Kosovo in October and November 1979 and on conversation with local officials, including the Provincial Communist party president Mahmut Bakalli. It includes selected economic and educational statistics and a map of the Kosovo province.

738. Saljiu, Kurteš. "The Development of Autonomy in Yugoslavia." *Socialist Thought and Practice* 22:8 (1982): 32-45.

This is a survey of the changes in the constitutional status of the two autonomous units within the Republic of Serbia, namely Vojvodina and Kosovo, since 1945. These units are the area of the Hungarian and Albanian minorities, respectively. The constitutional changes of 1963, 1968, and 1974 are analyzed in detail.

739. "What Happened in Kosovo?" *Socialist Thought and Practice* 21:8 (1981): 11-36.
    An interview with Sinan Hasani, vice president of the Assembly of the SFR of Yugoslavia, concerning the demonstrations in Kosovo during the spring of 1981.

Gypsies

740. Andrejić, Ljubomir. "Prilog bibliografiji o Ciganima" (A Contribution to the Bibliography on Gypsies). *Glasnik etnografskog muzeja* 33 (1970): 209-70.
    An annotated bibliography of Yugoslav and Western literature on the Gypsies of Yugoslavia.

741. Lutovac, Momčilo. "O Romima u Crnoj Gori" (On the Romanies in Montenegro). *Glasnik etnografskog instituta SANU* 24 (1977): 119-38.
    The contribution makes distinction between Madjupi, Kovači, and Babelji nomadic Romanies (Gypsies) in present-day Montenegro. In 1971 these people totaled 4,197. The Romanies settled in Serbia following the Turkish invasion of the fourteenth century and appeared in Montenegro in the eighteenth century. Today only the nomadic Romanies preserve their ethnic and linguistic identity.

742. Šiftar, Vanek. **Cigani: Minulost v sedanjosti** (The Gypsies: The Presence of the Past). Murska Sobota: Pomurska založba, 1970. 232p.
    The study reviews the settlement of Gypsies in Prekmurje and elsewhere in Slovenia, their tribes, language, customs, migration patterns, health, education, housing, and their attitudes toward work and organized government. The author provides demographic data by villages.

743. Štrukelj, Pavla. "Dolenjski Romi v zbranem delu Janeza Trdine" (Dolenjsko Gypsies in the Collected Works of Janez Trdina). In **Janez Trdina etnolog: Zbornik posveta ob 150 letnici rojstva Janeza Trdine, Novo mesto 25. 5. 1980**, pp. 57-65. Ljubljana: Slovensko etnološko društvo, 1980. 119p.
    A critical survey of the treatment of the folklore of the Gypsies of Dolenjsko, Lower Carniola, in the works of the Slovene writer and ethnographer Janez Trdina (1830-1905).

744. Štrukelj, Pavla. **Romi na Slovenskem** (Romanies in Slovenia). Ljubljana: Cankarjeva založba, 1980. 323p.
    Štrukelj provides historical background on the Indian nomads in Europe, specifically in Yugoslavia and Slovenia. The empirical part is based on ethnological fieldwork in Slovenia, covering occupation characteristics and life style of the Romanies (Gypsies). The study includes texts of several Romany folktales and a dictionary of Romany words appearing in the book. Romanies of the Prekmurje region who were given land in the Banat region of Yugoslavia in 1948 soon returned to their villages in Prekmurje. So did those who were taken from the Gorenjsko region to the Kočevje area of Slovenia.

745. Trifunoski, Jovan. "Prilog proučavanja Roma u Jugoslaviji. Romi Kočanske kotline" (A Contribution to the Study of Romanies in Yugoslavia: The Romanies of the Kočani Basin). *Glasnik etnografskog instituta SANU* 22 (1973): 161-76.

This essay surveys the Romany population of the Kočani Valley in eastern Macedonia. Of a total of approximately 2,400 Romanies, 85% live in the urban center of Kočani and Vinica. Those of Muslim religion (80%) speak Turkish and Romany. The remaining 20% are of Orthodox religion and speak either Macedonian (they are referred to as Karaci) or Romanian (Liguri). Most of the Turkish Romanies are tinsmiths, musicians, or horse traders or work as helpers. The Karaci are farmers, and the Liguri make wooden utensils and troughs.

Slovaks, Czechs, Ruthenians

746. Auerhan, Jan. **Československa větev v Jugoslavii** (The Czechoslovak Branch in Yugoslavia). Knihovna českosl. ústavu zahraničního, I. Prague: Nádkladem Českosl. ústavu zahraničního, 1930. 403p.

This survey of Slovak, Czech, and Ruthenian minorities in Yugoslavia includes demographic data as well as data on their religious affiliation, with Slovaks being shown as predominantly Protestant and Czechs as typically Catholic. Among topics covered are educational and cultural institutions, folklore, and economic and political activities. Illustrations and a fold-out map.

747. Bednarik, Rudolf. **Slováci v Juhoslávii; materiály k ich hmotnej a duchovnej kultúre** (Slovaks in Yugoslavia: Materials for Their Material and Spiritual Culture). 2nd ed. Bratislava: Vydavateľstvo Slovenskej akademie vied, 1966. 386p. Illus. Maps. Plans.

A cultural and social anthropological study of the Slovak minority in Yugoslavia.

748. Grulich, Rudolf. "Die Tschechen in Jugoslawien." *Europa Ethnica* 32:3 (1975): 122-25.

The Czech settlement in South Slavic areas started in 1823 and increased after the occupation of Bosnia and Herzegovina by Austrian troops in 1878. The author describes the activities of this ethnic group during the nineteenth century.

749. Lilge, Karol. **Stará Pazova; Monografija** (Stara Pazova: A Monography). Na Myjave: Nákladom D. Pažického, 1932. 261p.

This is a local history of Stara Pazova, Srem, which focuses on the Slovak community there. It describes economic conditions and cultural activities and includes statistical information and photos.

750. Mráz, Andrej. **Rozhovory o juhoslovanských Slovákoch** (Notes on Yugoslavian Slovaks). Bratislava: Nakladatelstvo Pravda, 1948. 126p.

This brief account contains historical and ethnographic notes on Slovaks in the Yugoslav autonomous province of Vojvodina.

751. Siracki, Jan. "Mesto i značaj jugoslovenskih Slovaka u istoriji čehoslovačko-jugoslovenskih odnosa" (The Significance of Yugoslav Slovaks in the History of Czechoslovak-Yugoslav Relations). *Zbornik za društvene nauke* 48 (1967): 40-52.

During the nineteenth century, in the face of increasing Hungarian chauvinism, the Slovak minority sided with the Southern Slavs. In 1869 the Slovak Vilian Pauliny-Tóth represented the Kulpin district in the Hungarian parliament. In 1919, a Slovak grammar school was founded in Bački Petrovac with the financial support of the Czechoslovak government. During World War II, Slovaks and Czechs in Yugoslavia formed guerrilla groups.

752. Siracki, Jan. "Slovaci u Vojvodini kao istoričko-etnografski fenomen" (The Slovaks in Vojvodina as a Historical and Ethnographic Phenomenon). *Zbornik za istoriju* 5 (1972): 109-17.

This is a survey of the historical and cultural development of the Slovaks in Vojvodina from the time of their settlement during the eighteenth and nineteenth centuries to modern times, including political, geographical, economic, and religious aspects.

753. Svetoň, Ján. **Slováci v europskom zahraniči** (Slovaks in European Foreign Countries). Bratislava: Slovenska akademia vied a umeni, 1943. 95p.

This volume contains chapters on the religious life, demography, economy, and education of Slovaks abroad and includes the treatment of Slovaks in Yugoslavia. It contains maps showing their distribution in towns and villages of Vojvodina.

754. **Tradicyjna kultura jogoslavjanskyh Rusynoh (Prylogy): Materyjali zoz Sovytovanja o tradycyjnej kultury vojvodjanskyh Rysynoh i Ukraïncoh, ortrymanogo u Novym Sadze y Ruskym Kerstyre od 30. junyja do 5. julyja 1970. roku** (Traditional Culture of Yugoslav Ruthenians [Contributions]: Materials of the Conference on the Traditional Culture of Ruthenians and Ukrainians in Vojvodina, Held in Novi Sad and in Ruski Kerstur, June 30-July 5, 1970). Novi Sad: "Rusko slovo" and Etnografski institut Srpske akademije nauka i umetnosti u Beogradu, 1971. 316p.

These are the conference proceedings containing essays dealing with the Ruthenian and Ukrainian minorities in Vojvodina. Topics include migratory movements of Ruthenians to and within the Bačka region, major Ruthenian and Ukrainian settlements, folklore, language and linguistic assimilation, and literature and its relation to folklore. A bibliography on Yugoslav Ruthenians comprises 432 titles, arranged by subjects. French summary.

Hungarians

755. Bromlei, Iu., and Kshuba, M. S. "Nekotorye aspecty etnicheskikh protsessov v Iugoslavii." *Sovetskaia ethnografiia* 1 (1969): 59-67.

The article observes a tendency of Serbianization among the members of the Hungarian national minority, especially those of mixed Hungarian-Serbian parentage.

756. Gower, Sir Robert. **The Hungarian Minorities in the Succession States**. London: Grant Richards, 1937. 123p.

In the chapter on Hungarians in Yugoslavia, the author asserts that annexation of Vojvodina by Serbia, in 1918, violated the principle of self-determination, that Hungarians are underrepresented in various political bodies, that the effect of the land reform was to reduce the amount of land owned by Hungarians by 50%, and that educational rights and privileges have been curtailed. The volume includes the section pertaining to minorities of the 1919 Treaty of Saint-Germain.

757. Hajós, Ferenc. "A nemzetségek jogi helyzete a Szlovén szocialista köztársaságban" (The Legal Situation of Minorities in the Socialist Republic of Slovenia). *Razprave in gradivo* 9-10 (1979): 41-53.

The essay surveys the legal norms applicable to Hungarian and Italian minorities in Slovenia. Current implementation of these norms is also discussed.

758. Nećak-Lük, Albina. "Oris položaja madžarske narodne manjšine v Prekmurju v obdobju od 1918 do 1945" (A Survey of the Hungarian Ethnic Minority in Prekmurje during the Period between 1918 and 1945). *Zgodovinski časopis* 35:3 (1981): 279-86.

Following the Trianon Treaty of 1920, the Prekmurje region, formerly under Hungarian administration, came under Yugoslav sovereignty. The area was inhabited by 74,000 Slovenes and 14,000 ethnic Hungarians. Hungarian civil servants were dismissed or transferred elsewhere. The agrarian reform legislation placed Hungarians at the lower end of the scale according to which land was distributed. Hungarian public education declined considerably during the interwar period.

759. Popov. Jelena. "Organizacija Komunističke partije Jugoslavije u Vojvodina 1945-1948" (Organization of the Communist Party of Yugoslavia in Vojvodina, 1945-1948). *Zbornik za istoriju* 19 (1979): 61-96.

Between 1945 and 1948 in Vojvodina, membership in the Communist party of Yugoslavia increased substantially. The majority of the members were of Serb nationality, with Hungarians a distant second.

760. Sándor, Varga. **20 let komisije za narodnosti – A Nemyetiségi Bizottság húsz éve** (Twenty Years of the Commission for Nationalities). Lendava-Lendva: Pomurski medobčinski svet SZDL, Komisija za narodnostna vprašanja v obmejne stike, 1980.

This is a report of the activities of the Commission for Nationalities of the Intercommunal Council of the Socialist Alliance of the Working People of Pomurje. It provides information on the use of Hungarian in public administration and in schools of the Lendava and Murska Sobota communes (counties) in Slovenia.

761. Seli, Ištvan. **Gradjansko nasledje u socialističkoj kulturi Madjara u Jugoslaviji i njegovo prevazilaženje** (The Bourgeois Heritage in the Socialist Culture of Hungarians in Yugoslavia and Its Transformation). Belgrade: Centar za istraživanja kot presedništva CK SKJ, 1976. 139p.

The study considers the interwar Yugoslav policy toward the Hungarians, which was "minority-oriented," as politically unstructured and defensive. The present situation is characterized by the evolution to a geographically, economically, and politically homogeneous "nationality" on an equal footing with a "nation."

7 _____ The Slovene and Croat Minorities in Italy and Austria, 1945-1980

Toussaint Hočevar

HISTORICAL SUMMARY

The Slovene Minority in Italy

For South Slavic minorities in Italy and Austria, the end of World War II brought promises of hope. However, their expectations were subsequently only partially realized. Although the border adjustment with Italy brought all Croat territory which had been under Italian administration during the interwar period and a major part of the Slovene-inhabited Coastland province under Yugoslav sovereignty, a substantial Slovene minority remained in the present provinces of Trieste, Gorizia, and Udine, first under Anglo-American and later under Italian administration.

The Slovene educational system which had been reintroduced in Trieste and Gorizia following the capitulation of Italy in 1943 was left in place and was even somewhat enlarged by the Anglo-American and subsequent Italian administrations. Today the system consists of elementary and secondary schools and a teachers college. The demands for minority schools in the Slovene-speaking area of the province of Udine have not yet been met by the Italian authorities.

The Slovene press and publishing flourish in all three Slovene-inhabited provinces, and there is a permanent Slovene theatrical company in Trieste. The state-supported Trieste radio maintains a special broadcasting service in Slovene, while Slovene television programming can be received directly from neighboring Yugoslavia.

The only Slovene political party, *Slovenska skupnost*, is represented in local and provincial governments as well as in the regional assembly of the autonomous region Venezia-Giulia, which is comprised of the provinces of Trieste, Gorizia, and Udine. Several other Italian political parties include representatives who speak the Slovene language.

In public administration the role of Slovene remains limited, despite numerous petitions and resolutions submitted by Slovenes through various channels over the years. Only recently, protests were raised against the postal administration in Trieste because it refused to accept telegrams written in Slovene. Moreover, in August 1982 the administrative court of the region Friuli-Venezia Guilia ruled against the use of Slovene in elected representative bodies after such use had been sanctioned in the Trieste Provincial Council.[1]

The Italian-Yugoslav Agreement of Osimo of 1975, through which Italy recognized the present boundary with Yugoslavia as definitive, failed to include specific provisions for the protection of the Slovene minority in Italy. Slovenes in Italy are demanding legislation which would assure uniform implementation of Slovene linguistic rights in the provinces of Trieste, Gorizia, and Udine. It appears that successive Italian governments have procrastinated adopting legislation which would offer the Slovene minority a comparable degree of protection as that enjoyed by the German-speaking minority of South Tirol. Such statutory guarantees could contribute significantly to international stability in a strategically important area.

The Slovene and Croat Minorities in Austria

In Austria, British occupational authorities introduced bilingual German-Slovene primary education in the Slovene-inhabited portion of Carinthia. However, in 1958 the Austrian administration allowed parents to withdraw children from Slovene classes. In 1959 instruction of Slovene was made subject to parental request and had to be taken in addition to the regular curriculum in German, which significantly reduced the number of children taking Slovene in primary schools. At the secondary education level, the federal government opened an eight-year secondary school (gymnasium) for Slovenes in Klagenfurt/Celovec, the Carinthian capital. The instruction in this school is in Slovene, but the students acquire proficiency in German as well.

Article 7 of the State Treaty concluded between the Allied Powers and Austria in 1955 contains provisions for the protection of Slovene and Croat minorities. However, the absence of a precise definition of the territory to which these provisions were to apply served the Austrian government as an excuse for implementing Article 7 in very few places, and even there only partially. Thus the provision for erection of bilingual town-limit signs was conveniently ignored for seventeen years, until the governor of Carinthia, Hans Sima, decreed in 1972 that such signs be erected in 205 localities. After forceful removal of bilingual signs by German-Austrian extremists, the federal chancellor Bruno Kreisky gave in to their demands, forcing Governor Sima to resign. At this point Slovene protest demonstrations in Klagenfurt and elsewhere brought the Carinthian minority problem to worldwide attention. Following a special language census, which was boycotted by the Carinthian Slovenes, bilingual signs were erected in a limited number of smaller places. Similarly, the provisions of the State Treaty for the use of Slovene in the courts and administration have been implemented only on a token basis. The federal law on minorities passed in 1976 with the intent of satisfying the provisions of Article 7 of the State Treaty has been declared unsatisfactory by the Slovene and Croat minority organizations, which are demanding its amendment (*Novellierung*).

The properties of Slovene cooperative and educational organizations, which had been confiscated by the National Socialists, gradually have been restored to their original use. There has been some new investment as well, for example, in a new business building in Klagenfurt which houses the central office of Carinthian Slovene lending cooperatives, in a Catholic printing plant, and in dormitories for out-of-town students attending the Slovene gymnasium in Klagenfurt.

The Croats of Burgenland have generally been the subject of less attention than the Slovenes of Carinthia. This is because the Croats live in an area in which urbanization has not made such inroads as in Carinthia. Also, in contrast to the Slovenes, the Croats appear to accept more readily the role of a folklore curiosity, rather than that of an ethnic group aspiring to their own educational and economic institutions.[2]

Notes

[1] *Gospodarstvo*, 22 October 1982. (Trieste)

[2] Cf. Wilhelm Filla, *Am Rande Österreichs: Ein Beitrag zur Soziologie der österreichischen Volksgruppen* (Vienna: Wilhelm Braumüller, 1982).

BIBLIOGRAPHY

Slovenes in Italy

General Reference Works

762. **Bibliografija zgodovinske razstave London 1915 – Osimo 1975** (Bibliography of the Historical Exposition London 1915 – Osimo 1975). Trieste: Narodna in študijska knjižnica v Trstu, 1978. 29p.

This is a select bibliography of works pertaining to the Italian-Yugoslav boundary questions and to the problems of Slovene and Croat minorities under Italian administration, 1915-1975.

763. Koleric̆, Antonija, in collaboration with Marjan Pertot. **Bibliografija slovenskega tiska v Italiji med dvema vojnama, 1918-30.IV. 1945** (Bibliography of Slovene Publications in Italy between the Two Wars, 1918-30-4-1945). Trieste: Narodna in študijska knjižnica v Trstu, 1966. 97p. mimeographed.

Koleric̆'s bibliography is of Slovene-language titles published within the interwar territorial boundaries of Italy during the interwar and World War II period. It includes periodicals but excludes all partisan clandestine publications produced during World War II. It further contains an explanatory index of pseudonyms. There are 1,035 entries, arranged chronologically.

764. **Per la tutela globale degli sloveni in Italia; dal Primorski dnevnik ed altre fonti**. Trieste: Editoriale Stampa Triestina, 1972. 59p.

This booklet contains documents published between 1970 and 1972 concerning the efforts of the Slovenes in Italy to obtain global protection, i.e., uniform minority rights applying within the provinces of Trieste, Gorizia, and Udine. Included are legislative proposals of the Italian Communist party, the Italian Socialist party, and the Slovene Alliance (Slovenska Skupnost).

765. Petric̆, Ernest. **Mednarodnopravni položaj slovenske manjšine v Italiji** (The Status of the Slovene Minority in Italy under International Law). Edited by the Slovenski raziskovalni inštitut v Trstu. Trieste: Založništvo tržaškega tiska, 1980. 122p.

Petric̆ surveys the rights of the Slovene minority in Italy in the light of international law. He views the 1975 Italo-Yugoslav Osimo Agreement as superseding the Special Statute appended to the 1954 London Memorandum, while at the same time obligating Italy to incorporate in her law the minority rights provisions contained in the Special Statute. Moreover, under the Osimo Agreement these rights are to be extended beyond the former Free Territory of Trieste to all Slovene-inhabited areas in Italy.

Monographs

766. **Atti del convegno "Linee per la rinascita et un diverso sviluppo della Slavia Friulana."** Edited by Slovenski raziskovalni inštitut. Trieste: Editoriale Stampa Triestina, 1980. 91p.

The volume contains the papers presented at a conference held at Passariano, Italy in 1980, focusing on problems of economic development in Venetian Slovenia. It includes historical demographic data by counties and a map of Slovene and Friulan counties within the autonomous region Friuli-Venezia Giulia.

767. **Atti del Simposio sui problemi socioeconomici e ambientali degli Sloveni in Italia.** Edited by Slovenski raziskovalni inštitut, Trieste. 2 vols. Trieste: Editoriale Stampa Triestina, 1978. 370p.; 102p.

Papers in the first volume range from general surveys of conditions in the Slovene-inhabited area of Italy to evaluations of specific projects such as the international industrial zone proposed under the Italo-Yugoslav Osimo Agreement of 1975. Papers by V. Z. Simonitti and F. Clavora, in the second volume, focus on problems of under-development and out-migration in Venetian Slovenia and discuss the considerable damage inflicted by the 1976 earthquake. Other contributors treat the ethnic structure and linguistic problems of the Kanalska dolina (Valcanale), in the northeastern corner of Italy, as well as problems of the counties of Bardo/Lusevere, Grmek/Grimacco, and Dreka/Drechia.

768. **Atti IV Incontro Geografico Italo-Sloveno (Pordenone, 28-29 ottobre 1973).** Part I: **Le minoranze etnico-linguistiche della frontiera italo-jugoslava.** Udine: Instituto di Geografia della Facolta di Lingue e Letterature Straniere dell'Universita di Trieste, Sede Staccata di Udine, 1974. 154p. (Summaries in English).

The proceedings of the Fourth Italo-Slovene Geographical Symposium held in Pordenone, Italy in 1973. Papers treat the situation of Slovenes in Italy and Italians in Yugoslavia, providing statistics on both groups. Also included is a gravitational analysis for some towns in Slovenia.

769. Boileau, Anna Maria, and Sussi, Emidio. **Dominanze e minoranze: Immagini e rapporti interetnici al confine nordorientale.** Udine: Editrice Grillo, 1981. 253p.

The authors present an empirical study of the relations between ethnic groups in northeastern Italy (Slovenes, Friulans, Italians). They analyze the images these groups have of themselves and of each other.

770. Bonamore, Daniele. **Disciplina giuridica delle istituzioni scholastiche a Trieste e Gorizia: Dalla Monarchia A.-U. al G.M.A. e dal Memorandum di Londra al Trattato di Osimo.** Biblioteca della Rivista giuridica della scuola, 2. Milano: Dott. A. Giuffrè Editore, 1979. 608p.

The account traces the history of education in the provinces of Trieste and Gorizia, Italy from 1787 until the Treaty of Osimo of 1975. Special emphasis is on the languages of instruction, i.e., Italian and Slovene.

771. Chronista Sontiacus (pseud.). "Slovenci v Italiji" (Slovenes in Italy). In **Slovenci v desetletju 1918-1928: Zbornik razprav iz kulturne, gospodarske in politične zgodovine,** edited by Josip Mal, pp. 62-117. Ljubljana: Leonova družba, 1928.

This is an overview of events in the Slovene-inhabited areas occupied by Italy in 1918 and annexed in 1920. The activities of the Slovene national government in Gorizia and of the Italian-Slovene Council in Trieste between the time of the breakdown of Austrian authority and the arrival of Italian troops are described in detail. Provides results of 1921 and 1923 elections.

772. Davis, James C. "A Slovene Laborer and His Experience of Industrialization, 1888-1976." *East European Quarterly* X:1 (1976): 3-20.

An oral history based on interviews with Franc Žužek, a retired laborer who has lived all of his eighty-seven years in a village on the Karst plateau near Trieste, Italy. A map of the area is included.

773. Debelli-Turk, Lida, ed. **Sv. Jakob; Zgodovinski razgledi po življenju Slovencev v tržaškem delavskem okraju Sv. Jakob** (Historical Glimpses of the Life of Slovenes in a Trieste Workers' District). Trieste: Založništvo tržaškega tiska, 1980. 325p.

This account presents a social history of the Trieste neighborhood of Sv. Jakob, including the post-1918 period. Illustrations enhance the report.

774. Ferenc, Tone; Kacin-Wohinz, Milica; and Zorn, Tone. **Slovenci v zamejstvu: Pregled zgodovine 1918-1945** (Slovenes beyond the Yugoslav Borders: A Survey of History between 1918 and 1945). Ljubljana: Državna založba Slovenije, 1974. 320p. Maps.

This history deals with the Slovene minority in Italy, Austria, and Hungary between 1918 and 1945. Bibliography.

775. Geržinič, Alojzij. **Pouk v materinščini – da ali ne? Delo za slovensko šolstvo na Tržaškem v zadnjih mescih nemške okupacije** (Instruction in the Mother Tongue – Yes or No? Work for Slovene Schools in the Province of Trieste during the Last Months of German Occupation). Buenos Aires: Založba Sij, 1972. 136p.

Between January and May 1945, the author served as superintendent of elementary Slovene schools in the German-occupied province of Trieste. He was responsible for reestablishing the Slovene educational system, which had been suppressed under Italian rule. Detailed information on his activities is based mainly on the author's diary.

776. Hočevar, Toussaint. **Slovenski družbeni razvoj: Izbrane razprave** (Slovene Social Development: Selected Essays). New Orleans: Založba Prometej, 1979. 191p.

This study includes an essay on the occupational structure of the Trieste Slovenes, originally published in *Ekonomska revija* (see entry 777), and a report on the effects of the changing economic environment on the Slovene minority in Italy.

777. Hočevar, Toussaint, and Lokar, Aleš. "Ekonomskopolitični aspekti diferencirane zaposlitvene strukture Slovencev in Italijanov v Trstu" (Economic Policy Implications of the Differentiated Occupational Structure of the Slovenes and Italians in Trieste). *Ekonomska revija* 25:4 (1974): 374-78.

The authors compare educational and occupational structures of the Slovene and Italian linguistic groups in Trieste province, based on 1961 and 1971 census data. The share of Slovenes in white-collar jobs falls short of that which would be expected based on education, suggesting mal-employment.

778. Komac, Miran. "Hrvaška jezikovna manjšina v italijanski pokrajini Molise" (The Croat Linguistic Minority in the Italian Province of Molise). *Razprave in gradivo* 9-10 (1979): 99-109.

In three villages at the foot of the eastern Apennines, the descendants of the sixteenth century migrants from Dalmatia preserve the Croatian Ikavian speech. Recently they have been voicing demands for the protection of their heritage.

779.   Lega democratica in collaborazione con Circolo cultural "Studenci" de S. Pietro al Natisone, Gruppo ricerca e presenza di Gorizia. **Atti convengo nazionale Le minoranze linguistiche in Italia: Comunità etnico-linguistiche non tutelate e stato democratico**, Udine 31 gennaio—1 febbraio 1981. 126p.

The proceedings include a paper and comments by several participants concerning the Slovene minority in the province of Udine, Italy.

780.   Levak, Ksenija, and Budal, Gojmir. **Longera; Lineamenti socio-geografici dell'abitato presso Trieste**. Edited by Slovenski raziskovalni inštitut. Trieste: Editoriale Stampa Triestina, 1981. 93p.

This sociogeographic study of the Slovene-inhabited village of Lonjer/Longera on the outskirts of Trieste analyzes the ethnic, demographic, occupational, and industrial structure of the population. It surveys employment and leisure-related activities. Tables and two photographs.

781.   **Lingua, espressione e letteratura nella Slavia italiana. Primo ciclo di conferenze degli Incontri culturali 1973-74 a Scrutto (S. Leonardo)**. San Pietro al Natisone-Trieste: Editoriale Stampa Triestina, 1978. 134p.

Linguistic and literary essays focusing on the Slovenes in the Udine province of Italy make up the first cycle of the 1973-1974 Cultural Encounters Conference. Treated are such subjects as the Slovene dialects (Tine Logar, Pavle Merkù), Slavic-Romance linguistic contacts (G. B. Pellegrini), folk poetry in Resia (Milko Matičetov), late medieval manuscripts (Pavle Merkù), and the role of the literary Slovene (Breda Pogorelec).

782.   Lokar, Aleš, and Thomas, Lee. "Socioeconomic Structure of the Slovene Population in Italy." *Papers in Slovene Studies* (1977): 26-39.

This is an empirical analysis based on occupational and educational data of counties with varying shares of the Slovene population. The authors conclude that statistical evidence is consistent with linguistic discrimination of a particular type: the lack of public institutions in the Slovene language. For this reason Slovenes are under-represented in public and administrative occupations. Until now the Slovenes have tried to find an escape from this situation by concentrating in free professions and entrepreneurship, but this is becoming increasingly difficult since the most dynamic sectors of development are to be found in publicly or semi-publicly managed enterprises and institutions.

783.   Novak, Bogdan. **Trieste, 1941-1954: The Ethnic, Political, and Ideological Struggle**. Chicago and London: University of Chicago Press, 1970. 526p.

The Trieste dispute involved—between the destruction of Austria-Hungary in 1918 and the Italian peace treaty in 1947—the entire region which the Italians call Venezia Giulia and the Yugoslavs the Julian March. From 1947 to 1954 the dispute was confined to the zone of the Free Territory of Trieste, which was created by the treaty but could not be put into operation because the Allied powers could not agree on the choice of a governor. Finally the most logical solution was reached. In October 1954 Yugoslavia received Zone B, with minor changes; Italy, Zone A. Both the big dispute (1918-1947) and the little one (1947-1954) were passionate because they involved nationalism. This book should be consulted for information on the diverse local political factions as well as on ethnographic composition of the area in question.

784.   Radetić, Ernest. **Istra pod Italijom, 1918-1943** (Istra under Italy, 1918-1943). Zagreb: n.p., 1944. 276p. Map.

This is a historical account of Croats and Slovenes in Istra during the interwar Italian administration. It includes a selective list of family names in their Croat and Italianized forms. In 1936, 17,000 family name changes were imposed in the Pula province alone. Radetić provides a detailed list of Croat and Slovene property (schools, businesses, homes) destroyed by Fascists during the twenties, mainly by fire, with monetary losses expressed in Italian lire. The uprising in Krnica and the proclamation of the "Labin Republic" by the coal miners of Labin, both in 1921, are described in detail.

785.   Rebula Tuta, Alenka. **La questione nazionale a Trieste in un'inchiesta tra gli operai sloveni**. Trieste: Editoriale Stampa Triestina, 1980. 183p.

This sociological study is based on interviews with a sample of 54 Trieste workers of Slovene nationality. The main focus is on attitudes concerning the use of Slovene. Analytical portions of the text are supplemented with extensive passages from interviews.

786.   Špekonja, H. **Rod za mejo: Zgodovinska in socialna slika Beneške Slovenije in Rezije** (Progeny across the Border: Historical and Social Picture of Venetian Slovenia and Rezija). n.p., 1954(?). 71p.

A survey of historical and contemporary conditions of the Slovene population inhabiting the valleys of Rezija (Resia), Ter (Tarcento), Nadiža (Natissone), and Kanal (Canale), Italy. Historically, home rule was exercised by a parliament of village mayors, called *višja sosednja*, or *arenga*. In 1419 this body accepted the sovereignty of the republic of Venice under the guarantee of continued autonomy. Under the peace treaty of Campoformio in 1797, the area came under Austria, but was ceded to Italy in 1866, following a plebiscite. The author surveys the Slovene cultural heritage and the measures to Italianize the area by both secular and church authorities, up to 1952. Census data are provided for selected years from 1811 to 1921, when 33,000 Slovenes were registered.

787.   Susič, Emidij, and Sedmak, Danilo. **Tiha asimilacija: Psihološki vidiki nacionalnega odtujevanja** (Silent Assimilation: Psychological Aspects of National Alienation). Trieste: Založništvo tržaškega tiska, 1983. 174p.

This volume offers an analysis of selected psychosociological mechanisms responsible for assimilation of individuals belonging to ethnic minority groups. It takes into consideration problems related to mass media, school, mixed marriages, and the use of leisure time. The applied portion of the study draws upon the contemporary experience of the Slovene minority in Italy.

Slovenes and Croats in Austria

General Reference Works

788.   Apovnik, Paul. **Das Volksgruppensesetz—eine Lösung?: Standpunkt der Kärntner Slowenen**. 3rd ed. Klagenfurt/Celovec: Slovene Information Center, 1980. 141p.

Apovnik presents information pertaining to the situation of linguistic minorities in Austria. He advocates greater tolerance *vis-à-vis* linguistic minorities in general and the

Slovenes of Carinthia in particular. Photographs of Slovene civil rights demonstrations during the 1970s and of related events are included.

789. Arbeitsgemeinschaft Volksgruppenfrage. **Kein einig Volk von Brüdern: Studien zum Mehrheiten-/Minderheitenproblem am Beispiel Kärntens.** Österreichische Texte zur Gesellschaftskritik, 9. Vienna: Verlag für Gesellschaftskritik, 1982. 443p.

Fourteen essays deal with the linguistic minority problems of the Carinthian Slovenes. The authors, all of whom are on the faculty of the University of Klagenfurt, treat the problems from the point of view of their disciplines: socio-linguistics, history, psychology, sociology, and political science.

790. Grafenauer, Bogo. **Ethnic Conditions in Carinthia.** Ljubljana: Research Institute, Section for Frontier Questions, 1946. 40p. Map.

A historical survey of ethnic conditions in Carinthia, Austria. Census data are analyzed, and a map showing ethnic distribution is included.

791. Klemenčič, Vladimir, ed. **Koroška in koroški Slovenci: Zbornik poljud-noznanstvenih in leposlovnih spisov** (Carinthia and Carinthian Slovenes: Popularizing Scientific and Literary Essays). Maribor: Založba Obzorja, 1971. 389p. Map.

Yugoslav and Austrian Slovene authors present sociogeographic, historical, and linguistic-literary essays. The volume includes the text of a memorandum submitted by Carinthian Slovene organizations to the Austrian government in 1955. A linguistic map of Carinthia is based on the 1951 census.

792. **Koroški zbornik** (Carinthian Essays). Ljubljana: Državna založba Slovenije, 1946. 658p.

This compendium consists of scholarly essays on geography, history, linguistics, and literature pertaining to the Slovenes of Carinthia.

793. **The Legal Status of Ethnic Groups in Austria.** Vienna: Federal Chancellery Austria, 1977. 107p.

This official publication contains the text of Article 7 of the Austrian State Treaty of 1955 as well as texts of notes between Austria and Yugoslavia pertaining to the Slovene and Croat minorities in Austria.

794. Osolnik, Bogdan, ed. **Problem manjšin v jugoslovansko-avstrijskih odnosih: Članki in dokumenti** (The Minorities Problem in Yugoslav-Austrian Relations: Articles and Documents). Belgrade: Medjunarodna politika, 1977. 197p. Maps.

These contributions discuss Austria's international obligations in regards to Slovene and Croat minorities, implementation of Article 7 of the Austrian State Treaty, and the Austrian law on the legal status of ethnic groups of 1976. The appendix contains Yugoslav notes to Austria of 1974 and 1976, the declaration of the Yugoslav Executive Council of 1975, and the declaration of Slovene organizations in Carinthia presented to the U.N. in 1977. There are also photographs of demonstrations in Austria by Slovene civil rights groups and by German-Austrian anti-Slovene extremists.

795. Rusinow, Dennison I. **Nationalism Today: Carinthia's Slovenes.** Part I: **The Legacy of History.** Southeast Europe Series, Europe vol. XXII, no. 4. Hanover, NH: The American Universities Field Staff, 1977. 9p. Part II: **The Story of Article Seven.** Southeast Europe Series, vol. XXII, no. 5. Hanover, NH: The American Universities

Field Staff, 1977. 9p. Part III: **"Let the Cat Die Quickly."** American Universities Field Staff Reports, 1978/no. 23 Europe. Hanover, NH: The American Universities Field Staff, 1978. 14p.

As a case study, the problem of the Carinthian Slovenes reveals the complexities of "the national question" in central Europe. It also sheds light on contradictory aspects of minority group options in political and economic life. Article 7 of the Austrian State Treaty of 1955 obligated Austria to guarantee both the survival and the equality of Slovene (and Croat) minorities. Dispute over implementation centers on the school system, use of Slovenian as a second language in the bureaucracy and courts, and bilingual topographical signs. Part 3 discusses census data on the number of Slovenes in Carinthia since 1980, German-Austrian assimilatory pressures, and the controversy surrounding the 1976 special census. If the disappearance of the Slovenes is, as some would believe, a foregone conclusion, the author asks why not do all that the State Treaty requires and much more besides.

796. Tischler, Josef, ed. **Die Sprachenfrage in Kärnten vor 100 Jahren und heute; Auswahl deutscher Zeitdokumente und Zeitstimmen.** Klagenfurt: Rat der Kärnter Slowenen, 1957. 116p.

A collection of German documents and newspaper articles spanning a period of 100 years and dealing with language-related topics in Austrian Carinthia. A large part of the texts date from the post-World War II period.

797. Zorn, Tone. "Bibliografija del o slovenski severni meji v letih 1918-1978" (Bibliography of Works about Slovenia's Northern Border, 1918-1978). *Jugoslovenski istorijski časopis* 18:1-2 (1979): 101-20.

This bibliography of works published in Yugoslavia and abroad, 1918-1978, on the subject of Slovenes in Carinthia and Styria (Austria) and in Hungary includes works on the Carinthian plebiscite of 1920, the struggle for cultural autonomy before World War II, and the Carinthian Slovenes' particular situation during the *Anschluss*. The post-World War II period is covered up to 1977 in works cited.

History

798. Barker, Thomas M. "The Carinthian Slovene Question in the Light of Recent German Austrian Scholarship." *Nationalities Papers* 7:2 (1979): 125-37.

Adapted mainly from the appendix of *The Slovene Minority of Carinthia* (see entry 799), Barker's article critically surveys recent historical and sociological literature on the Carinthian Slovenes by German Austrian authors.

799. Barker, Thomas, and Moritsch, Andreas. **The Slovene Minority of Carinthia.** 2nd ed. Social Science Monographs Brooklyn College Studies on Society in Change. New York: Columbia University Press, 1983. 516p.

This work, a completely revised and rewritten version of the monograph *The Slovenes of Carinthia: A National Minority Problem* (1960) by Thomas M. Barker, brings the history of this significant minority group up to date. The evolution of the "Carinthian question" over the two decades since the work's original publication prompted the author to follow up his research and to survey the post-1960 course of Austrian and Yugoslavian policies toward the Slovenes, and to present a current picture of the ethnic Carinthian situation.

800. Carantanus. **Jugoslavija in njene meje, I. Koroška** (Yugoslavia and Her Frontiers, 1. Carinthia). Ljubljana: Pisarna za zasedeno ozemlje v Ljubljani, 1919. 62p.

A brief survey of the historical role of Slovenes in Carinthia and a review of the contemporary Slovene-German linguistic boundary. The booklet also contains linguistic decennial census data by counties and villages of Carinthia for 1880 through 1910. It lists government officials by language (1913) and parishes by language used in church (1848 and 1918), and includes a 1910 census data linguistic map.

801. Einspieler, Valentin. **Verhandlungen über die der slowenischen Minderheit angebotene Kilturautonomie 1925-1930: Beitrag zur Geschichte der Slowenen in Kärnten.** Klagenfurt: published by the author, 1976. 171p. Map.

Einspieler presents documents, including minutes of the school commission of the Carinthian provincial assembly, pertaining largely to the role of the Slovene language in the educational system. The period 1920-1930 is covered, with emphasis on 1925-1930.

802. Grafenauer, Bogo. **The National Development of the Carinthian Slovenes.** Ljubljana: Research Institute, Section for Frontier Questions, 1946. 91p.

This survey of the history of Carinthian Slovenes provides data on the 1930 elections, the industrial structure of population (1880-1934), occupational levels (1934), and size of land holdings (1934).

803. Haas, Hanns, and Stuhlpfarrer, Karl. **Österreich und seine Slowenen.** Vienna: Locker & Wögenstein, 1977. 142p.

This is a documented coverage of the Germanization drive in coinhabited Carinthia, largely from 1920 to 1977.

804. **Koroška v borbi. Spomini na osvobodilno borbo v Slovenski Koroški** (Carinthia in the Struggle. Reminiscences on the Liberation Struggle in Slovene Carinthia). Klagenfurt: Zveza bivših partizanov Slovenske Koroške, 1951. 224p.

These contributions tell of the armed resistance of Carinthian Slovenes against the Third Reich. The volume contains documents on death sentences pronounced against 13 Slovenes by the People's Court in Klagenfurt in 1943. All 13 were subsequently decapitated in Vienna. Included are photographs of families who were deported to Thuringia, Germany from their native Carinthia.

805. Korotanec (pseud.). "Naša Koroška" (Our Carinthia). In **Slovenci v desetletju 1918-1928: Zbornik razprav iz kulturne, gospodarske in politične zgodovine,** edited by Josip Mal, pp. 1-62. Ljubljana: Leonova družba, 1928.

This essay surveys political and educational conditions as well as the prevailing situation of religious communities in the Slovene-inhabited areas of Carinthia between 1920 and 1928. An analysis of a 1925 map of parishes published by the Catholic diocese of Gurk (Krka) reveals 67,000 inhabitants in 82 parishes designated as Slovene; 26,000 in 16 parishes designated as Slovene-German; and 28,000 in 12 parishes designated as German-Slovene.

806. Moritsch, Andreas. "Zur Kärntner Minderheitenfrage." *Österreichische Osthefte* 17:2 (1975): 180-82.

The author reviews new publications on the problem of the Slovene minority with regard to censuses, ethnic development, discrimination of Carinthian Slovenes in the administration, and the sociopolitical situation of the Slovene population in Carinthia during the nineteenth and twentieth centuries.

807.   Ude, Lojze. **Koroško vprašanje** (The Carinthian Question). Ljubljana: Državna založba Slovenije, 1976. 363p.

This collection of previously published essays is by a historian specializing in the modern history of Carinthian Slovenes. The essays appeared between 1946 and 1973.

808.   Zwitter, Fran. **Die Kärntner Frage**. Disertacije in razprave, 2. Klagenfurt and Celovec: Slovenski znanstveni inštitut, 1979. 62p.

The Carinthian ethnic problem is viewed from a historical perspective, buttressed by socioeconomic data, in this translation of a paper first published in *Sodobnost* 5 (1937), Ljubljana. It is supplemented by a paper presented by the author at the Second Carinthian Cultural Symposium in 1970.

Politics and Government

809.   **Kärnten. Volksabstimmung 1920. Voraussetzungen — Verlauf — Folgen**. Studien zur Geschichte und Gesellschaft in Slowenien, Österreich und Italien, 1. Vienna: Löcker Verlag, 1981. 265p.

This volume incorporates the results of recent research by contributors who include German Austrian, Slovene Austrian, and Yugoslav specialists. International as well as political, economic, and social aspects are brought to bear on the 1920 Carinthian plebiscite issue. The socioeconomic variables as a determinant of the plebiscite outcome (59% for Austria against 41% for Yugoslavia) are treated empirically by Andreas Moritsch. The thesis advanced by some Yugoslav and Austrian historians according to which the Slovene Carinthian working class voted for Austria because they preferred a progressive republic to a Yugoslav monarchy is not borne out by Moritsch's data. Rather, economic considerations were decisive. Conservative farmers who supplied the local urban market did not relish the prospect of being separated from Klagenfurt by a customs border, while the Ferlach/Borovlje gunsmiths or the Viktring/Vetrinj textile workers perceived Yugoslavia as their natural market.

810.   Nećak, Dušan. "Volitve v kmetijske zbornice na Koroškem po drugi svetovni vojni" (Elections for the Agricultural Chambers in Carinthia after World War II). *Zgodovinski časopis* 28:1-2 (1974): 95-116.

The elections for the provincial agricultural chamber of Carinthia between 1951 and 1971 are analyzed, with particular reference to the participation of Carinthian Slovenes. Data for 1932 as well as 32 notes are included.

811.   Neumann, Wilhelm. **Abwehrkampf und Volksabstimmung in Kärnten 1918-1920: Legenden und Tatsachen**. Das Kärntner Landesarchiv, 2. Klagenfurt: Verlag des Kärntner Landesarchivs, 1970. 154p.

The author polemicizes against recent theses advanced by the Austrian historians Rudolf Neck and Karl Stuhlpfarrer concerning the 1920 Carinthian plebiscite. These authors underestimate the influence which the German-Austrian resistance against Yugoslav troops may have had on the decision of the Paris Peace Conference to conduct the plebiscite. Moreover, the decision was due mainly to Italian, rather than to American, efforts. Two-thirds of the volume contain official documents.

812.   Rigl, Miha, ed. **Koroška pota** (Carinthian Paths). Maribor: Založba Obzorja, 1978. 151p. Bilingual (Slovene-German) edition.

A travel guide through Slovene Carinthia, Austria, including a schematic, comparative representation of linguistic minority legislation and minority institutions in Austria (Carinthia, Styria, Burgenland), Italy (Trieste, Gorizia, Venetian Slovenia, South Tirol), Hungary (Vas and Zala districts), and Slovenia (Koper region, Prekmurje).

813. Rumpler, Helmut, ed. **Kärntens Volksabstimmung 1920. Wissenschaftliche Kontroversen und historisch-politische Diskussionen anlässlich des internationalen Symposiums Klagenfurt 1980.** Klagenfurt: Kärntner Druck- und Verlagsgesellschaft, 1981. 434p.

Contributors to this compendium include German Austrian, Slovene Austrian, and Yugoslav specialists. In a broad thematic sweep, the book covers the theory of nationalism and the specific forms nationalism assumed among the Slovenes, Carinthian Slovenes, other South Slavs, and German Austrians. Five essays treat the international political aspects bearing on the 1920 Carinthian plebiscite. A survey of the recent literature on Carinthia of the 1918-1920 period is included.

814. **Sodobna vprašanja slovenske in hrvaške manjšine v Avstriji—Suvremena pitanja slovenske i hrvatske manjine u Austriji** (Current Issues of the Slovene and Croat Minorities in Austria). Ljubljana: Inštitut za narodnostna vprašanja, Ljubljana and Zavod za migracije i narodnosti, Zagreb, 1976. 74p. Title of English edition: *Actual Questions of the Slovene and Croat Minorities in Austria.*

The proceedings of the Conference on Contemporary Problems of the Slovene and Croat Minorities in Austria, which was held in Ljubljana on May 26, 1976.

815. Veiter, Theodor. **Das Österreichische Volksgruppenrecht seit dem Volksgruppengesetz von 1976: Rechtsnormen und Rechtswirklichkeit.** Vienna: Wilhelm Braumüller, 1979. 192p.

The author discusses the 1976 Austrian legislation on ethnic minorities. The law of 1976 was passed in an attempt to implement Article 7 of the State Treaty of 1955, which pertains to the Slovene and Croat linguistic minorities. The integral text of the law of 1976 and related federal decrees passed in 1977 are appended.

816. Veiter, Theodor. **Das Recht der Volksgruppen und Sprachminderheiten in Österreich: Mit einer ethnosoziologischen Grundlegung und einem Anhang (Materialien).** Vienna and Stuttgart: Wilhelm Braumüller, 1970. 890p.

Veiter analyzes Austrian legislation with regard to minority rights and legal practice concerning the right of ethnic and linguistic minority groups, including minority complaints to international bodies. Because of their relative importance, the Slovene and Croat linguistic minorities occupy the largest part of the book. The work contains information on the deportation of Slovene farmers from Carinthia to Thuringia, Germany during World War II.

817. Veiter, Theodor. **Verfassungsrechtslage und Rechtswirklichkeit der Volksgruppen und Sprachminderheiten in Österreich.** Vienna: Wilhelm Braumüller, Universitäts-Verlagsbuchhandlung, 1980. 131p.

This study contains a chapter on the de-Slovenization of geographical names in Carinthia. During the interwar and World War II period this activity was carried out by the Klagenfurt section of the Austrian/German Alpine Association and the Military Geographic Institute. The campaign was given added emphasis and carried to completion under the auspices of the Cartographic Institute following World War II.

Geography and Demography

818. Randall, Richard R. "Political Geography of the Klagenfurt Basin." *Geographical Review* 47:3 (1957): 406-19.

A review of the physical, economic, and political geography of the Klagenfurt Basin in Austria, including maps of counties voting for Yugoslavia in the 1920 plebiscite, of the area claimed by Yugoslavia, 1945-1950, and of the area with bilingual (Slovene-German) schools, 1945 and 1953.

819. Zorn, Tone, "Ljudsko štetje z dne 7. marca 1923 na Koroškem" (The Census of 7 March 1923 in Carinthia). *Kronika* (Ljubljana) 16:2 (1968): 121-23.

The 1923 Austrian census grossly understated the number of Slovenes in Carinthia. The author supports his thesis with contemporary evidence showing that anti-Slovenes were deliberately appointed as census takers. Also, the results of the 1923 census show a downward bias when compared with those of the 1939 census conducted by the National Socialist authorities.

820. Zorn, Tone. "Slovenci na avstrijskem Štajerskem" (Slovenes in the Austrian Styria). *Casopis za zgodovino in narodopisje*, New Series 15:1-2 (1979): 430-47.

The article provides and analyzes census data on the number of Slovenes in Austrian Styria, particularly in the so-called Radgona Triangle. In this area Austria has failed to apply minority provisions contained in Article 7 of the State Treaty.

Social and Economic Conditions

821. Čuješ, Rudolf P. "Minorities: Methodological Questions in Relation to Slovenes in Carinthia." *Nationalities Papers* 7:2 (1979): 138-46.

The study relates primarily to the situation of the Slovenes in Carinthia, with emphasis on social facts which have a decisive influence on proper understanding and presentation of matter under investigation. Forced assimilation may exist even in the absence of outright coercion.

822. Flaschberger, Ludwig, and Reiterer, Albert F. **Der tägliche Abwehrkampf: Erscheinungsformen und Strategien der ethnischen Assimilation bei den Kärntner Slowenen**. Vienna: Wilhelm Braumüller, Universitäts-Verlagsbuchhandlung, 1980. 123p.

An examination of the social and political assimilatory pressures faced by the Carinthian Slovenes. In recent years, the Slovenes in Austria have shown greater resilience than expected. Qualitative analysis is followed by an empirical study based on a 2% sample of the population age 16-69 in the Völkermarkt/Velikovec district. Seventy-five percent of those interviewed had at least a passive knowledge of Slovene.

823. **Gospodarsko-socialni problemi koroških Slovencev: predavanja in razprave pozimi 1973/74 v Domu prosvete v Tinjah** (Economic and Social Problems of Carinthian Slovenes: Lectures and Discussions Held in the Cultural Center of Tinje during the Winter of 1973/74). Tinje/Tainach: Dom prosvete v Tinjah, 1974. 109p.

Proceedings of a symposium held in Tainach/Tinje, Austria in 1974. Most of the contributors belong to the post-World War II generation of specialists. During the preceding two decades the Slovene-inhabited counties of Carinthia had experienced a rapid decline of the agricultural labor force. The main problem resulting from this development is that the Slovene minority's institutional influence has failed to keep pace with rapid structural change and remains limited to agriculture— hence the strongly felt need for gaining representation in the existing semi-public bodies which regulate the activities of the nonagricultural sector.

824. **Raumplanungsgespräch Südkärnten**. Vienna: Slowenisches Wissenschaftliches Institut, 1977. 197p.

The publication provides the proceedings of a symposium on regional planning in the Slovene-inhabited region of southern Carinthia in Austria. The symposium was held in Vienna in January 1977.

Language and Literature

825. Detela, Lev. **Povojni slovenski koroški pesniki in pisatelji; obrazi sodobne koroške književnosti v slovenskem jeziku: Esejistična razmišljanja o slovenski povojni literaturi v Avstriji** (Postwar Slovene Carinthian Poets and Writers; Portraits from Contemporary Slovene Literature in the Slovene Language: Essay Reflections on the Slovene Postwar Literature in Austria). Celovec/Klagenfurt: Družba sv. Mohorja v Celovcu, 1977. 149p.

Offered here are essays on the work of nine contemporary Carinthian-Slovene literary figures, an introduction, and a concluding overview. There is a German summary as well as a bibliography of other essays on Carinthian-Slovene literature by the author, a literary critic and free-lance writer now living in Vienna.

826. Obid. Vida. **Die slowenische Literatur in Kärnten seit 1945**. Disertacije in razprave, 1. Klagenfurt/Celovec: Slovenski znanstveni inštitut, 1979. 63p.

The author surveys contemporary Slovene literature in Carinthia, Austria. Focus is on individual authors, in particular those of the group contributing to the literary review *Mladje* (Celovec/Klagenfurt).

Education and Cultural Affairs

827. Moritsch, Andreas. "History Teaching in Austria and Carinthia: A Slovene Perspective." *Nationalities Papers* 7:2 (1979): 147-53.

Moritsch, a Slovene-speaking native of Carinthia and a professor at the University of Vienna's Institute for Eastern European History and Balkan Studies, evaluates the treatment of Slovene history in the curriculum of Austrian and particularly Carinthian schools. He makes concrete proposals for improvements, particularly in regard to the treatment of the role of Slovenes in the history of Carinthia.

828. Zorn, Tone. "Manjšinska šolska problematika na avstrijskem Koroškem" (Problems about Minority Education in Austrian Carinthia). *Razprave in gradivo* 7-8 (1976): 125-33.

The discussion centers on the so-called utraquist schools of interwar Austria, which served the purpose of Germanizing the Slovene population. Mandatory bilingual education was introduced after World War II and discontinued in 1958, resulting in unfavorable consequences for the Carinthian Slovenes.

Religion

829. **Das gemeinsame Kärnten—Skupna Koroška: Dokumentation des deutsch-slowenischen Koordinationsausschusses der Diözese Gurk.** Klagenfurt: Deutsch-slowenischer Koordinationsausschuss des Diözesenrates, 1974. 154p.

A collection of contributions of German-Austrian and Slovene-Austrian authors pertaining to the Catholic religious community in Carinthia, Austria.

8 _____ National Minorities in Bulgaria, 1919-1980

Peter John Georgeoff,
with the assistance of David Crowe (Jews)

HISTORICAL SUMMARY

Bulgaria may be considered, in a sense, an exception among the Balkan nations, for its minority population constitutes only about 10% of the total. Compared to Yugoslavia, where no ethnic group has a majority, Bulgaria becomes almost a homogeneously ethnic state. In another sense, Bulgaria may be considered one of the most ethnically heterogeneous states in the Balkans. Unlike Yugoslavia, which is formed by a federation of constituent republics and autonomous regions which possess considerable internal administrative independence and whose political boundaries are based largely on ethnic nationality, Bulgaria is a centralized nation. Its administrative subdivisions, which in the past have been changed frequently, are largely determined on the basis of economic, geographic, historic, political, and administrative reasons, rather than ethnicity.

The distribution of the ethnic minorities in Bulgaria is such that the formation of political subdivisions on the ethnic principle is not feasible. Moslem Turkish villages, Moslem Bulgarian villages, and Bulgarian and Turkish Christian Orthodox settlements may exist in the same area. Indeed, Moslem and Christian, Bulgarian and Turk, and Romanian and Tatar often live side by side in the same village.

The heterogeneity of Bulgaria's population is due to at least two important factors. The first is Bulgaria's strategic location on one of the great world travel routes between Asia, Africa, and Europe. The second factor follows from the first: because Bulgaria is so situated, many peoples have passed through her territory as travelers, traders, invaders, and conquerors; and all have left their mark. Thracians, Greeks, and Romans all have been there, and all have left remains of their civilization. However, the Turks, by their conquest and subjugation of the Bulgarian people for nearly five hundred years, exerted the most profound effect upon the land and its inhabitants. Mosques and minarets are reminders of this time, as are the minorities that remain in Bulgaria.

The Ottoman invasion profoundly changed the characteristics of the population of the territory of contemporary Bulgaria. Turkish lords and managers of the newly acquired Bulgarian lands came to stay. Accompanying them were retinues of followers and a permanent force of soldiers to secure the fruits of their conquest. The Turks became, and remain, the largest ethnic minority in Bulgaria. This statement is all the more remarkable given the fact that, since Bulgaria's liberation, there has been a constant, though a numerically uneven exodus from Bulgaria to Turkey.

In addition, the Turkish conquest brought to Bulgaria other ethnic groups, for Turkish sovereignty opened up Bulgaria to them. Greeks from Byzantium, a state that previously had been at almost perpetual odds with the Bulgarian rulers, were now able to settle in Bulgaria because Byzantium, too, shortly became Ottoman. Armenians came when their ancient homeland was incorporated into the Ottoman empire. Later the Jews came, fleeing the fierce pogroms of the Spanish Inquisition.

The arrival of the Turks permitted still another ethnic element to enter the Balkans. Gypsies whose origins were in India came from Persia, Egypt, Syria, and other territories that had become part of the Ottoman empire as early as the fourteenth century through Constantinople to Bulgaria, where they have remained.

The indigenous Bulgarian population fell upon difficult days after the Turkish conquest. Suffering and misery abounded throughout the land. As *rayahs* (non-Moslem serfs), they were required to work the land for the Turkish overlords. At the same time, there remained an avenue of escape. They could become Moslems, in which case they would be granted Ottoman citizenship with all the rights and privileges which such citizenship entailed; and some chose this route. As soon as the land was conquered, some Bulgarians accepted Islam, thus preserving their lives and possessions. Others resisted, only to succumb later as the pressure for conversion to Islam increased until it peaked in the seventeenth century.

These Ottoman efforts at proselytizing succeeded most among the Bulgarian peasantry of the Rhodopi Mountains, where Islam was accepted on a grand basis. This group, known as the Pomaks, and as Bulgarian-Mohammedans, remains an important religious minority in Bulgaria. The Pomaks speak Bulgarian, not Turkish, and their customs, traditions, and culture are essentially Bulgarian.

Another large group in Bulgaria is the Macedonians. However, whether they are a separate ethnic group or not remains in dispute. The language that they speak is very similar to Bulgarian, and historically and presently the

Bulgarians consider it to be a dialect of Bulgarian. Macedonian history, customs, and traditions are similar to those of Bulgaria, except that Bulgaria was liberated from Turkish rule in 1878, while Macedonia became free only in 1912.

Bulgaria welcomed Macedonian immigrants, both political refugees and students, even before Bulgarian independence, and they have assumed an active role in Bulgarian life. At times, members of the Bulgarian cabinet, including prime ministers, have been of a Macedonian background. At the same time, not all Macedonians have considered themselves Bulgarian. Some have regarded themselves as Serbs, and others have accepted the Greek thesis that they are Greeks.

Given the confusion and conflicting claims, many Macedonians considered the best solution to be autonomy, an idea that gathered momentum in the twentieth century. The idea was seized upon during the Second World War by the Communist Partisan Fatherland Front, and a Macedonian republic was established for the part of historic Macedonia that was within Yugoslav territory. At the same time, attempts were made to encourage the expression of Macedonian ethnicity among Macedonians in Bulgaria, even to the extent of declaring themselves Macedonians in the Bulgarian census. After Tito's break with Stalin and Dimitrov's death, the Bulgarians began to suppress the idea of a separate Macedonian ethnicity, and the last census to include this item, or indeed any item regarding ethnicity, was the one of December 1956. Since that time there have been bitter denunciations and recriminations between Sofia and Belgrade over the question of a separate Macedonian ethnicity.

Another ethnic element in the Bulgarian population is the Romanians, of which there are several types. A few descendants of Romanians who settled in Bulgaria from the provinces of Wallachia and Moldavia are still found, primarily around Vidin, Kula, Svishtov, and in Southern Dobrudja, where they are known as "Vlachs" (*Vlasi* in Bulgarian). Their number is not large, for most Romanians living in Bulgaria were repatriated in population exchanges that took place during the first half of this century.

A second type of Romanian is a group of nomadic shepherds in the Rhodopi Mountains who also call themselves "Vlachs." Their real ancestry is in much dispute: they may be Romanized Dacians as the Romanians claim, or Romanized Greeks as some Greeks contend. At any rate, they speak a version of Romanian that is unlike that spoken by the inhabitants of Romania. The group is also known as *Latinci* or "Latins" among the Bulgarians, as Arumanians or "Aromanians" by the Romanians of Romania, as "Tsintsars" by the Serbs, as "Kuzovlachs" ("lame Vlachs") by the Macedonians, and as Sarakatchans by the Greeks after the village of Sarakovo in the Pindus Mountains where many of them lived. All of these names are used in the literature at one time or another in referring to these people.

A third related group that needs to be noted here is that of the nomadic "Karakatchans" (*Karakachani*), whose way of life and cultural patterns are similar to those of the Vlachs and with whom they may indeed well have common origins. This group has Greek as its mother tongue, and its first identifiable beginnings appear to be in the region of the Pindus Mountains of Greece. Their ethnicity being in question, the Greeks claim them as Greeks, the Bulgarians as Hellenized Thracians, and the Romanians as Hellenized Dacians.

Several distinctly Slav ethnic groups have also made their temporary or permanent home in Bulgaria. Contacts between Russia and Bulgaria at times have been very close. In fact, Bulgaria's independence from the Ottoman Turks can be attributed to a considerable extent to the support which the Bulgarians received from the Russians. As a result, Russians have lived in Bulgaria from the nineteenth century as businessmen, diplomats, and emigrés. However, their number drastically increased after the Russian Revolution, when a large group of "White" Russian political exiles found asylum in Bulgaria. Many left after a time, but some remained, only to be "repatriated" to the Soviet Union after Russian forces moved into Bulgaria during World War II. Presently the Russians that reside in Bulgaria are on temporary assignment in a military, diplomatic, economic, cultural, or other advisory capacity. Most intend to remain in Bulgaria only as long as their tour of duty requires.

Other Slavic ethnic groups in Bulgaria were the Czechs and to a lesser extent the Slovaks, both of whom had important "colonies" in Bulgaria beginning in the latter half of the nineteenth century. By the early 1920s a lively and prosperous Czech colony existed in Bulgaria, with its own businesses, banks, libraries, newspapers, schools, and churches, and the Slovaks were close behind. The end of World War II brought an end to the Czech and Slovak settlements in Bulgaria. In the postwar population adjustments, most of these groups were repatriated to Czechoslovakia.

Another minority group in Bulgaria, one of considerable importance, is the Armenians, whose coming to Bulgarian territory shortly after the Turkish conquest has already been noted. Engaged primarily in trade and commerce, Armenians lived mostly in larger towns and cities and constituted a small but important minority in Bulgaria throughout the Ottoman period as well as after Bulgaria's liberation. Their numbers increased significantly in Bulgaria after World War I as a consequence of the Armenian massacres. Located as Bulgaria is, in juxtaposition to Turkey, many Armenian refugees sought sanctuary there. As a result, the Armenian population in Bulgaria grew significantly during the early twenties, even though many of them used the country only as a stopover on their way to western Europe and North America. Today, the Armenian minority in Bulgaria has dwindled to insignificance. After World War II, a mass repatriation of the Armenian population from Bulgaria to the Soviet Union took place, mostly to Soviet Armenia.

The Greeks once were an important minority group in Bulgaria. Greek trading outposts had been established from antiquity on the territory of what was to become modern Bulgaria. With the establishment of Ottoman rule in the Balkans, Greek merchants were able to obtain various privileges from the Turks and so to penetrate into the larger Bulgarian towns, where, like the Armenians, they established themselves as a vital part of the mercantile community. As a result of the Ottoman conquest, Bulgarian society was disorganized, and in the centuries that ensued, Greek influence in Bulgaria's religious, educational, and cultural life became strong. Greek churches and schools were established not only in the towns but in some of the larger villages. Thus the number of Greeks in Bulgaria grew to rival that of the Turks, and Greek hegemony threatened to overpower the Bulgarians. The Bulgarian renaissance, which took place in the eighteenth and nineteenth centuries, was as much a cultural and educational struggle against Greek influence as it was opposition to the Ottoman empire.

As a result of the secession of the Bulgarian Church from the Greek Patriarchate of Constantinople in 1860, the Greek influence in Bulgaria waned, and after Bulgaria's liberation in 1878 a number of Greeks left Bulgaria. The question of the Greek minority took on added and more intense dimensions during the Second Balkan War and reached near-crisis proportions after World War I. The situation was defused through an agreement for mass repatriations, in which most of the Greeks were repatriated to Greece and the Bulgarians in Greece were returned to Bulgaria. Thus, by the beginning of World War II, only a few thousand Greeks remained in Bulgaria, most of whom lived near the Greek-Bulgarian border. Relative numbers changed little as a result of the war, since the boundaries between Greece and Bulgaria remained substantially the same after the conflict.

Three other minorities in Bulgaria should be considered here. The first is the Gagauzi, a Turkic ethnic group that speaks Turkish but that belongs to the Eastern orthodox faith. They live primarily in the area of Varna and are not more than a few thousand in number.

The Tatars and the Circassians, two other minorities, were transplanted into Bulgaria by the Porte in 1861 and 1864, respectively. Two purposes were served by resettlement: refuge and defense. As Moslems, they received sanctuary in the Moslem-ruled Ottoman Europe. The Circassians fought a valiant rebellion against the Russians, only to be defeated; and rather than submit, most left their ancient homeland to seek refuge and resettlement in Turkey and her provinces, which included Bulgaria. Furthermore, the Porte welcomed them as co-religionists and as a large, trustworthy group to serve as a countervailing force against the Bulgarian population, especially in areas where the Turkish population was diminishing and the Bulgarian one was increasing. Most now live in villages in Dobrudja near the Bulgarian-Romanian frontier.

The minority problem in Bulgaria has been further complicated by religion. As previously noted, the Pomaks, who are ethnically Bulgarian, are Moslem. Indeed, they are perhaps the "purest" Bulgarian stock existent today, since as Moslems their women and girls were not violated by the Turkish forces of occupation as the Christians sometimes were. Yet, because of religious difference they remained until recently outside of the mainstream of life of the Bulgarian majority. On the other hand, the Gaugauzi are of Turkic ethnicity but belong to the Eastern Orthodox Christian faith. And the Gypsies belong to either one or the other, with about 75% being Moslem and the rest Eastern Orthodox. The Jews as an ethnic and religious minority are discussed separately.

Prior to the seizure of power by the Bulgarian Communists, the Bulgarian Eastern Orthodox Church was the national church. However, there still are small minorities of Catholics and Protestants, the latter being divided into several denominations. Catholicism in Bulgaria has its modern roots in the Bulgarian reawakening of the nineteenth century.

Partly in an attempt to break the fetters of the Greek Church in Bulgaria, and partly in an effort to bring Western enlightenment to Bulgaria, a number of prominent Bulgarians during this period sought popular support to reunite the Bulgarian Church to Rome. The movement failed, but Catholicism gained a foothold in Bulgaria, which was strengthened by subsequent missionary activities, primarily in education and medicine. At the time of the suppressions of foreign Catholic activities by the Communists in Bulgaria in 1952, there were three dioceses — in Plovdiv, Sofia, and Ruse; and hospitals, experimental farms, and schools were being conducted by various Catholic orders, notably the Carmelites, Ascenionists, and Lucharests. Although there has now been some relaxation of restrictions against the church, most of Bulgarian Catholicism continues to be indigenous in nature, with the largest part of the Catholic minority being found in and around Plovdiv.

Protestantism in Bulgaria flows from the great missionary movement in the United States during the mid-nineteenth century. At that time, American missionaries arrived in Ottoman-ruled Bulgaria, where they founded schools and churches. Shortly they became a strong, pro-Bulgarian voice in the West in the furtherance of Bulgaria's struggles for independence. Although Protestantism never gained a significant number of adherents in Bulgaria, it nevertheless exerted an influence on Bulgarian development out of proportion to its size, for a number of Bulgarian leaders and intellectuals during the latter part of the nineteenth century and first half of the twentieth century had gone to schools established by the Protestant missionaries.

At the time the Communists assumed power in Bulgaria, there were five significant Protestant denominations in Bulgaria: the Pentecostal, Methodist, Baptist, Congregational, and Adventist. Because of their ties with the West, and the United States in particular, these churches were deemed subversive. A number of ministers were either jailed or executed. Protestantism continues to exist in Bulgaria, although it is supervised and restricted. Recently several Protestant pastors were tried for activities inimical to the Bulgarian state — the smuggling and distribution of Bibles.

Most Protestants today live in Bulgaria's larger cities: Sofia, Plovdiv, Varna, Ruse, and Turnovo. Their existence is tolerated to the extent that they retain in indigenous basis, maintaining only such contacts with the West as may be approved by, and of interest to, the regime. Taken together, Protestants constitute Bulgaria's smallest religious minority.

In the bibliography that follows, annotated bibliographic citations have been included for all the minority groups noted in the preceding discussion. However, the number of citations, as well as the topics considered, varies for each minority group. In some cases, such as the "Macedonian minority" in Bulgaria, the citations listed are intended to be suggestive, being selective and representative of a far greater volume of literature. In other instances, fewer studies and articles about a group are available, so that bibliographic material about the group is limited to a few of the topics included in the bibliography. For this reason, not all categories contain material relating to each of Bulgaria's minority groups considered in this introduction. Although many studies have been done of minorities in Bulgaria, much work remains.

Some limitations and cautions should also be noted regarding the statistical information that is presented in the bibliographic sources. Much of the historical demographic data on the ethnic populations of the Balkans is unreliable, due to either the poor methodological techniques used or the political purpose of the data, or both. With some exceptions, hard data on Bulgaria's ethnic populations during the Ottoman period are unreliable and hard to come by. After the conquest, the ethnicity of the empire's subjects was not of immediate paramount importance to the Porte. By the time the subject

(Text continues on page 282.)

Estimated Population of Bulgaria

Record of the Census of January 1, 1893

Bulgarians	2,505,326
Turks	569,728
Romanians	62,628
Greeks	58,518
Gypsies	52,132
Spanish-speaking Jews	27,531
Tatars	16,290
Armenians	6,445
Germans and Austrians	3,620
Albanians	1,221
Russians	928
Czechs	905
Serbians	818
Italians	803
Not specific	3,820

Source: John Scott Keltie, ed. *The Statesman's Year-Book; Statistical and Historical Annual of the States of the World for the Year 1901*. London: Macmillan and Company, p. 1143.

Ethnic Minorities in Bulgaria

Population of Bulgaria in 1910

Bulgarians	3,518,756
Turks	465,641
Romanians	79,429
Greeks	43,275
Gypsies	122,296
Jews	40,133
Germans	3,402
Russians	2,505
Other nationalities	62,076

Source: John Scott Keltie and M. Epstein, eds. *The Statesman's Year-Book: Statistical and Historical Annual of the States of the World for the Year 1921*. London: Macmillan and Company, 1921, p. 728. From the census of December 31, 1910.

National Composition According to Language or Ethnic Affiliation:
Bulgaria, 1934-1965

Native Tongue or Ethnic Affil.	1934		1946	1956	1965	
	I[a]	II[a]	II[b]	II[b]	II[b]	III[b]
Total Population	6,077,939	6,077,939	7,029,349	7,613,709	8,226,564	8,227,866
Percent	100.0%	100.0%	100.0%	100.0%	100.0%	100.0%
Bulgarian	5,274,854	5,204,217	6,073,124	6,506,541	7,259,147	7,231,243
Percent	86.8%	85.6%	86.4%	85.4%	88.2%	87.9%
Pomak	c	...	...	...	...	...
Percent		...	...	...	...	...
Turk	618,268	591,193	675,500	656,025	746,755	780,928
Percent	10.2%	9.7%	9.6%	8.6%	9.1%	9.5%
Jewish	28,026	...	...	...	...	5,108
Percent	0.5%	...	...	...	...	0.1%
Russian	11,928	...	...	...	...	10,815
Percent	0.2%	...	...	...	...	0.1%
Greek	9,601	...	...	...	...	8,241
Percent	0.2%	...	...	...	...	0.1%
Serb	172	...	...	...	...	577
Percent	0.0%	...	...	...	...	0.0%
German	4,171	...	...	...	...	795
Percent	0.1%	...	...	...	...	0.0%
Macedonian	...	...	...	187,789	8,750	9,632
Percent	...	...	...	2.5%	0.1%	0.1%
Armenian	23,045	...	...	...	...	20,282
Percent	0.4%	...	...	...	...	0.2%
Romanian	16,405	...	...	...	...	763
Percent	0.3%	...	...	...	...	0%
Tatar	4,377	...	...	...	...	6,430
Percent	0.1%	...	...	...	...	0.1%
Gypsy	80,532	...	...	...	...	148,874
Percent	1.3%	...	...	...	...	1.8%
Other	6,560	...	...	...	...	4,178
Percent	0.1%	...	...	...	...	0.0%
Undetermined	0	282,529	280,725	263,354	211,912	0
Percent	0%	4.7%	4.0%	3.5%	2.6%	0%
Unaccounted for	0	0	0	0	0	0
Percent	0%	0%	0%	0%	0%	0%

Notes: a: Nationality determined by native tongue. *b:* Nationality determined by ethnic affiliation. *c:* In 1934, 134,125 Moslems spoke Bulgarian; the majority of these persons were Pomaks. The 1926 census recorded 102,351 persons of Pomak ethnicity.

Source: Paul S. Shoup. *The East European and Soviet Data Handbook.* © 1981, Columbia University Press. Reprinted by permission.

became of real concern to the Ottomans, particularly during the nineteenth-century national revivals in the Balkans, population figures had become highly suspect, with each national group skewing the data to advance its own national purpose. The situation intensified after Bulgaria's independence and the national conflicts which ensued between Bulgaria and her Balkan neighbors.

The problem still confronts researchers studying the ethnic minorities of Bulgaria. For instance, after World War II, when diplomatic relations between Bulgaria and Yugoslavia were rather close, the population of the Pirin area of Bulgaria, in particular, was encouraged to call itself "Macedonian," and it was so designated in the census. As the situation worsened between the two countries, the number of "Macedonians" in Bulgaria diminished to insignificance. Indeed, the last census to include this information, or any other information regarding the size of Bulgaria's ethnic minorities, was the one for December 1956. Since that time, no figures on ethnicity have been published by the Bulgarians except those relating to emigration and immigration.

Even when population data on ethnicity were published, the question of what constituted an ethnic group was often a moot point for other groups besides the Macedonians. For instance, the Gypsies, who prefer to be known as "Romanies," consider themselves a separate ethnic group, but Bulgarian government policy regards them as "Bulgarians," and they have been identified as such in the census.

Perhaps the most reliable of the statistics on ethnicity are those relating to the exchanges of minorities during the 1920s and 1930s, since the exchanges were supervised by neutral international commissions. Even so, the usefulness of the data is limited, for they are concerned primarily with the ethnic populations that were transferred, not those that remained. Thus, the data on minorities, ethnic and religious, are subject to limitations and must always be used with care.

Jews

Bulgaria's Jewish community enjoyed a modicum of economic and cultural success until the Holocaust. Earliest statistics showed 14,342 Jews in Bulgaria in 1881. This number grew significantly with the Bulgarian acquisition of Eastern Rumelia six years later, and by 1900 the community had grown to 33,663. Proportionately, they made up 0.9% of the population at the turn of the century, with 95% in urban areas, particularly Sofia, which had over half of the country's Jewish population by 1934. By 1926, there were 46,558 Jews in Bulgaria; 48,398 in 1934; and 51,500 in 1943.[1]

Jewish life in Bulgaria, while modestly successful, did not find Jews well-integrated, since consistent government, social, and economic policies discouraged an active Jewish role in Bulgarian society. But by the end of the nineteenth century, stimulated primarily by Zionist influences, Jewish culture began to thrive. Zionists helped develop an educational system for the Bulgarian Jewish community that emphasized Jewish studies, and under the direction of the Jewish Central Consistory, Bulgarian Jews created a three-tiered educational system that began with kindergarten and ended with the *pro gymnasium*. The Jewish community provided 80% of the funding for this system, while the rest came from local and national governmental sources.

Enrollment in these schools grew impressively after World War I, and their success became a source of pride to the Jewish community.[2]

Another unique characteristic of Bulgaria's Jewish minority was its relatively insignificant role in the country's economic life. Those involved in Bulgaria's business life concentrated their efforts in the import/export business, and even then they made up only 2% of those engaged in commerce in Bulgaria. Few were involved in government or professional work, nor could many be found among the country's intellectuals. Consequently, while Bulgaria's Jewish community, concentrated mostly in its urban areas, enjoyed a comfortable social and political life, it was not deeply integrated into Bulgarian society, which helped temper anti-Semitic feelings against it.[3]

Anti-Semitism spread in Bulgaria after 1933 with the growing economic influence of Germany and the return of Bulgarian students from Germany and Austria who had been infected by Nazi propaganda.[4] In addition, a Fascist movement emerged under Khristo Kunchev that followed German anti-Semitic patterns and called for moves against Jewish economic interests and, oddly, for the "removal of Jews from positions of influence."[5] Regardless, a strong body of anti-Semitic sentiment did not emerge until Bulgaria began to drift towards Germany after the Munich agreement. This and the Nazi-Soviet pact convinced the nation's leaders that only Hitler could provide Bulgaria with the opportunities to expand her frontiers.[6]

In mid-1940, Premier Bogdan Filov announced that his government intended to limit the rights of Bulgarian Jews, and this attitude was promulgated into the Law for the Protection of the Nation. In 1942, the Bulgarian government obtained power, under parliamentary protest, to deal freely with the Jews, and created a Commissariat for Jewish Affairs.[7]

In early 1943, SS officials arrived to help set up a deportation program for Bulgarian Jews. On February 2, 1943, the Bulgarian government agreed to surrender all Jews in the Macedonian and Thracian areas acquired by Bulgaria earlier. The figure included 8,000 from Macedonia, 6,000 from Thrace, and 6,000 from Old Bulgaria. The Thracian and Macedonian Jews were sent to death camps in Poland.[8] However, political opposition tempered by concern over the impact of Bulgarian participation in the Nazi campaign against the Jews and strong international protests hindered further German efforts to ship Jews from Old Bulgaria to Poland. The Germans did, however, succeed in having most of Sofia's Jews shipped to the countryside, and used forced Jewish labor in public works programs.[9]

By the end of 1943, the new Bulgarian government of Dobri Bozhilov had eased these restrictions, and on August 31, 1944, the new government of Ivan Bagrianov nullified all anti-Jewish legislation. Within a week the Soviet Union declared war on Bulgaria and quickly occupied it. It removed the Bulgarian government of Kosta Muraviev and replaced it with the Fatherland Front, which, after peace was concluded between Moscow and Sofia, revived the Jewish communal network under a Central Jewish Consistory with 34 communities under it. The consistory published a weekly newspaper, *Evreiski Vesti* (Jewish News), and organized an anti-Nazi political organization, the "Ilya Ehrenburg." Most remarkable, according to the consistory, were Bulgaria's post-Holocaust figures published in 1945, which showed that, with few exceptions, its Jewish population had survived the war.[10]

The new communist rulers were faced with a dilemma not experienced in other east European countries, where most Jews had died during the Holocaust. Unfortunately, efforts by the Jewish community to have property, businesses, and other goods restored to them, failed for the most part, even after the passage of the 1945 Law of Restitution. In addition, Bulgarian Jews found that Bulgaria's new rulers were unwilling to allow them to enjoy the unique cultural status that they had prior to World War II. The Communist-organized Central Jewish Committee of the Fatherland Front oversaw the activities of the Central Jewish Consistory to insure that it adhered strictly to official government policy on community matters. Bulgarian Zionists struggled to maintain an independent status in these representative bodies, though the Communists always remained the dominant force. As a result, by 1948 Bulgaria's Jews had lost control of their most significant cultural organs, and what remained were organized to adhere strictly to guidelines of Bulgaria's Communist regime. This, combined with the deteriorating economic status of the nation's Jews, as well as concern over the rise of anti-Semitism, stimulated many to consider emigration to Israel.[11] Illegal emigration had gone on since World War II, and by the end of 1948 almost 7,000 Jews had left the country. Over the next few years, emigration intensified, and by December 1951 there remained only 7,676 Jews in Bulgaria, over half in Sofia. By 1952, Jewish cultural autonomy ceased to exist, and their organs came under the complete control of the government.[12]

Notes

[1]N. M. Gelber, "Jewish Life in Bulgaria," *Jewish Social Studies* VIII:2 (April 1946): 106; Nora Levin, *The Holocaust: The Destruction of European Jewry, 1933-1945* (New York: Schocken Books, 1875), pp. 715-18; Lucy Dawidowicz, *The War against the Jews, 1933-1945* (New York: Bantam Books, 1975), p. 544; Frederick B. Chary, *The Bulgarian Jews and the Final Solution, 1940-1944* (Pittsburgh: The University of Pittsburgh Press, 1972), pp. 29, 58. See also Appendix I, pp. 203-7. Chary uses demographic statistics from the official Bulgarian Direction Generale de la Statistique, *Annuaire Statistique* 27 (1935).

[2]Gelber, "Jewish Life in Bulgaria," p. 119; Chary, *The Bulgarian Jews*, pp. 30-32.

[3]Nissan Oren, "The Bulgarian Exception: A Reassessment of the Salvation of the Jewish Community," in *Yad Vashem Studies* VII, ed. Livia Rothkirchen (Jerusalem: Yad Vashem, 1968), pp. 85-87; Levin, *The Holocaust*, pp. 548-49; Peter Meyer, "Bulgaria," in *The Jews in the Soviet Satellites*, ed. Peter Meyer, et al. (Syracuse, NY: Syracuse University Press, 1953), p. 566.

[4]Levin, *The Holocaust*, p. 549; Meyer, "Bulgaria," p. 567.

[5]Gelber, "Jewish Life in Bulgaria," p. 125.

[6]Levin, *The Holocaust*, p. 549; Oren, "The Bulgarian Exception," p. 89.

[7]Chary, *The Bulgarian Jews*, pp. 36-41, 53-54; Frederick B. Chary, "The Bulgarian Writers' Protest of October 1940 against the Introduction of Anti-Semitic Legislation into the Kingdom of Bulgaria," *East European Quarterly* IV:1 (March 1940): 89-90.

[8]Levin, *The Holocaust*, pp. 553-54; Chary says 4,075 Jews from Thrace, 158 from Pirot, and 7,160 from Macedonia were shipped to Poland (Chary, *The Bulgarian Jews*, p. 127). For further information on Bulgaria's dealing with the Macedonian and Thracian Jews, see Alexander Matkovski, "The Destruction of Macedonian Jewry in 1943," in *Yad Vashem Studies*, III (Jerusalem: Yad Vashem, 1959), pp. 203-58; and the recollections of Nadejda Slavi Vasileva, "On the Catastrophe of the Thracian Jews," in *Yad Vashem Studies*, III (Jerusalem: Yad Vashem, 1959), pp. 295-302.

[9]Chary, *The Bulgarian Jews*, pp. 142-52; *Encyclopedia Judaica*, Vol. 4 (New York: The Macmillan Company, 1971), pp. 1487-88.

[10]Chary, *The Bulgarian Jews*, pp. 174, 176-77; Meyer, "Bulgaria," p. 575.

[11]Meyer, "Bulgaria," pp. 592-94, 600-601.

[12]Ibid., pp. 606-7.

BIBLIOGRAPHY

Reference Material and Sources

830. Bulgaria, Ministerstvo na vunshnite dela i na izpovedaniiata. **The Bulgarian Question and the Balkan States.** Sofia: State Printing Press, 1919. 305p.

The volume seeks to document Bulgaria's claims to Macedonia, Dobrudja, and Eastern Thrace on the basis of history and ethnography. Included are detailed ethnographic maps of the populations in these areas.

831. Bulgaria, Ministerstvo na vunshnite raboti. **La vérité sur les accusations contre la Bulgaria.** 2 vols. in 1. Sofia: Imprimerie de l'État, 1919. 600p. + 126p.

Demographic yearbooks after about 1956 do not give any data regarding the ethnic composition of Bulgaria's population. However, except for an occasional lapse, detailed data regarding emigration and immigration have been provided by nationalities, with this information often including age group, sex, and country of emigration.

832. Dinev, Lubomir, and Mishev, Kiril. "Naselenie" ("Population"). In **Bulgariia: Kratka geografiia** (Bulgaria: A Brief Geography), pp. 153-81. Sofia: Nauka i izkustvo, 1975. 336p.

This general volume on the geography of Bulgaria contains a brief discussion of the ethnic composition of the population as of the mid-1970s. Areas where these minorities live are cited, as well as their percentages of the total population.

833. **Dogovor za mir** (Treaty of Peace). Sofia: Durzhavna pechatnitsa, 1919. 124p.

This is the Bulgarian publication, in both Bulgarian and French, of the Treaty of Neuilly. The problem relating to minorities and their protection is covered in chapter III, section IV. In other sections of the chapter, Bulgaria renounces any further claims to territories in Thrace. The volume also contains a copy of the separate convention between Greece and Bulgaria signed at the same time at Neuilly, which attempted to guarantee the unrestricted, voluntary emigration of each country's minorities to the other country.

834. Institut National de la Statistique et des Études Économiques. **Les minorités ethniques en Europe Centrale et Balkanique.** Paris, 1946. pp. 22-23.

This publication gives detailed statistical data about the minorities of the Balkans, including those in Bulgaria, and provides data about Southern Dobrudja after its return to Bulgaria in 1940.

835. Kesiakov, B. **Prinos kum diplomaticheskata istoriia na Bulgariia, 1878-1925** (A Contribution toward the Diplomatic History of Bulgaria, 1878-1925). 3 vols. Sofia: Pechanitsa "Rodopi," T. Klisarov, 1925.

These three volumes contain some of the most important documents relating to Bulgarian diplomatic history from 1878 to 1925, including those relating to minorities.

836. **Observations de la délégation bulgare sur le projet du Traité de Paix.** Paris: Peace Conference—Bulgaria, 1919.

The volume presents the Bulgarian position regarding the ethnic composition of the population of Dobrudja, Macedonia, and Thrace. The documents included served as Bulgarian position papers for the conference.

837. **Settlement of Bulgarian Refugees. Reports of the Commission of the League of Nations.** Vol. I, nos. 1-52 (Economic and Financial). Geneva: League of Nations, 1926-1939.

Although the material in these reports relates primarily to the settlement of Bulgarian refugees in Bulgaria, useful information is provided concerning the general exchange of minorities. The reports are written either in English or French.

838. **Statisticheski godishnik na Bulgarskoto Tsarstvo. Annuaire statistique de Royaume de Bulgarie** (Statistical Yearbook of the Kingdom of Bulgaria). Volumes 1-34, 1909-1942. Sofia: Glavna direkstiia na statistikata, 1910-1942. (Volumes 5-14, 1913-1922; 15-16, 1923-1924; 21-22, 1929-1930 were issued together.)

The contents vary somewhat from year to year. Different volumes provide detailed data regarding ethnicity, nationality, and religious adherence.

839. **Statisticheski godishnik na Narodna Republika Bulgariia** (Statistical Annual of the People's Republic of Bulgaria). 1947-1948- . Sofia: Tsentralno statistichesko upravlenie, 1948(?)- . Annual.

This annual supersedes *Statisticheski godishnik na Bulgarskoto Tsarstvo*. Russian and English translations of the text to be used with the tables in the main volume are published separately. Early volumes contain rather thorough data on minorities in Bulgaria. However, since the census of 1956, no further statistical information of this type has been published.

840. **Statisticheski spravochnik na N. R. Bulgariia, 1958** (Statistical Handbook of the P(eople's) R(epublic) (of) Bulgaria, 1958). Sofia: Tsentralno statistichesko upravlenie pri Ministerskiia suvet, May 1959.

Included in this little handbook are data on the major nationalities of Bulgaria, both in absolute numbers and in percentage of the total population, based on the census of 1956. No such data have appeared in any of the later handbooks.

Monographs and Articles

841. Bell, H. T. Montague. **The Near East Year Book and Who's Who, 1927: A Survey of the Affairs, Political, Economic, and Social, of Yugoslavia, Roumania, Bulgaria, Greece, and Turkey.** London: The Near East, ltd., [1927]. 944p.

The volume includes a brief but excellent chapter on religion in Bulgaria and provides statistical and descriptive information regarding the "Mohammedans" (Muslims), Jews, Armenians, Protestants, and Catholics.

842. Cary, William. **Bulgaria Today: The Land and the People.** New York: Exposition Press, 1965. 139p.

This is essentially a descriptive travel book of Bulgaria—which includes, however, two entire chapters on Bulgarian minorities. The volume is very sympathetic to the present Bulgarian government and its activities among these minorities.

843. Dinekov, Petur, ed. **Folklor, ezik, i narodna sudba** (Folklore, Language and National Fate). Sofia: Publishing House of the Bulgarian Academy of Science, 1979. 213p.

The volume is a collection of scholarly articles on Bulgarian folk-lore and folk-literature and their relationship to popular views and beliefs. Although the dominant Bulgarian ethnic group is stressed, other ethnic subgroups are included.

844. Dinev, L. "Naselenie" ("Population"). In **Geografiia na Bulgariia. Vol. II. Ikonomicheska geografiia**, pp. 3-20. Sofia: Bulgarskata akademiia na naukite, 1961.

Included in the chapter on the population of Bulgaria is an analysis of Bulgaria's ethnic composition. Changes in this composition from Bulgaria's liberation from Turkey in 1878 to about 1956 are analyzed.

845. **Dobrogea** (Dobrudja). Bucharest: Academia Romana, 1940. 369p.

This is a general survey in English of the region of Dobrudja. In addition to sections on its physical geography and its history, the populations and cultures of the area are described. A French edition of this volume was also published.

846. **Etnogenezis i kulturno nasledstvo na bulgarskiia narod. Sbornik** (Ethnogenesis and the Cultural Inheritance of the Bulgarian People. Essays). Sofia: Izdatelstvo na Bulgarska akademiia na naukite, 1971. 160p.

The volume is a collection of papers presented at a conference in May 1968 on the topic given in the title of the book. Although much of the material relates to the majority Slavic Bulgarian population, two papers are directly concerned with minorities in Bulgaria: "Turkskata kolonizatsiia i demografskite promeni v bulgarskite zemi" (Turkish Colonizations and Demographic Changes on Bulgarian Lands) and "Niiakoi cherti iz obichainoto pravo na rodopskite bulgari" (Some Highlights of the Common Law of the Rhodopi Bulgarians).

847. Genov, Georgi P. **Bulgaria and the Treaty of Neuilly**. Sofia: H. G. Danov & Co., 1935. 186p.

The book is an attack on the Treaty of Neuilly. Much statistical data are produced in an effort to prove that large portions of territory inhabited by Bulgarian majorities were given to Greece, Romania, and Yugoslavia. The question of minorities in Bulgaria is also considered at length, again with extensive and detailed data. Genov's volume is perhaps one of the best expressions in English of Bulgaria's position on the minority question after World War I. The German version of this volume appeared later as: Genoff, Prof. G. P. *Das Schicksal Bulgarians: Sein Kampf gegen Friedensdiktat von Neuilly*. Berlin: Carl Heymanns Verlag, 1940. 160p.

848. Haskins, Charles Homer, and Lord, Robert Howard. **Some Problems of the Peace Conference**. Cambridge, MA: Harvard University Press, 1920. 308p.

This general volume relates to the problems that resulted from the peace conferences following World War I, including those of the minorities in the Balkans, to which an extensive part of the volume is devoted. The problems of Dobrudja, Thrace, and Macedonia as they affected Bulgaria are given particular consideration.

849. Ishirkov, Anastas. **Les Bulgares en Dobroudja: aperçu historique et ethnographique**. Berne: Pochon-Jent & Buhler, 1919. 189p.

The author, a professor at the University of Sofia, presents a support of Bulgarian claims to Dobrudja on historical and ethnographic grounds.

850. Kolev, Nikolai Ivanov. **Bulgarska etnografiia** (Bulgarian Ethnography). Parts I and II. Veliko Turnovo: n.p., 1973.

A compendium of lectures on the subject of Bulgarian ethnography, including material specifically on several ethnic subgroups of the Bulgarian population.

851. Ladas, Stephen Pericles. **The Exchange of Minorities: Bulgaria, Greece, and Turkey.** New York: Macmillan, 1932. 849p.

This is a very comprehensive volume on the subject of the exchange of minorities among the above-named countries as it took place during the dozen or so years following World War I. Extensive statistical tables, charts, maps, and documents are included.

852. Logio, George Clenton. **Bulgaria: Problems and Politics.** London: William Heinemann, 1919. 285p.

This is a political study of the situation in Bulgaria immediately following World War I, focusing primarily on the nationality issue and Bulgaria's lost territories. It contains a good analysis of Bulgaria's territorial claims during this period of the Bulgarian, Greek, Serbian, and Romanian conflicts regarding the nationality questions and the minorities within their respective jurisdictions.

853. Maday, Bela C., ed. "Anthropology in East-Central and Southeast Europe." *East European Quarterly* IV (1970): 237-367.

Based mainly on a symposium of east European anthropology held at the annual meeting of the American Anthropological Association in 1967 and on subsequently written articles by anthropologists in eastern Europe and in the United States, this is a collection of papers dealing with the structure and activities of ethnocultural anthropology in seven European countries, including Bulgaria. The article on Bulgaria is by Phillip V. R. Tilney and is entitled "Ethnographic Research in Bulgaria."

854. Manchev, Krust'o. **Bulgariia i neinite susedi, 1931-1939: Politicheski i diplomatischeski otnosheniia** (Bulgaria and Her Neighbors, 1931-1939: Political and Diplomatic Relations). Sofia: Izdatelstvo Nauka i iskustvo, 1978. 308p.

This is a diplomatic history of Bulgaria and her role in the Balkan Pact written from a contemporary Marxist Bulgarian ideological perspective. Considerable attention is devoted to the minority question as it affected Bulgaria's diplomatic policy and posture during this period.

855. Markham, Reuben H. **Meet Bulgaria.** Sofia, 1931. 390p.

Written by an American sympathetic to Bulgaria, this volume has chapters on "The People" and "The Molding of the Bulgaria Nation," providing detailed descriptive and statistical data about minorities in Bulgaria and the historical reasons for their presence. Notes at the end of the volume further discuss the questions of Dobrudja and Macedonia.

856. Ognjanoff, Christo von. **Bulgarien.** Nürnberg: Glock und Lutz Verlag, 1976. 496p.

This is a general introduction to Bulgaria, its land, history, economy, and culture. The chapter entitled "Land und Volk" includes material on Bulgaria's minorities up to about the mid-1960s.

857. Papacosma, S. Victor. "Minority Questions and Problems in East European Diplomacy between the World Wars: The Case of Greece." *Nationalities Papers* VIII:1 (1980): 1-8.

This is a study of Greek efforts to make Greece's population more homogeneous through the forced transfer after World War I of other ethnic groups that were within the country. Ethnic Greeks from Bulgaria thus were resettled on Greek land left vacant when ethnic Bulgarians were transferred to Bulgaria. Greece's minority problems with Albania, Yugoslavia, and Turkey are also considered.

858. Razboinikov, Anastas. "Keshanska okoliia: Poselishten i etnografski prinos" (The Keshan Region: A Demographic and Ethnographic Contribution). *Izvestiia na etnografskiia institut s muzei* VI (1963): 49-60.

In this historical study of the Keshan Okoliia (District), statistical data are provided for the Okoliia going back to the early eighteenth century. Land ownership is compared in terms of Moslem and Christian villages. Other ethnographic and occupational data are included.

859. **Seeds of Conflict. Series I: Irredentist and Nationalist Questions in Central Europe, 1913-1939.** Vol. 2 and 3 in the series. Bulgaria I and Bulgaria II. Nendeln: Kraus Reprint, 1973.

These two volumes contain a collection of articles, newspaper accounts, commission reports, and monographs relating to the minority question and Bulgaria, covering both the Bulgarian minority living in the neighboring states and the ethnic groups of those states living in Bulgaria. *Bulgaria I* contains material relating primarily to the period from about 1913 to 1920. All points of view that affect Bulgarian minority questions are included in an attempt to focus on the issues which have led to irredentist aspirations of the Balkan powers and their participation in the two world wars. Most of the materials included are in French, English, German, or Esperanto.

860. Seton-Watson, Hugh. "Minorities and Mixed Populations." In **Eastern Europe between the Wars, 1918-1941**, 3rd ed., pp. 268-319. Hamden, CT: Archon Books, 1962. 425p.

This chapter is a general review of the minority questions in eastern Europe. Seton-Watson considers the problems of population exchange, Macedonia, and the German and Jewish minorities in particular.

861. Vakarelski, Khristo. **Dobrudzha** (Dobrudja). Sofia: Bulgarska akademiia na naukite. Etnografski institut i muzei, 1964. 424p. Map. Illus.

This volume is a comprehensive study of the life and peoples of Dobrudja, including information on their dress, means of livelihood, tools and implements, household utensils, etc. Noted in the descriptions are the Turks, Tatars, Gagauzes, and other groups.

Jews

General Reference Material, Sources, Serials

862. **Annual.** Published by the Obshchestvena Kulturno-Prosvetna Organizatsija na Evreite v Narodna Republika Bulgariia. Sofia: Tsentralno Rukovodstvo, 1966- .

Though its articles on modern Bulgarian Jewry tend to be overly doctrinaire, this series is a valuable contribution to Bulgarian studies. Its contributions on the earlier history of Bulgarian Jews are often quite valuable. Articles touch on every aspect of Bulgarian Jewish history and culture, and reflect an effort by the government and the small Bulgarian Jewish community to underline the uniqueness of its heritage.

863. **Borbata na bulgarskiia narod za zashtita i spasiavane na evreite v Bulgariia prez Vtorata svetovna voina: dokumenti i materiali** (The Struggle of the Bulgarian People to Save the Jews in Bulgaria during the Second World War: Documents and Materials). Edited by P. Popova, et al. Sofia: Bulgarska akademiia na naukite, institut za istoriia, 1978. 350p.

This extensive documentary collection begins with a historical survey of Bulgaria-Jewish relations in World War II, though the core of it is a collection of 192 documents drawn from Bulgarian, German, and Russian files on the Holocaust in Bulgaria and the status of the Jewish community in Bulgaria after World War II.

864. Central Consistory of Jews in Bulgaria. **Evrei zaginali v antifashistkata borba** (Jews Killed in the Anti-Fascist Battle). Sofia: Natsionalen Komitet na Otechestveniia Front, 1958. 366p.

Published in honor of the Jews who fought and died in the Bulgarian underground against the Germans, this memorial volume provides details on their role and, at times, heroism. It also has excellent information on certain aspects of Bulgarian partisan activities against German forces.

865. Central Consistory of Jews in Bulgaria. **Izlozhenie po Zakona za zashtitata na natsiiata** (Report on the Law for the Defense of the Nation). Sofia, 1940. n.p.

Located in the Jewish record section of the Bulgarian Academy of Sciences, this important document was one of the official Jewish responses to strong anti-Fascist statements made against the Jewish role in Bulgarian society after the passage of the Law for the Defense of the Nation. Its value lies in the important demographic and other statistics that appear throughout.

866. **Godishink** (Yearbook). Published by the Obshchestvena Kulturno-Prosvetna Organizatsija na Evreite v Narodna Republika Bulgariia. Sofia: Tsentralno Rukovodstvo, 1966- .

The yearbook has been published annually since 1966 by the General Cultural-Educational Organization of Jews in the People's Republic of Bulgaria, once the Bulgarian Jewish Consistory. Its articles on the Holocaust and Bulgaria tend to be nationalistic and appaud the positive role of the Bulgarian people in saving its Jewish population. Included are articles on the seizure of Jewish property during World War II.

867. Grinberg, Natan, ed. **Dokumenti ... vzlaga sa na komisarstvoto za evreiskite vprosi da izseli za Polska 20,000 evrei** (Documents of the Commissiariat Concerning the 20,000 Jews Sent to Poland). Sofia: Izdavoa Tsentralnata konsistariia na evreite w Bulgarija, 1945. 200p.

This is a valuable collection of documents on the History of Jews in Bulgaria during World War II that traces in detail the constant shifts in Bulgarian governmental policies towards the Jews. Many of the documents are rare Bulgarian files difficult to locate except in official Bulgarian archives. The author also has information on Bulgarian dealings with Thracian Jews.

868. Grinberg, Natan, ed. **Khitleristkiiat natisk za unishtozhavane na evreite ot Bulgariia** (Hitler's Pressures for the Extermination of the Jews of Bulgaria). Tel Aviv: "Amal," 1961. n.p.

A documentary account written by Grinberg after he immigrated to Israel from Bulgaria. The main portion of this large documentary collection is drawn from German files located in the archives of Yad Vashem. Grinberg argues that the Jews were saved because of the intervention of the Bulgarian people led by the Communist party. He is critical of the role of King Boris III in this matter. Grinberg worked for the new Commissariat for Jewish Questions established after the Soviets occupied Bulgaria in the fall of 1944, and this collection alludes to documents used by this organization to investigate crimes against the Jews during World War II.

869. Kosier, Ljubomir Stefan. **Statistika Jevreja u Jugoslaviji i Bugarskoj** (Statistics of the Jews in Yugoslavia and Bulgaria). Zagreb, Belgrade, and Ljubljana: "Kankarstvo": Ekonomska Biblioteka Srba, Hrvata i Slovenaca, 1930. 60p.

The detailed statistical data about the Jews in Yugoslavia and Bulgaria presented in this volume are accompanied by the author's extensive discussion and analysis. Much of the data are historical and geographical in nature or comparative in terms of the religions and populations of the two countries.

Monographs and Articles

870. Adeney, Rev. J. H. **The Jews of Eastern Europe**. London: Central Board of Missions and Society for Promoting Christian Knowledge, 1921. 94p.

This volume is a review of Christian missionary activities among the Jews of eastern Europe. The work of missionaries to the Jews of Bulgaria is discussed briefly.

871. Arditi, Benjamin. **Roliiata na Tsar Boris III pri izselvaneta na Evreite ot Bulgariia** (The Role of King Boris III in the Deportation of the Jews of Bulgaria). Tel Aviv, 1952. n.p.

This book strongly accentuates the role played by King Boris III to save Bulgaria's Jews from transportation to death camps in Poland during World War II. Unfortunately, its view is uncompromising, which has a negative influence on the scholarly merits of the book.

872. Arditi, Benjamin. **The Bulgarian Jews in the Years of the Nazi Regime, 1940-1944** (in Hebrew). Tel Aviv: Israel Press, 1962. 436p.

Arditi's second, and more substantial, study on Bulgarian Jewry in World War II emphasizes the importance of King Boris III in saving the country's Jewish population from extermination. It provides excellent coverage of the history of the formulation and implementation of anti-Jewish legislation in Bulgaria, highlighted by the Law for the Protection of the Nation of January 23, 1941, and has good material on the organization and leadership of the Jewish underground community.

873.   Baruth, Eli. **Iz istoriiata na bulgarskoto evreistovo** (From the History of the Bulgarian Jews). Tel Aviv, 1960. n.p.

This is a history of Bulgaria's Jews, with important sections on their plight in World War II. For example, the author goes into some detail on the implementation and subsequent protest against the anti-Jewish Law for the Defense of the Nation.

874.   Blagoeva, Snezhana. **Bulgarian Jewellery** (sic). Sofia: Septemvri Publishing House, 1977. 88p.

This is a brief introduction in English to the subject of Bulgarian Jewry. The volume consists of an introductory survey of the topic followed by elaborate colored plates with detailed descriptions for each. Jewry from the Rhodopi Mountain region and from Macedonia are included, but unfortunately none from other ethnic groups and regions in the country.

875.   "Bulgaria." In **Hitler's Ten-Year War on the Jews**, pp. 112-26. New York: Institute of Jewish Affairs of the American Jewish Congress and World Jewish Congress, 1943.

A brief account of the Jewish situation in Bulgaria prior to World War II and up to the early months of 1943.

876.   Chary, Frederick B. **The Bulgarian Jews and the Final Solution, 1940-1944.** Pittsburgh, PA: The University of Pittsburgh Press, 1972. 246p.

This is the definitive study of the Holocaust in Bulgaria. It is based on records in the General Cultural-Educational Organization of the Jews in the People's Republic of Bulgaria, which draw on some material from the Bulgarian Central State Historical Archives as well as files from the Bulgarian Academy of Sciences. Equally important are records from the files in Bulgaria from Yad Vashem in Jerusalem plus German archives in the National Archives of the United States. Chary provides an excellent general survey of Jewish conditions in Bulgaria after 1934, though the core of his excellent study centers on a detailed analysis of the status of Jews in that country during World War II. This story is particularly significant because traditional Bulgarian Jewish population was the only one to survive World War II intact except for that exterminated in the Bulgarian occupied territories of Thrace and Macedonia who were sent to Hitler's death camps. It contains a valuable collection of charts and an important bibliography.

877.   Gelber, Natar Michael. "Jewish Life in Bulgaria." *Jewish Social Studies* VIII:2 (April 1946): 103-26.

An excellent early post-World War II article on the history of the Bulgarian Jewish community from 1878 through the early 1930s. The author used available demographic statistics to document the place and significance of Jews in Bulgarian society during this period. His work provides an important demographic and statistical overview of the Bulgarian Jewish community *vis-à-vis* Bulgarian society during the first 54 years of independence. The article contains a number of important charts as well as a good selection of footnotes.

878.   Koen, Albert, and Assa, Henri. **Le sauvetage des Juifs en Bulgarie: 1941-1944**. (Translation of *Spasiavaneto na evreite v Bulgariia*). Sofia: Editions Septemvri, 1977. 200p.

Koen and Assa present a history of the Jews in Bulgaria during World War II and describe the successful efforts of the Bulgarian nation to save them from extermination by the Nazis.

879.   Konfino, Barukh. **Aliyah Set: From the Shores of Bulgaria 1938-1940, 1947-1948; The End of the Bulgarian Diaspora 1948-1949** (in Hebrew). Jerusalem: Achiasal Publishing House, 1965. 135p.

This volume details the various emigrations of Bulgarian Jews to Palestine before, during, and after World War II.

880.   Kosier, Ljubomir Stefan. **Jevreji u Jugoslaviji i Bugarskoj** (The Jews in Yugoslavia and Bulgaria). Zagreb, Belgrade, and Ljubljana: Ekonomska Biblioteka Srba, Hrvata i Slovenaca, 1930. 408p.

Kosier's in-depth study of the Jews in Yugoslavia and Bulgaria includes a discussion of their religion and religious customs, nationality and assimilation, commerce, banking, trades, and social conditions, and a history of the Balkan Peninsula. A chapter presenting extensive statistical data is included. See also entry 869.

881.   Leviev, Misho, ed. **Natasha blagadar nost** (Our Thanks). Sofia: Sbornik "kadima," 1946.

This collection deals with the history of Bulgarian Jews during World War II.

882.   Levin, Nora. "Bulgaria." In **The Holocaust: The Destruction of European Jewry, 1933-1945**, edited by Nora Levin, pp. 548-60. New York: Thomas Y. Crowell, 1968.

This chapter is a brief, but comprehensive survey of developments in Bulgaria during World War II which resulted in the saving of Bulgaria's Jewish citizens and of the events in Bulgarian-occupied territory which culminated in the almost total extermination of the Jews there.

883.   Matkovski, Alexander. "The Destruction of Macedonian Jewry." *Yad Vashem Studies* III (Jerusalem, 1959): 203-58.

Matkovski's important article is based on official military files in Yugoslavia and official investigations of the Holocaust in Macedonia. Many of the documents are also available at Yad Vashem in Jerusalem.

884.   Matkovskj, Aleksander. **Tragediiata na evreite od Makedoniia** (The Tragedy of the Jews of Macedonia). Skopje: "Kultura," 1962. 101p.

This is an expanded version of the author's article that appeared in *Yad Vashem Studies* three years earlier (entry 883). Matkovski discusses in scholarly depth the incarceration and ultimate destruction of Macedonian Jews under Bulgarian occupation during World War II. He gives a vivid description of their life at Skopje, their principal concentration camp prior to their deportation to Poland in 1943.

885.   Meyer, Peter. "Bulgaria." In **The Jews in the Soviet Satellites**, edited by Peter Meyer, et al., pp. 557-621. Syracuse, NY: Syracuse University Press, 1953.

A section of the volume presents an overview of Jewish life in pre-World War II Bulgaria, the Jewish situation in Bulgaria during World War II, the postwar economic, social, and political conditions of the Jews there, and the reasons that most of them decided to emigrate to Israel.

886. Mezan, Saul. **Les Juifs Espagnols en Bulgarie**. Vol. 1: **Histoire, statistique, ethnographie**. Sofia: Imprimerie "Amischpat," 1925. 150p.

This volume deals with the history of Sephardic Jews in Bulgaria through the 1920s. It includes a valuable collection of statistics and other materials.

887. Miller, Marshall L. **Bulgaria during the Second World War**. Stanford, CA: Stanford University Press, 1975. 304p.

The author includes one brief chapter on the "Jewish question," which provides a balanced overview of the subject.

888. Oliver, Khaim D. **We Were Saved: How the Jews in Bulgaria Were Kept from the Death Camps**. Translation of *Nie spasenite*. Second revised supplemented edition. Sofia: Sofia-Press, 1978. 208p.

This volume is a history of the Jews in Bulgaria during the Second World War. It discusses how the Jews were able to avoid extermination by the Nazis, and is highlighted by collections of documents and photographs.

889. Oren, Nissan. "The Bulgarian Exception: A Reassessment of the Salvation of the Jewish Community." *Yad Vashem Studies*, VII (Jerusalem, 1968): 83-106.

This is one of the definitive short studies in English on Bulgarian Jews during the Holocaust. The author begins with an overview of Jewish life in Bulgaria during the interwar period, while the bulk of the study centers on the role played by the Bulgarian government, its political factions, and the Jewish community in efforts to keep Old Bulgaria's Jews from being shipped to death camps elsewhere. He also discusses the controversies that have emerged since World War II over the role played by King Boris and others in these successful efforts. This is a well-documented study that integrates the most significant scholarly works on the topic available at the time.

890. Oschlies, Wolf. **Bulgarien, land ohne Antisemitismus**. Erlangen, Germany: Ner-Tamid-Verlag, 1976. 168p.

This is an expanded version of the author's *Bulgariens Juden in Vergangenheit und Gegenwart* (1972). The early portion of the book deals with the history of Bulgarian Jewry between 1878 and 1939, while the core of it centers on their history during the Holocaust. Oschlies pays attention to the successful efforts of the government to save the Jews of Old Bulgaria and its failure to do the same for the Jews of Thrace and Macedonia. The documents and the bibliographical information in this study add to the history of Bulgarian Jewry.

891. Oschlies, Wolf. "Die Tragödie der mazedonischen Juden." In **Bulgarien, Land ohne Antisemitismus**, pp. 66-76. Erlangen, Germany: Ner-Tamid-Verlag, 1976. 168p.

A brief section that attempts to explain the reasons for the nearly total extermination of the Jews in Bulgarian-occupied Macedonia during World War II.

892. Piti, Buko, ed. **Bulgarskata obshtestvenost za rasizma i antisemitizma** (Bulgarian Public Opinion on Racism and Anti-Semitism). Sofia: n.p., 1937. 203p.

Published in the midst of growing anti-Semitism that was, for the most part, imported from other parts of Europe, this volume is a collection of comments by prominent Bulgarians who attacked this new mood. It attempts to explain the historical reasons for the lack of significant anti-Semitism in Bulgaria.

893.   **Prouchvaniia za istoriiata na evreiskoto naselenie v bulgarskite zemi XV-XX vek: (sbornik statii)** (Studies on the History of the Jewish Population on Bulgarian Lands [from the] XV-XX Centuries: A Collection of Articles). Edited by Nikolai Todorov, et al. Sofia: BAN, 1980. 319p.

A collection of essays on the history of Jews in Bulgaria from the fifteenth to the twentieth century.

894.   Pundarev, Aleksandr N. **Evreite v Bulgariia i v sveta** (The Jews in Bulgaria and in the World). Sofia, 1940. n.p.

An anti-Jewish pamphlet published after the implementation of the ZZN (Law for the Defense of the Nation) that tried to show through economic arguments that the Jews had played an inordinately powerful and exploitative role in Bulgarian society.

895.   Reitlinger, Gerald. "Bulgaria." In **The Final Solution: The Attempt to Exterminate the Jews of Europe 1939-1945**, edited by Gerald Reitlinger, pp. 379-84. New York: The Beechhurst Press, 1953.

This is a brief account of the saving of the Bulgarian Jews and of the extermination of the Jews in Bulgarian-occupied territory.

896.   Romano, Albert, et al., eds. **The Jews of Bulgaria** (in Hebrew). Jerusalem and Tel Aviv: Encyclopedia of the Jewish Diaspora, 1968.

This large memorial volume in Hebrew contains a number of valuable articles on Jewish history in Bulgaria. One of the more significant entries is a lengthy account by Chaim Kishales on the various questions and theories about the salvation of Bulgaria's Jews during World War II. Kishales' work is based on a larger study by him (*It Happened in Those Days: Notes on the Life of the Jews in Bulgaria during the Period 1939-1950*), in Hebrew, located at Yad Vashem in Jerusalem. This volume also includes an excellent study on Zionism in Bulgaria, and a good history of Jewish communities in that country.

897.   Tamir, Vicki. **Bulgaria and Her Jews: The History of a Dubious Symbiosis**. New York: Sepher-Hermon Press for Yeshiva University Press, 1979. 314p.

Tamir presents a history of Bulgarian Jewry from its inception in the seventh century until after World War II, of which two-thirds is devoted to the twentieth century. Though it lacks some scholarly virtues, it remains an important contribution to the history of the Bulgarian Jewish community. A section of bibliographical notes and a collection of documents are included.

898.   Tonchev, Todor. **Osnovatelen li e u nas antisemitizmut?** (Is Anti-Semitism Deep-Rooted among Us?). Sofia, 1938. 50p.

This little booklet is a defense of the Bulgarian Jews, in which their patriotism, as well as their contributions to Bulgarian economic, cultural, social, and religious life, is shown in historical perspective.

899.   Topalov, Vladislav. "L'opinion publique bulgare contre les persectuions des juifs (Octobre 1940—9, Septembre 1944)." In **Études Historiques a l'occasion du XXII Congrès Internationale des Sciences Historiques Vienna, août—septembre, 1965.** II. Sofia: BAN, 1965.

   Topalov's article discusses the role of Bulgarian public sentiment in efforts to halt the shipment of the country's Jewish population to death camps in other parts of eastern Europe.

900.   Tsion, Daniel. **Pet godini pod fashistki gnet: Spomeni** (Five Years under Fascist Terror: Memoirs). Sofia, 1945. 80p.

   Written by the former chief rabbi of Bulgaria, this account of Jewish life in Bulgaria during World War II includes an excellent study of life in the Somovit concentration camp. Rabbi Tsion was relieved of his position, according to this study, because he attempted to relay to Soviet and Orthodox leaders a warning from God about the persecution of the Jews.

Macedonians

901.   Anastasoff, Christ. **The Bulgarians from Their Arrival in the Balkans to Modern Times: Thirteen Centuries of History.** Hicksville, NY: Exposition Press, 1977. 380p.

   This history of Bulgaria devotes several chapters to the question of Macedonia and the Macedonians—from antiquity to the post-World War II period. Written in a highly partisan style, the volume is a good statement of the historic position of Bulgaria toward Macedonia and her inhabitants.

902.   Anastasoff, Christ, ed. **The Case for an Autonomous Macedonia: A Symposium.** Indianapolis, IN: Central Committee of the Macedonian Political Organization of the United States and Canada, 1945. 206p.

   The volume consists of statements, documents, maps, and ethnographic data favoring the thesis that the Macedonians are Bulgarians rather than a separate ethnic group and that autonomy would be a solution to the "Macedonian Question."

903.   Anastasoff, Christ. **The Tragic Peninsula: A History of the Macedonian Movement for Independence since 1878.** St. Louis, MO: Blackwell Wielandy, 1938. 369p.

   A history of Macedonia from about 1878 to the late 1930s that is highly sympathetic to Bulgarian claims on Macedonia.

904.   **Artǎ populara a aromanilor din Dobrogea** (Folk-Art of the Aromanians of Dobrudja). Bucharest: "Meridiane," 1979. 38p.

   This volume contains a brief description of Macedonian-Romanic folk-art of Dobrudja. Topics discussed include: costumes and clothing, tools, house decorations, utensils, and ornamental jewelry. A bibliography is included.

905.   Barker, Elisabeth. **Macedonia: Its Place in Balkan Power Politics.** London: Royal Institute of International Affairs, 1950. 129p.

   This is a study of Macedonia, her ethnography, and its effect on the politics of the Balkans. The period between the two World Wars is emphasized, as is the immediate aftermath of World War II.

906. Christowe, S. **Heroes and Assassins**. New York: R. M. McBride & Co., 1935. 290p. Illus.

Christowe describes the activities of the IMRO (Internal Macedonian Revolutionary Organization), particularly after World War I.

907. The Executive Committee of the Brotherhoods of the Macedonian Emigration in Bulgaria. **Memoir Presented to the Governments of the United States of America, of Great Britain and Ireland, of France, of Italy and Japan**. Sofia, 1919.

The *Memoir* is a plea by Macedonians living in Bulgaria to the Great Powers after World I to unite all of Macedonia with Bulgaria as part of the Treaty of Peace. An ethnographic map of Macedonia is included.

908. "Greek and Servian Assimilative Policies" and "The Peace Treaties and the Minorities." In **The Tragic Peninsula**, edited by Christ Anastasoff, pp. 245-54; 255-71. St. Louis, MO: Blackwell Wielandy, 1938.

The contributions are strongly pro-Bulgarian and pro-IMRO (Internal Macedonian Revolutionary Organization). The Macedonians are considered Bulgarians. Focus is on Greek and Serbian policies toward this group between world wars as well as the effect of the post-World War I peace treaties on the Macedonian minorities. The author of the volume is director of the Research and Information Bureau of the Macedonian Political Organization in the United States.

909. Kofos, Evangelos. **Nationalism and Communism in Macedonia**. Salonika: Institute for Balkan Studies, 1964. 251p.

Written from a political, military, and diplomatic perspective, this history of Macedonia and her minority problems emphasizes the policies and activities of the Balkan Communists with regard to the Macedonian question, and especially the Greek Communist party and its guerrilla war. Included are maps, a bibliography, and an index.

910. Kyriakides, Stilphon P. **The Northern Ethnological Boundaries of Hellenism**. No. 5 in a series. Thessalonika: Society for Macedonian Studies. Institute for the Study of the Haemos (Balkan) Peninsula, 1954. 63p.

This short study argues that "the northern ethnological boundaries of Hellenism both in Macedonia and Thrace have been during the Middle Ages, [sic] and still are today, the same as those established by the Hellenes during the victorious days of the Macedonian dynasty." The study therefore concludes that most of the population beyond the present Greek borders who live within this historic region is Greek, irrespective of the language spoken.

911. Mojsov, Lazo. **Okolu prashanjeto na makedonskoto natsionalno maltsinstvo vo Grcija** (On the Problem of the Macedonian Ethnic Minority in Greece). Skopje: Institut za natsionalna istorija, 1954. 392p.

Through the implementation of post-World War I treaties on the exchange of populations between Greece and Bulgaria and between Greece and Turkey, Greece had hoped to Hellenize northern Greece. However, since the criteria for determining populations to be exchanged were based on religious characteristics, the Macedonians remained numerically the strongest ethnic group in many localities of so-called Aegean Macedonia. Greece was able to avoid implementation of the 1920 Treaty for the Protection of Non-Greek Nationalities in Greece because of the diplomatic imbroglio with

Bulgaria and Yugoslavia: Yugoslavia insisted that the Macedonian minority be recognized as Serbian, while Bulgaria emanded that they be treated as Bulgarians. *Vis-à-vis* the Bulgarians, Greece maintained that the population in question was "Slavomacedonian."

912. Moore, P. "Macedonia: Perennial Balkan Apple of Discord." *World Today* XXXV (October 1979): 420-28.

Written by a senior analyst for Radio Free Europe, the article discusses the perennial problem between Bulgaria and Yugoslavia concerning Macedonia. The author presents an overview of the problem, especially in the context of post-World War II developments. He notes that it is the "uncertain ethnic character of the majority Slavic population" that has proved to be the source for the debate.

913. Ramet, Pedro. "Soviet Factor in the Macedonian Dispute." *Survey* XXIV (Summer 1979): 128-34.

This is a good, general survey of the Yugoslav-Bulgaria debate over Macedonia and of the question of whether the Macedonians are Bulgarians or a distinct ethnic group.

914. Solarov, Kosta. **La Bulgarie et la question Macédonienne**. Sofia: Imprimerie de l'État, 1919. 258p. Bulgarian edition: *Bulgariia i Makedonskiiat vupros: Prichinite na Balkanskite voini* (Bulgaria and the Macedonian Question: The Causes of the Balkan Wars). Sofia: Pechanitsa P. Glushkov, 1925. 180p.

The study analyzes the relationships since 1878 between Bulgaria and Macedonia and attempts to show that the Macedonians are Bulgarians. Maps and several important treaties relating to this period are included.

915. Stilianov, Khristo. **Osvoboditelnite borbi na Makedoniia** (Macedonia's Struggles of Liberation). Vol. I: **Ilindenskoto vuzstanie** (The Ilinden Insurrection); Vol. II: **Sled Ilindenskoto vuzstanie** (After the Ilinden Insurrection). Sofia: Durzhavna pechatnitsa, 1933; 1943.

The author, from a Bulgarian viewpoint, gives a history of the struggles in Macedonia since the uprising on St. Elias Day, in 1903. The role of the Balkan powers in these struggles is noted, as well as the complexities caused by the varied, heterogeneous minorities within the region.

916. Swire J. **Bulgarian Conspiracy**. London: Robert Hale, Ltd., 1939. 356p.

This is a detailed political study of Bulgaria during the period between world wars. A considerable part of the volume is devoted to a detailed analysis of the problem of Macedonia and its effect on internal Bulgarian politics as well as the country's foreign relations.

917. Veritas (pseud.). **Makedoniia pod igo, 1919-1929** (Macedonia under the Yoke, 1919-1929). Sofia: Makedonskiia natsionalen komitet, 1929(?). cxcvi, 580p. Maps. Illus.

This encyclopedic volume is a condemnation of Greece and Yugoslavia for their role in Macedonia during the decade noted above. The problem of minorities and their protection under various treaties is reviewed in considerable detail as a most important factor in the politics, diplomacy, and wars of the Balkans.

918.   Vishinski, Boris. "Denial: With No Argument." *Macedonian Review* VI:3 (1976): 221-24.

The author seeks to discredit Bulgarian statistical data which attempt to show that a Macedonian national minority does not exist in the Pirin region of Bulgaria. This is the controversy that has hindered Bulgarian-Yugoslav relations.

919.   Vishinski, Boris, ed. "Documents for Yugoslav-Bulgarian Relations." *Macedonian Review* VIII:8 (1978): 239-46.

Three documents are presented which relate to Bulgarian-Yugoslav relations during the 1970s: 1) a joint agreement between Todor Zhivkov and Josip Broz Tito; 2) a resolution by the parliament of Yugoslavia regarding the Bulgarian national minority in the country; and 3) Yugoslavia's pledge to regard the Yugoslav-Bulgarian frontiers as inviolable. The decisions effect also the situation of the Macedonians in the Pirin region.

920.   Wilkinson, H. R. **Maps and Politics: A Review of the Ethnographic Cartography of Macedonia**. Liverpool: University Press, 1951. 366p.

This volume presents an excellent comparative analysis of the use of maps to support the various Macedonian ethnic claims of the several Balkan states.

921.   Zarev, P. "Dimitur Talev." In **Istoriia na bulgarskata literatura** (History of Bulgarian Literature), vol. 4, pp. 721-52. Sofia: Izdatelstvo na Bulgarskata academiia na naukite. Institut za literatura, 1976.

The chapter includes a brief biographical sketch of Dimitur Talev, a noted Macedonian-Bulgarian writer, and a discussion of his famous trilogy of Macedonian novels: *Zhelzniiat svetilnik* (The Iron Candlestick), *Prespanskite kambani* (The Bells of Prespa), and *Ilinden* (Ilinden—i.e., "The Feast Day of St. Elias"). A bibliography of his works is included.

Turks and Moslems

922.   Ardenski, Vladimir. **Svoi, a ne chuzhdi (Ochertsi)** (Our Own, and Not Foreigners [Sketches]). Sofia: Partizdat, 1973. 144p.

This is a highly sympathetic account of the life of the Bulgarian Moslems and of the changes that have taken place in their villages under the present Communist government. The writer, himself a Bulgarian Moslem, describes the historical origins of his group and its separation from the mainstream of Bulgarian life. Written from a Marxist point of view, the work is highly critical of past Bulgarian governments in their policies toward this minority. Bibliography.

923.   Danailov, G. T. "Vliianie na plemennite i religiozni elementi vurkhu demo-grafiiata na Bulgariia ili demografski osobnosti na tursko-mokhamedanskoto naselenie (1879-1926 g.g.)" (The Influence of Racial and Religious Elements on the Demography of Bulgaria or Demographic Peculiarities of the Turkish-Mohammedan Population, 1879-1926). In **Bulgarska akademiia na naukite. Sbornik**, Book 24, Part III, Part 1 to 12, pp. 344-430. Sofia: Bulgarska akademiia na naukite, 1932.

The study provides very detailed demographic statistics, in absolute numbers, in percentages, and on a comparative basis, about the Moslem populations in Bulgaria. In particular, resettlement and vital statistics are provided.

924. "Expulsion of the Turkish Minority from Bulgaria." *World Today* VII (January 1951): 30-36.
The article describes the situation of the Turkish minority in Bulgaria between world wars and includes data regarding emigration of Turks from Bulgaria during this period. It includes information about post-World War II Bulgarian pressure on Bulgaria's Turks to leave the country and on Turkey to accept them, and concludes with a summary of the agreement signed on December 2, 1950 between Turkey and Bulgaria for the repatriation of Bulgarian Turks to Turkey.

925. Hazai, G. "Les dialectes turcs du Rhodope." *Acta orientalia* IX:2 (Budapest, 1959): 205-29.
This is a linguistic study of the particular dialects of the Turks in the Rhodope Mountains of Bulgaria, including their phonics and morphologies.

926. Hazai, G. "Textes turcs du Rhodope." *Acta orientalia* X:2 (Budapest, 1960): 185-229.
The article is a collection primarily of folktales of the Rhodopi region, followed by a French translation of each and an extensive Turkish-French glossary of words used.

927. Hoppe, F. M. "Die Gagauzen." *International Archives of Ethnography* IIL (1957): 119-29.
A German Protestant missionary, cognizant of ethnological methodology, who spent many years in Bulgaria working among the Turkish population there, provides a brief description of the history and customs of the Gagauzi of Bulgaria.

928. Hoppe, F. M. "Die türkischen Gagauzen-Christen." *Oriens Christianus* XLI (1957): 125-37.
The author gives a brief description of the Gagauzi of Bulgaria—their origin, history, Christian heritage, holidays, and customs.

929. Kakuk, S. "Le dialecte turc de Kazanlyk." *Acta orientalia* VIII:2 (Budapest, 1958): 169-87.
This is a linguistic study of the particularities of the dialect of the Turks of Kazanluk, including its phonetics, morphology, and syntax.

930. Khristov, Khristo, and Khadzhinikolov, V. **Iz minaloto na bulgarite mokhamedani v Rodopite** (From the Past of the Bulgarian-Mohammedans in the Rhodopi). Sofia: Bulgarska akademiia na naukite, 1958. 171p.
This is a short history of the Rhodopi Mountain Pomaks, from earliest times to around the early 1950s. A map is included.

931. Kiril, Patriarch of Bulgaria. **Bulgaromokhamedanski selishta v uzhni Rodopi: toponimno, etnografsko i istorichesko izsledvane** (Bulgarian Mohammedan Settlements in the Southern Rhodopi: A Toponymic, Ethnographic, and Historical Study). Sofia: Sinodalno kn-vo, 1960. 101p.
Presented here are the findings of a field study conducted by the Bulgarian prelate during 1943-1944. Official records of the *obshtini* and the *oblasts* and historic Turkish documents were used, and extensive field interviews with representative inhabitants in these villages were conducted.

932. Koev, I. "Prinos k"m izučavane na turskata narodna vezbenai t"kanna ornamentika v Ludgorieto" (Contribution to the Study of Turkish Ornamental Embroideries and Fabrics in Ludogorie). *Izvestiia na etnografiskia institut s muzei* III (1958): 65-118.

The author discusses the decorative fabrics and embroideries done by Turkish women in the region of Ludogorie.

933. Kostanick, Huey Louis. "Turkish Resettlement of Bulgarian Turks, 1950-1953." In **University of California Publications in Geography**, vol. VIII, no. 2, pp. 65-163. Maps. Tables. Berkeley: University of California Press, 1957.

This monograph is perhaps the definitive work in English on the subject of the resettlement of the Bulgarian Turks. The author includes voluminous general statistical data relating to the Turks in Bulgaria as well as to the other minorities in the country.

934. Kostanick, Huey Louis. "Turkish Resettlement of Refugees from Bulgaria, 1950-1953." *Middle East Journal* IX (Winter 1955): 41-52.

The resettlement of the Turkish refugees from Bulgaria during the period 1950-1952 is the subject of this detailed study. Topics covered include the location of Turkish settlements in Bulgaria, the history of previous Turkish-Bulgarian population exchanges, and the present exchange (its motives and purposes, scope, methods of operation, and Turkish reactions), with an evaluation of its outcome.

935. Kowalski, Tadeusz. **Les Turcs et la langue turque de la Bulgarie du nord-est.** Cracow: Nakl. Polskiej Akademji Umiejetnosci, 1933. 28p.

This is a brief linguistic study of the language of Turkish groups in northeast Bulgaria. However, the author, in an extended introduction, describes the various ethnic elements in this region, including the Turks, Tatars, and Gagauzes, that form the subject of his study.

936. Marinov, Vasil Aleksandrov. **Prinos kum izuchavaneto na bita i kulturata na turstite i gagauzite v severoiztochna Bulgariia** (Contributions toward the Study of the Life and Culture of the Turks and Gagauzes in Northeastern Bulgaria). Sofia: Bulgarska akademiia na naukite, 1956. 363p.

This is a comprehensive study of the history, culture, social life, and economic conditions of the Turks and Gagauzes of northeastern Bulgaria. Numerous photographs and illustrations, a detailed map, a good index, and an extensive bibliography add to the usefulness of the volume.

937. Marinov, Vasil, et al. "Prinos kum izuchavaneto bita i kulturata na turskoto naselenie v Severoiztochna Bulgariia" (Contributions towards the Study of the Life and Culture of the Turkish Population in Northeastern Bulgaria). In **Izvestiia na Etnografskiia institut s muzei**, vol. II, pp. 95-216. Bulgarska akademiia na naukite, Otdelenie za ezikoznanie, etnografiia i literature. Sofia: Izdanie na Bulgarskata akademiia na naukite, 1955.

The paper reports the results of three field studies made among the Turkish population of northeast Bulgaria during the years 1951, 1952, and 1953. Family trees showing village relationships, a village map depicting the growth and development of the village, and several house plans (with building methods illustrated and explained) are included. Also discussed are musical instruments, tools and methods of agriculture, household crafts, folk costumes, trades, animal husbandry, transportation, and economic cooperative life.

938. Memishev, Ivsein. **Uchastieto na bulgarskite turtsi v borbata protiv kapitalizma i fashizma, 1914-1944** (The Participation of the Bulgarian Turks in the Struggle against Capitalism and Fascism, 1914-1944). Sofia: Partizdat, 1977. 219p.

This is a description of the role played by Bulgarian Turks in opposition to the Bulgarian governments during the years cited above. The work of the Bulgarian Communist party among this group is recounted in detail and is credited for the support given to the party by this group at various critical times. Published by the press of the Bulgarian Communist party, the volume is highly uncritical and ignores the vast majority of Turks who were not in sympathy with the aims of the Communists.

939. Mizov, Nikolai. **Isliamut v Bulgariia** (Islam in Bulgaria). Sofia: Izdatelstvo na BKP, 1965. 232p.

Mizov discusses the dissemination of Islam in Bulgaria and its effects on the populace. He notes that communism must do more to combat the religion, which, unlike Christianity, it has tended to ignore. The book is published by the publishing house of the Bulgarian Communist Party.

940. Sanders, Irwin T. "The Moslem Minority of Bulgaria." *Moslem World* XXIV (1934): 356-69.

This is a descriptive survey, with some statistical data included, of Bulgaria's Moslem population as it existed during the mid-1930s. Written on the basis of first-hand experience by an American sociologist who spent many years in Bulgaria, the study describes the three main Moslem groups in Bulgaria at the time: the Turks, the Pomaks (Moslemized native Bulgarians), and the Gypsies. Extensive comments about each group are given.

941. Schechtman, J. B. "Compulsory Transfer of the Turkish Minority from Bulgaria." *Journal of Central European Affairs* XII (July 1952): 154-69.

The article is an excellent, rather detailed study of the reparation of members of Bulgaria's Turkish minority population to Turkey. Extensive background information is provided, political aspects of the reparation are considered, and the economic factors are noted. Some statistical data are also presented.

942. Shishkov, S. N. **Bulgaro-Mokhamedanite (pomatsi): istoriko-zemepisen pregled s obrazi** (The Bulgarian Mohammedans [Pomaks]: A Historical-Geographical Survey with Illustrations). Plovdiv: Turovska pechatnitsa, 1936. 118p.

Locations of villages and extensive statistical data about their populations are provided in this short, well-organized study of the Bulgarian Moslems. Discussions focus on cultural traditions, internal migration patterns, and the linguistic peculiarities of this group in the use of their native Bulgarian language.

943. Shukru, Takhirov. "Etnokulturni protsesi sred bulgarskite turtsi" (Ethnocultural Processes among the Bulgarian Turks). *Bulgarska etnografiia* V:4 (1980): 3-16.

The article notes the importance, from the viewpoint of the Bulgarian Communist party, of all ethnic groups being ideologically, politically, morally, and socially united for the patriotic development of the nation. Examples of the results of the communization of the Bulgarian Turks are given, in which the Moslem traditions, attitudes, and customs have been replaced by those of communism. Interesting data are provided on such topics as intermarriages between Bulgarian Turks and Slav Bulgarians, social integration, participation in sports, and housing.

944. Ülküsal, Müstecib. **Dobruca ve Türkler** (Dobrudja and the Turks). Ankara: Türk külturünü arastirma enstitüsü, 1966. 256p. Map. Illus.

This is a detailed historical account, by a Turk, of the life and culture of the Moslems in Dobrudja. Although the work concentrates on the Turkish inhabitants of this area, the Tartars and Gagauzi are also included.

945. Vakarelski, Khristo. "Pominutsi na bulgari mokhamedani i khristiiani v srednite rodopi" (Occupations of Bulgarian-Mohammedans and Christians in the Middle Rhodopi). *Izvestiia na etnografskiia institut i muzei* XII (1969): 39-68.

In this article on the occupations of the inhabitants of the Central Rhodopi Mountains, special attention is given to the methods used in agriculture and animal husbandry by both Moslems and Christians. Illustrations and a map show specific practices in each village and area.

946. Vasilev, Kiril. **Rodopskite bulgari-mokhamedani: istoricheski ocherk** (The Rhodopian Bulgarian-Mohammedans: A Historical Outline). Plovdiv, Bulgaria: Khristo G. Danov, 1961. 288p.

This is a history of the Pomaks who live in the Rhodopi Mountains. The volume unfortunately lacks an index and maps.

947. Vasileva, Margarita. "Skhodstva i otliki v Bulgarskata i Turskata svatba v grupa sela na razgradski okrug" (Similarities and Differences in the Bulgarian and Turkish Wedding in a Group of Villages of the Razgradski Okrug). *Izvestiia na etnografskii institut i muzei* XII (1969): 161-90.

The article describes reciprocal cultural influences between Bulgarian and Turkish villages, with marriage customs being used for illustrative purposes. The study is seen as having a theoretical importance in determining the ways in which socialist values can be transmitted. Thirteen similarities in the marriage ritual were identified. A lesser number of differences were found, primarily in the bridal dress and in the role of the members of the respective wedding parties.

948. Veleva, M., and Lepavtsova, Il. **Bulgarski narodni nosii: Tom II. Bulgarski narodni nosii v sredna zapadna Bulgariia i srednite zapadni Rodopi ot kraia na XVIII do sredata na XX v.** (Bulgarian Folk Costumes: Vol. II. Bulgarian Folk Costumes of Middle Western Bulgaria and the Middle and Western Rhodopes from the End of the Eighteenth to the Middle of the Twentieth Century). Sofia: Bulgarska akademiia na naukite, 1974. 252p.

This is a well-illustrated, in-depth analysis of the folk costumes of the above noted regions, for both males and females, Moslem and non-Moslem. Each item of cothing is discussed separately. Material of a historical and contemporary nature is included, and a map adds greatly to the volume's usefulness.

Other Minorities

949. Academie Roumanine. **Connaisance de la terre et de la pensée Roumaines.** Vol. V: **Les Macedo-Roumains: Esquisse historique et descriptive des populations Roumaines de la péninsule Balcanique,** edited by Th. Capidan. Bucharest: Academie Roumanine, 1937. 79p. Maps. Photographs.

This is a monograph on the Macedonian Vlachs by a Romanian scholar. Topics include origins of the name and its variants, the geographical distribution of the Vlachs, their history, language, occupations and trades, culture, and religion.

950.   Auerhan, Jan. **Čechoslovaci v Jugoslavii, v Rumunsku, v Madarsku a v Bulharsku** (Czechoslovaks in Yugoslavia, in Rumania, in Hungary, and in Bulgaria). Prague: "Melantrich," 1921. 207p.

The volume includes informative data regarding the history and cultural and economic status of the Czechoslovak colonies in each of the countries cited in the title.

951.   Auerhan, Jan. **Československé jazykové menšiny v evropském zahraniči** (Czechoslovaks Scattered in European Lands). Prague: Orbis, 1935. 105p.

The author describes the political, linguistic, educational, and religious status of the Czechoslovak minorities in each of the European countries where a sizable colony existed. Bulgaria is one of the states included.

952.   Bercovici, Konrad. "The Macedonian Gypsy." In **The Story of the Gypsies**, pp. 32-48. New York: Cosmopolitan Book Corporation, 1928. 294p.

This is a popularly written volume about Gypsies. In terms of the Macedonian Gypsies, fact seems to be mixed uncritically with fiction and legend, so as to create a more interesting and readable chapter.

953.   Bozhikov, Bozhidar. "Promeni v etnicheskiia sustav na naselenieto na Kurdzhali" (Changes in the Ethnic Composition of the Population of Kurdzhali). *Izvestiia na etnografskiia institut i muzei* VI (1962): 39-48.

The article is a case study of the changes of the ethnic composition of Kurdzhali. Data from 1884 through 1962 are displayed in a series of tables, and a brief analysis is included.

954.   **Chekhoslovashki obzor (Československý obzor)** (Czechoslovak Survey). Sofia: vols. I-V, 1920-1925. 5 vols. in 4. Frequency varies: volumes I-IV are semi-monthly; volume V is monthly. Written in both Bulgarian and Czech.

Published in Sofia during the 1920s, the survey recounts the activities of the Czechoslovaks in Bulgaria at the time. Included are news items about Czechoslovak schools, churches, and businesses in Bulgaria, events in the mother country, and the activities of Czechoslovak immigrants throughout the world.

955.   Frumkin, Grzegorz. **Population Changes in Europe since 1939: A Study of Population Changes in Europe during and since World War II as Shown by the Balance Sheets of 24 European Countries**. London: George Allen and Unwin, 1951. 191p.

This is a country-by-country analysis of European population shifts during and after the Second World War. The section on Bulgaria is concerned primarily with the Romanian-Bulgarian population changes in Southern Dobrudja after it was reincorporated into Bulgaria.

956.   Georgieva, Ivanichka. "Izsledvaniia vurkhu bita i kulturata na bulgarskite tsigani v Sliven" (Investigations on the Life and Culture of the Bulgarian Gypsies in Sliven). *Izvestiia na etnografskii institut i muzei* IX (1966): 25-50.

Georgieva's historical survey of Gypsy life in Sliven includes some historical statistical data regarding the number of Gypsies in the town and their occupations for particular periods as well as photographs of their dwellings and activities.

957. Gilliat-Smith, B. J. "The Dialect of the Moslem Kalajdzhis (Tinners) of the Tatar Pazardzhik District." *Journal of the Gypsy Lore Society*, Third Series, XIV (Part I) (1935): 25-43.

A linguistic study of the dialect of the Moslem Kalaidzhis Gypsies of the Tatar Pazardzhik area, who once practiced the tinner's trade, after which they, as a subgroup, and their dialect are named.

958. Gilliat-Smith, B. J. "Two 'Erlides' Fairy-Tales." *Journal of the Gypsy Lore Society*, Third Series, XXIV:1-2 (January-April 1945): 17-26.

These are two tales in the Erlides dialect, that spoken by the Gypsies of Sofia and environs. The original and an English translation are included in each case.

959. **Jahrbuch der Dobrudschadeutschen.** (1956 and 1957). Compiled by Otto Klett. Gerlingen, Germany: Verlag Heilbronner Stimme, 1956(?); 1957. 168p.; 188p.

Issued by displaced Germans, formerly residents of Dobrudja, the yearbooks commemorate the life and culture they once enjoyed there. Historical, religious, cultural, and statistical data are included. Although much of this information relates to the period between World Wars, when all of Dobrudja was under Romanian jurisdiction, Bulgaria's involvement in the region and her relationship with this German group are also examined.

960. **Jubilejńi ročenka Českosloven ské kolonie v Bulharsku, 1868-1928** (Jubilee Yearbook of the Czechoslovak Colony in Bulgaria, 1868-1928). Sofia: Družstva Československého národního domu T. G. Masaryka, 1928(?). xvi, 297p.

This is a jubilee yearbook published by the Czechoslovak colony in Bulgaria in commemoration of its fiftieth anniversary. Data are provided on its leaders, schools, sports (i.e., Sokol activities), culture, financial affairs, and commercial enterprises. Some rare photographs are included.

961. Karateev, Mikhail D. **Belogvardeitsy na Balkanakh: vospominaniia belogo ofitsera** (White Russians on the Balkans: Memoirs of a White Russian Officer). Buenos Aires: Talleres Graficos Dorrego, 1977. 230p.

This is an autobiography by a White Russian officer cadet, now living in Uruguay, in which he describes his experiences in the Balkans as a refugee after the Russian Revolution. Although the volume is not restricted to Bulgaria, a significant part of the book relates to his adventures there, with much valuable information being given about the life of these Russian emigrés in Bulgaria at that time. The dilemma of the Bulgarian government in dealing with this group is described humorously and insightfully. In view of the relative dearth of material on this group in Bulgaria, the volume assumes an added importance.

962. Kenrick, Donald. "Notes on the Gypsies in Bulgaria." *Journal of the Gypsy Lore Society*, Third Series, VL (1966): 77-84.

A brief but detailed description of the life of the Gypsies in present-day Bulgaria.

963.   Marinov, Vasil. "Nabludeniia vurkhu bita na tsigani v Bulgariia" (Observations on the Life of the Gypsies in Bulgaria). *Izvestiia na etnografskiia institut i muzei* V (1962): 227-76.

Marinov's article is a good descriptive account of the contemporary life of Bulgarian gypsies. Older, traditional nomadic patterns of existence are contrasted with those which now require them to live in fixed communities. Old crafts and tools are described and illustrated. In addition, musical instruments, methods of transportation, and dwelling construction are illustrated and discussed.

964.   Marinov, Vasil Aleksandrov. **Prinos kum izuchavaneto na proizkhoda, bita i kulturata na karakachanite v Bulgariia** (Contributions toward the Study of the Origin, Life, and Culture of the Karakachani in Bulgaria). Sofia: Bulgarska akademiia na naukite, 1964. 138p.

This is one of the very few studies by a Bulgarian of the nomadic ethnic group in Bulgaria that is called Karakachani, and it is by far the best and the most detailed. Topics covered include economic and social structures, cultural patterns and customs, animal husbandry, food, clothing and ornamentation, dwellings, and the recent changes that outside forces have effected upon them.

965.   Marinov, Wasil. "Die Schafzucht der nomadisierenden Karakatschani in Bulgarien." In **Viehzucht und Hirtenleben in Ostmitteleuropa: Ethnographische Studien**, edited by Màrta Belényesy and Béla Gunde, pp. 147-96. Budapest, 1961.

This is a brief but well-done study of the Karakachani in Bulgaria which describes their method of sheep raising and their pastoral, nomadic way of life.

966.   **Naše Zahranici** (Our Emigrants). Prague, 1919-1932(?).

Issued from 1919 to the early 1930s, the annual detailed news about the activities of the Czechoslovak immigrants throughout the world. Included in some, but not all, of these annuals are items about the Czechoslovak colony in Bulgaria.

967.   Nešović, Slobodan. **Jugoslaviǎ-Bugarska, ratno vreme 1941-1945** (Yugoslavia-Bulgaria: War Time 1941-1945). Belgrade: Narodna knjiga, 1978. 382p.

The last chapter (pp. 325-47) treats the position of Georgi Mihailov Dimitrov (1882-1949), president of Bulgaria and secretary general of the Bulgarian Communist party, *vis-à-vis* the attachment of the Pirin district of Bulgaria to the Yugoslav republic of Macedonia. It deals with the discussion within the Central Committee of the Bulgarian Workers' Party concerning the Pirin question between 1944 and 1946 and includes the correspondence between Dimitrov and Tito. The volume has an index of persons and a bibliography.

968.   Papahagi, Tache. **Antologie aromǎneascǎ** (An Aromanian Anthology). Bucharest: Tip. Rômania nouǎ, 1922. 519p.

The volume contains a variety of material relating to the Aromanians: their language, history, present settlements (with map), poetry, folktales, literature, and folksongs.

969.   Peyfuss, Max Demeter. **Die aromunische Frage: Ihre Entwicklung von den Ursprüngen bis zum Frieden von Bukarest (1913) und die Haltung Österreich-Ungarns.** Vienna: Böhlau Verlag, 1974. 166p.

In this history of the Vlachs in the Balkans, the emphasis is on the factors leading to their national reawakening in the nineteenth century, their development of a national consciousness, and the role that the Romanian governments have played in bringing about the collapse of Austria-Hungary.

970.   Schechtman, Joseph. "Transfer of the Germans from Bulgaria." In **European Population Transfers, 1939-1945**, pp. 250-51. Ithaca, NY: Cornell University Press, 1946.

This brief article describes the resettlement of ethnic Germans who were living in Bulgaria. Considerable factual and statistical data are included, despite space limitations. The article is especially valuable because relatively little has been written about this migration.

971.   Wurfbain, Andre. **L'échange gréco-bulgare des minorités ethniques**. Lausanne: Payot & Co., 1930. 217p.

The author discusses the problems and procedures involved in the exchange of the Bulgarian and Greek minorities during the 1920s as part of the provisions of the peace treaty of Neuilly.

9 _____ National Minorities in Albania, 1919-1980

Stephan M. Horak

HISTORICAL SUMMARY

Albania, since 1946 the People's Republic of Albania, has been the most homogeneous nation in the Balkan Peninsula since its proclamation of independence on November 28, 1912. Her problem with respect to the issue of the national minorities is not internal but rather is an external problem involving large number of Albanians (1,309,523 as of 1971) residing in Yugoslavia. Some 35% of Albanians live outside their country—the highest percentage of any divided nation in Europe, with 2,550,000 Albanians residing in Albania.

The ethnic minority population in Albania, in fact, is estimated at 80,000.[1] In round numbers, according to the 1961 census, there are 35,000 Greeks (2.2%), 10,000 Macedonians and Montenegrins (0.8%), 35,000 Vlachs (2.2%), and about 5,000 Gypsies living in Albania. Regrettably, the political isolation, together with hard-to-come-by official or unofficial information, makes it difficult to obtain precise data or objective knowledge regarding non-Albanian ethnics.

While the Greek minority of southern Albania, living in compact settlements near the border, still maintains its ethnic identity and at one time even had its own newspaper, *To vima*, the Vlachs, for instance, are rapidly undergoing denationalization because they lack ethnic material in print, educational institutions, and contacts with Vlachs abroad. The process of denationalization reveals itself in the declining population of ethnic groups, from 3% in 1955 to only 1% in 1976. In the early 1970s, in several Macedonian villages along Ohrid Lake, the Macedonian language was maintained as the language of instruction and the textbooks used were from the Macedonian People's Republic. However, worsening relations between Belgrade and Tirana in the late 1970s brought these limited concessions to an end.

According to John Kolsti, of all ethnic groups, only the Greeks constitute a serious ethnic problem inside Albania. "The Greek presence in South Albania was a threat to the security of the country in the late 1940s; tensions along the Greek-Albanian border lasted long after the end of the Greek Civil War.... In 1971, however, when the Greek government officially gave up all territorial claims to South Albania, it was no longer viewed as a serious threat to the internal security of the country."[2]

Another factor contributing to ethnic distinction is religious affiliation. To a significant degree, religion used to be a part of ethnic identity, at least in the case of the Greeks, the Vlachs, and, in part, the Montenegrins and Macedonians, before the total destruction of organized religion in 1967. Pre-World War II data indicated the population to be 70% Muslim, 20% Orthodox, and 10% Catholic. Now, it is impossible to deduce from these numbers the percentage of non-Albanians from each faith or denomination. However, it is true that all ethnic minorities were once represented in these groups.

Finally, it should be noted that Article 43 of the new constitution recognizes the rights of national minorities living in Albania. On December 28, 1976, the People's Assembly approved the constitution, which guarantees ethnic Greeks "the protection and development of their culture, the use of their language and the teaching of it in the school." Yet, in spite of the legal settlement, a hostile exchange of accusations regarding the Greeks in Albania continues on the highest level.

National Composition in
Albania According to Ethnic Affiliation

Ethnic Affiliation	1945	1950	1955
TOTAL POPULATION	1,122,044	1,218,943	1,391,499
Percent	100.0%	100.0%	100.0%
Albanian	1,075,467	1,186,123	1,349,051
Percent	95.8%	97.3%	97.0%
Greek	26,535	28,997	35,345
Percent	2.4%	2.4%	2.5%
Yugoslav	14,415	3,474	5,770
Percent	1.3%	0.3%	0.4%
Other	5,627	349	1,333
Percent	0.5%	0%	0.1%
Undetermined	...	...	...
Percent	...	...	...
Unaccounted for	0	0	0
Percent	0%	0%	0%

Source: Paul S. Shoup. *The East European and Soviet Data Handbook.* © 1981, Columbia University Press. Reprinted by permission.

Notes

[1]Peter R. Prifti, *Socialist Albania since 1944: Domestic and Foreign Developments* (Cambridge, MA: The MIT Press, 1978), p. 2. See also Paul S. Shoup, *The East European and Soviet Data Handbook,* (New York: Columbia University Press, 1981), p. 135.

[2]John Kolsti, "Albanism: From the Humanists to Hoxha," in *The Politics of Ethnicity in Eastern Europe*, eds. George Klein and Milan J. Reban, pp. 40-41 (Boulder, CO: East European Monographs, 1981).

BIBLIOGRAPHY

972. Dragl, Stefanija. "Makedonske šole v Albaniji" (Macedonian Schools in Albania). *Razprave in gradivo* 11-12 (1980): 73-78.

The author surveys Macedonian schools in the lake area of Ohrid and Prespan in Albania. She evaluates the language used in Macedonian elementary-school textbooks published in Tirana. The information is based largely on reports by individual teachers.

973. Faensen, Johannes. **Die albanische Nationalbewegung**. Osteuropa-Institut an der Freien Universität Berlin, Balkanologische Veröffentlichungen, 4. Berlin: in Kommission bei Otto Harrassowitz, Wiesbaden, 1980. 186p.

Utilizing recent Albanian literature, this volume is the most up-to-date study on Albania. Of special interest is the biographical section, which includes 44 biographies of individuals involved in the Albanian national awakening. Albania's national minorities are discussed only marginally.

974. Kastrati, Jup. **Bibliografi shqipe** (Albanian Bibliography). Tiranë: "Naim Frashëri" Publ. Hse, 1959. 408p.

An extensive bibliography of materials published in the Albanian language.

975. Keefe, Eugene K., et al. **Area Handbook for Albania**. Washington, DC: U.S. Government Printing Office, 1971. 223p. Bibliography, pp. 197-207.

This volume is one of a series of handbooks prepared by Foreign Area Studies of the American University, providing valuable information about Albania. Six co-authors discuss the general character of the society, the historical setting, the physical environment, the people, social system, government structure and political system, communications and cultural development, the economic system, and internal and external security, and an extensive bibliography will assist the reader in research and additional detailed study. Three maps and several tables add to the value of the handbook.

976. Lagoreci, Anton. **The Albanians: Europe's Forgotten Survivors**. Boulder, CO: Westview Press, 1978. 230p.

One-third of this book consists of an overview of Albanian history from the fourteenth-century Ottoman invasion to the end of World War II. The major portion of the work is devoted to a discussion and analysis of political, diplomatic, economic, social, and cultural developments from 1945 to the early 1970s.

977. Marmullaku, Ramadan. **Albania and the Albanians**. Translated from Serbo-Croation by Margot and Boško Milosovjevič. Hamden, CT: Archon Books, 1975. 178p.

The author, a Yugoslav Albanian from Kosovo, is a senior adviser on Balkan affairs for the Commission on International Relations of the Presidency of the Yugoslav League of Communists. His perspective is that of an Orthodox party intellectual, and he basically approves of the techniques for "building socialism" in Albania. The special section on the Albanians of Kosovo contains some valuable critical insights.

978.   Pano, Nicholas C. **The People's Republic of Albania**. Baltimore, MD: Johns Hopkins Press, 1968. 185p.

This volume is part of the Integration and Community Building in Eastern Europe series. It serves well as an introduction to Albanian modern history and politics, especially for the interested layperson and the beginning student in this field.

979.   Popovski, Tosso. **Macedonian National Minorities in Bulgaria, Greece and Albania**. Skopje: Makedonska knjiga, 1981. 292p.

The author argues that the 500,000 Macedonians living in Bulgaria, Greece, and Albania are deprived of their national rights.

980.   Prifti, Peter R. **Socialist Albania since 1944: Domestic and Foreign Developments**. Studies in Communism, Revisionism, and Revolution, 23. Cambridge, MA: The MIT Press, 1978. 311p.

Prifti bases his study mostly on Albanian sources and offers the most up-to-date reference works on the developments in that country. He also provides information on Albanians in Yugoslavia.

981.   Skendi, Stavro, ed. **Albania**. East Central Europe under the Communists Series, Robert F. Byrnes, ed. New York: Praeger, 1956. 389p.

Designed for the general reader and for reference use, the handbook includes biographical data on 27 leading Communists, a brief chronology for 1944-1955, a list of treaties, and an impressive bibliography. Also, information on Albania's national minority is offered.

982.   Skendi, Stavro. **The Albanian National Awakening, 1878-1912**. Princeton, NJ: Princeton University Press, 1967. 498p.

The author, a native of Albania, traces the progress and setbacks of Albanians in their history and struggle for national independence. This publication is a good textbook presentation for college students and the general reader.

10 —————— Nationality Research Centers in Eastern European Countries*

Theodor Veiter

In the countries of the Danube River region, to which Poland, the USSR, and Italy could be marginally included, there are to this day research centers that investigate nationality matters, including the legal status of ethnic and linguistic minorities. A complete list of these centers cannot be furnished due to the difficulty involved in obtaining the needed information.

Within the countries in question, the term *Volksgruppen* (nationality groups) is seldom used when referring to the ethnic population, although in the Soviet Union the word *etnitscheska grupa* has begun to be utilized.[1] By and large the term *nationalities* is widely accepted, and in the Croatian language one finds more recently the term *nationality group* (*narodna grupa*, plural: *narodne grupe*).[2] In the five-language dictionary by Golias,[3] a 1974 Yugoslavian publication, one finds the term *Volksgruppe* in the German version and a comparable expression used in the remaining five languages (Serbo-Croatian, Slovenian, English, French, and Italian). The expression *national minority* is either missing or rarely used, particularly when taking the word *national* into consideration. The exception is in the Russian language, in which the expression *natsional'nyi* (e.g., *natsional'naia grupa*), for example, is

*Translated from German by Siegfried E. Heit, this essay was first published in *Der Donauraum* 25:1 (1980).

ethnic and analogous to the Serbo-Croatian and Slovenian word *narod*, i.e., *narodni*. The term *nation* is rarely used in Serbo-Croatian and Slovenian, whereas in the USSR the customary term for the individual Soviet (national) groups is *natsiia*.

For the most part, when *narod* is used in assorted variations, such as the Slovenian *narodnost* (which could be translated as "nationality group") or *narodna skupina* (likewise translated as "Volksgruppe") or the Serbo-Croatian *roditelji* (parents), one sees therein a derivative which expresses a natural element. Not as conclusive is *natsiia, even though this word is related to the Latin term natio* and thus does show that it, too, originally is derived from the natural element (nasci = to be born).

HUNGARY

Hungary has various research centers for nationality issues—the most important being the Committee for Eastern European and Nationalities Complex of the Hungarian Academy of Sciences, whose president is a German-Hungarian, Dr. Emil Niederhauser. The Ministry of Culture has its own nationalities department. The National Institute of Pedagogy has a professional chair of nationalities, whose purpose is to publish textbooks for the various ethnic schools as well as to conduct research on the ethnic groups. Included among these nationality-based schools are ethnic kindergartens, preschools, grammar schools, middle schools, and high schools, all of which use the corresponding national language as the language of instruction, namely German, Romanian, Serbo-Croatian, Slovakian, and Slovenian. A number of schools are also bilingual (utraquist) in that they use Magyarian (officially known as Hungarian in the non-Magyarian languages) as well as one of the other ethnic languages as the language of instruction. Designated for every important nationality are regional inspectors—four altogether. A breakdown of inspectors on the country level would include nine for German, one for Romanian, five for Serbo-Croatian, five for Slovakian, and one for Slovenian. For the past twenty-five years, the Hungarian Textbook Publishing Company has published texts in the minority languages.[4] Good relations exist with the Yugoslavian textbook publishing firms which deliver books from Skolska Knjiga in Zagreb, with the textbook publisher in Belgrade, and with the Regional Publishing House in Novi Sad. It should be noted, though, that the expression "Croatian" is not used, even though a part of the Croatian ethnic group in Hungary, i.e., West Hungary, makes exclusive use of Čakaviš, a Croatian language. The education of teachers for the ethnic schools takes place in separate departments offering a distinct course of study, including specialized preparation for those planning to teach in ethnic kindergartens. An effort is made to research laws pertinent to nationalities and policies affecting national minorities.[5]

The various ethnic newspapers examine their own nationality-related political situations. For the German ethnic group, there is the *Neue Zeitung* (in 1974 the circulation dropped to 4,018), for the Slovakians the *Ludove Noviny* (circulation of 1,506 and presently experiencing growth), for the Croats, Serbs, and Slovenes the *Narodne Novine* (circulation of 3,310 and growing), and for the Romanian ethnic group *Foaia Noastra* (circulation of 960 and growing). That the *Narodne Novine*, which is not circulated in the

Burgenland, has become a paper for the Slovenian ethnic group living mostly in the area of the Raab River can be explained by the fact that this is such a small minority.

On the part of the Hungarians, ethnic research is conducted by the Ministry of Culture (Kulturális Minisztérium). This can at best be classified as scholarly research only. The committee of the Hungarian Academy of Sciences, under the direction of Dr. Niederhauser, coordinates research on east European history as well as nationality issues. First organized in 1977, it does not constitute a research consortium or institute but was established for autonomous research. Included among its areas of responsibility is the research of Hungarian nationalities since 1945. In charge of nationality issues is the well-known expert in this field and the presiding secretary of the committee, Dr. Laszlo Kövago.

Among the institutes actively engaged in research concerning nationalities in Hungary is the MTA Dunántúli Tudományos Intézete in Pécs (Fünfkirchen). The director is the academician Dr. Otto Bihari (Pécs, Kulich Gyula utca 22). This institute deals with the German and south-Slavic minorities in the Trans-Danubian area. During the interwar years, the University of Pécs had the Institute of International Law, which, under the leadership of Ivan Nagy and Ferencz Faluhélyi, examined minority issues. During this time the institute published a series of books on minority rights in general, in particular the minorities in the Burgenland. A total of twenty-six works had been published by 1937.

Another institution dealing with the Slovakian and Romanian minorities of the Great Plain exists at the University of Szeged—Jósef Attila Tudományegyetem, Bölszézettudományi Kar. Uj- és legujabbkori egyetemes történeti tanszék (Szeged, Tancsics Mihály u. 2). The institute is attached to the chair of modern history and headed by Professor Daniel Csatári.

The former Institute for Minorities at the University of Budapest, under the leadership of the ethnic German from Zips, Dr. Ernst Flachbarth, internationally known advocate of nationality rights, was closed in 1940. From there, Professor Flachbarth moved to the University of Pécs, where he remained until his death at the end of the 1950s.

The Slovak Ludwig von Goglàk taught history of the nationalities in Hungary at the University of Budapest until the revolt of 1956. No successor was found for his position after he fled to Vienna in 1956. He continued his research of Slovakian history at the University of Vienna.

The individual nationalities have their own associations. Magyarországi Délszlávok Demokratikus Szövetsége (Democratic Association of South Slavs in Hungary) and Magyarországi Német Dolgozók Demokratikus Szövetsége (Democratic Association of Slovaks in Hungary) share the same address: H-1065 Budapest, VI. Nagymezö u. 49. Another association is Magyarországi Románok Demokratikus Szövetsége (Democratic Association of Romanians in Hungary), H-5700 Gyula. These associations constitute political representation for the nationalities. The attendant agency in the government is the Department for Nationalities in the Ministry of Culture (Kulturális Minisztérium, Nemzetiségi Osztály, H-1055 Budapest, V. Szalay László u. 10-14). The department head is Dr. Ferenc Boros. Newspapers are published independently by each association. Besides those already mentioned, the *Ludové Noviny* for the Slovaks and *Foaia Noasträ* for the Romanians should be cited. Definite documentation about the actual state of affairs of the nationalities is gathered by the national Gorkij Library (Áilami Gorkij Könyvtár. H-1056 Budapest, V. Molnár u. 11., Director: Dr. Gyula Tóth).

Finally, to supplement the list, reference should be made to the Hungarian Ethnographic Society in Budapest, which has a Department for Nationalities. Under the editorship of Professor Iván Balassa, it has published in the respective languages collective volumes of ethnography and folklore of the different nationalities. To date, ten volumes have appeared (Magyar Néprajzi Társaság, H-1087 Budapest, VIII. Könyves Kálmán krt. 40).

CZECHOSLOVAKIA

Institutes that are concerned only with the ethnic and linguistic relationship between Czechs and Slovaks are not included here, since neither Czechs nor Slovaks are classified as minorities. According to the nation-state concept, only the whole is a nation; thus both constitute the nation, i.e., the Czechs comprise two-thirds of the 15 million inhabitants and the Slovaks one-third. The official theory of the existence of a Czechoslovakian people, promulgated during 1919-1938, is no longer valid since World War II. As far as nationalities go, only the following are considered as such: approximately 600,000 Magyars (Hungarians), 60,000 Ukrainians (Ruthenians), and 77,000 Poles. The Germans, officially still listed at 77,000 (approximately 3.5 million were expelled or transferred), were recognized as a nationality minority and given the right to constitute themselves as such during the "Prague Spring" of 1968. Even today they are officially listed as a nationality minority in official reports published for foreign consumption. The constitution of 1968 in the section pertaining to the rights of nationalities in the ČSSR also guarantees them ethnic equality.

Ethnopolitical self-representation is possible through certain organizations. For the Poles it is the Polish Cultural and Educational Association (PRKO); for the Magyars (usually called Hungarians) it is the Social and Cultural Association for Hungarians in the ČSSR (Csemdok) (although the original Czech text specifies Magyars and not Hungarians); for the Germans it is the Cultural Association for Citizens of German Nationality in the ČSSR; and for the Ukrainians the Cultural Association of Ukrainian Workers (KZUP). These ethnic groups also have their own newspapers, and the Poles have a theatre, the Polish Theatre in Český Těšin (the former Silesian Teschen) in north Moravia.

A Council of Nationalities functions within the governmental agencies of the ČSR and the SSR. The chairman of this council is the first deputy to the chairman of the government of the ČSSR. Scholarly work is not done there.

The Polish, Magyar, and Ukrainian ethnic groups have elementary as well as secondary schools in which the language of instruction is their native language. These schools have textbooks in their languages, but lessons in the official language, i.e., Czech or Slovakian, are also given. The Germans, who no longer are classified as Sudeten-Germans,[6] and most of whom were deported, now live scattered among other ethnic groups. The government uses this as an excuse for not opening German nationality schools, even though these were planned during the "Prague Spring" of 1968. Only forty-five nine-year elementary schools were opened as "Learning Centers for the German

Language." German textbooks were written and published by various educational publishing houses in the ČSSR. Learning centers were opened for children of Greek (Macedonian) descent in northern Moravia, where their parents, most of whom had been followers of the Communist Markos regime in Macedonia, had found asylum after leaving their homeland in the years following the war.[7]

A research institute of the Silesian Academy of Science is concerned primarily with minority issues, especially with the history of the Sudeten Germans and emigration of the nationalities from Czechoslovakia.[8] It has published the best and most comprehensive bibliography on the Sudeten issue.

The Slovakian Academy of Sciences is involved in issues pertaining to nationalities. One need merely mention its monumental work concerning the Austro-Hungarian Compromise of 1867.

ITALY

Because of its borderlands, Italy belongs, in a restricted sense, to the Danube region. However, it should not be overlooked that from 1918 up to the Second World War, Italy was directly involved in what is today the Yugoslavian coastal region (rightly called "altra sponda") and in parts of the Danube region, i.e., Zara, Logosta, Fiume with the Quarnero Islands, Istria, Terra dei Cicci, West-Krain with Postumia/Postojna/Adelsberg, as well as the hinterland to a certain extent of Trieste, Görz/Gorica/Gorizia, and the Isonzo valley.[9] During World War II, Italian forces invaded the entire Dalmatian coast, with the exception of Ragusa/Dubrovnik, and thereby severely limited the territory of the Independent Croatian State (*Nesavizna Drzava Hrvatska*).[10] In addition, Italy obtained from the Third Reich the southern part of the former Drau-Banat, which today is the Slovenian Socialist Republic, with Ljubljana (Laibach) as its provincial capital. Hereby, Italy encroached directly on the Danubian region and underscored its interest in the area by signing the Treaty of Osimo in 1975,[11] which theoretically would secure a shipping route, i.e., navigation rights, from the Gulf of Trieste via the Save to the Danube. Finally, Italy has an active Slovenian ethnic group in Venezia-Eriuli, i.e., the provinces of Trieste, Gorizia, and Udine, where regional research institutes have established contact with Yugoslavia.

Here one should mention the Slovenski raziskovalni Institute in Trieste. This Slovenian research institute is concerned with the history as well as the legal status of the Slovenians in Italy. It also concerns itself with minority issues in general. An excellent series of books in Italian bears witness to its efforts.

Located in Gorizia/Gorica is the ISIG (Instituto Internazionale di Sociologia di Gorizia), under the leadership of Raimondo Strassoldo, which examines problems of nationalities in the frontier areas, South Tyrol for example. It also delves into topics of an ethnopolitical nature regarding southeastern Europe. A number of remarkable books, pro-minority without exception, are published by the LINT Publishing House in Trieste.[12]

Many Slovenian newspapers and magazines are published in the autonomous region Venezia-Giulia-Friuli. They are not generally scholarly in nature, although the Catholic Slovenian cultural journal *Most*, published in Trieste, does print scholarly articles. Also, the *Bollettino d'informazioni degli Sloveni in Italia* in Trieste regularly prints documentary materials concerning the Slovenian minority.

The provincial government of the province of Trieste had an advisory council for minority questions. In 1978, Dr. Brezigar, a Slovenian, was appointed to head this council while he was at the same time the editor of the Slovenian daily newspaper *Primorski Dnevnik*. Although as a result of the 1980 elections he withdrew from this position, the advisory council should survive.

The Society of Slovenian Academicians (freely translated from "Društvo slovenskih izobražencev") in Trieste can be considered a minority research institution. The existence of this Catholic institution was prohibited prior to World War II, when all minority organizations were proscribed in Italy. During that time it was known as the Catholic Academician Association of Zarja in Bohinj, Slovenia. In 1939, at Sv. Janež ob Bohinjskem jezeru, the first conference of Catholic academicians was convened. Since World War II, these conferences have taken place in Draga near Trieste. The topic for the fourteenth conference, which met in September 1979, was "National Characteristics in Theology and the Church before the Year 2000." This research group issues the journal *Draga*, a supplement to the Slovenian Catholic literary journal "*Mladika*" of Trieste.

Various universities within the Italian-Yugoslavian and Italian-Austrian border areas have research institutes dealing with nationality matters of southeastern Europe. The University of Trieste, with its Instituto di Studi e decumentazione sull'Est Europeo (ISDEE) (Corso Italia, 27) and its journal *Est-Ovest*, is an example. In Trieste the Societá Trentina di scienze storiche, under the direction of Umberto Corsini, more and more concerns itself with minority rights in Austria-Hungary and especially the position of the Trieste Italians in the Crown land of Tyrol. Moreover, the institute focuses upon the nationality rights in Old Hungary as well as in the area of the former Dual Monarchy. At the University of Padova (Padua), there is a research institute under the direction of Professor Milan Stanislao Ďurica which specializes in the Sudeten issue as well as the history of Slovakia. Dr. Lisa Guarda-Nardini is the specialist at the institute, while Francesco Leoncini, a lecturer at the University of Venice, is concentrating on the Sudeten-German issue. Outstanding publications about nationality problems in southeastern Europe have been produced there.

YUGOSLAVIA

That Yugoslavia, which designates itself a multinational state, should place special emphasis on scholarly research of minorities is probably understandable. This work refers only to the ethnic and linguistic minorities and not to the major nationalities which comprise the state and are constituent nations, called socialist republics, or better known as component republics.[13] The following research centers should be mentioned.

The Inštitut za narodnostna vprašanja (Institute for Nationality Questions) in Ljubljana was founded during the interwar period, when it directed its research toward the situation of the oppressed Slovenian people in Italy. The driving force behind this work was Dr. Lavo Čermelj, the present-day Nestor of ethnopolitical research. At present, however, all nationality questions within the Slovenian region are examined, even such problems as the Magyar national group in the Prekmurje. The institute's resident expert, Albina Lük, is a Magyar native of that region. The institute publishes a scholarly yearbook for nationality questions, *Razprave in gradivo* (freely translated as *Proceedings and Materials*), containing some outstanding contributions, and in recent years issued some special publications on the Carinthian Slovenian problem.

The Zavod za Migragije i Narodnosti in Zagreb is an institute comparable to the Slovenian Institute. Both have provided publications about minority issues with parallel Serbo-Croatian and Slovenian texts.

In Zagreb the Čakavski Sabor (Čakavish Council) deals expressly with the ethnic issues involving the Burgenland Croatians; these, with the exception of a few villages, belong to the Čakavish branch of the Croatian language.

A typical research institute for nationality questions is located in Ljubljana—the Zgodovinsko društvo za Slovenijo (Historical Society for Slovenia). Its quarterly journal, *Zgodovinski časopis*, is concerned with nationalities in the past and present. Again, the focus is on the Slovenian problems in Italy and Carinthia. The journal possesses an excellent scholarly reputation, although at times it does reflect biases.

Loosely affiliated with the above-mentioned is the institute in Belgrade, the Zveza društev zgodovinarjev Jugoslavije (Association of Yugoslavian Historical Societies). Its publication, *Jugoslovenski istrijiski časopis*, is less involved with nationality questions.

The Inštitut za zgodovino delavskega gibanja (Institute for the History of the Workers' Movement) in Ljubljana publishes a journal, *Prispevki za zgodovino delavskega gibanja* (Contributions to the History of the Workers' Movement), which occasionally deals with issues relating to the Slovenian minority. The journal *Časopis za zgodovino in narodopisje* (Journal for History and Ethnography), published in Maribor located on the Drava River, deals with the minority issues of lower Styria (and the Austrian southern Styria) district and the Prekmurje region. The periodical *Naši razgledi* (Our Views), published in Ljubljana, continues to focus on the problems of national minorities (even those of countries other than Yugoslavia). A scholarly research center is located there.

The significant Muslim population in Bosnia and Herzegovina, officially[14] considered neither as a religious, ethnic, nor national minority but rather as a branch of the Southern Slavs, together with the Montenegrins, represents the "relatively indigenous nation." Housed in the Bosnian-Herzegovinian Academy of Science in Sarajevo is a research center for Muslim questions. Also in Sarajevo, the Esperantist League of Bosnia-Herzegovina, together with the Bosnian UNESCO Commission, engages in serious, scholarly research in the area of nationality rights and language policies.[15] This is accomplished with the assistance of internationally recognized experts from Western Europe.

In Belgrade, the Center for Demographic Research, in conjunction with the publishing house Medjuna-rodna Politika, is engaged in researching ethnopolitical and nationality-related questions. Furthermore, the *Jugoslovenska Stvarnost*, also in Belgrade, is involved with nationality questions. The Savez udruženja pravnika Jugoslavije of Belgrade and the Institute of Socio-Political

Science and Jurisprudence at the School of Law in Novi Sad should also be mentioned.

Although the history departments of Yugoslavian universities pursue the history of nationality problems, and law faculties concern themselves with the legal aspects of public and international law with respect to the nationalities, systematic research is not pursued by the universities. The number of publications dealing with nationality questions is vast, but tendentious. Even basic works, published in the United States and Western Europe, dealing with the international aspect of nationality rights, such as those directly concerned with the problems of the Slovenian minorities in countries other than Yugoslavia, are systematically suppressed.[16] The only known exception, and a model of objectivity, is a new work by Ernest Petrič.[17]

ROMANIA

Since Romania is a multiethnic country, research in nationality policies and nationality rights plays a significant role. To be sure, on the part of the Communist party of Romania there is the attempt to build a "Socialist Nation"[18] ethnic superstructure based on party ideology and patterned on the example of the USSR. According to the official party viewpoint, the first step toward a unified national state was taken when Romania became independent in 1877. During the 1977 centennial celebration, this position was promulgated in conjunction with a strong anti-Habsburg and anti-Hungarian sentiment, all with disregard to historical facts. To be sure, the nationalities still receive attention, despite the fact that in the future there may be a fully integrated, even linguistically and ethnically unified Romanian nation in which the individual nationalities and ethnic groups (other than the Romanians) will cease to exist. These nationalities include the Hungarians, Germans, Serbians, and Ukrainians. According to the words of Nicolae Ceauşescu, a "unity between the Romanian people and other co-inhabiting nationalities" should become a reality through Marxist-Leninist brotherhood. Innate national sentiments, especially those of the Germans and the Hungarians, are considered obsolescent and thus expendable.

The foremost authority on nationalities in Romania is the Academy for Socio-Political Sciences in Bucharest. Within the framework of this academy, as a direct result of a speech given on March 12, 1971, by Nicolae Ceauşescu, to the assembly of the Council on Workers of Hungarian Nationality, an institute was established which investigates special problems of coinhabiting nationalities. The workers' councils of the Hungarian, German, and Ukrainian nationalities have no particular scientific research assignments to pursue, although the councils of the Hungarian and German workers, due to the dimension of these ethnic groups, play a certain role in assessing problems that may arise. To this end, plenary sessions of these councils are being held and corresponding publications are issued.[19] The Council on Cultural and Socialist Education includes members of the German and Hungarian minorities who serve in an advisory capacity on nationality matters.

In states where minorities exist, instruction in the mother tongue is a prerequisite to specializing in nationality research. Romania has a network of educational institutions with German as the language of instruction, including kindergartens, elementary and secondary schools, and girls' high schools

(Ordinance of the Ministry of Education and Instruction, No. 278/1973). During the 1977/78 school year, 692 school units and departments used the German language during regular daytime instruction, and two girls' secondary schools and three college preparatory schools utilized German as the language of instruction in their night courses. Some 13,712 children attended the German kindergartens, 39,662 the elementary schools, and 5,112 the high schools. There are also institutions with a classical-humanistic emphasis,[20] as well as one school with an agricultural-industrial curriculum, seven offering programs in mathematics/physics, one in philology and history, and one school specializing in pedagogy. Romanian must be taught at all levels, and certain subjects—Romanian history, geography of the Romanian Socialist Republic, government and patriotism, economics and business law, etc.—must be taught exclusively in Romanian.[21]

Similar numbers are reported for the Hungarian minority. This, too, is reported in the plenary sessions. Lately, more and more research work about the Magyars (Szeklers) abroad is being made known, some with absolute objectivity, as for example that of the London Minority Rights Group.[22] At the universities and other schools of higher education, instruction, too, is offered in the German and Magyar languages, which is the case at Babeş-Bolyai University in Cluj-Napoca.

The Romanian Academy of Science is the leading authority on the history of the nationalities of Romania. Outside of Romania the Societas Academia Dacoromana in Munich can claim this role, with its publication *Acta Historica*.[23]

AUSTRIA

In Austria, various institutions and societies explore, at least partially, the topic of minorities in southeastern Europe. Among these is the Austrian Ost- und Südostinstitut in Vienna, which publishes the periodical *Österreichische Osthefte*. The Forschungsinstitut für den Donauraum, which publishes the journal *Der Donauraum*, is sometimes mistaken for the Donaueuropäische Institut because both are located in Vienna. The latter does not, however, deal with nationality problems but focuses on matters of economics.

Austrian universities are involved in east European research, including research on the question of nationalities in the region east and southeast of present-day Austria (Institut für Österreichische Geschichtsforschung an der Universität Wien; Institut für Zeitgeschichte in Wien; Institut für Zeitgeschichte an der Universität Salzburg). Also touching on this topic is the work done by the Wissenschaftliche Kommission, which, in conjunction with the National Archives, investigates Austrian history from 1918 through 1938, with emphasis on the question of the ethnic groups in Burgenland and Carinthia. At the University of Innsbruck, more attention is being given the history of the Italians in Trentino, a region not included in east-southeast-Europe.

The topic of Carinthian Slovenes is dealt with by various scholarly establishments of the minority group itself, above all by Slovenski Znanstveni Inštitut in Klagenfurt/Celovec, where the beginnings of Slovenian scholarly research can be observed.[24] The Slovenian information center (Slovenski informacijski center—SIC) in Klagenfurt/Celovec attempts to investigate the issues of the Carinthian minority. Moreover, the Institut für Slawistik at the

University of Graz has recently begun an extensive compilation on the Slovenian mother tongue in Carinthia.

The Dom prosvete v Tinjah (in Teinach/Tinjah), a Catholic cultural center with a pronounced ethnopolitical character, has issued a large number of publications, religious as well as minority-political in scope. It also sponsors symposia with an accent on minority issues.

The Mladje club in Klagenfurt publishes a literary magazine of the same name which frequently contains essays related to the problem of the Carinthian Slovenes. Of the two leading Slovenian weekly newspapers, only the politically Left *Slovenski Vestnik* of Klagenfurt regularly includes relevant scholarly articles on questions about minority and minority language issues, whereas *Naš Tednik*, issued by the Christian People's Council, rarely, if ever, does so.

The official historiography of Carinthia discourages any research on ethnic groups due to its rejection of Slovenian positions. The one exception is the work done by the University of Klagenfurt, a federal institution. The German-language press of the province has a predominantly anti-Slovenian orientation.

The Croats of Burgenland at the present do not have a scholarly, ethno-political institute, although there was an attempt in 1974 by the "Symposion Croaticon" to research their own identity.[25] Through the Hrvatsko Kulturno Društvo u Gradišći (the Croatian Cultural Association of Burgenland) in Eisenstadt/Željezno and the Hrvatski Akademski Klub (Croatian Academic Club) in Vienna, the Croats of Burgenland have made initial scholarly inquiries into the subject of ethnic minorities. And the weekly newspaper *Hrvatske novine* of Eisenstadt and Trausdorf/Trajstof has, since about 1978, been dealing with general ethnopolitical issues. The official historiography and the minority policy of the Burgenland are not receptive to the issues of the ethnic minorities, but are not necessarily hostile either.

POLAND

According to the official Polish view, there are no longer any ethnic or linguistic minorities in Poland since, as a result of the Warsaw Agreement between Poland and the Federal Republic of Germany, those Germans who remained in Poland after the World War II population transfer were resettled in West Germany.[26] This official view has been refuted by Alfred Bohmann, a former official in the Foreign Ministry in Bonn, but estimates of the number of Germans still in Poland vary greatly (between 180,000 and 1.2 and as high as 1.8 million). Besides the Germans, Czechs also reside in the Olza region. The number of Ukrainians is relatively high, although it would appear that the cession to the USSR of areas in the east, predominantly settled by Ukrainians (East Galicia, Volhynia, Brest-Litovsk), would have decreased their number significantly. Finally, mention must be made of the linguistic minorities of the Mazurs and the Kashubs in former East Prussia.[27]

Only a few scholarly institutions examine topics related to ethnic minorities in Poland, namely: the Instytut Zachodni in Poznań,[28] and the Instytut Śląski in Opole under the direction of Józef Byczkowski, a minority specialist with rather pro-German views. The Geographic Institute of the

Polish Academy of Science (Geografii Polskiej Akademii Nauk) in Warsaw compiles data on linguistic minorities.[29]

BULGARIA

Although the Danube makes up its northern boundary, Bulgaria traditionally is not included in the Danube region, but belongs to the Balkans. With Austria and Hungary she had no conflicting territorial claims. Bulgaria, too, if one does not designate the Macedonians as an ethnic minority but as a branch of the Bulgarian nation (an official stance of Bulgaria but unacknowledged by both Yugoslavia and Greece), has a number of ethnic and linguistic minorities. Among these are the Aromanians,[30] the Pomaks, the Vlachs, and the Albanians. The once numerous Greeks and Turks in Bulgaria fell victim to mass repatriation and expulsion. Since Bulgarians still reside in the Romanian Banat, the Bulgarian Academy of Sciences is the scholarly authority on this particular group, as the question on minorities is within the scope of its Etnografski Institut.[31]

NOTES

[1]A. K. Aziian, *Leninskaia natsionalnaia politika v razvitii i deistvii* (Moscow: "Nauka," 1972).

[2]See the journal *Hrvatske novine*, Eisenstadt/Željezno, Austria.

[3]Janko Golias, *Petježicni glosar ustave in samoupravljenja SFRJ* (Ljubljana: Društvo znanstvenih in tehničnih prevajalcev Slovenije s sofinanciranjem kulturne skupnosti Slovenije, 1976).

[4]László Kövágó, ed., *Nationalitäten in der Ungarischen Volksrepublik* (Budapest: Kulturalis Miniszterium Nemzetisegi Osztalya, 1979).

[5]Béla Bellér, *Az ellenforradadalom nemzetiségi politkájának kialakulasa* (Budapest: Akadémiai Kiadó, 1975); Rudolf Joó, *The Question of National Minorities in European Interstate Documents after 1945* (Budapest: Külpolitika I016 Budapest, Bérc utca 23, 1979).

[6]The literature about the Sudeten issue and the advocacy of the viewpoint of the Sudeten Germans is vast, well-funded, and scholarly researched, though not unbiased. The expulsion has received a rather positive interpretation in the work by Rudolf Jaworski, *Vorposten oder Minderheit? Der Sudetendeutsche Volkstumskampf in den Beziehungen zwischen der Weimarer Republic und der CSR* (Stuttgart: Deutsche Verlagsanstalt, 1977).

[7]Bohumil Hubinek, "Lösung der Nationalitätenfrage in der ČSSR," in *Tschechoslowákisches Leben* (Prague, 1979); Stilpon P. Kyriakides, *The Northern Ethnological Boundaries of Hellenism* (Thessaloniki: Society for Macedonian Studies, 1955).

[8]Arnošt Mazur, *Národnostní vývoj na území ČSSR*, 2 vols. (Opava: Českoslovènska akademia vĕd v Opavé, 1969).

[9]Andreas Moritsch, *Das nahe Triester Hinterland* (Vienna, Graz, and Cologne: Böhlau Verlag, 1969).

[10]See the official map of the Geographic Institute of the Independent State of Croatia indicating the new borders, Zagreb, 1942; also the outstanding study by Jere Jareb, *Pola stoljeća hrvatske politike* (Buenos Aires: Knjižnia Hrvatske Revije, 1960).

[11]Manlio Udina, *Gli accordi di Osimo* (Trieste: LINT, 1979); Ernest Petrič, "Nekateri mednarodnopravni vidiki določil o manjšinah v osimski pogodbi," in *Teorija in Praska Revija za družbena vprašanja*, vol. 15, pp. 1055-68 (Ljubljana, 1978).

[12]See Renzo Gubert, *La situazione confinaria* (Trieste: LINT, 1972); *Atti della Conferenza* (Trieste, vol. 1, 1979; vol. 2, 1980).

[13]Koca Jončić, ed., *Nations and Nationalities of Yugoslavia* (Belgrade: Medjunarodna Politika, 1974); *Ustavi i ustavni zakoni* (Zagreb: Informator, 1974).

[14]Atif Purivatra, "On the National Phenomenon of the Moslems of Bosnia-Herzegovina," in Jončić, pp. 303-29; Dominik Mandic, *La historia etnica y religiosa de Bosnia y Herzegovina* (Buenos Aires: Studia Croatica, 1973).

[15]Senada Colic, ed., *Jezik is Rasizam* (Sarajevo: Savez za esperanto BiH, 1978). (Basic study).

[16]Anton Podstenar's basic study, *Koroški slovenci in civilna oblast: Razlogi za izredno zaščito. Zbornik Svobodne Slovenije* (Buenos Aires: Svobodna Slovenija, 1966-1975), is not allowed into the Slovenian Socialist Republic and is not officially cataloged. A certain relaxation appears to have become a reality with the new edition of Thomas Barker's *The Slovenes of Carinthia: A National Minority Problem* (New York and Washington, DC: League of CSA, 1960), being printed in Slovenia.

[17]Ernest Petrič, *Mednarodnopravno varstvo narodnih manjšin* (Maribor: Založba obzorja, 1977).

[18]Nicolae Ceauşescu, ed., *Die sozialistische Nation* (Bukarest: Politischer Verlag, 1973); Istvan Zolcsak, *Forced Assimilation of the Minorities in Rumania* (São Paulo, Brazil: Transylvanian World Federation, 1980).

[19]See *Plenartagungen der Räte der Werktätigen ungarischer und deutscher Nationalität in der Sozialistischen Republik Rumänien* (Bukarest: Politischer Verlag, 1978); "Revue roumaine des sciences sociales," in *Série de sciences juridiques* (Bukarest: Editura Academiei Republicii Socialista România), 1956- .

[20]Hermann Schmidt in *Plenartagungen* (see note 19), "Bericht über die Neugestaltung und Vervollkommnung des Unterrichts in der Muttersprache."

[21]Franz Storch, "Bericht über die kulturell-erzieherische und künstlerische Tätigkeit in den Reihen der Bevölkerung deutscher Nationalität," p. 71, in *Plenartagungen* (see note 19).

[22]George Schöpflin, *The Hungarians of Rumania, Report No. 37 of the Minority Rights Group* (London, 1978); see also Elémér Illyés, *Siebenbürgen im Wandel* (Vienna: Braumüller, 1980).

[23]The Academia Republicii Socialiste România of Bukarest enjoys an excellent scholarly reputation, although one of its publications on nationality policies, *Die Unabhängigkeit Rumäniens, 1877-1977* (1978), is fraught with pro-Romanian biases and scholarly discrepancies. See also: Walter König, "Die gegenwärtigen Schulverhältnisse der Deutschen in Rumänien," *Korrespondenzblatt des Arbeitskreises für Siebenbürgische Landeskunde* 3-4 (1977): 81-137; Carl Göllner, ed., *Studien zur Geschichte der mitwohnenden Nationalitäten in Rumänien und ihrer Verbrüderung mit der rumänischen Nation*, Vol. I: *Die deutsche Nationalität* (Bukarest: Politischer Verlag, 1976).

[24]Wolfgang Brunbauer, ed., *Raumplanungsgespräch Südkärnten*. Klagenfurt: Slowenisches Wissenschaftliches Institut, 1977. This is the most important publication to date.

[25]Franz Palkovits, ed., *Symposion Croaticon: Die burgenländischen Kroaten* (Vienna: Braumüller, 1974).

[26]Hans Harmsen, *Sozialer Dienst für Spätaussiedler* (Bonn: Eichholz, 1976); Wolfgang G. Beitz, *Die Eingliederung junger Zuwanderer (Spätaussiedler und Asylanten* (Bonn: Otto Benecke-Stiftung, 1979); Hans Joachim von Merkatz, ed., *Aus Trümmern wurden Fundamente* (Düsseldorf: Walter Rau Verlag, 1979).

[27]For the Polish point of view, see Remigiusz Bierzanek, "Volksgruppenrecht und Heimatrecht" (Translated from *Sprawny Miedzynarodowe*, Warsaw, 1960), in *Heimatrecht in polnischer und in deutscher Sicht* (Leer: Rautenberg, 1962).

[28]Janusz Ziólkowski, "Die Bevölkerung der Westgebiete," in *Die polnischen Westgebiete* (Poznan: Westinstitut, 1960). (In German).

[29]Agnieszka Zurek, ed., *Bibliografia polskich prac o migraciach stalych, wewnetrznych ludności w Polsce (lata 1916-1969/70)* (Warsaw: Instytut Geografii, 1979). (Zeszyt 1).

[30]Max Demeter Peyfuss, *Die aromunische Frage* (Vienna, Graz, and Cologne: Böhlau Verlag, 1974).

[31]K. Telbnzor and M. Vekova, *Traditsionen byt i kultura na banatskite Bulgari*. Sofia: Bulgarska akademiia na naukite, 1963. 230p.

About the Contributors

Stephan M. Horak received his Ph.D. in 1949 in East European history at the University of Erlangen. Since 1965 he has been a professor of history at Eastern Illinois University, and he was a research fellow at Osteuropa Institut, University of Tübingen, 1953-1956. In addition to numerous essays and articles, he has authored *Poland and Her National Minorities*; *Poland's International Affairs, 1919-1960*; *Russia, the USSR and Eastern Europe: A Bibliographic Guide*; and other books. He is the editor of *Guide to the Study of the Nationalities: Non-Russian Peoples of the USSR* and the journal *Nationalities Papers*, and is the chairman of the Association for the Study of the Nationalities (USSR and East Europe).

Richard Blanke received his Ph.D. from the University of California at Berkeley in 1970. He is currently professor of history at the University of Maine, Orono. His articles have appeared in such journals as *Journal of Modern History*, *Slavic Review*, and *Slavonic and East European Review*, and he is the author of *Prussian Poland in the German Empire* (1981). He is currently working on the book *German Minority in Poland between the Wars*.

David M. Crowe, associate professor of history at Elon College, North Carolina, received his Ph.D. from the University of Georgia (1974). He has contributed essays on Baltic studies and Jewish and Russian history to *Guide to the Study of the Nationalities: Non-Russian Peoples of the USSR* and *The Baltic States in War and Peace, 1917-1945*, and articles to *Nationalities Papers*, *East European Quarterly*, *American Jewish History*, *Universitas*, *Lituanus*, *Journal of Baltic Studies*, and *The Modern Encyclopedia of Russian and Soviet History*.

Kenneth C. Farmer, assistant professor of political science at Marquette University, Milwaukee, Wisconsin, received his Ph.D. from the University of Wisconsin in 1977. He is the author of *Ukrainian Nationalism in the Post-Stalin Era* (1980), and contributor to the *Guide to the Study of Soviet Nationalities: Non-Russian Peoples of the USSR* (1982). He is also the author of numerous articles and reviews on Soviet nationalities policies, Soviet domestic and foreign policies, and defense issues.

Stephen Fischer-Galati received his Ph.D. in East European history from Harvard University in 1949. He is currently Distinguished Professor of History at the University of Colorado and editor of the *East European Quarterly* and *East European Monographs*. His publications include *Ottoman Imperialism and German Protestantism*; *The New Rumania: From People's Democracy to Socialist Republic*; and *The Balkan Revolutionary Tradition*, and he contributed to the *Guide to the Study of Soviet Nationalities: Non-Russian Peoples of the USSR*.

Peter John Georgeoff is professor of comparative and international education at Purdue University, Lafayette, Indiana. He received his Ph.D. from Peabody College, Vanderbilt University. He is the author of several books and monographs, including *The Social Education of Bulgarian Youth*; *The Yugoslav Elementary School Curriculum and the Social Studies*; *Education in Bulgaria*; and *The Yugoslav School System*, and numerous book chapters and articles on southeastern Europe, such as "The Role of Education in the Bulgarian National Revival," "Educational and Religious Rivalries in European Turkey before the Balkan Wars," and "The Bureaucracy of Contemporary Bulgarian Educational Institutions."

Toussaint Hočevar received his doctorate in economics from the University of Innsbruck and is currently a professor of economics at the University of New Orleans. His publications include *The Structure of the Slovenian Economy, 1848-1963* (1965); *Economic History of Slovenia, 1828-1918: A Bibliography* (1978); "Economics of Preferential Border Zones: The Austro-Italian Case" (*Southern Economic Journal*); "Equilibria in Linguistic Minority Markets" (*Kyklos*); and "Economic Costs of Linguistically Alternative Communication Systems: The Case of Uzbekistan" (*Nationalities Papers*).

Josef Kalvoda received his Ph.D. in public law and government from Columbia University in 1960, and is currently professor of history and political science and chairman of the Department of Political Science, Saint Joseph College, West Hartford, Connecticut. Among his books are *Czechoslovakia's Role in Soviet Strategy* (1978). He has contributed case studies, essays, articles, and reviews to Czech- and English-language books and periodicals, such as *The American Historical Review*, *The American Political Review*, *The Journal of Politics*, *Yale Review*, *Slavic Review*, *Nationalities Papers*, *Kosmas*, and others.

Martin L. Kovacs, Ph.D., is professor of history at the University of Regina, Saskatchewan. His recent publications include *Esterhazy and Early Immigration to Canada* (1974); *Immigrants and Society* (1975); *Ethnic Canadians: Culture and Education* (1978); and *Roots and Realities among Eastern and Central Europeans* (1983). He is one of the founders of the Central and East European Studies Association of Canada, associate editor of *Nationalities Papers*, as well as the author of numerous articles and papers.

Theodor Veiter, Dr.iur., University of Vienna (1931), is currently a professor at the Faculty of Law, University of Innsbruck. He is editor of *A.W.R.-Bulletin*, Vienna, and co-editor of *Europa Ethnica*, Vienna, and *Canadian Review of Studies in Nationalism*. His publications include *Die Slowenen in Kärnten* (1936); *Das Recht der Volksgruppen und Sprachminderheiten in Österreich* (1970); *Nationalitätenkonflikt und Volksgruppenrecht im ausgehenden 20. Jahrhundert* (1973); and *Bibliographie zur Südtirolfrage* (1983). He is a contributor to *Sprachen und Staaten* (1976), *Scritti in onore di Manlio Udina* (1975), and the periodical *Canadian Review of Studies in Nationalism*.

Author/Short Title Index